MENTAL HEALTH IN SPORT AND PHYSICAL ACTIVITY

Bringing together the most prestigious writings on mental health in sport and physical activity from the International Society of Sport Psychology's flagship journal, *International Journal of Sport and Exercise Psychology*, this volume provides an essential reference for the field of sport and exercise psychology.

Carefully selected for their popularity and impact on the field, the chapters in this volume feature an international range of contributions. Each chapter has been closely updated to ensure its relevance in current research and maintain its position as a piece of state-of-the-art scholarship. Chapters cover a range of topics, including the mental health of high-performance athletes, assessment methods and screening tools, adjustment patterns in the junior to senior transition, the role of perfectionism, body shaming, mindfulness, and exercise addiction. The book concludes with a discussion of key takeaways from the preceding chapters and suggestions for future opportunities. Endorsed by the Society's Academy of Science, this volume is an authoritative series of writings on mental health in sport and physical activity.

Brought together in a single volume for the first time, the book is a must-have for graduate students, scholars, and professions in sport and exercise psychology.

Robert J. Schinke is President for the International Society of Sport Psychology (ISSP) and a Past President of the Association for Applied Sport Psychology (AASP). Robert is a Full Professor and the Canada Research Chair of Multicultural Sport and Physical Activity at Laurentian University, in Canada, and a Distinguished Honorary Professor at Tsing Hua University, in Taiwan. Robert has worked extensively with world champion professional boxers featured on major television networks, consults also with an assortment of professional sport athletes across disciplines, and has served as Mental Training Consultant with several Canadian male and female national teams each Olympic cycle since 1996.

Alessandro Quartiroli is a current member of the International Society of Sport Psychology (ISSP) and previously a member of the Executive Board of the Association for Applied Sport Psychology (AASP, USA). Ale is a Professor of Psychology at the University of Wisconsin-La Crosse (US) and a Visiting Reader at the University of Portsmouth (UK). A transnational scientist-practitioner, Ale provides applied services to a variety of clients from different performing domains, levels of competition, and geographical locations. He supervises trainees' applied and scholarly practice in the US, UK, and other countries. Ale's scholarly work is centered around the training, development, and practice of sport, exercise, and performance psychology scientist-practitioners.

International Perspectives on Key Issues in Sport and Exercise Psychology

Series Editors Robert J. Schinke, Thomas Schack, and Athanasios Papaioannou

International Perspectives on Key Issues in Sport and Exercise Psychology is a series of edited books published in partnership with the International Society of Sport Psychology. Each title reflects cutting edge research in the psychological study of high-level sport, written by key researchers and leading figures in the field of sports psychology.

Encyclopedia of Sport and Exercise Psychology
Volume 1: Theoretical and Methodological Concepts
Edited by Dieter Hackfort and Robert J. Schinke

Encyclopedia of Sport and Exercise Psychology
Volume 2: Applied and Practical Measures
Edited by Dieter Hackfort and Robert J. Schinke

Advancements in Mental Skills Training
Edited by Maurizio Bertollo, Edson Filho and Peter C. Terry

Mental Health in Elite Sport
Applied Perspectives from Across the Globe
Edited by Carsten Hvid Larsen, Karin Moesch, Natalie Durand-Bush, Kristoffer Henriksen

Mental Health in Sport and Physical Activity
Selected Writings from the ISSP Academy of Science
Edited by Robert J. Schinke

For more information about this series, please visit: www.routledge.com/ISSP-Key-Issues-in-Sport-and-Exercise-Psychology/book-series/KISEP

MENTAL HEALTH IN SPORT AND PHYSICAL ACTIVITY

Selected Writings from the ISSP Academy of Science

Edited by Robert J. Schinke
With Assistant Editor Alessandro Quartiroli

Routledge
Taylor & Francis Group
LONDON AND NEW YORK

Designed cover image: © Getty Images

First published 2024
by Routledge
4 Park Square, Milton Park, Abingdon, Oxon OX14 4RN

and by Routledge
605 Third Avenue, New York, NY 10158

Routledge is an imprint of the Taylor & Francis Group, an informa business

British Library Cataloguing-in-Publication Data
A catalogue record for this book is available from the British Library

Library of Congress Cataloguing-in-Publication Data
Names: Schinke, Robert J., editor.
Title: Mental health in sport and physical activity : selected writings from the ISSP academy of science / Edited by Robert J. Schinke.
Description: Abingdon, Oxon ; New York, NY : Routledge, 2024. | Series: ISSP key issues in sport and exercise psychology | Includes bibliographical references and index.
Identifiers: LCCN 2023049461 (print) | LCCN 2023049462 (ebook) | ISBN 9781032605845 (hardback) | ISBN 9781032603964 (paperback) | ISBN 9781003459750 (ebook)
Subjects: LCSH: Sports--Psychological aspects. | Exercise--Psychological aspects. | Athletes--Mental health. | International Society of Sports Psychology.
Classification: LCC GV706.4 .M4565 2024 (print) | LCC GV706.4 (ebook) | DDC 796.01/9--dc23/eng/20231213
LC record available at https://lccn.loc.gov/2023049461
LC ebook record available at https://lccn.loc.gov/2023049462

ISBN: 978-1-032-60584-5 (hbk)
ISBN: 978-1-032-60396-4 (pbk)
ISBN: 978-1-003-45975-0 (ebk)

DOI: 10.4324/9781003459750

Typeset in Times New Roman
by MPS Limited, Dehradun

CONTENTS

CONTRIBUTORS

Rachel Arnold, Department for Health, University of Bath, UK.

Jennifer Breithecker, Department of Sports Sciences, University of Augsburg, Germany.

Gavin Breslin, School of Psychology, Queen's University Belfast, Belfast, UK.

Danran Bu, Hubei Institute of Sport Science, Wuhan, China.

Chen Chang, Department of Physical Education and Sport Sciences, National Taiwan Normal University, Taipei, Taiwan.

Yu-Kai Chang, National Taiwan Normal University, Taiwan.

Chiung-Ling Chu, Department of Physical Education and Sport Sciences, National Taiwan Normal University, Taipei, Taiwan.

Patrick Clifton, Australian Football League, Melbourne, Australia.

Nikos Comoutos, University of Thessaly, Greece.

Suzanne Cosh, Faculty of Medicine and Health, School of Psychology, University of New England, Armidale, Australia.

Jennifer Cumming, School of Sport, Exercise and Rehabilitation Sciences, University of Birmingham, and Institute for Mental Health, University of Birmingham, Birmingham, UK.

Martin Daumiller, Department of Psychology, University of Augsburg, Germany.

Kitrina Douglas, Carnegie School of Sport, Leeds Beckett University, Leeds, UK.

Sarah-Jane Fenton, Institute for Mental Health, University of Birmingham, and School of Social Policy, University of Birmingham, Birmingham, UK.

David Fletcher, School of Sport, Exercise and Health Sciences, Loughborough University, UK.

Alina Franck, School of Health and Welfare, Halmstad University, Halmstad, Sweden.

Frank L. Gardner, School of Health Sciences, Touro University, New York, NY, USA.

Hannah L. Graham, School of Science and Technology, Nottingham Trent University, UK.

Cole Giffin, School of Kinesiology and Health Sciences, Laurentian University, Sudbury, Canada.

Mike Gross, University Health Services, Princeton University, Princeton, NJ, USA.

Donncha Hanna, School of Psychology, Queen's University Belfast, Belfast, UK.

Peter Harcourt, Australian Football League, Melbourne, Australia.

Chris Harwood, School of Science and Technology, Nottingham Trent University, Nottingham, UK.

Tandy Haughey, Sport and Exercise Sciences Research Institute, Ulster University, Newtownabbey, UK.

Kristoffer Henriksen, Institute of Sport Science and Clinical Biomechanics, University of Southern Denmark, and Team Denmark, Denmark.

Tibor Hortobágyi, Department of Kinesiology, Hungarian University of Sports Science, Budapest, Hungary; Department of Sport Biology, Institute of Sport Sciences and Physical Education, University of Pécs, Pécs, Hungary; Department of Neurology, Somogy County Kaposi Mór Teaching Hospital, Kaposvár, Hungary; Center for Human Movement Sciences, University of Groningen Medical Center, Groningen, The Netherlands; Institute of Sport Research, Sports University of Tirana, Tirana, Albania.

Zhijian Huang, School of Physical Education, Hubei University, Wuhan, China.

Tsung-Min Hung, Department of Physical Education and Sport Sciences, National Taiwan Normal University, Taipei, Taiwan.

Andreas Ivarsson, School of Health and Welfare, Halmstad University, Halmstad, Sweden.

Gretchen Kerr, Faculty of Kinesiology and Physical Education, University of Toronto, Toronto, Canada.

YoungHo Kim, Seoul National University of Science and Technology, South Korea.

Masataka Kiryu, Department of Human Sciences, Waseda University, Saitama, Japan.

Hirofumi Kobayashi, Graduate School of Arts and Sciences, The University of Tokyo, Tokyo, Japan.

Alex Kountouris, Cricket Australia, Melbourne, Australia.

Rita Kovacsik, Institute of Health Promotion and Sport Sciences, ELTE Eötvös Loránd University, Budapest, Hungary.

Kazutoshi Kudo, University of Tokyo, Japan.

Carsten Hvid Larsen, Institute of Sport Science and Clinical Biomechanics, University of Southern Denmark, and the Danish Football Association, Denmark.

Gerry Leavey, School of Psychology, Queen's University Belfast, Belfast, UK.

Xin Li, School of Physical Education (Main Campus), Zhengzhou University, Zhengzhou, China.

Hao Liu, Department of Physical Education, Shenzhen University, Shenzhen, China.

Jing-Dong Liu, Department of Physical Education, Sun Yat-Sen University, Guangzhou, China.

Michael Lloyd, Cricket Australia, Melbourne, Australia.

Daniel J. Madigan, School of Science, Technology, and Health, York St John University, UK.

Donald R. Marks, Nathan Weiss Graduate College, Kean University, Union, NJ, USA.

Daveena Mawren, Orygen, Melbourne, Australia.

Sean McCann, United States Olympic and Paralympic Committee, USA.

Patrick D. McGorry, Orygen, Melbourne, and Centre for Youth Mental Health, The University of Melbourne, Australia.

Ella McLoughlin, Department for Health, University of Bath and School of Science and Technology, Nottingham Trent University, UK.

Karin Moesch, Department of Sport Sciences, Malmö University, and Swedish Sports Confederation, Sweden.

Lee J. Moore, Department for Health, University of Bath, UK.

Zella E. Moore, Department of Psychology, Manhattan College, New York, NY, USA.

Madoka Nakamura, Department of Human Sciences, Waseda University, Saitama, Japan.

Drew Neill, Student Support, Ulster University, Newtownabbey, UK.

Athanasios Papaiounnou, School of Psychology, University of Thessaly, Volos, Greece.

William D. Parham, Department of Specialized Programs in Professional Psychology, Center for Trauma-Informed Education, Loyola Marymount University, and the Mental Health and Wellness Program of the National Basketball Players Association, USA.

Alexandra G. Parker, Orygen, Melbourne, Centre for Youth Mental Health, the University of Melbourne, and Institute of Sport, Exercise and Active Living, Victoria University, Melbourne, Australia.

Rachel Pess-Gross, Private Practice, Clark, NJ, USA.

Rosemary Purcell, Orygen, Melbourne, and Centre for Youth Mental Health, the University of Melbourne, Australia.

Alessandro Quartiroli, University of Wisconsin – La Crosse, USA and School of Sport, Health and Exercise Science, University of Portsmouth, Portsmouth, UK.

Daniel Rhind, School of Sport, Exercise, and Health Sciences, Loughborough University, Loughborough, UK.

Simon M. Rice, Orygen, Melbourne, and Centre for Youth Mental Health, the University of Melbourne, Australia.

Raven Rinas, Department of Psychology, University of Augsburg, Germany.

Roberto Ruíz-Barquín, Department of Developmental and Educational Psychology, Autonomous University of Madrid, Madrid, Spain.

Stephen Shannon, Sport and Exercise Sciences Research Institute, Ulster University, and Bamford Centre for Mental Health and Well-Being, Derry, UK.

Takashi Shimazaki, Department of Public Health and Environmental Medicine, the Jikei University School of Medicine, Tokyo, Japan and Advanced Research Center for Human Sciences, Waseda University, Saitama, Japan.

Saul Shrom, School of Sport, Exercise and Rehabilitation Sciences, University of Birmingham, Birmingham, UK.

Gangyan Si, Sport Psychology Center, Hong Kong Sports Institute, Hong Kong SAR, China.

George M. Slavich, Department of Psychiatry and Biobehavioral Sciences, University of California, Los Angeles, USA.

Ben Smith, AFL Players' Association, Melbourne, Australia.

István Soós, Department of Education, Hungarian University of Sports Science, Hungary.

Natalia B. Stambulova, School of Health and Welfare, Halmstad University, Halmstad, Sweden.

Shuji Suzuki, Faculty of Human Sciences, Waseda University, Saitama, Japan.

Attila Szabo, Institute of Health Promotion and Sport Sciences, ELTE Eötvös Loránd University, Budapest, Hungary.

Peter C. Terry, School of Psychology and Wellbeing, and Centre for Health Research, University of Southern Queensland, Australia.

Azusa Uematsu, Faculty of Sociology, Otemon Gakuin University, Osaka, Japan.

Ricardo de la Vega, Department of Physical Education, Sport, and Human Movement, Autonomous University of Madrid, Madrid, Spain.

Dandan Wang, Research Department, Ersha Sports Training Center of Guangdong Province, Guangzhou, China.

Yuan Wang, Department of Sports, Guangzhou Polytechnic of Sports, Guangzhou, China.

Erin Willson, Faculty of Kinesiology and Physical Education, University of Toronto, Toronto, Canada.

Andrew T. Wolanin, Wolanin Consulting and Assessment, Inc., Bala Cynwyd, PA, USA.

Chun-Qing Zhang, Department of Psychology, Sun Yat-sen University, Guangzhou, China.

Daliang Zhao, Department of Education and Psychology, Guangzhou Sport University, Guangzhou, China.

1

INTRODUCTION

The International Society of Sport Psychology Academy of Science

Robert J. Schinke, Alessandro Quartiroli, YoungHo Kim, Kazutoshi Kudo, Yu-Kai Chang, and Nikos Comoutos

The *International Journal of Sport and Exercise Psychology* celebrated its 20th anniversary in 2023. The International Society of Sport Psychology's leadership is exceedingly proud of the monumental achievements that have marked the evolution of our flagship journal. We have actively grown this journal from a modest submission rate of less than 50 in its earliest years, through its progress onward from 100 submissions, through 300, to where we presently find ourselves, where several submissions are received daily. These submissions arrive from every country where sport and exercise psychology are practiced. The vastness of international diversity is also mirrored in a breadth of subject areas and how these are approached, often distinctly nuanced, in relation to their geographic regions. The abundant openness and exchange of ideas is something the International Society of Sport Psychology (n.d.) values and encourages through our various projects, including those submitted to the *International Journal of Sport and Exercise Psychology* (*IJSEP*).

The *IJSEP*'s success is partly the result of well-read and cited scholarship from the vastness of international scholars. Each year, the accepted manuscripts are monitored in terms of number of reads and citations, as well as their acquired Altmetric score. These numeric indices help to inform the *IJSEP*'s impact factor, along with further journal metrics whilst we also value the vastness of perspectives that span traditional through contentious subject areas, methodological approaches, and interventions (Papaioannou & Schinke, 2023). The breadth of submissions gaining these scores extend beyond a wide number of countries, to a variety of accepted approaches, with many yet to be considered. The accepted manuscripts include empirical studies, systematic reviews, theoretical contributions, practical contributions,

DOI: 10.4324/9781003459750-1

position stands, consensus statements, commentaries, and editorials. Each format and accompanying orientation have a place in the *IJSEP*.

Charting the Course for the ISSP Academy of Science

With the expansive collections of accepted manuscripts to the *International Journal of Sport and Exercise Psychology*, spanning 20 years, we pondered what the next step could be in advancing written knowledge in our rapidly evolving field through ISSP publishing projects? We sought to move beyond past practices, to emerging and unforeseen possibilities. Surely there would have to be higher levels of scrutiny and exactness than accepted manuscripts released bi-monthly? Early one morning, the first author of this introduction, also found as an editorial in the *IJSEP* (Schinke et al., 2023), received an email from a colleague from Asia that helped modify my thinking. Discussions and an associated grant application were underway with a National Academy of Science and Engineering so that cooperative work could continue among a group of colleagues, which included the first author. The grant application, particularly the agency it was targeting, ignited an idea that brought us to the present endeavour. It is serendipitous how discussions about one work task can stimulate a new direction of thinking, leading to new possibilities and growth for a professional field. The question I pondered was: "Why is there no Academy of Science for the field of sport and exercise psychology?" Certainly, if science and engineering hold such a high threshold for scholarly ideas, so too should sport and exercise psychology as its own legitimate domain. After all, this field already has well-established peer-reviewed journals and a growing number of accreditation possibilities for practitioners and scientist practitioners (Schinke et al., 2018). Though we are certain that further societies will follow the ISSP's leadership and generate their own national and regional Academies of Science, the International Society of Sport Psychology (ISSP) is the founding society within our field, and this is a foundational and pioneering action. The ISSP's proud history traces back to geopolitical challenges, and the willingness, and in fact, the conviction of sport and exercise psychologists to discuss ideas, germinate thoughts, and engage in collaborative projects despite diverse ideologies, philosophies, beliefs, and cultures, within and across nations. Ideological barriers can dissipate when professionals sit at a table and begin to dialog about a common interest or shared concern such as global mental health or equally a pressing concern such as the status of our physical environment (i.e., the scarcity of water, progressively hot climates, and pollution).

The ISSP has supported, and then collaborated with most every national and continental sport and exercise psychology society from our inception to present day. Part of our mission, and in fact, our responsibility, is to forge, and support new paths of inquiry and practice in sport and exercise psychology, and to stimulate an open exchange of these ideas across vast continents. If we, as sport and exercise psychologists, wish to be at the crest of discovery, and for our domain to further in its legitimacy, the International Society of Sport Psychology Academy of Science must be a cornerstone. The ISSP, with a foundation deeply rooted in scholarship, has now also expanded to include an ISSP-Registry and ISSP-Supervisory status for practicing professionals, a World Hall of Fame, global think tanks, an ambassador's program, and much more (see ISSPonline.org). However, the roots of everything we do must be steeped in theory and science, inclusive of local, national, and international perspectives.

Process

The process to this pioneering effort, continued from an insight one fine morning, and a tangential research funding possibility, into a much more important initiative, that we believe furthers our field's legitimacy. The question that ensued from the notion of an Academy became "Who could serve in the ISSP of Academy of Science, to recognize exceptional scholarly performance?" Recently, the ISSP launched the *World Sport Psychology Hall of Fame*, inclusive of eminent professionals. Once these people were inducted early in 2023, it became logical that four active members be enlisted to adjudicate potential manuscripts from the ISSP's journal. The sequential development of the project then led to a question of which manuscripts should be included in this inaugural admission and how might they be identified? Our first inclination was to select the most popular manuscripts within the *IJSEP* across topics, based on volume of reads, citations, and Altmetric score, with each weighted at 1/3. As exciting and straight forward as it would have been to proceed with a vastness of topics, we also wished to have the commemorative writings published with our print partner, Routledge/Taylor & Francis. Upon discussion with the publisher, negotiations ensued, and considerations eventually turned to viability of readership sales, which then led our team in a slightly modified direction from our initial concept and the vastness of topics to a hot subject area where the International Society of Sport Psychology has led discussions and think tanks, as well as commentaries. We combed through accepted *IJSEP* manuscripts and identified those pertaining to mental health, before and during COVID, leading into the current endemic state of our global community. Mental health, the academy's inaugural focus, broadly defined, is a timely discussion to pursue across sport and physical activity.

With a set pathway, Zoe Thomson and Adam Burbage from Routledge/Taylor & Francis assisted with the identification of potentially eligible manuscripts, deepening their endorsement of this project. Based on the numeric indices, we narrowed our selection to the leading 100 manuscripts. The ISSP Publishing Committee, comprised of Robert Schinke, Alessandro Quartiroli, YoungHo Kim, Yu-Kai Chang, Kazutoshi Kudo, and Nikos Comoutos, examined the manuscripts collaboratively, engaged in a series of virtual discussions, and narrowed the selection list further to those most closely aligned with our topic, from topics which were tangential. Forty manuscripts were solidified into a data set. These manuscripts were sent to the Academy of Science's four adjudicators to rate independently. The results were aggregated, which led to a rank order of eligible manuscripts. Invitations were then extended to the potential authors on a tight timeline. Explicit instructions were provided to retain each manuscript's existing structure, as it was part of each contribution's successful recipe, with only a request to update the scholarship, meaning lines of thinking and key references, to state-of-the-art status. The ensuing chapters reveal 14 carefully curated and refined manuscripts from the *IJSEP*. This model of updating existing scholarship is as new to Routledge, as the Academy of Science is to the ISSP and the domain at large.

You might wonder why this moment is the correct one to launch an ISSP Academy of Science, and the ensuing stringent approach to scholarship? Academies of Science are found in various domains, such as business management, science, and engineering. These "academies" might be national or international. What these "academies" reinforce is an exacting standard among scholars and knowledge production, intended to stimulate positive and profound societal impact. Sport and exercise psychology has its foundational scholars; people who understand the past and present well enough to recognize timely, coherent, and systematic scholarship, that in turn, could manifest in a healthier future, based on a prolific past. These learned historians are the people we have turned to in this legacy project.

Mental Health – The Academy's Inaugural Theme

Mental health has been central to the ISSP for some time. Interest began with submissions relating to the broader topic, furthered through position stands about athletes' career transitions, cultural competence, athlete mental health, occupational health, and safety in elite sport environments, acute athlete care, commentaries on adaptation to COVID in sport and physical activity contexts, and through consensus statements on elite athlete mental health more generally, and temporally situated within an Olympic quadrennial. These endorsements of the umbrella topic of mental health, found in the publications drop down window of our ISSP website, reflect a broad and expanding interest in the subject area, not just in a reactive sense, but also in a proactive sense, as people seek to thrive through sport and physical activity in everyday life. Mental health, as we envision it, is not only about diagnosis and treatment, but also about how people can thrive through personal and social actions. The content that follows in this compilation will reveal an emergence of physical activity and mental health writings, beyond the previously identified sport and mental health topics. The *IJSEP*'s current submission rates suggest physical activity in relation to the topic is expanding rapidly, so much so that we presently have five associate editors assigned to triaging manuscripts in this general area. Hence, the selected manuscripts will span sport and physical activity, as stressor, antidote, or inoculation to compromised mental status, offset by discussions of how one might thrive psychologically, emotionally, and spiritually through movement. This topic is essential within our field, among our professionals, as much as among sport and exercise psychology consumers. For the current project, we thank the successful authors, and the inaugural adjudicators (alphabetically): Diane Gill, Dieter Hackfort, Glyn Roberts, and Len Zaichkowsky, for their generous time, expertise, and endorsement. The Publications Committee also wishes to thank Routledge Publishers for their support of this inaugural ISSP activity.

Structure

What follows is a structure of manuscripts that reflect an ordering by topic, as opposed any form of performance indication, other than being successfully awarded entry into this inaugural compilation. Chapter 2 features a compilation of writings with the ISSP's inaugural consensus statement led by Kristoffer Henriksen and colleagues on improving the mental health of high-performance athletes. This inaugural contribution reflected the International Society of Sport Psychology's launch into its World Think Tank series. Chapter 3 authored by Robert Schinke and colleagues reveals one of several multinational ISSP Position Stands, the current one focused on mental health through occupational health and safety in high-performance sport. Chapter 4 reveals the work of Gangyan Si and colleagues where the authors revisit assessment methods and a managerial framework when working with Chinese elite athletes. In Chapter 5, the reader finds the work of Simon Rice and colleagues from Australia, pertaining to the preliminary validation of a brief mental health screening tool for elite athletes. In Chapter 6, Martin Daumiller and colleagues from Germany focus on elite athletes' achievement goals, burnout levels, psychosomatic stress symptoms, and coping strategies among elite athletes. For Chapter 7, the focus moves to Alina Frank and colleagues' manuscript about junior to senior transitions among Swedish athletes. In Chapter 8, the reader will find the work of Ella McLoughlin and colleagues from England, focused on the cumulative lifetime stressor exposure and health in elite athletes. Chapter 9 is provided by Erin Wilson and Gretchen Kerr from

Canada, focused on body shaming as a form of emotional abuse in sport, with a group of Canadian National Team athletes. In Chapter 10, Saul Shrom and colleagues from England consider lifestyle challenges and mental health of professional tennis players. Chapter 11 manuscript is authored by Stephen Shannon and colleagues from Ireland, pertaining to mindfulness and mental health outcomes in university level athletes. Chapter 12 is written by Zella Moore and colleagues from the United States, pertaining to a mindfulness acceptance commitment approach with university level athletes. Attila Szabo from Hungary and colleagues authored Chapter 13, and the authors consider the topic of passion and exercise addiction in relation to team and individual sports as the thirteenth contribution. Takashi Shimazaki and colleagues from Japan provide Chapter 14 and consider the use of long-term qi-gong practice in relation to the improvement of self-perceived health and quality of life among adults ages 50 and above. Chapter 15 features the work of Chang and colleagues from Taiwan, where exercise is considered as a potential benefit for patients with schizophrenia. Chapter 16 concludes this project with a convergence of postulates derived from the manuscripts. We now turn to this series of learned international contributors to contribute to and advance the dialog about mental health in sport and physical activity.

References

International Society of Sport Psychology. (n.d.). Welcome to the International Society of Sport Psychology. https://issponline.org

Papaioannou, A., & Schinke, R. J. (2023). What constitutes editorial virtuous leadership. *International Journal of Sport and Exercise Psychology*, *21*(5), 761–765. 10.1080/1612197X.2023.2235220

Schinke, R. J., Si, G., Zhang, L., Elbe, A. M., Watson, J., Harwood, C., & Terry, P. (2018). Joint position stand of the ISSP, ASPASP, FEPSAC, and AASP on professional accreditation. *Psychology of Sport and Exercise, 38*(5), 107–115. 10.1016/j.psychsport.2018.06.005

Schinke, R. J., Quartiroli, A., Kim, Y., Kudo, K., Chang, Y. K., & Comoutos, N. (2023). Introducing the international society of sport psychology academy of science. *International Journal of Sport and Exercise Psychology*, 1–4. https://doi.org/10.1080/1612197X.2023.2251769

2

UPDATED CONSENSUS STATEMENT ON IMPROVING THE MENTAL HEALTH OF HIGH-PERFORMANCE ATHLETES

Kristoffer Henriksen, Robert J. Schinke, Karin Moesch, Sean McCann, William D. Parham, Carsten Hvid Larsen, and Peter C. Terry

The present chapter is an updated version of the original statement, updated in 2023 specifically for the International Society of Sport Psychology Academy of Science. Research within the field of athlete mental health has grown considerably since the initial consensus statement, as witnessed in several research reviews (e.g., Gouttebarge et al., 2019; Prior et al., 2022) and position stands (Vella et al., 2021). Attention has been devoted to the role of specific stakeholders in athlete mental health (such as coaches, e.g., Bissett et al., 2020), to help seeking behavior (Castaldelli-Maia et al., 2019), to specific groups of athletes (such as student athletes; Kegelaers et al., 2022, and Olympic and Paralympic athletes; Henriksen et al., 2020). The COVID-19 pandemic impacted mental health worldwide and triggered specific research on the mental health of athletes during this period (Reardon et al., 2021; Wagemans et al., 2021). In addition, other events with global implications, including but not limited to the Russia-Ukraine war, escalated political tensions in several regions of the world (Center for Sports and Human Rights, 2022; Murray & Price, 2023), the rise in targeted hate crimes in the United States, and climatological catastrophes represent inextricably salient bigger-picture environmental contexts within which the expanding field of athlete mental health is now situated. The disruptive and distressing nature of these events and enhanced focus on varied and nuanced impacts on the lived experiences of athletes, sport psychologists, and researchers merits ongoing investigation.

Major sport organizations such as the IOC have developed toolkits to support Olympic Movement Stakeholders to develop and implement initiatives to protect and promote mental health and well-being in elite athletes

DOI: 10.4324/9781003459750-2

(IOC, 2021). The National Basketball Players Association (USA) convened an inaugural Global Summit on the Mental Health and Wellness of Elite Athletes in September 2023 in New York and will publish a "Playbook" with implications for direct service, research and evaluation, policy, and advocacy. A comprehensive review of all developments in the field is beyond the scope of the present chapter. With that said, the central messages in the statement still stand.

Members

A consensus statement is a summary of the opinions of a panel of experts. Selection procedures for membership of the Think Tank were used to secure applied experience, research expertise, global representation, and collaboration between key organizations. The International Society of Sport Psychology (ISSP), the European Federation of Sport Psychology (FEPSAC), the Association of Applied Sport Psychology (AASP) and the Asian-South Pacific Association of Sport Psychology (ASPASP) were each asked to nominate an expert from their organization. Selected professional sport organizations and National Olympic Committees were also offered a seat on the Think Tank. This process led to the selection of the following panel of seven experts, listed alphabetically:

- Kristoffer Henriksen (PhD) is a Professor at the University of Southern Denmark. He is a Sport Psychologist in Team Denmark, a member of the ISSP Managing Council and the Think Tank co-organizer residing in Denmark.
- Carsten Hvid Larsen (PhD) is an Associate Professor at the University of Southern Denmark. At the time of the Think Tank, he was a Sport Psychologist in Team Denmark, representing the Local Organizing Committee as a co-organizer. Today Carsten is the Head of Psychology in the Danish Football Association. He resides in Denmark.
- Sean McCann (PhD) is a Licensed Psychologist and a Sport Psychologist with the United States Olympic Committee. He was nominated by AASP and resides in the United States.
- Karin Moesch (PhD) is a Senior Lecturer at Malmö University. She is employed as a Sport Psychologist for the Swedish Sports Confederation, was during 2015–2022 in the Managing Council of, and nominated by FEPSAC, and resides in Sweden.
- William D. Parham (PhD, ABPP) is a Licensed Psychologist, Professor at Loyola Marymount University, Director for the Center of Trauma-Informed Education (CTIE), and Director of Mental Health and Wellness Program at the National Basketball Players Association (NBPA), who resides in the United States.

- Robert Schinke (PhD) is a Professor at Laurentian University, a Canada Research Chair, President of the ISSP, a distinguished Honorary Professor at several universities, and an experienced mental performance consultant who resides in Canada.
- Peter C. Terry (PhD) is a Registered Psychologist, a Professor at the University of Southern Queensland, and Dean of Graduate Studies. He is an experienced Sport Psychology practitioner, originally nominated by ASPASP, who resides in Australia.

The contributors present six propositions and recommendations to inspire researchers in their efforts to understand and investigate athlete mental health, and to assist elite sport organizations to create an environment that optimally nourishes athlete mental health and provides thorough care for athletes experiencing mental health disorders.

PROPOSITION 1: Mental health is a core component of a culture of excellence.

Increasingly competitive international sport has led to increased pressure on elite, Olympic, Paralympic, and professional athletes. Increasing training loads and performance demands present potential threats to athlete mental health. Several studies have demonstrated significant levels of mental ill-health among athlete populations and therefore present cause for concern (e.g., Foskett & Longstaff, 2018; Gouttebarge et al., 2019; Tahtinen et al., 2021). Just as physical training must be balanced with adequate recovery to see progress, so too, psychological demands must be balanced with strategies to support mental health. Winning "at any cost" is incompatible with a modern responsible sport system that values the human behind the performer. We regard supporting mental health as a core component of any culture of excellence. Notably, many elite sport organizations are presently focusing on athlete mental health and solutions through their sport resources and organizational environments.

Recommendation. *Sporting organizations, practitioners and researchers should pay due attention to athlete mental health in their efforts to promote athletic performance, and this should be stated explicitly in procedure and protocol manuals.*

PROPOSITION 2: Mental health in a sport context should be better defined.

The World Health Organization (WHO) has defined mental health as "a state of well-being in which every individual realizes his or her own potential, can cope with the normal stresses of life, can work productively and fruitfully, and is able to make a contribution to her or his community" (WHO, 2014). Kuettel and Larsen (2020) suggested an athlete-specific definition of mental health as "a dynamic state of well-being in which athletes can realize their potential, see a purpose and meaning in sport and life, experience trusting personal relationships, cope with common life stressors and the specific stressors in elite sport, and are able to act autonomously according to their values" (p. 23). Moving beyond the conceptualization of mental health as an absence of mental illness, these two definitions represent significant progress toward a more holistic view of mental health. The contributors to this consensus statement identify three key notions that should inform a definition of mental health in sport.

First, mental health is more than the absence of mental ill health. Within the sport science literature, mental health researchers often survey the prevalence of specific mental disorders, such as depression, anxiety, and eating disorders (Schinke et al., 2017). Mental health is indirectly conceptualized as the absence of such conditions. Assuming that all athletes who do not present with clinical disorders are healthy is overly simple. Mental health is a human lived experience and a highly dynamic feature of life. All athletes experience challenging life situations, ups and downs, and a full range of emotions. This is part of the human condition. We must therefore be careful not to pathologize normal human experiences. We need to distinguish between *clinical mental health disorders* (diagnosed according to recognized criteria), *subclinical mental ill health* (not severe enough to meet diagnostic criteria), *the human condition* (periodic experiences of adversity and unpleasant thoughts and emotions because of living a full life), and *the athlete condition* (periodic experiences of unpleasant thoughts and emotions, such as performance anxiety, because of engaging in athletic pursuits).

There can be many reasons why sport practitioners, including athletes, coaches, and managers, want mental health conditions to be diagnosed (insurance, financial support); why mental health professionals prefer diagnoses (clear treatment plans); and why researchers focus on diagnoses (clear inclusion and exclusion criteria). We issue a word of caution; language creates reality, and diagnostic language can potentially pathologize normal aspects of the human condition as well as cause practitioners to overlook athletes with mental health problems that do not meet diagnostic criteria. Athletes do not need to have a clinical mental disorder to need help to manage their mental health.

Second, mental health is contextualized. Mental health is about alignment between the individual and the context. An athlete may thrive in one sport environment or area of life and struggle in another, pointing to the importance of the person-environment fit. Behaviors considered dysfunctional in one context may be considered functional in another. For example, perfectionism may be considered functional in some elite sport settings but less so in life. What may look like mentally unsound behaviors may reflect a normal reaction to abnormal circumstances. At the same time, mental health and how it is fostered will vary depending on contexts. Contexts include the individual context (e.g., race, gender, religion, ethnicity), environmental context (e.g., national, organizational, political, sport specific) and developmental context (e.g., age, career phases, and transitions). These contexts shape motives, self-reflections, and the intrapersonal lived experience of mental health. Understanding the complexity of identity in situ (i.e., in relation to training environments and sport sub-culture) is key to understanding mental health, as the positive recognition of identity is a precondition for flourishing (Schinke et al., 2017).

The third notion that should inform a definition of mental health in sport is that it is related to, but separate from, performance (Moesch et al., 2018). Athletes with good mental health stand a better chance of performing well, particularly over the long term, and have reduced risk of experiencing career-ending issues. At the same time, sound mental health is not a prerequisite for performance. Some athletes achieve world-class performances despite mental health issues and clinically diagnosable disorders. Although some contemporary psychological scientists propose a mental health continuum from active mental illness to peak performance (Lardon & Fitzgerald, 2013), with degrees of psychological wellness/distress and effective/reduced functioning between the two, we recognize that mental health and performance, while related, should be understood as separate.

Recommendation. *Researchers should develop a clear definition of mental health in sport (1) as more than the absence of mental ill health, (2) as contextualized, (3) as decoupled from performance, and (4) in ways that acknowledge the full range of human emotions.*

PROPOSITION 3: Research on mental health in sport should broaden the scope of assessment.

Much of the current research and applied initiatives, such as screening, employ standardized tests based on recognized diagnostic criteria (e.g., DSM V, ICD11; Moesch et al., 2018). Although standardized tests certainly make important contributions, we issue words of caution. First, current scales tend to measure mental illness (e.g., Gorczynski et al., 2017) rather than mental health. Second, standardized tests inevitably delimit what we find. When we use scales to assess eating disorders, depression, and anxiety, those are the only constructs we identify. Related, scales to assess mental ill health fail to consider contextual variables (e.g., gender, race, culture, social class) that influence the way the mental ill health condition is expressed. There are a multitude of mental health issues that practitioners see in their applied work that may never be expressed, such as loss of identity, relationship issues, lack of sense of purpose, isolation, or domestic violence issues. Third, although sport specific instruments are being developed (Rice et al., 2020), scales are often decontextualized rather than adapted to specific sport and/or socio-cultural contexts. Fourth and finally, standardized tests typically measure symptoms, not the underlying issues (e.g., Nixdorf et al., 2013). Employing multiple methods (e.g., surveys, clinical intake interviews and broader qualitative inquiries, including observations) would allow a broader appreciation of the complexity of athlete mental health.

Recommendations. *Sport organizations should call for and financially support research aimed at developing sport relevant mental health research and screening programs. Researchers should (1) develop sport-specific measures of mental health; (2) develop tools to screen both athletes and organizations for risk and protective factors; (3) employ multiple methods; (4) provide room for individual narratives that may expand our conceptualization of mental health; and (5) recognize the contextual nature of mental health.*

PROPOSITION 4: Athlete mental health is a major resource for the whole athletic career and life post-athletic career.

Athletic careers are uneven and involve progressions, stagnations, and decays. Mental health is an important resource for athletes when they make career decisions and need to cope with various athletic and non-athletic transitions, whereas a lack of mental health is a barrier to effective decision-making and transition coping (Schinke et al., 2017; Stambulova et al., 2020). Sport-specific phases and transitions such as injuries, periods of high training load and extensive travel, or relocation to new cultural settings call for extra attention to the mental health of the athletes. Career termination is a particularly difficult transition that can trigger pre-existing and previously unrecognized or unacknowledged life challenges and issues that exacerbate the transition process. Although many elite athletes enjoy a healthy transition into retirement from high-performance competition, a proportion of elites experience a more difficult switch to a non-athlete status. Factors including premature retirement due to a range of unforeseen factors such as injury and de-selection or having failed to plan and make post-career financial and other lifestyle provisions can cause athletes to suffer transition distress (Kuettel et al., 2018; Stambulova et al., 2021).

Athlete challenges are fueled by generational identity. For example, growing up in the fast-paced, ever-evolving age of technology, social media, and artificial intelligence, the Gen Z population experiences pressures that are sometimes difficult to comprehend for older generations. Generationally influenced responses to coaching and training practices and protocols likely impact athletes' expectations and subsequent experiences in their competitive environments.

Recommendations. *Sport organizations should view their athletes as whole persons from a life-span perspective and be especially vigilant in reducing threats to mental health during difficult career transitions. Researchers are recommended to pay more direct attention to how mental health may affect athletic careers and how career transitions may affect mental health.*

PROPOSITION 5: The environment can nourish or malnourish athlete mental health.

An elite sport organization or environment (e.g., structure, personnel, and culture) does not *cause* mental health problems per se. Individuals respond differently to different environments. The environment can, however, nourish or malnourish athlete mental health (Kuettel & Larsen, 2020).

We have seen examples where sport organizations have publicly acknowledged that they have allowed cultures to arise that compromised athlete mental health and have since taken measures to remedy these situations (e.g., Swimming Australian, British Cycling, USA Gymnastics). From such examples, it becomes clearer how the elite sport system and the "medals at all costs" mantra is a potential threat to athlete mental health. Environments undoubtedly jeopardize athletes' mental health when they allow bullying, condone excessive weight control, or fail to prevent sexual abuse.

We also need to consider the potential impact of more accepted practices and characteristics such as a pressure to specialize and invest at an early age, pressure to train and compete while injured, pressure to forego academic pursuits and non-sport friendships, and periods of intense training without sufficient recovery. Responding to social media in all forms remains a constant and ever-present pressure to which athletes must respond (David et al., 2018; FIFPRO, NBPA & WNBPA, 2022). Under the camouflage of free speech, social media allows audiences to say what they want, when they want, how they want. Unbridled barrages of personal opinions, some of which are toxic and abusive (Ruser et al., 2022), impact on the lived experiences of athletes. Daily hazards have cumulative deleterious effects on mental health.

A recent position stand (Schinke et al., 2021) situated athlete mental health and treatment within a discussion of occupational health and safety. Regarding sport contexts as workplaces points to a need to ensure that people who work within high-performance sport are as safe as possible from occupational hazards.

At the same time, environments can actively nourish athlete mental health, and young athletes who regard their talent development environments as high quality report higher well-being (Ivarsson et al., 2015). Research findings in athletic talent development, athlete safeguarding, organizational psychology in sport, and cultural psychology, allow us to hypothesize that environments supportive of athlete mental health are integrated, values based and psychologically safe, send clear messages, and engage in practices that are coherent with these values, allow multiple identities, and empower the athletes (Henriksen & Stambulova, 2023; Mountjoy et al., 2015).

Pressure to win and the potential financial rewards of successful performance may press athletes, coaches, and managers to compromise, to not pay due attention to mental health and the potential human cost of medals, and even to collude in unhealthy practices. Everyone in the sport environment is morally, ethically, and sometimes legally bound to speak up when sport cultures normalize toxic practices. Overlooking athlete mental health is a primer for a dysfunctional environment.

Recommendations. *Sport organizations should consider mental health as a key indicator of their effectiveness and develop guidelines to openly and critically review the degree to which their environment is a resource for their athletes' mental health. Researchers should investigate the features of sporting environments that nourish and malnourish athletes' mental health with the aim to inform sport environments, such as federations, clubs, and talent academies.*

PROPOSITION 6: Mental health is everybody's business but should be overseen by one or a few specified members.

Everyone in a sport organization who intersects with athletes, including coaches, sport psychologists, medical staff, managers, dual career support providers, and other integrated support team members, has a responsibility to be aware of the person behind the performer, including their mental health status. Organizations have a responsibility to create an elite sport environment that supports athlete mental health, which includes building and promoting cultures that encourage inclusivity, identity centralization, and positive pathways.

Diverse and always present co-existing personal identities of athletes include, but are not limited to, dimensions of gender, race and ethnicity, culture, socioeconomic status, nationality, country of origin, regional location, sexual orientation, age/generational classification, religious or spiritual orientation, and ability status. These dimensions continuously frame the lived experiences of each sport participant. Thus, sport psychology professionals have an ethical responsibility to engage in self-reflection to understand, appreciate, and value intrapersonal factors that influence their clients in all their complexities and their interactions with them.

Sport organizations should (1) be open to discussing mental health; (2) provide the structures and resources to promote early identification and effective treatment of athletes at risk or mentally unwell and ensure that all involved persons have knowledge about these structures and resources; (3) encourage testimonials from athletes who have suffered from mental health problems to normalize and promote openness; (4) take steps to cultivate help-seeking behaviors, which includes identifying and removing barriers and reducing stigma; (5) set up educational initiatives for athletes, coaches and other stakeholders to increase mental health literacy; and (6) provide athletes with the opportunity to give back to the sport and thus experience meaning and purpose beyond their own results. We recognize that the systems set in place to support athlete mental health worldwide must vary to account for cultural and organizational differences, yet we encourage sport systems to seek inspiration from good examples (Henriksen et al., in 2023; Larsen et al., 2021; Moesch et al., 2018).

Mental health should be *one or a few people's assigned responsibility* to manage. Many roles are involved in helping athletes cope with mental health challenges, including sport psychology consultants, licensed clinical psychologists, psychiatrists, sports medicine specialists, and the athlete's general practitioner. Athletes may also be involved in more than one intervention of a psychological nature at a time, for example a performance enhancement initiative and a mental ill-being treatment. These interventions are often carried out by different service providers and are not coordinated. Moreover, athletes might experience interventions in several contexts simultaneously, such as in the case of an athlete who is involved in a club team and a national team at the same time. Within these circumstances, athletes run a further risk of having uncoordinated assistance, which in turn could compromise the quality of interventions whilst causing the athlete confusion.

Sometimes "everybody's business" means "nobody's responsibility" and there is a risk that no systematic attention is paid to mental health. Mental health officer(s) (MHO, or similar title) is a relatively new addition to the athlete support staff. We advocate that, having primary responsibility to address mental health issues, the MHO is a core component of a healthy elite sport system. The main functions of MHOs are to *manage, monitor, and evaluate* a structure to support athlete mental health, which includes designing, implementing, and evaluating a system for assessing its effectiveness, ongoing relevance, and strict adherence to professional, ethical, and moral standards. The cornerstones of such a system are confidentiality and an athlete-centered approach.

The functions of MHOs typically include (1) education of key stakeholders (coaches, athletes, experts, medical staff) to increase mental health literacy; (2) building and maintaining a network of service providers and setting up a system of referral; (3) being the main point of contact for athletes; (4) setting up a system of screening for athlete vulnerability and organizational risk factors; (5) overseeing that case management and communication between different people involved in an athlete's mental health work within the boundaries of confidentiality; (6) informing and educating coaches and athletes about the possibilities of getting help, possibly in the general national health care system; and (7) following athletes through their transition to career end. Everybody in the sport system should know the role and functions of the MHO.

To fulfill these functions, MHOs must have a range of competencies and resources. First, they should have training and experience in treating mental health issues and possess clinical skills as evidenced by traditional markers such as a national license or accreditation. Although these people will not necessarily engage in treatment as part of the job, knowledge of how to refer athletes, of what mental health issues are best treated how and by whom, and of ethical issues is important. Second, MHOs should have the organizational skills to support communication and collaboration with a range of providers (including medical doctors, physiotherapists, and sport psychology consultants) as well as several layers of management, in an environment characterized by high goals and expectations. Third, MHOs should have a solid familiarity with the sports world as a basis to build a system that is sensitized to the specific culture. Fourth, MHOs should have a strong network that includes specialists in several mental health areas and good relationship skills to maintain it.

Recommendations. *Sport organizations should (1) employ one or a few well-trained, licensed, or certified and experienced professionals who have the mental health of the athletes as a primary focus, (2) collaborate with universities to develop specific courses to ensure properly educated people are available to fulfill the role, and (3) educate all people in the sport system to increase their mental health literacy. Researchers should investigate the functions, competencies, and challenges involved in the successful fulfillment of the role as an MHO to support organizations' recruitment and education initiatives.*

Conclusion

The topic area of athlete mental health has become increasingly prominent due to the range of healthy and unhealthy manifestations that occur during athletic careers. This consensus statement is intended to inform and inspire future initiatives focused on athlete mental health, whilst also sparking discourse among high-performance sport communities regarding the salience of mental health as a core principle in elite athlete training programs. With the increasing recognition of what elite sport can, but sometimes does not, afford the athlete, there is a powerful need to improve understanding of what mental health is in a sport context, how researchers may investigate it, and how sport organizations can provide environments that support it.

Together, we recommend that researchers unite to develop a more contextualized definition of athlete mental health and more comprehensive strategies of assessment, as well as join forces with sporting organizations to investigate sustainable elite sport environments and the role of the mental health officer. We recommend that sport organizations recognize athlete mental health as a core component of a healthy elite sport system and a key indicator of their effectiveness, support research initiatives, and promote the mental health literacy of all their staff while engaging a mental health officer with the responsibility to oversee a system to support athlete mental health.

Acknowledgments

The Think Tank that led to this consensus statement was supported by grants from Team Denmark and the University of Southern Denmark.

Note

We recognize that mental health is too complex a topic for any group of experts to grasp in its nuanced entirety during a two-day think tank. We also recognize that, as a result of procedures for selection and invitation, the inaugural Think Tank was gender biased and the participants mostly represented organized systems in modernized societies (of note, one female participant was a last-minute cancellation). Future think tanks on the topic will recruit a broader diversity of global representation, culture and ethnicity, gender, and sexual orientation. Finally, we acknowledge that this consensus statement represents a snapshot in time and should be updated regularly to account for scientific and applied progress in relation to athlete mental health.

References

Bissett, J. E., Kroshus, E., & Hebard, S. (2020). Determining the role of sport coaches in promoting athlete mental health: A narrative review and Delphi approach. *BMJ Open Sport & Exercise Medicine*, *6*, 10.1136/bmjsem-2019-000676

Castaldelli-Maia, J. M., Gallinaro, J. G. M., Falcão, R. S., Gouttebarge, V., Hitchcock, M. E., Hainline, B., Reardon, C. L., & Stull, T. (2019). Mental health symptoms and disorders in elite athletes: A systematic review on cultural influencers and barriers to athletes seeking treatment. *British Journal of Sports Medicine*, *53*, 707–721, 10.1136/bjsports-2019-100710

Center for Sports and Human Rights. (2022). 5 Sport and Human Rights Issues to Look Out for in 2022, https://www.sporthumanrights.org/library/5-sport-and-human-rights-issues-to-look-out-for-in-2022

David, J. L., Powless, M. D., Hyman, J. E., Purnell, D. M., Steinfeldt, J. A., & Fisher, S. (2018). College student athletes and social media: The psychological impacts of twitter use. *International Journal of Sport Communication*, *11*(2), 10.1123/ijsc.2018-0044

FIFPRO, NBPA & WNBPA (2022). Decoding online abuse of players: Collective responses by players and unions. fifpro-nbpa-wnbpa-decoding_online_abuse.pdf

Foskett, R. L., & Longstaff, F. (2018). The mental health of elite athletes in the United Kingdom. *Journal of Science and Medicine in Sport*, *21*, 765–770. 10.1016/j.jsams.2017.11.016

Gorczynski, P. F., Coyle, M., & Gibson, K. (2017). Depressive symptoms in high-performance athletes and non-athletes: A comparative meta-analysis. *British Journal of Sports Medicine*, *51*, 1348–1354. 10.1136/bjsports-2016-096455

Gouttebarge, V., Castaldelli-Maia, J. M., Gorczynski, P., Hainline, B., Hitchcock, M. E., Kerkhoffs, G. M., Rice, S. M., & Reardon, C. L. (2019). Occurrence of mental health symptoms and disorders in current and former elite athletes: A systematic review and meta-analysis. *British Journal of Sports Medicine*, *53*(11), 700–706. 10.1136/bjsports-2019-100671

Henriksen, K., Diment, G., & Kuettel, A. (2023). The Team Denmark applied model of athlete mental health. *International Journal of Sport and Exercise Psychology*, 10.1080/1612197X.2023.2281525

Henriksen, K., Schinke, R., McCann, S., Durand-Bush, N., Moesch, K., Parham, W. D., Larsen, C. H., Cogan, K., Donaldsen, A., Poczwardowski, A., Noce, F., & Hunziker, J. (2020). Athlete mental health in the Olympic/Paralympic quadrennium: A multi-societal consensus statement. *International Journal of Sport and Exercise Psychology*, *18*(3), 391–408. 10.1080/1612197x.2020.1746379

Henriksen, K., & Stambulova, N. (2023). The social environment of talent development in youth sport. *Frontiers in Sports and Active Living*, *5*. 10.3389/fspor.2023.1127151

IOC. (2021). IOC mental health in athlete toolkit. Retrieved from: https://stillmed.olympics.com/media/Document%20Library/IOC/Athletes/Safe-Sport-Initiatives/IOC-Mental-Health-In-Elite-Athletes-Toolkit-2021.pdf

Ivarsson, A., Stenling, A., Fallby, J., Johnson, U., Borg, E., & Johansson, G. (2015). The predictive ability of the talent development environment on youth elite football players' well-being: A person-centered approach. *Psychology of Sport and Exercise*, *16*, 15–23. 10.1016/j.psychsport.2014.09.006

Kegelaers, J., Wylleman, P., Defruyt, S., Praet, L., Stambulova, N., Torregrossa, M., Kenttä, G., & De Brandt, K. (2022). The mental health of student-athletes: A systematic scoping review. *International Review of Sport and Exercise Psychology*. 10.1080/1750984X.2022.2095657

Kuettel, A., Boyle, E., Christensen, M. K., & Schmid, J. (2018). A cross-national comparison of the transition out of elite sport of Swiss, Danish and Polish athletes. *Sport & Exercise Psychology Review*, *14*, 3–22.

Kuettel, A., & Larsen, C. H. (2020). Risk and protective factors for mental health in elite athletes: A scoping review. *International Review of Sport and Exercise Psychology*, *13*(1), 231–265. 10.1080/1750984x.2019.1689574

Lardon, M. T., & Fitzgerald, M. W. (2013). Performance enhancement and the sport psychologist. In D. Baron, C. Reardon, & S. Baron (Eds.),

Clinical sport psychiatry: An international perspective (pp. 132–146). Chichester, UK: Wiley Blakwell.
Larsen, C. H., Moesch, K., Durand-Bush, N., & Henriksen, K. (2021). *Mental health in elite sport: Applied perspectives from across the globe*. London: Routledge.
Moesch, K., Kenttä, G., Kleinert, J., Quignon-Fleuret, C., Cecil, S., & Bertollo, M. (2018). FEPSAC position statement: Mental health disorders in elite athletes and models of service provision. *Psychology of Sport and Exercise*, *38*, 61–71. 10.1016/j.psychsport.2018.05.013
Mountjoy, M., Rhind, D. J. A., Tilbas, A., & Leglise, M. (2015). Safeguarding the child athlete in sport: A review, a framework and recommendations for the IOC youth athlete development model. *British Journal of Sports Medicine*, *49*, 883–886. 10.1136/bjsports-2015-094619
Murray, S., & Price, G. (2023). Athlete activists, sports diplomats and human rights: Action versus agency. *Societies*, 13(2), 27. 10.3390/soc13020027
Nixdorf, I., Frank, R., Hautzinger, M., & Beckmann, J. (2013). Prevalence of depressive symptoms and correlating variables among German elite athletes. *Journal of Clinical Sport Psychology*, *7*, 313–326. 10.1123/jcsp.7.4.313
Prior, E., Papathomas, A., & Rhind, D. (2022). A systematic scoping review of athlete mental health within competitive sport: Interventions, recommendations, and policy. *International Review of Sport and Exercise psychology*. 10.1080/1750984X.2022.2095659
Reardon, C. L., Bindra, A., Blauwet, C., Budgett, R., Campriani, N., Currie, A., Gouttebarge, V., McDuff, D., Mountjoy, M., Purcell, R., Putukian, M., Rice, S., & Hainline, B. (2021). Mental health management of elite athletes during COVID-19: A narrative review and recommendations. *British Journal of Sports Medicine*, *55*(11), 608. 10.1136/bjsports-2020-102884
Rice, S. M., Parker, A. G., Mawren, D., Clifton, P., Harcourt, P., Lloyd, M., Kountouris, A., Smith, B., McGorry, P. D., & Purcell, R. (2020). Preliminary psychometric validation of a brief screening tool for athlete mental health among male elite athletes: The Athlete Psychological Strain Questionnaire. *International Journal of Sport and Exercise Psychology*, *18*, 850–865. 10.1080/1612197x.2019.1611900
Ruser, J. B., Steinfeldt, J., & Friedman, E. J. (2022). Exploring the impacts of social media use on highly visible student-athletes well-being in the NIL-era. Association for Applied Sport Psychology (AASP) 37th Annual Conference, Fort Worth, TX.
Schinke, R. J., Giffin, C., Cosh, S., Douglas, K., Rhind, D., Harwood, C., Si, G., & Papaiounnou, A. (2021). International Society of Sport Psychology position stand: Mental health through occupational health and safety in high performance sport. *International Journal of Sport and Exercise Psychology*, *20*(6), 1711–1733. 10.1080/1612197X.2021.1992857
Schinke, R. J., Stambulova, N. B., Si, G., & Moore, Z. (2017). International Society of Sport Psychology position stand: Athletes' mental health, performance, and development. *International Journal of Sport and Exercise Psychology*, *16*(6), 622–639. 10.1080/1612197X.2017.1295557
Stambulova, N. B., Ryba, T. V., & Henriksen, K. (2020). Career development and transitions of athletes: The International Society of Sport Psychology position stand revisited. *International Journal of Sport and Exercise Psychology*, *19*, 524–550. 10.1080/1612197X.2020.1737836

Stambulova, N. B., Ryba, T. V., & Henriksen, K. (2021). Career development and transitions of athletes: The International Society of Sport Psychology position stand revisited. *International Journal of Sport and Exercise Psychology*, *19*(4), 524–550.

Tahtinen, R. E., Shelley, J., & Morris, R. (2021). Gaining perspectives: A scoping review of research assessing depressive symptoms in athletes. *Psychology of Sport and Exercise*, *54*. 10.1016/j.psychsport.2021.101905

Vella, S. A., Schweickle, M. J., Sutcliffe J. T., & Swann, C. (2021). A systematic review and meta-synthesis of mental health position statements in sport: Scope, quality and future directions. *Psychology of Sport and Exercise*, *55*. 10.1016/j.psychsport.2021.101946

Wagemans, J., Catteeuw, P., Vanderhounten, J., Jansen, J., De Corte, X., Ceusters, C. M., & Vissers, D. (2021). The impact of COVID-19 on physical performance and mental health: A retrospective case series of Belgian male professional football players. Frontiers in Sports and Active Living. https://www.frontiersin.org/articles/10.3389/fspor.2021.803130/full

World Health Organization. (2014). Mental health: A state of well-being. Retrieved from http://www.who.int/features/factfiles/mental_health/en/

3

INTERNATIONAL SOCIETY OF SPORT PSYCHOLOGY POSITION STAND

Mental Health through Occupational Health and Safety in High-Performance Sport

Robert J. Schinke, Cole Giffin, Suzanne Cosh, Kitrina Douglas, Daniel Rhind, Chris Harwood, Gangyan Si, and Athanasios Papaiounnou

Sport psychology professionals are devoting considerable attention to athlete treatment (e.g., Mountjoy et al., 2015, Seanor et al., 2023). Athlete treatment has been a long-standing consideration among sport professionals given the prevalence of maltreatment across participants' sport levels and age ranges. We find common and elaborate reporting measures for athletes and coaches in terms of safeguarding/safe play policies (International Olympic Committee, 2017) and underpinning the necessity and further development of such policies, expansive reports of athlete maltreatment evidenced within media outlets, worldwide (e.g., Seanor et al., 2023). Though variations of how safe sport environments are considered from one country to the next are unavoidable given cultural practices and national sport systems, much of the international sport community is moving toward versions of athlete safeguarding (see Mountjoy et al., 2015). We propose that discussions and solutions are a long way from sufficiently advanced. Though considerable attention has been paid to athlete maltreatment, fewer discussions pan to the organizational level, where the focus is proactive, effective structures and processes, fostering psychological and emotional growth.

This commentary expands discussions about safety, particularly in high-performance sport environments, given the weekly hours invested in training and competition for those working onsite. We seek to move beyond contextualized cases of maltreatment, to considerations of what nourishing processes entail and how these can be designed (Biswas et al., 2021). Sport psychology professionals have already produced position stands

DOI: 10.4324/9781003459750-3

(Moesch et al., 2018; Schinke et al., 2018) and consensus statements (Henriksen et al., 2020a, 2020b; Reardon et al., 2019) focused on athlete mental health in high-performance environments. These recent contributions have extended discussions beyond malnourishment, toward the generation of nourishing sport environments for athletes and staff (Henriksen et al., 2020a). However, much work is left to be done, particularly through the provision of support structures that develop athletes' coaches, and support staffs' holistic health (International Olympic Committee, 2023). We seek to further the discourse by framing this ISSP Position Stand in Occupational Health and Safety (OHS)[1], considering sport environments as employment sites. Viewing high-performance sport environments through the lens of OHS involves proactive approaches, where safety in training and competition environments are fostered through systemic, organizational structures, including, but also extending beyond, the training of management, frontline staff, and athletes. Drawing upon the expertise of international experts from four continents who actively work with youth and adults in high-performance environments, we have structured this position stand into four sections. We begin with a general overview of OHS, introducing general concepts and narrowing their relevance to nourishing environments within sport. We then consider athlete mental health, building the case for OHS from the vantage of a clinical psychologist with expertise in mental health. We then focus on youth sport, given the expanding reports of youth maltreatment contextualized in scientific and practical outlets. Though convergences exist when considering the safety of youth and adults in high-performance sport, there are also nuances. We then draw upon the ideological expertise of two cultural authors, one versed in individualism, one in collectivism, to consider OHS uptake.

Occupational Health and Safety in Elite Sport Contexts

OHS is focused on how workplaces promote or hinder employee well-being and safety (Burton, 2010; Tetrick & Peiró, 2012). We align with the World Health Organization's (2020) definition of health – a state of complete physical, mental, and social well-being, and not merely the absence of disease or infirmity. OHS is a multidisciplinary perspective focused on developing structurally safe workplace environments through hazard prevention and health promotion (Burton, 2010). While some occupational safety initiatives are supported within sports contexts, such as conduct/professionalism policies (see Safe Sport Policies; e.g., International Olympic Committee, 2017), personal protective equipment (PPE in the form of helmets, shinpads, mouthguards, and padding), and the employment of certified sports psychology practitioners versed in health-conducive athlete training, the lack of sustainable, and physically and psychologically safe sport environments is surprising given the parallels of athletes and employees and mounting recognition of unsafe sport environments, where aspiring athletes invest years of commitment (Henriksen et al., 2020b; Moesch et al., 2018; Schinke et al., 2018). We recognize professional (see Ekos Research Associates, 2010) and high-performance amateur athletes (Stambulova & Wylleman, 2019) spend approximately 34–42 hours in sports training each week. These efforts provide employment, financial security, and part of each athlete's personal identity (Schinke et al., 2021). When paired with daily meetings, recovery sessions, travel time, and extracurricular technical demands, such as studying film, high-performance athletes undertake an allotment of time akin to a standardized work week.

OHS is a disciplinary approach sport psychology researchers and practitioners, sport scientists, coaching staff, and organizational authorities (e.g., high-performance directors and general managers) can utilize to create structurally safe environments that nourish elite athletes' health. Creating physical and psychological safety allows athletes and staff to dedicate attention and energy toward sport-specific objectives and personal development, rather than protecting themselves and those within the environment from work hazards, such as stress and burn-out (Fan et al., 2020). When paired with health-conducive interventions, such as stress management classes, nourishing, structurally safe environments can empower athletes and staff with tools to develop their health while buffering against subclinical ill-health (Schinke et al., 2018).

Despite global frameworks (Burton, 2010), the development and effectiveness of OHS programs should be approached contextually to account for macro- and micro-level factors that influence a program's effectiveness. Macro-level factors, such as national culture and a country's wealth and policies, are concerned with the societal structures that shape how health and safety is approached nationally (Fan et al., 2020). Countries that value health and safety, such as those that prioritize universal healthcare and concrete occupational health and safety policies, showcase less occupational fatality rates when compared to countries lacking safety structures (Stoffregen et al., 2019) and contribute to a culture of safety by educating employees on risks that may threaten individual safety (Starren et al., 2013). Researchers and practitioners must recognize that safety, like performance, should be approached through culturally designed projects that account for differences at the national, organizational, occupational, and individual levels (Ryba et al., 2013). This endeavor can be challenging given organizations are comprised of culturally diverse individuals, each with intersecting safety perceptions and behaviors (Ryba et al., 2013; Starren et al., 2013), a point we return to. Practitioners and researchers applying cultural praxis, where theoretical knowledge production is used to prioritize practical social change, can create localized safety pursuits nuanced to sport organizations, empowering organizational members to contribute to creating safe training and performance environments (Blodgett et al., 2015). Additionally, wealth-developed countries, such as Sweden and France, have financial resources to contribute to robust OHS incentives within their organizations, resulting in comprehensive safety policies and reduced occupational fatality rates compared to underdeveloped nations (Fan et al., 2020; Stoffregen et al., 2019). Building upon recommendations for showcasing cultural sport psychology within emerging countries (Papaioannou et al., 2019), researchers and practitioners can be reflexive in considering how their social positioning, including wealth, creates opportunities and challenges when fostering safe sport environments; as sport leaders we must use our privileges to enact social justice (Blodgett et al., 2015).

Micro-factors are concerned with manageable aspects of occupations, organizations, interpersonal interactions, and athletes and sports staff's perceptions relating to health and safety (Fan et al., 2020), and can be targeted within health and safety interventions. At the occupational level, the safety risks within an occupation determine how OHS is approached, with enhanced safety precautions applied to riskier workplaces (Fan et al., 2020). High-risk sports have varying safety procedures used to mitigate their risk factors. At the organizational level, company leaders, such as high-performance directors, managers, and coaches, influence how safety is pursued, prioritizing, or neglecting safety through exceeding or adhering to the minimum requirements set by provincial/state and national sport organization safety policies (Burton, 2010). Leaders create a psychosocial safety climate (PSC) when they promote comprehensive safety policies, provide employee incentives (e.g., rewards for safe work) and health promotion activities (e.g., lunchtime physical activity), empower employees, listen to OHS contributions of employees, provide adequate resources, show support for stress prevention, and actively seek areas of workplace improvement to produce environments where safe working practices are engrained in employees' daily practices (Dollard & Bakker, 2010; Kim et al., 2016). These initiatives could be reflected in sport environments through safety policies, athlete, and sport staff incentives for safe work practices, such as promoting safe behavior (e.g., resting when injured), empowering athletes and sport staff by listening to their suggestions for OHS, and equipping sports personnel with health promotion initiatives like stress management classes, as sport environments can contribute to stress inside and outside of sport (Fletcher & Arnold, 2017).

Leaders who disregard safety contribute to systemic OHS failure within organizations, leading to miscommunication between staff, ignorance toward hazards, and failure to learn from experiences (Barling & Frone, 2003). A leader's perceived power can also influence relationships within the workplace, with power distance – the distribution of workplace power between employees – significantly contributing to how unsafe tasks are mitigated (Fan et al., 2020). Power distance between athletes and coaches can contribute to poor coach-athlete relationships (Wachsmuth et al., 2018), possibly expanding into athlete maltreatment if not effectively managed. When high-power distance is not managed, either directly through reducing leaders' power, or indirectly through empowering employees, individuals' willingness to question leaders' unsafe or inappropriate behaviors (e.g., workplace harassment) and commands becomes weakened, sometimes pressuring athletes into unsafe behaviors through fear and intimidation (Stoffregen et al., 2019).

Individual factors, such as demographics, age, risk perception, job insecurity, and perceived control, impact feelings and effort toward safety within sport (Choudhry & Fang, 2008; Fan et al., 2020). Such focus is important within elite sports contexts comprised of transnational (Ryba et al., 2016), immigrant (Schinke et al., 2017), and refugee athletes (Giffin et al., 2023), whose perceptions of safety are influenced by their cultural backgrounds, contextual interactions, and previous life experiences. For example, refugee athletes' forced migration experiences (e.g., conflict, war, persecution) result in vastly different perceptions of safety when compared with native-born athletes (Giffin et al., 2023). Compounding language proficiencies, cultural differences, and underdeveloped relationships with peers result in a reduced capacity to voice their safety concerns to employers (Yanar et al., 2018), making them vulnerable to environmental hazards. Effective OHS safety initiatives must bridge interventions that enhance newcomer athletes' capacities to share their perceptions of safety whilst contributing to health-promoting activities that empower athletes' adaptations within their new contexts.

The interacting and contextual micro and macro factors that differ between cultures, countries, workplaces, and individuals add complexity to creating physically and psychologically safe environments. Sports psychology practitioners versed in context-driven practice may be well suited to aid organizations in developing occupationally safe sport environments through nuanced – relevant interventions (Schinke & Stambulova, 2017). Safety interventions consist of proactive and reactive initiatives tailored to pressing safety requirements, identified through needs assessment (Burton, 2010). Proactive initiatives are influential in mitigating health and safety concerns before they occur, whilst reactive interventions help improve health and safety threats afterward (Fan et al., 2020; Giffin et al., 2021). Organizations must develop proactive and reactive interventions, as safety threats are ever-changing (e.g., COVID-19 resulted in vast safety initiatives to protect athletes' health at the 2020 Tokyo Olympics; Schinke et al., 2020).

One effective proactive and empowering initiative is comprehensive safety training, which enhances employees' awareness of how to complete potentially dangerous tasks within their workplace, the risks and hazards association with each, safety precautions that should be taken, and who to report to if safety threats are witnessed (Fan et al., 2020). Active safety training, where individuals engage in applied workshops, is more effective at producing safety values and behaviors compared to passive modes of training, such as self-directed learning through computer modules (Konijn et al., 2018). Post-accident reviews, proper medical and first aid (e.g., IED provided to Christian Erikson after he collapsed from cardiac arrest at the 2020 European Championships), and audits of workplace safety measures are reactive interventions that contribute to safe workplaces (Fan et al., 2020).

Some safety initiatives are more comprehensive than others and simultaneously address safety proactively and reactively. Comprehensive safety policies signed, promoted, and enforced by the highest organizational authority, such as high-performance directors and managers are proactive in conveying structure while pursuing safe work, and reactive in providing anticipatory instructions when an accident occurs (Burton, 2010; Tetrick & Peiró, 2012). Examples of safety policies in sport include the Universal Code of Conduct to Prevent and Address Maltreatment in Sport and Safe Sport Policies designed by National Sporting Organizations, each differing depending on country of origin. While policies are the first step in providing safety structure, their effectiveness is not guaranteed unless followed by members of a sporting organization (Burton, 2010). Joint health and safety committees (JHSC) comprised of employees, managers, unions, and OHS representatives and/or an Internal Responsibility System (IRS)[2] – a system where organizational employees have the role and responsibility for identifying unsafe work hazards – provides outlets that empowers employees to communicate proactive safety or health promotion ideas that may benefit the workplace and reactive ideas to combat current safety threats (Burton, 2010). Cultural diversity within these JHSC is important in representing athletes of different cultural compositions and life experiences. The IOC Athletes' Commission, comprised of former Olympic athletes, offers an athlete-driven perspective on various topics, including doping, women in sport, and the Olympic Games, and reflects the idea that athletes can create committees dedicated toward identifying unsafe hazards within sport environments (International Olympic Committee, n.d.). Finally, an integrated worker health promotion approach is beneficial in protecting athletes from safety threats while also providing opportunity to advance health and well-being (Biswas et al., 2021). Health promotion activities develop athletes' capacities to adapt to workplace stressors, improving their mental health and well-being (e.g., IOC, 2023).

Context Setting: Sporting Environments and Athlete Mental Health

Recently, there has been increased attention on athlete mental health (Henriksen et al., 2020b; Reardon et al., 2019), with reports suggesting a point prevalence of 18–30% for symptoms of depression and anxiety (Gouttebarge et al., 2017) and a career-prevalence of up to 46% of at least one disorder (Gulliver et al., 2015). Employee mental health is gaining salience in workplaces (Kirsh et al., 2018); however, an occupational mental health focus has not typically extended into elite sport environments. While many sporting organizations have increased support for retirement preparation (Torregrosa et al., 2020), less attention has been paid to the mental health of current athletes, though we see an uptick. Yet supporting well-being and promoting mental health throughout athletic careers is necessary to mitigate functional impairments and equip athletes to cope with stressors, which may also better enable them to manage transitions into the future. Consideration of athlete mental health during careers may be especially critical as the age at which athletes are entering and engaging in high-level competition (Allen & Hopkins, 2015) tends to be when many psychological disorders first develop and present (APA, 2013). Further, this is an age during which coping resources and skills are still developing (Carr, 2015), thus athletes may be especially vulnerable to sporting-related stressors and risk factors.

Although often understood as an individual pathology, the etiology of psychological disorders is multifaceted and arises in a complex interplay of biological, individual, and environmental factors (Carr, 2015). Within a biopsychosocial understanding of mental health, social and environmental factors are necessarily interlinked in the development and maintenance of psychological disorders. Therefore, there is a need to better contextualize athlete mental health within sporting environments, which are underscored by findings that sporting stressors and environments may contribute to athletes' mental health outcomes (Rice et al., 2016). There are numerous ways in which sport environments may function to predispose individuals to, as well as precipitate or perpetuate, mental health symptoms. Organizational stressors, over-training, poor performance, extended periods of travel, and injury are sport-related precipitating factors (Gulliver et al., 2015; Purcell et al., 2019; Rice et al., 2016). High training loads also increase injury risk and thus the likelihood of subsequent mental health symptoms (Palmer et al., 2021). A growing body of evidence also highlights the increased risk for athletes of experiencing distress and depression following concussion (Kilic et al., 2019). Relationships within sport, including team dynamics (Fletcher & Wagstaff, 2009), coaching expectations and climate (Pensgaard & Roberts, 2000), loneliness, and unsupportive social environments (Brownrigg et al., 2018) also contribute to the development of psychological disorders among elite athletes.

Furthermore, sporting organizations are typically guided by a strong (and often exclusive) performance focus (Hulme et al., 2019), with a performance narrative dominant and recurrently reproduced within elite sport settings (e.g., Cosh et al., 2019; Douglas & Carless, 2009). This focus results in performance goals being prioritized to the detriment of well-being, with evidence linking the performance narrative with disordered eating (Busanich et al., 2016; Papathomas, 2018). Further, in a "win at all costs" environment, pressure to return to sport quickly after an injury or playing through an injury is common (Roderick et al., 2000), which is associated with longer term physical and mental health sequelae (Kilic et al., 2019). A performance focus also drives practices around athletes' bodies, which may contribute to athlete overtraining and subsequent burnout (Rice et al., 2016). There has long been the notion of optimizing athletes' body composition to improve performance outcomes, with practices of body regulation and monitoring commonplace in elite sport (Miller, 2012). These regulatory practices, as well as interactions with coaches and staff, contribute to body dissatisfaction, low self-confidence, and poor body image (Coppola et al., 2014; Porter et al., 2013). Consequently, athletes engage in various body surveillance and dietary restraint behaviors (Boudreault et al., 2021; Lang, 2015; McMahon & Dinan-Thompson, 2011) which become normalized in elite sport environments (Cosh et al., 2015; Papathomas, 2018). Such practices and associated body dissatisfaction contribute to the development of disordered eating amongst athletes (de Bruin & Oudejans, 2018; Diaz et al., 2018). Although a focus on many guidelines in sport has been on perceived pressure around body shape, the role of sport settings and performance focus in contributing to body-related distress and psychological disorders such as disordered eating cannot be overlooked.

This performance focus can also result in maladaptive behaviors that place athletes at risk for psychological disorders being reinforced within elite sport environments when they are seen as conducive to performance. Such reinforcement is seen with weight control behaviors and perfectionistic strivings. These strivings develop within competitive sport environments (Rasquinha et al., 2014), where perfectionism is reinforced within everyday interactions (Cosh et al., 2015). Perfectionistic strivings are viewed as improving performance, yet are maladaptive for athletes (Hill et al., 2018) and are related to poorer well-being and development of various psychological disorders (Jensen et al., 2018; Sellars et al., 2016).

A strong performance focus also results in mental health only being considered a concern where performance is affected (Coyle et al., 2017). Compounding this issue is that mental health literacy typically remains low in sport settings, with coaches having limited awareness and understanding of mental health symptoms (Bird et al., 2020; Gorczynski et al., 2019). Therefore, symptoms and disorders may not be recognized where performance is not impacted. Further, a range of symptoms or subthreshold disorders may be viewed as contributing to performance and thus, reinforced. High training loads may be reinforced as dedicated behavior aimed at improving performance. However, training and exercise can become compulsive and a view that this signifies dedication and commitment may overlook that such behaviors can be symptomatic of presentations, including compulsive exercise and obsessive-compulsive disorder (Cromer et al., 2017; Lichtenstein et al., 2017). High training loads may also be a manifestation of high energy levels associated with mania, with high exercise levels potentially also exacerbating manic and hypomanic episodes (Sylvia et al., 2013). Rituals and pre-game routines may also represent obsessions and compulsions but are typically viewed as undertaken to improve performance (Cromer et al., 2017). What may be viewed positively in certain contact sports as competitive aggression may be manifestations of externalizing disorders or reflect an emerging internalizing disorder, especially in adolescents and males where depression and anxiety often manifest as aggression (Carr, 2015). Maladaptive behaviors and mental health symptoms are therefore often undetected in elite sport and can be reinforced via a performance focus.

Within sport settings there is scope for coaches and staff to monitor well-being, aid in identification of psychological disorders, and facilitate early intervention through referral to a mental health clinician (e.g., Rice et al., 2016; Schinke et al., 2020). This approach would require enhanced mental health literacy to aid in the identification of symptoms (Gorczynski et al., 2019). In instances where psychological disorders are identified, sporting organizations may be best placed to refer athletes for treatment as athletes are typically unsure of where to seek help (Coyle et al., 2017). Even where mental health literacy and identification of disorders is improved, this strategy in isolation may remain limited for promoting athlete mental health.

Firstly, athletes are less likely to seek help for their mental health than non-athletes (Bird et al., 2020; Gorczynski et al., 2019) with stigma – a key barrier to disclosure and help seeking in sport settings (Castaldelli-Maia et al., 2019). Athletes report concerns around perceptions from peers and coaches and losing status within the team and sport environment (Delenardo & Terrion, 2014). Vignette-based research has further highlighted the stigma surrounding mental health in sport environments, demonstrating that athletes with a history of any mental health disorder were less likely to be signed and more likely to be paid less than players with no mental health history (Merz et al., 2020). Such stigma perpetuated within the sport environments may limit access to help even after a disorder is identified, suggesting that identification and referral may not be sufficient as an isolated strategy.

An identification and referral-based approach to managing mental health is also focused on pathology. However, sport participation has the potential to enhance coping skills and resilience (Belcher et al., 2021) and thereby be a protective factor for mental health. Within elite sport settings, there have increasingly been shifts toward a holistic approach to supporting the "whole person" (Torregrosa et al., 2020). However, what the holistic approach constitutes is often less clearly defined, especially in relation to mental well-being. Strategies around mental health can often remain limited in terms of promoting well-being through the development of coping skills and resilience. Thus, there is scope for sporting organizations to adopt a broader definition of mental health, which encompasses protective factors.

Managing mental health through identification and referral also constitutes a reactive approach (Torregrosa et al., 2020). Whilst this approach may support some individual athletes, it fails to (a) consider the sporting environment including culture, stigma, and the performance focus, and (b) perpetuates an individualized perspective of mental health which limits recognition of how sport settings contribute. Further, prevention of disorders is better placed to reduce associated burden of disease and improve long-term outcomes (WHO, 2004). Thus, broader changes that address the sport environment and are geared toward prevention rather than treatment may be better placed to promote athlete mental health and well-being. Workplace policies and practices that adopt an integrated approach focusing on reducing stress, preventing harm, promoting health, and fostering empowering psychosocial environments tend to achieve the best well-being outcomes (Cooklin et al., 2017). To complement approaches that support individual athletes after they present with a disorder, prevention of disorders through broader organizational and cultural shifts in sport environments are needed. These should be guided by a comprehensive understanding of the environmental and sporting factors that affect mental health.

Organizational culture shifts may be needed to facilitate well-being (Purcell et al., 2019), especially to ensure that athlete mental health is viewed as a concern of the sport setting. Sporting organizations are focused on maximizing performance, albeit potentially to the detriment of athletes' well-being. However, a performance focus without fostering well-being through health conducive practices may be counterproductive. This kind of performance focus potentially contributes to development and maintenance of psychological disorders and, especially where treatment is delayed, psychological disorders result in functional impairments (Iorfino et al., 2018) that may impact performance. It has also been suggested that organizations should be guided by a focus on growing performance rather than avoiding poor performance (de Waal, 2003). Therefore, a shift in the culture of sporting organizations away from purely performance outcomes and to a broader focus on performance growth that also encompasses well-being may be beneficial, especially given that a focus on supporting athlete well-being is argued to foster the performance of sport organizations (Hulme et al., 2019).

Changes in the culture of sport settings may also be critical to facilitate stigma reduction and thereby promote disclosure and help seeking where needed. Part of achieving this may be to shift and diversify discourse around athletes, performance, and mental health within sport settings and in communications between sport staff and athletes. Normalizing psychology and related services would also be of benefit, especially as athletes are typically encouraged to access services with immediate and physical health benefits over mental healthcare (Stambulova & Ryba, 2014).

Reduction of stress and demand in workplaces are needed to promote employee well-being (Basu et al., 2017), thus there remains a greater need to consider the ways in which sport organizations may place athletes at risk and revise organizational structures and policies to mitigate these risks. For instance, given the possible detrimental consequences of body regulation practices and the limited evidence linking these practices with performance enhancement (Plateau et al., 2014), such practices may need to be reviewed. A shift away from institutional ownership over athletes' bodies (Cosh et al., 2012), as well as further infrastructure and guidance for coaches and sport staff on how to talk about athletes' bodies may be valuable (Plateau et al., 2014; Sabiston et al., 2020). Providing a broader approach to body management that locates food and exercise practices within health and nutrition-based discourses rather than performance narratives might also better promote physical and psychological well-being.

Recognition of the organizational responsibility, including of sport staff, also appears to be necessary to promote athlete mental well-being. Recent approaches in Australia include the instalment of dedicated well-being officers in sport environments (Australian Sports Commission, 2020). Having dedicated staff managing and targeting mental health is likely necessary to guide practices and oversee a shift to a well-being focus. However, engagement from all staff and athletes with regards to how they might impact or promote mental health is also needed. For example, coaches locate responsibility for eating practices in athletes rather than consider their own coaching practices (Plateau et al., 2014) and interactions within sport settings between staff and athletes can perpetuate unhealthy body and weight management practices (e.g., Boudreault et al., 2021; Cosh et al., 2015). Thus, supporting mental health may remain limited where it is not viewed as the responsibility of sporting organizations and the individuals who work within these settings. Collaborative efforts between sport staff and mental health professionals would be beneficial (Purcell et al., 2019; Rice et al., 2016).

A large range of sporting-related stressors, as well as features of sporting environments including culture and practices, contribute to the development and maintenance of athletes' psychological disorders. While the mental health of athletes continues to be viewed as an individual pathology that fails to conceptualize the role of environmental factors and sport settings, it is unlikely that the prevalence of psychological disorders in athlete populations will change. The current focus on detecting pathology limits opportunities for prevention and changing sporting environments to make them safer for athletes.

Safe Youth Sport Environments

Any discussion on OHS in sport must extend to youth sport. The investment of the sport system (e.g., financial and coaching resources), the investment of many parents (e.g., financially and emotionally), and the personal investment of children themselves, can result in children experiencing environments and relationships which do not prioritize their safety (Harwood & Knight, 2009; Rhind & Owusu-Sekyere, 2020). These environments are evident in the ongoing discussions around repeated cases of athlete maltreatment (Mountjoy et al., 2015), which can impact athletes far into their post-sport lives (Seanor et al., 2023). The United Nations Convention on the Rights of the Child (United Nations, 1989) outlines children's rights in three broad areas: rights to protection (e.g., from violence and harassment), rights to participation (e.g., leisure), and rights to provision (e.g., healthcare). Ensuring that a child is safe is fundamental to respecting these rights. Of relevance are the following two articles:

Article 3: States parties shall ensure that the institutions, services, and facilities responsible for the care or protection of children shall conform with the standards established by competent authorities, particularly in the areas of safety, health, in the number and suitability of their staff, as well as competent supervision.

Article 19: Governments must do all they can to ensure children are protected from all forms of violence, abuse, neglect, and bad treatment by their parents or anyone else who looks after them.

These rights should be respected in all contexts, including sport. Over recent years, there has been a growing body of evidence which illustrates how relationships in youth sport can become physically, emotionally, or sexually abusive (Mountjoy et al., 2015). In response, there has been a focus on how we can create and maintain safe sport for children. Safety in the context of youth sport has been defined as "An athletic environment that is respectful, equitable and free from all forms of non-accidental violence to athletes" (Mountjoy et al., 2015, p. 1). A key development in this regard has been the launch of the International Safeguards for Children in Sport, which outline the strategies which all organizations should have in place to achieve safe sport (Rhind & Owusu-Sekyere, 2020). The Safeguards recommend that sports organizations have a safeguarding policy; procedures for managing safeguarding concerns; accessible advice and support; strategies to identify and mitigate risks; guidelines for behavior; procedures to ensure safe recruitment and ongoing safeguarding training; effective relationships with partners and a system to monitor and evaluate these safeguarding strategies.

The focus of the International Safeguards is on adopting a proactive approach to creating and maintaining safe sport for children. Through analyzing the experiences of organizations working toward these international Safeguards, Rhind et al. (2017) identified eight CHILDREN pillars, which should underpin safe sport:

1 Cultural sensitivity strategies should be developed to create safe sport and need to consider the cultural, social, political, and legislative context in which they are being applied if they are to be effective.
2 A holistic approach should be adopted where safeguarding should be integrated into all aspects of an organization (e.g., within recruitment procedures, policies, and training).
3 People should be incentivized to behave safely with appropriate mechanisms in place to reward those who do and intervene for those who do not.
4 There should be effective leadership at all levels of an organization.
5 Safeguards need to be reviewed and adapted dynamically to maintain their relevance.
6 There needs to be appropriate resources (e.g., human, time, and financial).
7 A democratic approach should be adopted which promotes engagement with all stakeholders in and around the sport (e.g., children, parents, coaches).
8 Safe sport is facilitated by organizations developing partnerships (i.e., networks) with other stakeholders in and around sport (e.g., social services, charities).

Inversely, unhealthy cultures have been cited as facilitating cases of abuse in sport (Phelps et al., 2017). Safety culture has been defined as "… the assembly of underlying assumptions, beliefs, values, and attitudes shared by members of an organization, which interact with an organization's structures and systems and the broader contextual setting to result in those external, readily visible, practices that influence safety" (Edwards et al., 2013, p. 77). Moreover, Psychosocial Safety Climate (PSC) has been defined as "policies, practices, and procedures for the protection of employees' psychological health and safety" (Dollard & Bakker, 2010, p. 580). Psychosocial safety includes freedom from psychological and social risk or harm.

Safe sport is not just about preventing negative experiences; it also concerns how well sport actively promotes positive experiences and psychosocial outcomes for everyone involved, applied to all stages of athletic journeys. Sweeney et al. (2021) offered a persuasive narrative around the premature professionalization of youth sport in the context of elite UK academy soccer to the detriment of the young players aged as young as nine. Of the 265 million people who regularly play soccer, only 0.04% play in a professional league (Haugaasen & Jordet, 2012). There is strong advocacy for sport organizations to consider their moral responsibilities to children and families who specialize and invest early in a sport because of the competitive structure and talent pathway politics that promote early specialization. Scholars within the fields of positive youth development and life skills actively encourage a holistic approach to athlete development, whereby young people are provided with the intrapersonal and interpersonal tools and coping resources to develop as people within and outside of their sport (Camiré, 2015; Larsen et al., 2014; Sweeney et al., 2021).

How life skills and psychosocial development initiatives become formal elements of an occupational health and safety program in youth sport is particularly pertinent for the potential mental health and identity challenges that a young person may face if their transition to professional sport is unsuccessful (see Blakelock et al., 2016; Wilkinson, 2020). The predominant challenge for a youth sport organization is how they integrate an emphasis on young athletes' personal development within a more performance-oriented culture (see Camiré, 2015; Harwood, 2008), not only to mitigate risk of poor psychosocial and identity enrichment, but also to facilitate athletic development as a by-product. Hardcastleet al. (2015) explored stakeholders' perceived experiences and effectiveness of a life skills program integrated into multiple high-performance sports (e.g., netball, surfing) to develop athletes' self-regulation and coping skills necessary for balancing the demands of their sport, academics, and social lives. While athletes reported positive improvements in intrapersonal skills (e.g., goal setting, planning, time management), the program was delivered by external facilitators with minimal involvement from coaches. The lack of coach engagement was perceived to limit sustained teaching, practicing, and reflection on such skills.

What is becoming clear is sport organizations either do not value the holistic development of young athletes as a "safe sport" strategy enough, or where they tacitly acknowledge its importance, there remains a lack of organizational culture change to strategically deliver on the value. Support staff (e.g., psychologists; performance lifestyle practitioners) and coaches as key facilitators are not provided with sufficient time or education, nor is there the emphasis on intentional and explicit strategies for athletes' psychosocial development in the overall program (e.g., McCallister et al., 2000; Preston et al., 2021). Beyond ensuring children are safe throughout their athletic journey across all competitive levels, safe sport should also consider how children can be kept safe around and after sport through helping to develop psychosocial skills which help them to achieve a fulfilling life, as opposed to creating vulnerabilities that can jeopardize their well-being in the future. In conclusion, Safe Sport is the right of all children, the duty of all sports organizations and a mechanism through which we can optimize children's participation and performance in sport. Within the conversation around what youth sport should be about, and how youth sport should be delivered, "Safe sport" should consider the positive psychosocial outcomes that can comprise an adaptive lifelong legacy.

Occupational Health and Safety Ideologies

There are several interrelated complex factors currently impeding the integration of occupational health and safety within high-performance sport (Chen et al., 2019). These include, but are not restricted to, philosophical, cultural, structural, and practical issues that infuse sport and underpin the broader function of societies. One obvious way in which Western ideology continues to influence how we think about sport, and the implications for safer environments for athletes, is the value placed on individual autonomy; the capacity to "be" agentic and self-determining. Regardless of whether this be a myth or delusion, the belief that an individual sports person has the capacity to be self-directing and responsible for personal choices, remains somewhat embedded within Western culture. From such a perspective, the wider public believe individuals exercise their rights when taking on dangerous or risky behaviors that threaten their own health. It is the athlete who is believed to push the boundaries and who decides to extend training when he or she should rest, or to "fight on" when injured. It is a belief that if an individual wants to risk personal life, one should be empowered to do so, to ride the biggest waves, conquer the highest mountain and the state should not interfere. Likewise, if an individual does not want to be in sport, one can leave. Individualism also underpins a belief that the person will take responsibility for becoming better educated about what actions might improve longer-term health and well-being (or not). This ideology is problematic as it tends to reduce the burden on and the expectations of sport organizations to consider their duty of care toward athletes.

From an Eastern ideological perspective, athletes are part of a Whole-Nation system with collectively oriented values that stress the needs of the group over the needs of the individual. A collectivist orientation views athletes not at independent and self-directed individuals, but as athletes who are interdependent and represent a collective identity through social relationships. This collectivist perspective is also embedded into Western sport environments through newcomer athletes (i.e., immigrant, trans-national, refugee) following their relocations (see Giffin et al., 2023).

Within the Whole-Nation system, collective interests are a priority that override individual interests (Si et al., 2011). Similarly, the purpose of mental health management for Chinese people has emphasized the values of improving public mental health and promoting social stability while mental health services in Western cultures affirmed individualistic values (Si et al., 2021). Through a collective perspective, safety can be effective when approached by improving the outcome for the common good, consisting of individuals sacrificing to achieve common good and adhere to health guidelines (Maaravi et al., 2021). At the same time, when safety is being threatened at the individual level, such as through athlete injury, a collective perspective can be detrimental to individual health when safety needs (e.g., injury recovery) are not justifiable from the group perspective (Kawabata, 2013). This collective safety perspective is evident in Chinese athletes sacrificing their physical health and safety to achieve national glory to the common good (Si et al., 2015). Reflected within Westernized occupational health acts but not within sport, conceptualizing athlete rights (e.g., the right to refuse unsafe activities) could be an intervention spanning several Eastern and Western cultures where individual safety is prioritized over individual or collective success.

Within the philosophical realm "Western" ideology has also historically valued in sports people behaviors that align with hegemonic masculinity – athletes are therefore often called to enact aggression, exhibit shows of strength and power, and evaluate risk taking as prerequisites for discovery and pioneering behavior. In tandem, individualism has demonized weaknesses, stress, and cowardly behavior. Comparatively, much of "Eastern" ideology frames stressful events as opportunities for growth that facilitate positive experiences, resulting in expectations that Chinese athletes' performance only increases with high levels of stress. Despite varying cultural perspectives of stress, we must acknowledge that stress transcends culture and may pose safety hazards for athletes, such as training/competing beyond their boundaries of acceptability (physical and mental health), not informing on rule breakers, and not disclosing weaknesses, pain, or injury (Houlihan, 1997; Nixon, 1993). Further, these underpinning cultural ideologies provide context to understand how injuries in sport become hidden, normalized, and naturalized from a young age (i.e., Western ideology, Douglas, 2014; Roderick, 2006) or why athletes will forego their health and well-being for the greater good of a National System (Si et al., 2015). When working toward athlete safety, practitioners should consider how cultural aspects of safety hazards may be perceived through diverse athletes and staff.

Layered upon philosophical moorings are culturally specific practices that circulate through narrative and discourse (Douglas & Carless, 2015). While research has shown a variety of ways narrative scripts impede healthy participation in sport and hinder the uptake of occupational health and safety, chief among these is the performance narrative (Carless & Douglas, 2009; Douglas & Carless, 2009, 2015). This is a narrative script where dedication, sacrifice, and winning are highly valued, where self-worth is linked to performance outcomes, a monologue seen as the only way to be in sport, where all athletes must behave this way. Underpinned by the Western ideology, the performance narrative supports stories about playing with injuries, not reporting mental health concerns, valuing strength and power, life being a roller coaster, and you must be this way (Houlihan, 1997; Nixon, 1993). Although not directly explored within the Whole-Nation sport context, the performance narrative within China may be similarly performance based, filled with gold medal expectations and national/provincial pressure that is directly placed onto athletes' performance outcomes (Si et al., 2015), leading to fear of failure and performance anxiety if expectations are not met (Si et al., 2011). Through providing individuals and communities with narrative "scripts" that follow this template, particular ways of "being an athlete" and "experiencing the sporting journey" are amplified. Stories that fail to align with this template are silenced, hidden, and their legitimacy maligned. Though several alternative narrative templates exist within sport (discovery narrative, relational narrative being two) with trajectories that lead to valuing the journey over the destination, that winning is not everything, that contribute to a multidimensional identity, and mental health and well-being, these are often silenced by a dominant narrative which is "storied" as the only way to excel and succeed in sport. Thus, to bring about healthier sport, we also need to change the story.

Equally problematic, is the language in sport. Numerous studies have shown how sport and military language are interchangeable (Jansen & Sabo, 1994; Jenkins, 2013). Sporting contests therefore become narrated as battlefields where the "weak" are "trampled" and where (some) coaches (and fans, and parents at the touch line) tell children, youth, and senior players alike to "go in for the kill", and "take no prisoners" (Douglas & Carless, 2015). Within this environment, athletes are supplied with ready-made counters to those who may question excessive behaviors (be it force, injury, stress, mental health, and trauma); "no pain no gain".

Opie and Smith (1992) identified OHS has been hindered in Western society by a historical failure to accept that "sport" is "work", a failure to include sport in occupational law and policy and a judiciary who have neglected to see athletes within commercial terms with regards to sport development. Further, sport related injuries for athletes are treated differently to injuries in other occupations, which makes it understandable that most high-performance sport people fail to realize sport injuries are occupational injuries and are therefore determined by OHS rules (Chen et al., 2019). Windholz (2015) suggested there has also been an absence of transparency regarding the investigation of serious sporting incidents, with no tangible process that all injury investigations follow across sport environments. That said, there are examples of a changing landscape of acceptability regarding injury as the recent legal cases regarding head injury against World Rugby, the Rugby Football Union and Welsh Rugby, the NFL in the USA and in soccer in the UK show. In these cases, organizations have been criticized over alleged failures to protect players from risks caused by head injuries in rugby, given (in the 1900s–2000) no steps were taken to warn or educate players about the risk of brain injury. While we may think brain injury risk awareness to be a recent phenomenon, this is not the case. Harrison (2014) pointed out: “the crisis in fact began more than a century ago” (p. 822).

The pace of change is a moot point however, if, for example, more legal pressure had been brought to bear among world rugby unions and associations and more robust mental health support systems adopted internationally following the death by suicide of Rugby League player Terry Newton in 2010, would five National Rugby League players all aged between 18 and 20 years of age have taken their own lives between 2013 and 2015? One young player taking his life is tragic but five young men taking their lives within one sport raises many questions. While it is important to note that these suicides have provoked research into suicide, for the most part change seems to be slow and reactive rather than proactive, antithetical to OHS. There has been a feeling for several years that promoting safer working practices, introducing enhanced welfare for athletes, and taking mental health concerns seriously remains a “tick box” affair.

A final structural impediment is the huge differences between governing organizations regarding employment status of athletes. Given athletes’ employment status includes those (a) who are independent contractors, those who are “self-employed”, (b) are part of a professional team or squad, or/and (c) are paid through a National Governing Organization scheme, the level of intervention required is contested, especially in an individualist culture where athletes often believe their sport careers do not need undue or additional policing. For athletes claiming, independent contractor status (e.g., tennis, snooker, BMX, and surfing), self-employed status is determined through “application of the legal tests” as opposed to an individual deciding he or she is independent. While independent status brings a great deal of freedom, it also removes the burden from governing organizations to fully consider the working conditions, health, and safety of athletes. Neither does it provoke sport organizations to explore how the wider sport environment, sport-specific cultural beliefs and stereotypes, influence player behavior, and mental health risks. While players’ representative bodies input their ideas and preferences, these are not always heeded or/and can be misinformed and seen from a narrow viewpoint.

For the athlete who is signed by a professional team, or who has an employment contract, there are legal implications for both the individual as well as the organization. Though as Opie and Smith (1992), noted the benefits are usually in favor of the sport organization as opposed to the performer. Contractual terms therefore make it possible for the sport organization to exert a great deal of control over the athletes (employees) and include assurance the player will play sport whenever, wherever as directed by the club, attend training, and carry out instructions of the coach and performance team. These power imbalances and the threat to remove funding or/and position on the squad also inhibit athletes' agency regarding their legal right of redress. But it is also fair to say that many athletes become blind to practices in their own sport which in any other context would be seen as abusive or unacceptable. Once a young person has been enculturated into a closed-loop system where abusive practices are normalized, it becomes almost impossible to be aware of and challenge these (Anderson, 2005). In recent years, there has been a proliferation of "player" associations and unions, particularly in professional sports, which have given rise to "collective bargaining" of contracts and collective actions/lawsuits. It thus seems rather ironic that in an individualist culture, ultimately it is through collective bargaining that sport people are best protected.

Our last area which is more relevant within Western culture relates to whether the athlete competes in an "individual" sport or is part of a team, whether the sport and/or athlete are professional or amateur. Given professionalism has and is occurring at different times in different sports, these issues remain in flux (Opie & Smith, 1992) and makes a universal stand difficult. In recent years, new interventions and policy changes have been implemented in both Olympic and professional sports. We are seeing profiling for mental illnesses being introduced and specific roles (such as education and mental health) being incorporated into professional clubs. Furthermore, in some professional clubs (e.g., Manchester United Football club, UK) workshops which focus on mental health are not only being delivered to youth teams but have been introduced for parents. Of concern within China is that within national and provincial elite sports training centers, only a small number of athletes' mental health management training has been undertaken. Further, this understanding is fueled through external academic research needs (e.g., university-based research projects) rather than internally driven by the needs of sports training centers, resulting in poor mental health literacy. Yet, despite these and other interventions, it is also fair to say that there has only been modest progress relating to stigma and discrimination surrounding mental health (Douglas & Carless, 2015; Gulliver et al., 2012; Lebrun & Collins, 2017). Fear among athletes regarding career threatening consequences of disclosing a mental illness or health concerns related to mental distress still exist. Sharing information with a club doctor or psychologist might be relayed to a performance director or manager and may, consequently, negatively affect team selection and career prospects. Additionally, any mental health issue in professional sport is recorded on a player's medical record. Whether this is a "one off event" or a condition that is being managed, it could hinder future signings, transfers or moves, and therefore may put the athlete's career in jeopardy.

Conclusion

Upon reflection of established and emerging scholarship in relation to the mental health of athletes and those who support them in sport organizations and national sport systems, there is a proliferation of scholarship emphasizing an ethic of care. Sport systems must have embedded processes to nourish human performance, and as part of healthy functioning, excellence within the sporting realm. Much of the emerging discussion is focused on athlete mental health and how sport systems must safeguard sport participants, be they youth or adult, from the strains posed by a quest for performance excellence as part of daily life. These discussions must continue as sport psychology professionals and those they work with to seek better ways of supporting growth throughout athletes' careers. Much of the discussion is to present, either reactive in terms of the need for more support mechanisms, or conceptual, where resources and pathways are proposed as part of mental health literacy. We seek to extend current discussions by situating mental health and athlete treatment within a discussion of occupational health and safety, where elite sport environments are envisioned as places of work. Athletes and those who support them devote considerable hours within their work weeks in a quest for sporting excellence. With sport contexts regarded as workplaces, we must then embark on contextually derived proactive and react strategies to ensure that people who work within high-performance sport settings, develop their craft with the knowledge they are as safe as possible from occupational hazards, and moreover, when foreseeable, these hazards are minimized and become negligible. Circling back to what has been written, sport professionals could benefit from (a) a deepened understanding of OHS, (b) its relevance to athlete mental health, (c) an appreciation of the needs of aspiring youth, beyond high-performance adult performers, (d) considering the sport systems and their associated ideologies where safety should be embedded.

Disclosure Statement

No potential conflict of interest was reported by the author(s).

References

Allen, S. V., & Hopkins, W. G. (2015). Age of peak competitive performance of elite athletes: A systematic review. *Sports Medicine*, *45*(10), 1431–1441. 10.1007/s40279-015-0354-3

Anderson, E. (2005). *In the game*. SUNY Press.

APA. (2013). *Diagnostic and statistical manual of mental disorders (DSM-5)*. APA Publishing.

Australian Sports Commission. (2020). Australian Sports Commission Annual Report: 2019–2020. https://www.sportaus.gov.au/__data/assets/pdf_file/0004/975442/4ab986bed7392b8074608c7aa1f3cddfa24ea85f.pdf

Barling, J., & Frone, M. R. (Eds.). (2003). *The psychology of workplace safety*. American Psychological Association.

Basu, S., Qayyum, H., & Mason, S. (2017). Occupational stress in the ED: A systematic literature review. *Emergency Medicine Journal, 34*(7), 441–447. 10.1136/emermed-2016-205827

Belcher, B. R., Zink, J., Azad, A., Campbell, C. E., Chakravartti, S. P., & Herting, M. M. (2021). The roles of physical activity, exercise, and fitness in promoting resilience during adolescence: Effects on mental well-being and brain development. *Biological Psychiatry: Cognitive Neuroscience and Neuroimaging, 6*(2), 225–237. 10.1016/j.bpsc.2020.08.005

Bird, M. D., Chow, G. M., & Cooper, B. T. (2020). Student-athletes' mental health help-seeking experiences: A mixed methodological approach. *Journal of College Student Psychotherapy, 34*(1), 59–77. 10.1080/87568225.2018.1523699

Biswas, A., Begum, M., Van Eerd, D., Smith, P. M., & Gignac, M. A. M. (2021). Organizational perspectives on how to successfully integrate health promotion activities into occupational health and safety. *Journal of Occupational & Environmental Medicine, 63*(4), 270–284. 10.1097/JOM.0000000000002087

Blakelock, D. J., Chen, M. A., & Prescott, T. (2016). Psychological distress in elite adolescent soccer players following deselection. *Journal of Clinical Sport Psychology, 10*, 59–77. 10.1123/jcsp.2015-0010

Blodgett, A. T., Schinke, R. J., McGannon, K. R., & Fisher, L. A. (2015). Cultural sports psychology research: Conceptions, evolutions, and forecasts. *International Review of Sport and Exercise Psychology, 8*(1), 24–43. 10.1080/1750984X.2014.942345

Boudreault, V., Gagnon-Girouard, M.-P., Carbonneau, N., Labossière, S., Bégin, C., & Parent, S. (2021). Extreme weight control behaviors among adolescent athletes: Links with weight-related maltreatment from parents and coaches and sport ethic norms. *International Review for the Sociology of Sport, 53*(3). 10.1177/10126902211018672

Brownrigg, A., Burr, V., Bridger, A., & Locke, A. (2018). 'You shut up and go along with it': An interpretative phenomenological study of former professional footballers' experiences of addiction. *Qualitative Research in Sport, Exercise and Health, 10*(2), 238–255. 10.1080/2159676x.2017.1396557

Burton, J. (2010). WHO healthy workplace framework and model. World Health Organisation.

Busanich, R., McGannon, K. R., & Schinke, R. J. (2016). Exploring disordered eating and embodiment in male distance runners through visual narrative methods. *Qualitative Research in Sport, Exercise and Health, 8*(1), 95–112. 10.1080/2159676X.2015.1028093

Camiré, M. (2015). Reconciling competition and positive youth development in sport. *STAPS, 109*(3), 25–39. 10.3917/sta.109.0025

Carless, D., & Douglas, K. (2009). 'We haven't got a seat on the bus for you' or 'all the seats are mine': Narratives and career transition in professional golf. *Qualitative Research in Sport and Exercise, 1*(1), 51–66. 10.1080/19398440802567949

Carr, A. (2015). *The handbook of child and adolescent clinical psychology: A contextual approach*. Routledge.

Castaldelli-Maia, J. M., Gallinaro, J. G. d. M. e., Falcão, R. S., Gouttebarge, V., Hitchcock, M. E., Hainline, B., Reardon, C. L., & Stull, T. (2019). Mental health symptoms and disorders in elite athletes: A systematic review on cultural influencers and barriers to athletes seeking treatment. *British Journal of Sports Medicine*, *53*(11), 707–721. 10.1136/bjsports-2019-100710

Chen, Y., Buggy, C., & Kelly, S. (2019). Winning at all costs: A review of risk-taking behaviour and sporting injury from an occupational safety and health perspective. *Sports Medicine – Open*, *5*(1), 15. 10.1186/s40798-019-0189-9

Choudhry, R. M., & Fang, D. (2008). Why operatives engage in unsafe work behavior: Investigating factors on construction sites. *Safety Science*, *46*(4), 566–584. 10.1016/j.ssci.2007.06.027

Cooklin, A., Joss, N., Husser, E., & Oldenburg, B. (2017). Integrated approaches to occupational health and safety: A systematic review. *American Journal of Health Promotion*, *31*(5), 401–412. 10.4278/ajhp.141027-LIT-542

Coppola, A. M., Ward, R. M., & Freysinger, V. J. (2014). Coaches' communication of sport body image: Experiences of female athletes. *Journal of Applied Sport Psychology*, *26*(1), 1–14. 10.1080/10413200.2013.766650

Cosh, S., Crabb, S., Kettler, L., LeCouteur, A., & Tully, P. J. (2015). The normalisation of body regulation and monitoring practices in elite sport: A discursive analysis of news delivery sequences during skinfold testing. *Qualitative Research in Sport, Exercise and Health*, *7*(3), 338–360. 10.1080/2159676X.2014.949833

Cosh, S. M., Crabb, S., LeCouteur, A., & Kettler, L. (2012). Accountability, monitoring and surveillance: Body regulation in elite sport. *Journal of Health Psychology*, *17*(4), 610–622. 10.1177/1359105311417914

Cosh, S. M., Tully, P. J., & Crabb, S. (2019). Discursive practices around the body of the female athlete: An analysis of sport psychology interactions in elite sport. *Psychology of Sport and Exercise*, *43*, 90–104. 10.1016/j.psychsport.2018.12.021

Coyle, M., Gorczynski, P., & Gibson, K. (2017). "You have to be mental to jump off a board any way": Elite divers' conceptualizations and perceptions of mental health. *Psychology of Sport and Exercise*, *29*, 10–18. 10.1016/j.psychsport.2016.11.005

Cromer, L., Kaier, E., Davis, J., Stunk, K., & Stewart, S. E. (2017). OCD in college athletes. *American Journal of Psychiatry*, *174*(6), 595–597. 10.1176/appi.ajp.2017.16101124

de Bruin, A. P., & Oudejans, R. R. D. (2018). Athletes' body talk: The role of contextual body image in eating disorders as seen through the eyes of elite women athletes. *Journal of Clinical Sport Psychology*, *12*(4), 675–698. 10.1123/jcsp.2018-0047

de Waal, A. A. (2003). Behavioral factors important for the successful implementation and use of performance management systems. *Management Decision*, *41*(8), 688–697. 10.1108/00251740310496206

Delenardo, S., & Terrion, J. L. (2014). Suck it up: Opinions and attitudes about mental illness stigma and help-seeking behavior of male varsity football players. *Canadian Journal of Community Mental Health*, *33*(3), 43–56. 10.7870/cjcmh-2014-023

Diaz, I., Godoy-Izquierdo, D., Navarrón, E., Ramírez, M. J., & Dosil, J. (2018). Eating disorders in sports and football: An updated review. *Cuadernos de Psicología del Deporte*, *18*, 43–56.

Dollard, M. F., & Bakker, A. B. (2010). Psychosocial safety climate as a precursor to conducive work environments, psychological health problems, and employee engagement. *Journal of Occupational and Organizational Psychology*, *83*(3), 579–599. 10.1348/096317909X470690

Douglas, K. (2014). Challenging interpretive privilege in elite and professional sport: One [athlete's] story, revised, reshaped and reclaimed. *Qualitative Research in Sport, Exercise and Health*, *6*(2), 220–243. 10.1080/2159676X.2013.858369

Douglas, K., & Carless, D. (2009). Abandoning the performance narrative: Two women's stories of transition from professional sport. *Journal of Applied Sport Psychology*, *21*(2), 213–230. 10.1080/10413200902795109

Douglas, K., & Carless, D. (2015). *Life story research in sport: A narrative approach to understanding the experiences of elite and professional athletes*. Routledge.

Edwards, J. R. D., Davey, J., & Armstrong, K. (2013). Returning to the roots of culture: A review and reconceptualization of safety culture. *Safety Science*, *55*, 70–80. 10.1016/j.ssci.2013.01.004

Ekos Research Associates. (2010). 2009 status of the high performance athlete. https://www.ekospolitics.com/articles/0519.pdf

Fan, D., Zhu, C. J., Timming, A. R., Su, Y., Huang, X., & Lu, Y. (2020). Using the past to map out the future of occupational health and safety research: Where do we go from here? *The International Journal of Human Resource Management*, *31*(1), 90–127. 10.1080/09585192.2019.1657167

Fletcher, D., & Arnold, R. (2017). Stress in sport: The role of the organizational environment. In C. R. D. Wagstaff (Ed.), *The organizational psychology of sport: Key issues and practical applications* (pp. 83–100). Routledge/Taylor & Francis Group.

Fletcher, D., & Wagstaff, C. R. D. (2009). Organizational psychology in elite sport: Its emergence, application and future. *Psychology of Sport and Exercise*, *10*(4), 427–434. 10.1016/j.psychsport.2009.03.009

Giffin, C. E., Schinke, R. J., Kerr, G., Kao, S. F., & Larivière, M. (2021). Interventions for improving the staff cancer role within varsity team sport contexts. *Journal of Sports Psychology in Action*, *13*(4), 215–229. 10.1080/21520704.2021.1931593

Giffin, C. E., Schinke, R. J., Larivière, M., Coholic, D., & Li, Y. (2023). Migration and meaning: An exploration of elite refugee athletes' transitions into the Canadian sports system. *International Journal of Sport and Exercise Psychology*. Advance online publication. 10.1080/1612197X.2023.2219460

Gorczynski, P., Gibson, K., Thelwell, R., Papathomas, A., Harwood, C., & Kinnafick, F. (2019). The BASES expert statement on mental health literacy in high-performance sport. *The Sport and Exercise Scientist*, *59*, 6–7.

Gouttebarge, V., Hopley, P., Kerkhoffs, G., Verhagen, E., Viljoen, W., Wylleman, P., & Lambert, M. I. (2017). Symptoms of common mental disorders in professional rugby: An international observational descriptive study. *International Journal of Sports Medicine*, *38*(11), 864–870. 10.1055/s-0043-114010

Gulliver, A., Griffiths, K., & Christensen, H. (2012). Barriers and facilitators to mental health help seeking for young high-performance athletes: A qualitative study. BMC Psychiatry, *12*(1). 10.1186/1471-244X-12-157

Gulliver, A., Griffiths, K. M., Mackinnon, A., Batterham, P. J., & Stanimirovic, R. (2015). The mental health of Australian elite athletes. *Journal of Science and Medicine in Sport*, *18*(3), 255–261. 10.1016/j.jsams.2014.04.006

Hardcastle, S. J., Tye, M., Glassey, R., & Hagger, M. S. (2015). Exploring the perceived effectiveness of a life skills development program for high-performance athletes. *Psychology of Sport and Exercise*, *16*(3), 139–149. 10.1016/j.psychsport.2014.10.005

Harrison, E. (2014). The first concussion crisis: Head injury and evidence in early American football. *American Journal of Public Health*, *104*(5), 822–833. 10.2105/AJPH.2013.301840

Harwood, C. (2008). Developmental consulting in a professional football academy: The 5Cs coaching efficacy program. *The Sport Psychologist*, *22*(1), 109–133. 10.1123/tsp.22.1.109

Harwood, C. G., & Knight, C. J. (2009). Stress in youth sport: A developmental investigation of tennis parents. *Psychology of Sport and Exercise*, *10*(4), 447–456. 10.1016/j.psychsport.2009.01.005

Haugaasen, M., & Jordet, G. (2012). Developing football expertise: A football-specific research review. *International Review of Sport and Exercise Psychology*, *5*(2), 177–201. 10.1080/1750984X.2012.677951

Henriksen, K., Schinke, R. J., Moesch, K., Mccann, S., Parham, W., Terry, P., & Larsen, C. (2020a). Consensus statement on improving the mental health of high performance athletes. *International Journal of Sport and Exercise Psychology*, *18*(5), 391–408. 10.1080/1612197X.2019.1570473

Henriksen, K., Schinke, R. J., Durand-Bush, N., Moesch, K., McCann, S., Parham, W. D., Larsen, C. … et al. (2020b). Athlete mental health in the Olympic/Paralympic quadrennium: A multi-societal consensus statement. *International Journal of Sport and Exercise Psychology*, *20*(3), 391–408. 10.1080/1612197X.2020.1746379

Hill, A. P., Mallinson-Howard, S. H., & Jowett, G. E. (2018). Multidimensional perfectionism in sport: A meta-analytical review. *Sport, Exercise, and Performance Psychology*, *7*(3), 235–270. 10.1037/spy0000125

Houlihan, B. (1997). Sport, national identity and public policy. *Nations and Nationalism*, *3*(1), 113–137. 10.1111/j.1354-5078.1997.00113.x

Hulme, A., McLean, S., Read, G. J. M., Dallat, C., Bedford, A., & Salmon, P. M. (2019). Sports organizations as complex systems: Using cognitive work analysis to identify the factors influencing performance in an elite netball organization. *Frontiers in Sports and Active Living*, *1*. 10.3389/fspor.2019.00056

International Olympic Committee. (2017). Safeguarding athletes from harassment and abuse in sport: IOC toolkit for IFs and NOCs. https://stillmed.olympics.com/media/Document%20Library/OlympicOrg/IOC/What-We-Do/Promote-Olympism/Women-And-Sport/Boxes%20CTA/IOC_Safeguarding_Toolkit_ENG_Screen_Full1.pdf

International Olympic Committee. (2023). Mental health action plan. https://stillmed.olympics.com/media/Documents/News/2023/07/Mental-Health-Action-Plan-2023.pdf?_ga=2.177835557.126713604.1692112815-1779695323.1692112815

International Olympic Committee. (n.d.). Athletes' commission. https://olympics.com/ioc/athletes-commission

Iorfino, F., Hermens, D. F., Cross, S. P. M., Zmicerevska, N., Nichles, A., Badcock, C.-A., Groot, J., Scott, E. M., & Hickie, I. B. (2018). Delineating the trajectories of social and occupational functioning of young people attending early intervention mental health services in Australia: A longitudinal study. *BMJ Open*, *8*(3), e020678. 10.1136/bmjopen-2017-020678

Jansen, S. C., & Sabo, D. (1994). The sport/war metaphor: Hegemonic masculinity, the Persian Gulf War, and the new world order. *Sociology of Sport Journal*, *11*(1), 1–17. 10.1123/ssj.11.1.1

Jenkins, T. (2013). War – the militarization of American professional sports: How the sports intertext influences athletic ritual and sports media. *Journal of Sport and Social Issues*, *37*(3), 245–260. 10.1177/019372470686

Jensen, S. N., Ivarsson, A., Fallby, J., Dankers, S., & Elbe, A.-M. (2018). Depression in Danish and Swedish elite football players and its relation to perfectionism and anxiety. *Psychology of Sport and Exercise*, *36*, 147–155. 10.1016/j.psychsport.2018.02.008

Kawabata, M. (2013). Is collectivism good for health promotion? Experiences of day labourers in Japan. *Global Health Promotion*, *20*(4), 44–51. 10.1177/1757975913503384

Kilic, Ö, Hopley, P., Kerkhoffs, G. M. M. J., Lambert, M., Verhagen, E., Viljoen, W., Wylleman, P., & Gouttebarge, V. (2019). Impact of concussion and severe musculoskeletal injuries on the onset of mental health symptoms in male professional rugby players: A 12-month study. *BMJ Open Sport & Exercise Medicine*, *5*(1), e000693. 10.1136/bmjsem-2019-000693

Kim, Y., Park, J., & Park, M. (2016). Creating a culture of prevention in occupational safety and health practice. *Safety and Health at Work*, *7*(2), 89–96. 10.1016/j.shaw.2016.02.002

Kirsh, B., Krupa, T., & Luong, D. (2018). How do supervisors perceive and manage employee mental health issues in their workplaces? *Work*, *59*(4), 547–555. 10.3233/wor-182698

Konijn, A. M., Lay, A. M., Boot, C. R. L., & Smith, P. M. (2018). The effect of active and passive occupational health and safety (OHS) training on OHS awareness and empowerment to participate in injury prevention among workers in Ontario and British Columbia (Canada). *Safety Science*, *108*, 286–291. 10.1016/j.ssci.2017.12.026

Lang, M. (2015). "None of the kids are allowed to eat junk at the pool": Discourses of 'optimal' nutrition in competitive youth swimming and the impact on athlete welfare. *The International Journal of Sport and Society: Annual Review*, *5*(1), 11–22. 10.18848/2152-7857/CGP/V05/54117

Larsen, C. H., Alfermann, D., Henriksen, K., & Christensen, M. K. (2014). Preparing footballers for the next step: An intervention program from an ecological perspective. *The Sport Psychologist*, *28*(1), 91–102. 10.1123/tsp.2013-0015

Lebrun, F., & Collins, D. (2017). Is elite sport (really) bad for you? Can we answer the question? *Frontiers in Psychology*, *8*, 10.3389/fpsyg.2017.00324

Lichtenstein, M. B., Hinze, C. J., Emborg, B., Thomsen, F., & Hemmingsen, S. D. (2017). Compulsive exercise: Links, risks and challenges faced. *Psychology Research and Behavior Management*, *10*, 85–95. 10.2147/PRBM.S113093

Maaravi, Y., Levy, A., Gur, T., Confino, D., & Segal, S. (2021). "The tragedy of the commons": How individualism and collectivism affected the spread of the COVID-19 pandemic. *Frontiers in Public Health*, *9*, 37. 10.3389/fpubh.2021.627559

McCallister, S. G., Blinde, E. M., & Weiss, W. M. (2000). Teaching values and implementing philosophies: Dilemmas of the youth sport coach. *Physical Educator*, *57*, 33–45.

McMahon, J. A., & Dinan-Thompson, M. (2011). 'Body work-regulation of a swimmer body': An autoethnography from an Australian elite swimmer. *Sport Education and Society*, *16*(1), 35–50. 10.1080/13573322.2011.531960

Merz, Z. C., Perry, J. E., Brauer, A. H., Montgomery, T. L., Shulze, J., & Ross, M. J. (2020). The cost of mental illness: The public's derogation of athletes with psychological distress. *Stigma and Health*, *5*(4), 442–450. 10.1037/sah0000213

Miller, T. (2012). *NSCA's guide to tests and assessments: Science of strength and conditioning series*. Human Kinetics.

Moesch, K., Kenttä, G., Kleinert, J., Quignon-Fleuret, C., Cecil, S., & Bertollo, M. (2018). FEPSAC position statement: Mental health disorders in elite athletes and models of service provision. *Psychology of Sport and Exercise*, *38*, 61–71. 10.1016/j.psychsport.2018.05.013

Mountjoy, M., Rhind, D. J. A., Tiivas, A., & Leglise, M. (2015). Safeguarding the child athlete in sport: A review, a framework and recommendations for the IOC youth athlete development model. *British Journal of Sports Medicine*, *49*(13), 883–886. 10.1136/bjsports-2015-094619

Nixon, H. L. (1993). Accepting the risks of pain and injury in sport: Mediated cultural influences on playing hurt. *Sociology of Sport Journal*, *10*(2), 183–196. 10.1123/ssj.10.2.183

Opie, H., & Smith, G. (1992). The withering of individualism: Professional team sports and employment law. *University of New South Wales Law Journal*, *15*(2), 313–355.

Palmer, D., Cooper, D. J., Emery, C., Batt, M. E., Engebretsen, L., Scammell, B. E., Schamasch, P., Shroff, M., Soligard, T., Steffen, K., Whittaker, J. L., & Budgett, R. (2021). Self-reported sports injuries and later-life health status in 3357 retired Olympians from 131 countries: A cross-sectional survey among those competing in the games between London 1948 and PyeongChang 2018. *British Journal of Sports Medicine*, *55*(1), 46–53. 10.1136/bjsports-2019-101772

Papaioannou, A. G., Schinke, R. J., & Schack, T. (2019). Sport psychology in emerging countries, special section two: Introduction. *International Journal of Sport and Exercise Psychology*, *17*(1), 1–4. 10.1080/1612197X.2019.1575071

Papathomas, A. (2018). Disordered eating in sport: Legitimized and stigmatized. In M. Atkinson (Ed.), *Sport, mental illness, and sociology* (Vol. 11, pp. 97–109). Emerald Publishing Limited.

Pensgaard, A. M., & Roberts, G. C. (2000). The relationship between motivational climate, perceived ability and sources of distress among elite athletes. *Journal of Sports Sciences*, *18*(3), 191–200. 10.1080/026404100365090

Phelps, A., Kelly, J., Lancaster, S., Mehrzad, J., & Panter, A. (2017). Report of the independent review panel into the climate and culture of the world class programme in British cycling. https://www.sportsthinktank.com/uploads/cycling-independent-review.pdf

Plateau, C. R., McDermott, H. J., Arcelus, J., & Meyer, C. (2014). Identifying and preventing disordered eating among athletes: Perceptions of track and field coaches. *Psychology of Sport and Exercise*, *15*(6), 721–728. 10.1016/j.psychsport.2013.11.004

Porter, R. R., Morrow, S. L., & Reel, J. J. (2013). Winning looks: Body image among adolescent female competitive swimmers. *Qualitative Research in Sport, Exercise and Health*, *5*(2), 179–195. 10.1080/2159676x.2012.712983

Preston, C., Allan, V., & Fraser-Thomas, J. (2021). Facilitating positive youth development in elite youth hockey: Exploring coaches' capabilities, opportunities, and motivations. *Journal of Applied Sport Psychology*, *33*(3), 302–320. 10.1080/10413200.2019.1648327

Purcell, R., Gwyther, K., & Rice, S. M. (2019). Mental health in elite athletes: Increased awareness requires an early intervention framework to respond to athlete needs. *Sports Medicine – Open*, *5*(1), 46. 10.1186/s40798-019-0220-1

Rasquinha, A., Dunn, J. G. H., & Causgrove Dunn, J. (2014). Relationships between perfectionistic strivings, perfectionistic concerns, and competitive sport level. *Psychology of Sport and Exercise*, *15*(6), 659–667. 10.1016/j.psychsport.2014.07.008

Reardon, C. L., Hainline, B., Aron, C. M., Baron, D., Baum, A. L., Bindra, A., Budgett, R., Campriani, N., Castaldelli-Maia, J. M., Currie, A., Derevensky, J. L., Glick, I. D., Gorczynski, P., Gouttebarge, V., Grandner, M. A., Han, D. H., McDuff, D., Mountjoy, M., Polat, A., … Engebretsen, L. (2019). Mental health in elite athletes: International Olympic Committee consensus statement (2019). *British Journal of Sports Medicine*, *53*(11), 667–699. 10.1136/bjsports-2019-100715

Rhind, D. J. A., Kay, T., Hills, L., & Owusu-Sekyere, F. (2017). Building a system to safeguard children in sport: The 8 CHILDREN pillars. *Journal of Sport and Social Issues*, *41*(2), 151–171. 10.1177/0193723517696966

Rhind, D. J. A., & Owusu-Sekyere, F. (2020). *International safeguards for children in sport: Developing and embedding a safeguarding culture*. Routledge.

Rice, S. M., Purcell, R., De Silva, S., Mawren, D., McGorry, P. D., & Parker, A. G. (2016). The mental health of elite athletes: A narrative systematic review. *Sports Medicine*, *46*(9), 1333–1353. 10.1007/s40279-016-0492-2

Roderick, M. (2006). *The work of professional football*. Taylor & Francis.

Roderick, M., Waddington, I., & Parker, G. (2000). Playing hurt: Managing injuries in English professional football. *International Review for the Sociology of Sport*, *35*(2), 165–180. 10.1177/101269000035002003

Ryba, T. V., Stambulova, N. B., & Ronkainen, N. J. (2016). The work of cultural transition: An emerging model. *Frontiers in Psychology*, *7*. 10.3389/fpsyg.2016.00427

Ryba, T. V., Stambulova, N. B., Si, G., & Schinke, R. J. (2013). ISSP position stand: Culturally competent research and practice in sport and exercise psychology. *International Journal of Sport and Exercise Psychology*, *11*(2), 123–142. 10.1080/1612197X.2013.779812

Sabiston, C. M., Lucibello, K. M., Kuzmochka-Wilks, D., Koulanova, A., Pila, E., Sandmeyer-Graves, A., & Maginn, D. (2020). What's a coach to do? Exploring coaches' perspectives of body image in girl's sport. *Psychology of Sport and Exercise*, *48*, 101669. 10.1016/j.psychsport.2020.101669

Schinke, R. J., Blodgett, A. T., McGannon, K. R., Ge, Y., Oghene, O., & Seanor, M. (2017). Adjusting to the receiving country outside the sport environment: A composite vignette of Canadian immigrant amateur elite athlete acculturation. *Journal of Applied Sport Psychology*, *29*(3), 270–284. 10.1080/10413200.2016.1243593

Schinke, R. J., Henriksen, K., Petersen, B., Wylleman, P., Si, G., Zhang, L., McCann, S., & Papaioannou, A. (2021). Pathways through acute athlete care during training and major tournaments: A multinational conceptualised process. *International Journal of Sport and Exercise Psychology*, *19*(3), 295–309. 10.1080/1612197X.2021.1892940

Schinke, R. J., Papaioannou, A., Maher, C., Parham, W. D., Larsen, C. H., Gordin, R., & Cotterill, S. (2020). Sport psychology services to professional athletes: Working through COVID-19. *International Journal of Sport and Exercise Psychology*, *18*(4), 409–413. 10.1080/1612197X.2020.1766182

Schinke, R. J., & Stambulova, N. (2017). Context-driven sport and exercise psychology practice: Widening our lens beyond the athlete. *Journal of Sport Psychology in Action*, *8*(2), 71–75. 10.1080/21520704.2017.1299470

Schinke, R. J., Stambulova, N. B., Si, G., & Moore, Z. (2018). International Society of Sport Psychology position stand: Athletes' mental health, performance, and development. *International Journal of Sport and Exercise Psychology*, *16*(6), 622–639. 10.1080/1612197X.2017.1295557

Seanor, M., Giffin, C. E., & Schinke, R. J., Coholic, & Lariviere. (2023). Pixies in a windstorm: Australian elite gymnasts' stories of maltreatment through media data. *Sport in Society*, *26* (3), 553–572. 10.1080/17430437.2022.2060825

Sellars, P., Evans, L., & Thomas, O. (2016). The effects of perfectionism in elite sport: Experiences of unhealthy perfectionists. *The Sport Psychologist*, *30*(3), 219–230. 10.1123/tsp.2014-0072

Si, G. Y., Duan, Y. P., Li, H. Y., & Jiang, X. B. (2011). An exploration into social-cultural meridians of Chinese athletes' psychological training. *Journal of Clinical Sport Psychology*, *5*(4), 325–338. 10.1123/jcsp.5.4.325

Si, G. Y., Duan, Y. P., Li, H.-Y., Zhang, C.-Q., & Su, N. (2015). The influence of the Chinese sport system and Chinese cultural characteristics on Olympic sport psychology services. *Psychology of Sport and Exercise*, *17*(2), 56–67. 10.1016/j.psychsport.2014.08.008

Si, G. Y., Li, X., Huang, Z. J., Wang, D. D., Wang, Y., Liu, J. D., … Zhang, C. Q. (2021). The mental health of Chinese elite athletes: Revisiting the assessment methods and introducing a management framework. *International Journal of Sport and Exercise Psychology*. Advanced online publication. 10.1080/1612197X.2021.1907769

Stambulova, N. B., & Ryba, T. V. (2014). A critical review of career research and assistance through the cultural lens: Towards cultural praxis of athletes' careers. *International Review of Sport and Exercise Psychology*, *7*(1), 1–17. 10.1080/1750984X.2013.851727

Stambulova, N. B., & Wylleman, P. (2019). Psychology of athletes' dual careers: A state-of-the-art critical review of the European discourse. *Psychology of Sport and Exercise*, *42*, 74–88. 10.1016/j.psychsport.2018.11.013

Starren, A., Hornikx, J., & Luijters, K. (2013). Occupational safety in multicultural teams and organizations: A research agenda. *Safety Science*, *52*, 43–49. 10/1016/j.ssci.2012.03.013

Stoffregen, S. A., Giordano, F. B., & Lee, J. (2019). Psycho-socio-cultural factors and global occupational safety: Integrating micro- and macro-systems. *Social Science & Medicine*, *226*, 153–163. 10.1016/j.socscimed.2019.02.046

Sweeney, L., Horan, D., & MacNamara, Á. (2021). Premature professionalisation or early engagement? Examining practise in football player pathways. *Frontiers in Sports and Active Living*, *3*, 158. 10.3389/fspor.2021.660167

Sylvia, L. G., Salcedo, S., Bernstein, E. E., Baek, J. H., Nierenberg, A. A., & Deckersbach, T. (2013). Nutrition, exercise, and wellness treatment in bipolar disorder: Proof of concept for a consolidated intervention. *International Journal of Bipolar Disorders*, *1*(1), 24. 10.1186/2194-7511-1-24

Tetrick, L. E., & Peiró, J. M. (2012). Occupational safety and health. In S. Kozlowski (Ed.), *The Oxford handbook of organizational psychology* (Vol. 2, pp. 1228–1244). Oxford University Press.

Torregrosa, M., Reguela, S., & Mateos, M. (2020). Career assistance programs. In D. Hackfort & R. J. Schinke (Eds.), *The Routledge international encyclopedia of sport and exercise psychology* (Vol. 2, pp. 73–88). Routledge.

United Nations. (1989). Convention on the rights of the child. https://www.unicef.org.uk/what-wedo/un-convention-child-rights/?sisearchengine=284&siproduct=Campaign_G_02_Our_Work&gclid=EAIaIQobChMI6d-Pl-Du8QIVgtrICh0VIgTAEAAYAyAAEgJKJvD_BwE

Wachsmuth, S., Jowett, S., & Harwood, C. G. (2018). Managing conflict in coach—athlete relationships. *Sport, Exercise, and Performance Psychology*, *7*(4), 371–391. 10.1037/spy0000129

Wilkinson, R. J. (2020). A literature review exploring the mental health issues in academy football players following career termination due to deselection or injury and how counselling could support future players. *Counselling and Psychotherapy Research*, *21*(4), 859–868. 10.1002/capr.12417

Windholz, E. (2015). Professional sport, workplace health & safety law and reluctant regulators. *Sports Law E Journal*, No. 2015. https://www.cabdirect.org/cabdirect/abstract/20163304663

World Health Organization. (2004). Prevention of mental disorders: Effective interventions and policy options. https://apps.who.int/iris/handle/10665/43027

World Health Organization. (2020). Basic documents (49th ed.).

Yanar, B., Kosny, A., & Smith, P. M. (2018). Occupational health and safety vulnerability of recent immigrants and refugees. *International Journal of Environmental Research and Public Health*, *15*(9), 2004. 10.3390/ijerph15092004

4

THE MENTAL HEALTH OF CHINESE ELITE ATHLETES

Revisiting the Assessment Methods and Introducing a Management Framework

Gangyan Si, Xin Li, Zhijian Huang, Dandan Wang, Yuan Wang, Jing-Dong Liu, Hao Liu, Daliang Zhao, Danran Bu, and Chun-Qing Zhang

Introduction

Elite sport is a typically high-stress occupation, various occupational stressors such as overtraining, competitive anxiety, injury, and retirement transitions. Previous research into elite athletes has demonstrated that the elite athletes may be more vulnerable compared to the general population (Foskett & Longstaff, 2018; Gouttebarge et al., 2019; Gulliver et al., 2015). Indeed, there are several sport-specific issues such as injuries, overtraining, burnout, and retirement that might lead athletes more susceptible to mental health disorders (Rice et al., 2016) and create barriers to elite athletes seeking mental health treatment due to stigma, low mental health literacy, and negative past experiences (Castaldelli-Maia et al., 2019). That said, it seems that the percentage of elite athletes who have had mental health disorders is not less than the general population (Moesch et al., 2018). Likewise, the Chinese elite athletes also demonstrated high levels of mental health disorders (Liu, 2019; Tan et al., 2014; Yan, 2020). Compared to the scale of high-performance sport in China and the number of elite athletes nationwide, the mental health-related research and applied interventions on Chinese elite athletes are still relatively limited.

Over the past five years, the mental health of elite athletes has indeed attracted much attention worldwide. For example, the International Society of Sports Psychology (ISSP; Henriksen, Schinke, Moesch et al., 2020; Schinke et al., 2018), European Federation of Sport Psychology (FEPSAC; Moesch et al., 2018), American Medical Society for Sports Medicine (AMSSM; Chang et al., 2020), and Canadian Centre for Mental Health and Sport (CCMHS; Van Slingerland et al., 2019) called attention on mental

DOI: 10.4324/9781003459750-4

health problems of athletes. In 2018, the International Society of Sport Psychology (ISSP) issued a position statement on athletes' mental health which highlighted the importance of assessing athletes' mental health using the continuum-type models by associating both mental health and mental illness with athletes' top performance, treating athletes' career development as a whole when dealing with their mental health issues, and implementing cultural appropriate mental health-related interventions (Castaldelli-Maia et al., 2019; Schinke et al., 2018). The European Federation of Sport Psychology (FEPSAC) also issued a position statement on mental health disorders in elite athletes and models of service provision, in which the models of service provision by six European countries were systematically reviewed and summarized into seven aspects, including professional service providers, support systems, diagnostic assessments, clinical treatment, performance during treatment, screening, and education system (Moesch et al., 2018). This statement provides a great resource for researchers and practitioners to have a better understanding of status and approaches of the athletes' mental health management in Europe. That said, both these statements have highlighted how important it is that stakeholders, such as coaches, athletes, managers, sport psychologists, and medical doctors, focus their attention on the mental health of elite athletes. Likewise, the International Olympic Committee (IOC) has also issued a consensus statement calling for the development of management strategies to address the indicators and symptoms of mental health issues (Reardon et al., 2019). This statement indeed provides researchers and practitioners evidence- and consensus-based guidelines for the diagnosis and management of mental health disorders. It also indicates that the IOC has officially called on the world to face up to the mental health disorders of elite athletes.

To address the urgent issues of mental health among elite athletes, the ISSP organized two athlete mental health Think Tank meetings in 2018 and 2019 to summarize the opinions of expert panels from the ISSP, FEPSAC, the Association of Applied Sport Psychology (AASP), the Asian-South Pacific Association of Sport Psychology (ASPASP), and the United States Olympic and Paralympic Committee (USOPC). The first consensus statement provided six propositions and recommendations related to how to improve mental health of elite athletes, which also emphasized the importance of developing contextualized mental health definition in sports context, broadening the scope of assessment on athletes' mental health using multiple methods, stakeholders working with sport organizations to develop a nurturing environmental and sustainable environment, as well as specifying the role of mental health officer (Henriksen, Schinke, Moesch et al., 2020). Then, the second statement on the mental health of athletes involved in the Olympic/Paralympic quadrennium, in which the opportunities and challenges of mental health pre-, during-, and post-Olympic Games were reviewed

(Henriksen, Schinke, McCann et al., 2020). This statement also proposed an initiative to improve psychological support for post-Game period, including improving psychological safety, reducing unnecessary stress, optimizing recovery, destigmatizing mental health, and increasing help-seeking. Overall, these two statements provide guidance for research and applied practice by summarizing the status, challenges, and future directions of athlete mental health.

The importance of athlete mental health has also been recognized by the Chinese government. For example, the Chinese sports psychology community submitted a proposal on "Strengthening the Construction of the High-performance Athletes' Mental Health System" through representatives from the academic community at the 13th National People's Congress (i.e., Chinese highest legislature) in April 2019. This initiative was accepted by the General Office of the Standing Committee of the National People's Congress, which was handed over to the General Administration of Sport of China to handle it separately. In January 2020, an official reply was issued by the General Administration of Sport of China promising that they will continue to vigorously promote the construction of the mental health system for elite athletes and consider four main aspects (General Administration of Sport of China, 2020). The four main aspects include (a) establishing an institutional policy for protecting and promoting mental health of elite athletes; (b) assessing the status quo of mental health among elite athletes; (c) conducting evidence-based research that focusing on the mental health of elite athletes; and (d) developing a multi-discipline professional task force on mental health of elite athletes. This highlights the necessity of developing a comprehensive mental health management framework for Chinese athletes along with some high-quality empirical research to inform policy making and resource allocation. Under the Chinese Whole-Nation system, this is a memorable official document that marks a new phase in history into which the mental health management of Chinese athletes has entered.

There has been increased attention on the mental health of Chinese elite athletes during the last 10 years. Chinese sport psychology researchers have explored the mental health of Chinese elite athletes and preliminary evidence has been established via quantitative (e.g., Yang, 2015) and qualitative studies (e.g., Yan, 2020). However, most of the studies are descriptive in nature and lack a systematic investigation of the mental health situation and rather solely focused on the negative dimensions of mental health. To better understand the mental health issues of Chinese elite athletes, a systematic investigation is required. Therefore, the current chapter describes an exploratory endeavor hopeful in achieving this purpose. Specifically, the two main purposes of this chapter are (a) to revisit the assessment methods used for measuring mental health among Chinese elite athletes and (b) to introduce our recent development of a contextually appropriate mental health management framework for Chinese elite athletes with some practical examples.

Assessment Methods of Mental Health among Elite Athletes

Although potential protective factors (e.g., feeling of autonomy, positive relations in sport and private life, and adequate recovery) were highlighted in qualitative studies (Küttel & Larsen, 2020), past research heavily focused on the negative dimensions of mental health for elite athletes (Reardon et al., 2019). Likewise, the most frequently used mental health tools with Chinese elite athletes are the Symptom Checklist 90 (SCL-90; Derogatis et al., 1973), and the Psychological Health Inventory (PHI; Livson & Peskin, 1967) during the last 30 years. Both these tools are typical measures of psychopathology. Using the SCL-90, previous research focused on descriptive analysis of the negative mental health symptoms among a certain type of sports (e.g., Ying & Tang, 2010) or in a certain region (e.g., Liu et al., 2007; Tan et al., 2014). It should be noted that the PHI is revised from the Minnesota Multiphasic Personality Inventory (MMPI; Graham, 1987) and it has been applied in the population of elite athletes with internal consistency reliabilities examined (Zhou & Guo, 2007). In addition, self-reported measures for depression such as the Self-Rating Depression Scale (SDS; Zung, 1965), and for anxiety such as the Self-Rating Anxiety Scale (SAS; Zung, 1971) have also been used. Overall, the assessment of mental health for Chinese elite athletes only focused on the psychopathology indicators for a long period of time.

Regarding the positive dimensions of mental health for elite athletes, Lundqvist and colleagues (Lundqvist, 2011; Lundqvist & Sandin, 2014) developed an integrated model of global well-being and context-specific well-being related to sport that is modified and extended from a model for the well-being of employees (Page & Vella-Brodrick, 2009). Specifically, this framework comprises subjective well-being (e.g., satisfaction with training, positive emotion in sports), psychological well-being (e.g., self-acceptance as an athlete and positive relation to coach and teammate), and social well-being (e.g., social acceptance in sport, social coherence in sport) in a sport context. A key strength of this well-being framework is that it provides insights into the construction of the positive dimensions of mental health among athletes. However, it should be noted that this framework did not take athletes' negative aspects of mental health into consideration.

Under the influence of positive psychology, the Dual-Factor Model of Mental Health, including both positive and negative mental health, was proposed (Greenspoon & Saklofske, 2001). The Dual-Factor Model states that mental health is not solely an absence of mental illness or having high levels of subjective well-being but the combination of both (Suldo & Shaffer, 2008). In other words, the positive and negative indicators of mental health are independent but simultaneously inter-related. That said, the Dual-Factor Model of Mental Health emphasizes active prevention and advocates the use of a two-dimensional classification standard to identify individuals who may need to improve their sense of well-being to actively prevent mental illness, and who might need intervention (Keyes & Lopez, 2005). Building on the Dual-Factor Model of Mental Health, Yang (2015) developed a positive dimension in addition to the dimension of psychopathology for measuring the mental health of Chinese athletes. Yang defined the positive dimension of mental health as comprising three main aspects: willpower, social adaptability, and sports cognition. However, this definition contains an ambitious but too broad a scope, which lacks a clear conceptual structure of the elements of mental health. In addition, this tool has not been through strict scale development processes and it includes too many dimensions that are not consistent with the key dimensions of athletes' mental health. That said, it might provide more useful information if both the positive and negative dimensions can be measured simultaneously although the previous common practice is to measure the mental health separately with a focus on the psychopathology.

In line with the suggestions of dual-continua model of mental health and mental illness (Keyes, 2002), the assessment of Chinese athletes' mental health assessment should include both positive and negative dimensions. The negative dimension can be assessed using the existing tools, such as SCL-90, PHI, the Patient Health Questionnaire (PHQ; Spitzer et al., 2006), and the Generalized Anxiety Disorder scale (GAD-7; Spitzer et al., 2006), all of which had been validated and used in Chinese populations, including the athletic population. The positive dimension can be measured using tools such as athletes' training and competition well-being scale (e.g., Zhang & Liang, 2002) and flourishing scale (Küttel et al., 2021). Furthermore, we highly recommend the use of the more sport-specific assessment tools: the Sport Mental Health Assessment Tool 1 (SMHAT-1) and the Sport Mental Health Recognition Tool 1 (SMHRT-1) developed by the IOC Mental Health Working Group (Gouttebarge et al., 2021).

With the comprehensive assessment of athletes' mental health in terms of positive and negative mental health levels, tailor-made mental health interventions can be developed for different types of athletes (Schinke et al., 2018). For example, strength-based interventions (Wagstaff & Leach, 2015) targeting the improvement of positive mental health can be applied to deal with athletes having low negative mental health but at the same time low positive mental health (partial mental health). In contrast, mindfulness- and acceptance-based (e.g., Gardner & Moore, 2007; Myall et al., 2023; Si et al., 2016) or compassion-based interventions (e.g., Mosewich et al., 2019) for reducing the negative mental health can be developed to help athletes with high negative mental health but also high positive mental health (i.e., partial mental disorder). For athletes with high negative mental health and low positive mental health (i.e., complete mental disorder), an integrated mental health intervention program targeting both negative and positive mental health can be applied with maximum effectiveness as compared to any type alone. Taking the key role of sporting environment into consideration (Küttel & Larsen, 2020), mental health interventions should be integrated as part of the mental health management within the sports training centers for Chinese elite athletes.

Mental Health Management of Chinese Elite Athletes

Given the scale and numbers of elite athletes in China, currently there seems to be a dearth of systematic research on the management of mental health among Chinese elite athletes. A major concern is that there are only a small number of athletes' mental health management work had been specifically carried out at the national and provincial elite sport training centers in China. Even though there are some ongoing mental health screening projects, these were driven by external academic research needs (e.g., university-based research projects) rather than internally driven by the needs of athletes at the training centers. In addition, mental health literacy intervention projects have rarely been conducted in Chinese sport training centers (Bu, 2020). These limitations might be related to the lack of awareness and perceived importance of elite athletes' mental health issues, which highlights the importance for researchers, teams, and center management working together to tackle this issue (Henriksen, Schinke, Moesch et al., 2020). The first step might be to develop a sport-center based mental health management framework to support and respond to the mental health needs of elite athletes (Purcell et al., 2019).

Developing a Sport Training Center-Based Mental Health Management Framework

Why we need to develop a sport training center-based mental health management framework for Chinese elite athletes? The sport training system and environments for Chinese athletes are different from their Western counterparts that most of the elite athletes in China training in government-fully funded and centrally managed sport training centers (Si et al., 2011). In contrast, Western athletes most likely train in sport clubs or government-partly funded and openly managed bases. In addition, there is usually a research or science and technology department within each of the Chinese national and provincial sport training centers. Within the research or science and technology department there are sports psychology or psychological counseling professionals. These consultants can generally act as coordinators for the mental health management of elite athletes. For example, organizing mental health screening, organizing mental health literacy education, recommending experts, referring athletes with mental health issues to specialized external hospitals, and so on. It should be noted that currently there are no specialized sport psychiatrists in China and elite athletes with these needs are referred to hospital psychiatrists.

Another reality in the Chinese medical system is that there are no clinical psychologists, instead there are registered psychological consultant/therapists. When athletes in need see a hospital psychiatrist, there is little chance that athletes will be followed up by a licensed psychotherapist. Once the athletes return to the team after diagnosis and/or treatment, it can be a great challenge for training center-based sport psychology consultants, coaches, and management teams. For example, the challenges can be whether and how the athletes in such conditions can participate in training and competition in a normal way. Given that sport doctors in Chinese sports training centers are responsible for the training and competition-related issues such as prevention and treatment of the injuries and sports fatigue, usually they will not be directly involved with the mental health issues.

Considering the aims and structures of the existing mental health services and management recommended by the IOC (Reardon et al., 2019) and taking the unique working mechanism of Chinese sport system into consideration, we propose that a sport training center-based mental health management framework for Chinese elite athletes comprised three main components: (a) annual mental health screening, (b) follow-up and mental health emergency intervention, and (c) mental health literacy education (see Figure 4.1). The three main components need to be coordinated by specialized agencies (i.e., research or science and technology department of the training center or a sports science institute) or persons at the sport training center to make sure the management work well. Hereafter, we refer it as a center-based mental health team. That said, the research or science and technology department of sport training centers can appoint internal or external sport psychology professionals working together as a mental health team to coordinate the above three aspects of support. The research or science and technology department appoint sport psychology professionals with competence requirements, including sport psychology or counseling/clinical psychology with master's degree or above, and with at least three years working experience in the area, given that in the Chinese sport psychology qualification system, at least three years of applied experiences is required. In addition, the Olympics happened every quadrennial and three years of applied experiences can make sure that the sport psychology professionals be familiar with the operation in the training centers' sports systems. To ensure all three aspects of support are met, resourceful sport training centers can set up their own mental health taskforce, in which

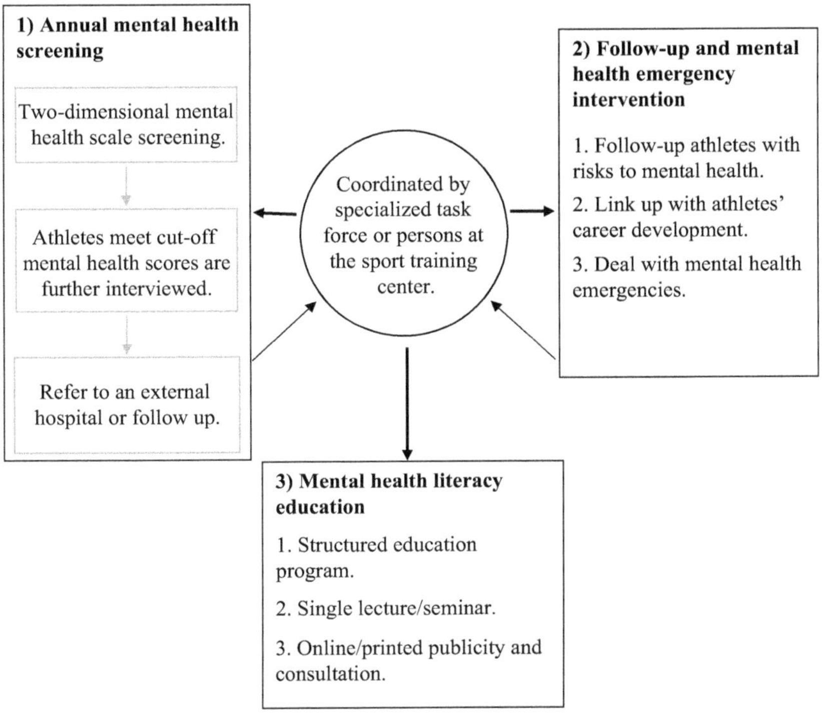

FIGURE 4.1 Sport training center-based mental health management framework for Chinese elite athletes.

external personnel can be recruited as part-time staff. It should be noted that in Chinese elite sports context there are no mental coaches, but each sports training center normally will have one or two sport psychology consultants. Further explanations of each component are provided in the following sections.

Annual Mental Health Screening

The first core component of this mental health management framework is an institutionalized screening procedure and standardized screening process. Given the mental health screening is training center-based rather than in national level, an annual screening is feasible taking the scale of screening and manpower into consideration. That is, all elite athletes based in the sport training centers should be screened for mental health at a certain time each year. The complete screening procedure can be divided into three steps. Step 1: Screening all training center-based athletes with reliable and valid self-report measures that assess both the negative and positive dimensions of mental health. Step 2: For athletes with negative mental health indicators exceed a certain threshold, follow-up interviews need to be conducted. Based on a standardized protocol, two psychological professionals then interview athletes meet certain cut-off values and further assess the mental health status of athletes, independently. Step 3: For those athletes who are assessed as high risk, the mental health team should advise the center's management to refer the athlete to an external partner hospital for further diagnosis and treatment. For athletes with low to moderate levels of mental health risk, the mental health team will follow-up with them for four weeks, which we explain next.

Follow-up and Mental Health Emergency Intervention

There are two types of situations for the mental health team to follow-up. First, for those athletes with mental health symptoms that are below the clinical standard after screening, the mental health team need to work closely with coaches, team medical, and other support staff to meet the requirements of follow-up support. Face-to-face or online-based mental health interventions can be provided to increase the positive mental health and decrease the negative mental health among athletes with mild to moderate mental health risks. Second, for those athletes who are diagnosed with mental health disorders (e.g., depression, bipolar disorder, and eating disorder), great efforts should be made when they return to the sport training centers from psychiatric consultation at external partner hospitals. For example, athletes still have symptoms and are unwilling to take medication might jeopardize the team's regular training schedules, continuous guidance, and supervision from the psychiatrist are required along with the cooperation of coaching team. Based on our previous applied experience, athletes who are unwilling to take medication are largely lacking mental health literacy. For example, athletes may have the stigma of taking medication equals to confirmed mental illness, beliefs of taking medication will sabotage their training, and medication does not work.

In certain situations, career planning team might have to be involved dealing with athletes' mental health issues related to career development and career transition (Wylleman et al., 2015). This is because athletes' mental health disorders such as sleep disorders and mood disorders might be related to the absence of clear career goals, sports performance ups and downs, and chaotic values (Schinke et al., 2018). Therefore, well-planned career development and transition can help prevent the mental health disorders. That said, follow-up work can also cooperate with center-based staff responsible for athletes' career planning to deal with the career development and transition-related mental health issues.

Mental health emergency refers to immediate risk in the context of a disturbed mental state (Reardon et al., 2019). Follow-up support should also include dealing with any mental health emergencies or any urgent major psychological crisis events. For example, the sudden accidental death of a coach or athlete, the outbreak of a pandemic, the unexpected and not performance-based disqualification of the Olympic Games. The mental health team should provide immediate psychological support (e.g., grief counseling and stress/emotion management) to help athletes adjust their emotions and adapt to their environment. The mental health emergency service should also be independent from the annual screening and the mental health team should be ready for providing urgent assistance to the teams of the sport training centers.

Mental Health Literacy Education

As previously mentioned, part of reasons that athletes do not seek help is because they lack mental health literacy (Bu et al., 2020). Therefore, it is also important to increase athletes' mental health literacy levels, particularly for those athletes with low levels of mental health literacy. That said, it is also suggested that annual screening can include the indicator of mental health literacy in addition to the mental health indicators. The mental health literacy education of Chinese elite athletes can be conducted via structured education courses that are suitable for non-competition, seasonal group teaching. For example, the education course can consist of 4–5 lessons, with each lesson lasts for one hour targeting a certain topic. In other situations, a single lecture or seminar can be conducted which is suitable for situations like the sudden outbreak of pandemics (e.g., the COVID-19) that closed training required (Reardon et al., 2021). Of course, the traditional approach is to advertise the importance of mental health literacy and educate athletes via the online/print publicity. That said, consultations can also be used to increase athletes' mental health literacy levels.

In general, mental health literacy education aims to increase mental health knowledge, to teach individuals how to recognize symptoms related to problematic mental health, to reduce stigma, and to promote help-seeking attitudes (Bu et al., 2020; Diamond et al., 2022). Based on the Dual-Factor Model of Mental Health, we also recommend including positive dimensions into the structured education curriculum. It is better that the mental health literacy interventions can be delivered at least once a year in the sport training centers. In addition to the format of courses and lectures, such education can be implemented via the internet-delivered interventions (Gulliver et al., 2012).

Practical Examples of Applying the Mental Health Management Framework

Annual Mental Health Screening

The research team consists authors of the current chapter applied this mental health management framework in the G sport training center, located at the

South China. We conducted the annual mental health screening for athletes of the G training center during the COVID-19 pandemic in July 2020. Part of the other purpose for conducting this screening is to evaluate the impact of lockdown on athletes' mental health, given the fact that lockdown caused serious impacts on the mental health of elite athletes (Carnevale Pellino et al., 2022). This screening is coordinated by a core mental health team consists of one full-time center-based sport psychology consultant (DW) and three part-time certified sport psychology consultants (GS, YW, and DZ), with one part-time professional (GS) serving as the leader of the team. It should be noted that within this team there are also two interns who were pursing master's degrees in sport psychology under the supervision of team leader (GS). The G sports training center also has a taskforce for elite athletes' career development planning which consists of two part-time sport psychology counselors (JL, HL).

Guided by the sport training center-based mental health management framework (see Figure 4.1), the screening consists of three steps. During Step 1, we screened 700 elite athletes using the SCL-90 inventory and found that approximately 11% elite athletes showed moderate to high levels of mental health disorders. During Step 2, we further assessed the 11% athletes individually via face-to-face interviews. Using a standard form developed by the research team, each athlete was interviewed and evaluated by two sport psychology professionals (DW and YW), independently. Then, the interview resulted approximately 3% high-risk athletes, 15% moderate-risk athletes, and 82% low-risk athletes. During Step 3, we made recommendations to the training center's management for transferring high-risk athletes to the psychiatric doctors of the external partner hospital to receive further diagnosis and treatment.

Follow-up and Mental Health Emergency Intervention

For athletes with moderate-level mental health risks at the G sports training center, our mental health team continued to follow-up with them for four weeks. We provided consultation and observational assessments at least once per week, and at the same time gathering feedback from coaches and team medical staff. Specifically, the mental health symptoms for two-thirds of the athletes with moderate level of mental health risk gradually disappeared after four weeks of follow-up intervention. For another one-third of athletes, their mental health symptoms did not disappear but at the same time did not get worse, and therefore they were continuously monitored to prevent the conditions getting worse.

For the low mental health risk athletes, we reported their general conditions to team managers and coaches. We also mentioned to the team that the mental health team can be requested to follow-up with certain athletes if needed. If athletes' mental health problems were related to career development and transition, they were referred to the athlete career planning and development working group with the athletes' consent. For the performance-related matters, the career development group continually communicated with the mental health team to address such matters.

The high mental health risk athletes who were diagnosed with mental health disorders by the external partner hospital received treatments from hospital psychiatrists. Then, they were released from the hospitals and returned to the G sports training center for four weeks without having to join scheduled regular training of their teams or competitions if any. The mental health team at G sports training center continued to maintain their communication with the hospital psychiatrists concerning these athletes.

While the mental health team was conducting the mental health screening, an athlete of a team sport at the G sports training center suddenly passed away during training due to heart attack. This led to serious psychological turmoil among all the other athletes in the team. Our research group considered this as a mental health emergency issue. Two members of the mental health team (GS and DW) immediately provided group grief counseling for the entire team. The team was trained to accept the facts, express grief, and re-adapt to the environment without the deceased athlete. The acceptance- and compassion-based intervention worked well, with both coaches and athletes participated in the intervention. With the coaches and athletes established a sense of trust in the mental health team, we conducted a follow-up intervention on helping the athletes to cope with adversities and build up team cohesion. Then, the head coach of the team requested the mental health team to further provide psychological support for the whole team to prepare for the forthcoming national championships in the next two months.

Mental Health Literacy Education

Recently, our team member (DB), under the research team's support, conducted a mental health literacy intervention for elite athletes at H province in the winter training period from December 2019 to January 2020. It should be noted that this is an independent training without mental health screening. A total of 60 elite badminton and table tennis athletes (35 males and 25 females) were recruited. The design of randomized controlled trial was used and the intervention lasted eight weeks with one 120-minute training session per week. Findings demonstrated that the intervention significantly improved athletes' mental health literacy, help-seeking attitudes, and intentions, as well as reduced stigma in both post-intervention and follow-up tests. Although there were no significant intervention effects on athletes' help-seeking behaviors at both post- and follow-up tests, this demonstrates that the center-based mental health literacy interventions for Chinese elite athletes are feasible and can be integrated into the management framework.

Reflections

In line with the Dual-Factor Model (Greenspoon & Saklofske, 2001; Keyes & Lopez, 2005; Suldo & Shaffer, 2008), the assessment of mental health should include both positive and negative mental health and treat them as related but distinct phenomena. Sport-specific tools for measuring positive mental health such as well-being scale (e.g., Zhang & Liang, 2002) and flourishing in sports context (e.g., Küttel et al., 2021) should therefore be developed. It should be noted that the psychopathology measurement tools of mental health such as SCL-90 (Derogatis et al., 1973) and PHI (Livson & Peskin, 1967) are continued to be used to assess the negative dimensions of mental health given the limitations. Very recently, the IOC mental health group developed the SMHAT-1 (Gouttebarge et al., 2021). Our research group just completed the validation of the scale package and psychometric validation of the Multicomponent Mental Health Literacy Scale (MMHLS) among Chinese elite athletes (Wang et al., 2022). Based on the Dual-Factor Model, the mental health of Chinese elite athletes can be divided into four categories: (a) complete mental health (i.e., low negative mental health – high positive mental health), (b) partial mental health (i.e., low negative mental health – low positive mental health), (c) partial mental disorder (i.e., high negative mental health – high positive mental health), and (d) complete mental disorder (i.e., high negative mental health – low positive mental health). Based on this classification, specific interventions can be developed and applied to athletes with different types of mental health.

In line with the sport-focused mental health care model proposed by the Canadian Centre for Mental Health and Sport (Van Slingerland et al., 2019), the key part of the sport training center-based mental health program for Chinese athletes is to set up a specialized task force or find center-based persons to coordinate the three main components from annual mental health screening to follow-up and mental health emergency intervention, and then mental health literacy education. Therefore, resources are needed for the research or science and technology departments at sport training centers to appoint sport psychology professionals to coordinate the management of elite athletes' mental health. Better, long-term contracts can be provided to those key mental health team members no matter in full-time or part-time formats. It seems that at least one full-time sport psychology consultant should be center-based staff. As we recommended sport training centers should conduct annual mental health screening for the center-based elite athletes to detect and further prevent the mental health symptoms getting worse, a more frequent screening on a short period of interval (e.g., half year) might also be feasible. Another solution might be a specific arrangement of the screening within a certain time frame. That said, this depends on the manpower, resources, and necessities of the centers. Furthermore, coordination is required to become an integrated support mechanism and the medical and psychological resources within the training centers including team medical staff, sport psychologists, and career development professionals should be able to work closely with each other (Henriksen, Schinke, Moesch et al., 2020). Regarding the follow-up work of athletes with serious mental health risks, the coordination between the mental health team and outside psychiatric and psychological experts is extremely important. Sport training centers should have established a cooperative relationship with the contractual or partner hospitals for the diagnosis and treatment of mental health disorders for elite athletes. Nonetheless, the follow-up work for athletes with mental health disorders requires close cooperation between the mental health team, coaches, and team medical staff no matter whether those concerned athletes are still in training and competition or just returned to the team after treatment.

With regards to the improvement of mental health literacy for both Chinese athletes and coaches, it is suggested that a structured literacy education course can be designed, which can be implemented in sport training centers flexibly (Bu, 2020). Resourceful sport training centers can conduct at least one mental health literacy education course each year. In addition to the face-to-face educational interventions, online interventions for improving athletes' mental health literacy would also be beneficial with the ability to reach more athletes (Gulliver et al., 2012). In sports training centers, it is important to establish an atmosphere in which everyone values the mental health and mental health literacy of the center-based elite athletes. We also highlight the importance of screening the mental health literacy of elite athletes and call for the implementation of context-specific mental health interventions for those athletes who really need the help.

Conclusion

To sum up, we proposed that the assessment methods for Chinese elite athletes should be based on the Dual-Factor Model of Mental Health and introduced our recently developed mental health management framework for Chinese athletes. We have also preliminarily applied this framework at two provincial level high-performance sport training centers with satisfactory results. Future studies should consider expanding the scale of implementation, nationwide, at an increasing number of sport training centers to test its feasibility and effectiveness in different contexts. Further studies are also needed to examine and confirm the functions and mechanisms related to the prevention or reduction of the negative dimension and the promotion of positive dimension of mental health.

Disclosure Statement

No potential conflict of interest was reported by the author(s).

Acknowledgments

Gangyan Si, Zhijian Huang, Danran Bu, and Chun-Qing Zhang's contribution was supported by the National Natural Science Foundation of China (No. 31800948). The authors would like to thank Dr Amanda J. Pitkethly for editing and proofreading the manuscript.

References

Bu, D. (2020). Mental health literacy and help seeking in Chinese elite athletes (Unpublished Thesis). Hong Kong, China: Hong Kong Baptist University.

Bu, D., Chung, P. K., Zhang, C. Q., Liu, J., & Wang, X. (2020). Mental health literacy intervention on help-seeking in athletes: A systematic review. *International Journal of Environmental Research and Public Health*, *17*, 7263. DOI: 10.3390/ijerph17197263

Carnevale Pellino, V., Lovecchio, N., Puci, M. V., Marin, L., Gatti, A., Pirazzi, A., … Vandoni, M. (2022). Effects of the lockdown period on the mental health of elite athletes during the COVID-19 pandemic: A narrative review. *Sport Sciences for Health*, *18*(4), 1187–1199. 10.1007/s11332-022-00964-7

Castaldelli-Maia, J. M., e Gallinaro, J. G. D. M., Falcão, R. S., Gouttebarge, V., Hitchcock, M. E., Hainline, B., … & Stull, T. (2019). Mental health symptoms and disorders in elite athletes: A systematic review on cultural influencers and barriers to athletes seeking treatment. *British Journal of Sports Medicine*, *53*(11), 707–721. 10.1136/bjsports-2019-100710

Chang, C., Putukian, M., Aerni, G., Diamond, A., Hong, G., Ingram, Y., … Wolanin, A. (2020). Mental health issues and psychological factors in athletes: Detection, management, effect on performance and prevention: American Medical Society for Sports Medicine Position Statement-Executive Summary. *British Journal of Sports Medicine*, *54*(4), 216–220. 10.1136/bjsports-2019-101583

Derogatis, L. R., Lipman, R. S., & Covi, L. (1973). SCL-90: An outpatient psychiatric rating scale–preliminary report. *Psychopharmacology Bulletin*, *9*, 13–28.

Diamond, S., Wallace, L., English, M., & Caperchione, C. M. (2022). The impact of mental health literacy initiatives on youth elite athletes: A systematic review. *Performance Enhancement & Health*, *10*(3), 100226. 10.1016/j.peh.2022.100226

Foskett, R. L., & Longstaff, F. (2018). The mental health of elite athletes in the United Kingdom. *Journal of Science and Medicine in Sport*, *21*, 765–770. DOI: 10.1016/j.jsams.2017.11.016

Gardner, F., & Moore, Z. (2007). *The psychology of enhancing human performance: The Mindfulness-Acceptance-Commitment (MAC) approach*. New York, NY: Springer.

General Administration of Sport of China. (2020). Reply to Recommendation No. 5136 of the Second Session of the 13th National People's Congress. (In Chinese). Retrieved from: http://www.sport.gov.cn/n315/n10701/c941327/content.html

Gouttebarge, V., Bindra, A., Blauwet, C., Campriani, N., Currie, A., Engebretsen, L., … Purcell, R. (2021). International Olympic Committee (IOC) Sport Mental Health Assessment Tool 1 (SMHAT-1) and Sport Mental Health Recognition Tool 1 (SMHRT-1): Towards better support of athletes' mental health. *British Journal of Sports Medicine*, *55*, 30–37. DOI: 10.1136/bjsports-2020-102411

Gouttebarge, V., Castaldelli-Maia, J. M., Gorczynski, P., Hainline, B., Hitchcock, M. E., Kerkhoffs, G. M., … Reardon, C. L. (2019). Occurrence of mental health symptoms and disorders in current and former elite athletes: A systematic review and meta-analysis. *British Journal of Sports Medicine*, *53*, 700–706. DOI: 10.1136/bjsports-2019-100671

Graham, J. R. (1987). *The MMPI: A practical guide* (2nd ed.). Oxford, England: Oxford University Press.

Greenspoon, P. J., & Saklofske, D. H. (2001). Toward an integration of subjective well-being and psychopathology. *Social Indicators Research*, *54*, 81–108. DOI: 10.1023/A:1007219227883

Gulliver, A., Griffiths, K. M., Christensen, H., Mackinnon, A., Calear, A. L., Parsons, A., … Stanimirovic, R. (2012). Internet-based interventions to promote mental health help-seeking in elite athletes: An exploratory randomized controlled trial. *Journal of Medical Internet Research*, *14*, e69. DOI: 10.2196/jmir.1864

Gulliver, A., Griffiths, K. M., Mackinnon, A., Batterham, P. J., & Stanimirovic, R. (2015). The mental health of Australian elite athletes. *Journal of Science and Medicine in Sport*, *18*, 255–261. DOI: 10.1016/j.jsams.2014.04.006

Henriksen, K., Schinke, R., McCann, S., Durand-Bush, N., Moesch, K. … Hunziker, J. (2020). Athlete mental health in the Olympic/Paralympic quadrennial: A multi-societal consensus statement. *International Journal of Sport and Exercise Psychology*, *18*, 391–408. DOI: 10.1080/1612197X.2020.1746379

Henriksen, K., Schinke, R., Moesch, K., McCann, S., Parham, W. D., Larsen, C. H., & Terry, P. (2020). Consensus statement on improving the mental health of high performance athletes. *International Journal of Sport and Exercise Psychology*, *5*, 553–565. DOI: 10.1080/1612197X.2019.1570473

Keyes, C. L. M. (2002). The mental health continuum: From languishing to flourishing in life. *Journal of Health and Social Behavior*, *43*, 207–222. DOI: 10.2307/3090197

Keyes, C. L. M., & Lopez, S. J. (2005). Toward a science of mental health: Positive directions in diagnosis and intervention. In C. R. Snyder & S. J. Lopez (Eds.), *Handbook of positive psychology* (pp. 45–59). New York, NY: Oxford University Press.

Küttel, A., & Larsen, C. H. (2020). Risk and protective factors for mental health in elite athletes: A scoping review. *International Review of Sport and Exercise Psychology*, *13*(1), 231–265. 10.1080/1750984X.2019.1689574

Küttel, A., Pedersen, A. K., & Larsen, C. H. (2021). To flourish or languish, that is the question: Exploring the mental health profiles of Danish elite athletes. *Psychology of Sport and Exercise*, *52*, 101837. DOI: 10.1016/j.psychsport.2020.101837

Liu, J. (2019). Suicidal ideation of elite athletes and its implications (Unpublished Thesis). Beijing, China: Beijing Sports University. (In Chinese)

Liu, J.-Q., Hu, Y.-X., & Yang, X.-J. (2007). Comparative research on mental health condition and correlative factors of some elite athletes in Shanghai. *China Sport Science and Technology*, *43*, 54–58. (In Chinese)
Livson, N., & Peskin, H. (1967). Prediction of adult psychological health in a longitudinal study. *Journal of Abnormal Psychology*, *72*, 509–518. DOI: 10.1037/h0025236
Lundqvist, C. (2011). Well-being in competitive sports – the feel-good factor? A review of conceptual considerations of well-being. *International Review of Sport and Exercise Psychology*, *4*, 109–127. DOI: 10.1080/1750984X.2011.584067
Lundqvist, C., & Sandin, F. (2014). Well-being in elite sport: Dimensions of hedonic and eudaimonic well-being among elite orienteers. *The Sport Psychologist*, *28*, 245–254. DOI: 10.1123/tsp.2013-0024
Moesch, K., Kenttä, G., Kleinert, J., Quignon-Fleuret, C., Cecil, S., & Bertollo, M. (2018). FEPSAC position statement: Mental health disorders in elite athletes and models of service provision. *Psychology of Sport and Exercise*, 38, 61–71. DOI: 10.1016/j.psychsport.2018.05.013
Mosewich, A. D., Ferguson, L. J., McHugh, T. L. F., & Kowalski, K. C. (2019). Enhancing capacity: Integrating self-compassion in sport. *Journal of Sport Psychology in Action*, *10*, 235–243. DOI: 10.1080/21520704.2018.1557774
Myall, K., Montero-Marin, J., Gorczynski, P., Kajee, N., Sheriff, R. S., Bernard, R., … Kuyken, W. (2023). Effect of mindfulness-based programmes on elite athlete mental health: A systematic review and meta-analysis. *British Journal of Sports Medicine*, *57*(2), 99–108. 10.1136/bjsports-2022-105596
Page, K. M., & Vella-Brodrick, D. A. (2009). The 'what', 'why' and 'how' of employee wellbeing: A new model. *Social Indicators Research*, *90*, 441–458. DOI: 10.1007/s11205-008-9270-3
Purcell, R., Gwyther, K., & Rice, S. M. (2019). Mental health in elite athletes: Increased awareness requires an early intervention framework to respond to athlete needs. *Sports Medicine-Open*, *5*(1), 46. 10.1186/s40798-019-0220-1
Reardon, C. L., Bindra, A., Blauwet, C., Budgett, R., Campriani, N., Currie, A., … Hainline, B. (2021). Mental health management of elite athletes during COVID-19: A narrative review and recommendations. *British Journal of Sports Medicine*, *55*(11), 608–615. DOI: 10.1136/bjsports-2020-102884
Reardon, C. L., Hainline, B., Aron, C. M., Baron, D., Baum, A. L., Bindra, A., … Engebretsen, L. (2019). Mental health in elite athletes: International Olympic Committee consensus statement (2019). *British Journal of Sports Medicine*, *53*, 667–699. DOI: 10.1136/bjsports-2019-100715
Rice, S. M., Purcell, R., De Silva, S., Mawren, D., McGorry, P. D., & Parker, A. G. (2016). The mental health of elite athletes: A narrative systematic review. *Sports Medicine*, *46*, 1333–1353. DOI: 10.1007/s40279-016-0492-2
Schinke, R. J., Stambulova, N. B., Si, G., & Moore, Z. (2018). International society of sport psychology position stand: Athletes' mental health, performance, and development. *International Journal of Sport and Exercise Psychology*, *16*, 622–639. DOI: 10.1080/1612197X.2017.1295557
Si, G., Duan, Y., Li, H. Y., & Jiang, X. (2011). An exploration into socio-cultural meridians of Chinese athletes' psychological training. *Journal of Clinical Sport Psychology*, *5*(4), 325–338.

Si, G., Lo, C.-H., & Zhang, C.-Q. (2016). Mindfulness training program for Chinese athletes and its effectiveness. In A. Baltzell (Ed.), *Mindfulness and performance* (pp. 235–267). New York, NY: Cambridge University Press.

Spitzer, R. L., Kroenke, K., Williams, J. B., & Löwe, B. (2006). A brief measure for assessing generalized anxiety disorder: The GAD-7. *Archives of Internal Medicine, 166*, 1092–1097. DOI: 10.1001/archinte.166.10.1092

Suldo, S. M., & Shaffer, E. J. (2008). Looking beyond psychopathology: The dual-factor model of mental health in youth. *School Psychology Review, 37*, 52–68. DOI: 10.1080/02796015.2008.12087908

Tan, Y.-B., Cao, Z., & Wu, Y-E. (2014). Current research of psychological health of high-level athletes in Guangdong province. *Journal of Sports Adult Education, 30*, 48–51. (In Chinese)

Van Slingerland, K. J., Durand-Bush, N., Bradley, L., Goldfield, G., Archambault, R., Smith, D., … Kenttä, G. (2019). Canadian Centre for Mental Health and Sport (CCMHS) position statement: Principles of mental health in competitive and high-performance sport. *Clinical Journal of Sport Medicine, 29*, 173–180. DOI: 10.1097/JSM.0000000000000665

Wagstaff, C. R., & Leach, J. (2015). The value of strength-based approaches in SERE and sport psychology. *Military Psychology, 27*, 65–84. DOI: 10.1037/mil0000066

Wang, X., Liang, W., Liu, J., Zhang, C. Q., Duan, Y., Si, G., … Zhao, D. (2022). Further examination of the psychometric properties of the Multicomponent Mental Health Literacy Scale: Evidence from Chinese elite athletes. *International Journal of Environmental Research and Public Health, 19*(19), 12620. 10.3390/ijerph191912620

Wylleman, P., Rosier, N., & De Knop, P. (2015). Transitional challenges and elite athletes' mental health. In J. Baker, P. Safai, & J. Fraser-Thomas (Eds.), *Health and elite sport. Is high performance sport a healthy pursuit?* (pp. 99–116). New York, NY: Routledge.

Yan, L. (2020). Emotional disorders of Chinese elite athletes: A qualitative study. (Unpublished Thesis). Wuhan, China: Wuhan Sports University. (In Chinese)

Yang, S. (2015). Investigation and intervention of mental health on elite athlete – In view of the dual-factor model of mental health. (Unpublished thesis). Shanghai, China: Shanghai Sports University. (In Chinese)

Ying, H., & Tang, W.-B. (2010). Comparison on the status quo and the related factors of the mental health of top-notch martial arts athletes. *Zhejiang Sport Science, 32*, 93–96. (In Chinese)

Zhang, L. W., & Liang, Z. P. (2002). Athletes' life satisfaction: The contributions of individual self-esteem and collective self-esteem. *Acta Psychologicha Sinica, 34*, 160–167. (In Chinese)

Zhou, Y.-G., & Guo, Y.-J. (2007). Research on the actuality and correlativity of social support and mental health for elite athletes. *Journal of Guangzhou Sport University, 27*, 82–85. (In Chinese)

Zung, W. W. (1965). A self-rating depression scale. *Archives of General Psychiatry, 12*, 63–70. DOI: 10.1001/archpsyc.1965.01720310065008

Zung, W. W. (1971). A rating instrument for anxiety disorders. *Psychosomatics, 12*, 371–379. DOI: 10.1016/S0033-3182(71)71479-0

5

PRELIMINARY PSYCHOMETRIC VALIDATION OF A BRIEF SCREENING TOOL FOR ATHLETE MENTAL HEALTH AMONG MALE ELITE ATHLETES

The Athlete Psychological Strain Questionnaire

Simon M. Rice, Alexandra G. Parker, Daveena Mawren, Patrick Clifton, Peter Harcourt, Michael Lloyd, Alex Kountouris, Ben Smith, Patrick D. McGorry, and Rosemary Purcell

Introduction

Elite professional sportspeople are exposed to a wide array of stressors that make them potentially susceptible to psychological distress (Gorczynski et al., 2017; Moesch et al., 2018). Recent years have witnessed increasing interest in screening processes for the identification of mental ill-health among athlete (Gouttebarge et al., 2021; Mountjoy et al., 2023). There is a need for targeted research into how impaired wellbeing in elite athletes may manifest. Intense physical activity performed at the elite athlete level may compromise aspects of mental wellbeing (Peluso & Andrade, 2005), and when combined with other stressors, including injury, performance, selection, or retirement/transition out of sport concerns, it is likely that elite athletes will experience fluctuating periods of increased vulnerability to mental ill-health or impeded wellbeing (Hughes & Leavey, 2012).

For professional sporting bodies to provide optimal support to their athletes and playing groups, and maintain performance excellence and cultures of achievement, attention must be given to athlete mental health (Taylor et al., 2012). Interest in the domain of elite athlete mental health is reflected in recent consensus statements outlining mental health symptom identification and management in sports-specific and elite environments (Henriksen et al., 2019; Moesch et al., 2018; Reardon et al., 2019). There is also growing interest in the development of athlete-specific screening and identification processes for the early identification of mental health problems

DOI: 10.4324/9781003459750-5

in this population (Donohue et al., 2019; Hussey et al., 2019). While a number of athlete mental health-related measures currently exist, they are relatively lengthy. For example, the Recovery Stress Questionnaire (RESTQ-Sport) (Kellmann & Kallus, 2001) was developed as a 77-item scale, though recent research has validated a shortened 36-item version (Kallus & Kellmann, 2016). Similarly, the Profile of Mood States (POMS) was originally 65 items (McNair, 1971), and has been abbreviated to 40-item (Grove & Prapavessis, 1992) and 24-item versions (Terry et al., 1999). The POMS in particular uses an adjective-checklist, and there is conjecture in the field regarding the psychometric validity of this measurement approach (Sliter & Zickar, 2014). While the RESTQ-Sport and POMS have significantly furthered research in the field (Beedie et al., 2000), their length has prohibited regular (i.e., weekly) monitoring or screening use in the sports environment (Taylor et al., 2012). Furthermore, much of the research undertaken to date on elite athlete mental health, including psychometric validation studies, has been with non-representative samples (Rice et al., 2016). Hence, selection bias and low study response rates (often <40%) limit the conclusions that can be drawn.

Salient to the development of mental health symptoms in athletes is the concept of psychological strain (Bhagat et al., 2010), characterised by a combination of perceived stress and difficulty coping. Psychological strain can be characterised on a continuum of emotional exhaustion and reaction to stressful experiences (Boswell et al., 2004), and is likely to occur in situations where an individual believes they do not have sufficient resources to cope (King & Beehr, 2017). Where coping resources are extended beyond an athlete's capacity, stress-related symptoms of psychological strain may emerge (Raedeke & Smith, 2004). Strain theory articulates three contributors to psychological strain, namely, failure to achieve positively valued goals, the removal of positively valanced stimuli, and presentation with negatively valanced stimuli – each of which produce a range of negative emotions (e.g., anger, frustration, hopelessness) that the individual can only manage by employing effective coping mechanisms (Agnew, 1992; Eitle et al., 2013). Data from elite athletes experiencing distress highlights a tendency for some to conceal difficulties from coaching staff and teammates (Doherty et al., 2016). Additionally, elite athletes who engage in externalising coping strategies, such as problematic alcohol use (Gouttebarge et al., 2018; O'Brien et al., 2005; Schuring et al., 2017) may experience these coping responses as ineffective in the longer term, potentially enhancing psychological distress through cascading problems associated with heavy substance use.

Athletes are known to be a population that demonstrate stoicism and withhold disclosure of mental health problems (Breslin et al., 2017; Kerr et al., 2016), and it has been suggested that athletes may experience depression in ways beyond current diagnostic (e.g., DSM-5-TR) criteria

(Doherty et al., 2016). Assessment of somatic or externalising symptoms of depression may improve the detection of mental health problems in populations less likely to openly discuss emotional functioning (Brownhill et al., 2006). From a theoretical perspective, the 'big build' model characterises escalating behaviours of avoidance, numbing, risk-taking, and anger or aggression as potential transdiagnostic markers of psychological distress (Brownhill et al., 2005). In the 'big build' model, psychological distress is associated with difficulties in self-regulation, including irritability and anger (Möller-Leimkühler & Yücel 2010), which is especially true among younger adult populations (Fava et al., 2010; Massimiliano et al., 2018), as well as problems with goal-directed behaviour and motivation (Gillan et al., 2016), and coping through use of substances (Lai et al., 2015).

Much of this line of research has focussed on male samples (e.g., Genuchi & Valdez, 2015; Martin et al., 2013), and relates to socialisation processes prohibiting expression of symptoms or behaviours associated with vulnerability or weakness (Seidler et al., 2016). Nonetheless, evidence also supports the salience of externalising symptoms among females (Rice et al., 2013; Möller-Leimkühler & Yücel, 2010). Coupled with concerns related to external stressors experienced by many athletes, including worries related to performance (Moen et al., 2017), selection (Robertson et al., 2017) and transition beyond a competitive identity (Torregrosa et al., 2015), it is possible that a broad conceptualisation of athlete strain indicators, consistent with the 'big build' model, may assist in earlier identification of athletes experiencing distress through non-internalising symptoms. In line with strain theory, it is possible that some athletes experiencing significant and ongoing psychosocial pressures beyond their natural coping resources, and who are simultaneously striving for ideals of competitive excellence, may experience early distress symptoms as a combination of performance and self-regulation difficulties. Identification may be further compromised as sports practitioners report less comfort in discussing psychological health with athletes relative to physical health and conditioning (Rao & Hong, 2016).

In a broad sense, symptoms of psychological strain in athletes reflect difficulties of adaptation or adjustment to a change in circumstances, and are characterised by impairments in social and athletic functioning, and mood-related and impulse control problems (Glaesmer et al., 2015). Stressors that elite athletes experience during their competitive years may be role related (e.g., maladjustment to training pressures and maintaining an athletic career or position security) or personal in nature (e.g., non-sporting issues such as the work-life interface, financial problems, or relationship difficulties) (Jones & Tenenbaum, 2009; Mellalieu et al., 2009; Sarkar & Fletcher, 2014). Additionally, contemporary elite athletes may experience role-related and personal stressors becoming increasingly intertwined through traditional and social media pressures and obligations associated with sponsorship (Filo et al., 2015; Sanderson et al., 2015).

Regardless of the cause, or perceived impact of a given stressor for an athlete, early identification and management of stress-related problems or mental health symptoms is an effective means to facilitate intervention in an earlier illness phase (Ferguson et al., 2018; Sebbens et al., 2016). If instances of externalising responses are indeed early indicators of athlete distress, assessment of these domains may improve early detection and intervention for impacted athletes. Given existing screening tools that assess psychological distress (e.g., K-10; Kessler et al., 2002) or depression (e.g., PHQ-9; Kroenke et al., 2001) have a strong focus on internalising symptoms, these measures may not be sufficiently sensitive to early manifestations of distress experienced by elite athletes, leading to less than optimal detection rates.

The purpose of the present study was to develop and validate a brief measure of sports-related psychological strain in a representative sample of elite-level Australian male athletes.[1] Secondary aims were to establish convergent and divergent validity benchmarked against established measures of global psychological distress and psychological wellbeing, and examine outcome differences for athletes likely to be experiencing psychological strain. Consistent with psychological strain theory, it was hypothesised that athletes unable to compete due to injury would report significantly higher scores on the measure domains than those able to currently compete.

Methods

Participants

A total of 1,007 male elite, professional athletes from three national Australian sporting codes (Australian football, cricket, soccer) provided data, constituting 78.6% of the contracted athletes across these codes. All athletes were aged 18 years and over (M = 23.67, SD = 4.16 years). No exclusion criteria were applied.

Measures

Athlete Psychological Strain Questionnaire

The Athlete Psychological Strain Questionnaire (APSQ) was conceptualised to be a brief, self-report rating scale specific to the athletic context. Candidate items for the APSQ were developed based on clinical and consulting experience in the field. Item development was further informed by our previous systematic review into elite athlete mental health indicating sources of stress and maladaptive avoidance coping patterns in this population (Rice et al., 2016), and other relevant studies highlighting that athletes experiencing psychological strain report relationship challenges within and outside sports settings (Doherty et al., 2016), problems with substance involvement (Donohue et al., 2013; Dunn & Thomas, 2012), performance concerns, including life after elite competitive sport (Torregrosa et al., 2004), and externalising behaviours such as anger or aggression and risk-taking (Doherty et al., 2016). Author Rice developed the initial item pool of 12 items. While larger candidate item pools are recommended when developing new scales (Carpenter, 2018), the present study was nested within a broader project into athlete wellbeing, and it was necessary to limit any time imposition for the participating athletes. Authors Purcell and Parker reviewed the final wording of the item pool authors Rice, Purcell, and Parker are all registered psychologists with significant experience in the fields of athlete and youth mental health. Candidate APSQ items were developed to assess for difficulties with team-based interactions, impaired impulse control and frustration tolerance, worries related to athletic performance and training stress, and transition to life beyond professional athletic pursuits. Items followed key recommendations for scale development, including brevity, reading level and tone (DeVellis, 2016; Worthington & Whittaker, 2006) and were designed to use the same response scale (i.e., 1 = 'None of the time'; 5 = 'All of the time') and timeframe as the Kessler-10 distress scale.

Psychological Distress

The *Kessler-10* (K-10; Kessler et al., 2002) is among the most widely used measures of global psychological distress and was used in the current study to assess convergent validity with the APSQ. Scores are categorised to indicate respondents' distress over the past four weeks. Responses to items (i.e., *'About how often did you feel hopeless?'*) are made on a 5-point scale (i.e., 1 = 'None of the time'; 5 = 'All of the time'). The K-10 was developed and validated using epidemiological samples, and is widely recommended as a useful screening tool or simple outcome measure for assessing treatment progress for common mental disorders such as anxiety and depression (Slade et al., 2011). The K-10 demonstrates robust psychometric properties (Sunderland et al., 2012) across varying populations (e.g., Sampasa-Kanyinga et al., 2018) and cultures (Hajebi et al., 2018). In the current study, the K-10 reported satisfactory reliability $\alpha = 0.86$.

Psychological Wellbeing

The Warwick-Edinburgh Mental Well-Being Scale (WEMWBS) (Stewart-Brown et al., 2009) is a 14-item self-report scale that assesses positive aspects of mental health (i.e., *'I've been feeling good about myself'*). The WEMWBS was used in the current study to assess convergent validity with the APSQ.

Responses are made relative to the last two weeks, in the form of a 5-point scale (i.e., 1 = 'None of the time'; 5 = 'All of the time'). Population-level studies support the psychometric properties of the WEMWBS as a measure of mental wellbeing (Clarke et al., 2011; Lloyd & Devine, 2012), including cross cultural studies (Taggart et al., 2013; Trousselard et al., 2016). The WEMWBS is inversely related to measures of common psychopathology assessing symptoms of depression and anxiety (Smith et al., 2017) and is positively related to favourable psychosocial working conditions (Bartram et al., 2011). In the current study the WEMWBS reported satisfactory reliability $\alpha = 0.95$.

Procedure

Ethical approval for the study was granted by the University of Melbourne Human Research Ethics Committee (ID: 1442705). All participants were invited to complete an anonymous online survey, which took approximately 15 minutes to complete. Participants were approached by the researchers, with the support of the participating sporting codes, consistent with the approved research ethics procedures. The first page of the survey included informed consent information, including the voluntary nature of participation. This first page of the survey stated that consent was inferred based on provision of data. Participants were reminded of any missing items prior to progressing to the next page, resulting in no missing outcome data. The survey was completed in a group setting, with two researchers present to introduce and oversee the data collection. Participants were provided with individual access to a tablet or laptop computer to complete the survey. Data collection occurred locally, at each of the participant clubs/associations.

Data Analysis

Descriptive statistics were used to characterise the sample. A two-stage process was undertaken to validate the factor structure of the APSQ using exploratory factor analysis (EFA) and parallel analysis in a randomly partitioned calibration sample, and confirmatory factor analysis (CFA) in a separate validation sample. Firstly, iterative exploratory factor analysis (principal axis factoring) was undertaken to determine the underlying factor structure of the APSQ (i.e., scale calibration) (DeVellis, 2016; Worthington & Whittaker, 2006). To enable this, the sample of $N = 1{,}007$ was partitioned into two datasets according to random numbers allocated in SPSS. This resulted in a calibration sample ($n = 497$), and a validation sample ($n = 510$). In line with recent guidelines (Carpenter, 2018), oblique rotation (promax) was adopted as it is identified as providing more robust factor solutions (Thompson, 2004), and involves an oblique factor rotation where factors are permitted to correlate. Following this, the included APSQ items, as identified through the principal axis procedure, were subject to CFA to validate the reported factor structure within the separate calibration sample (Byrne, 2001). We adopted the typically accepted criteria to assess model fit CFI > 0.95, TLI > 0.95, RMSEA and SRMR < 0.50 (Byrne, 2001), in addition to the sample size adjusted Bayesian Information Criterion (BIC) to judge improved model fit for a second-order model. Here, Δ BIC > 10 was the criteria to identify a 'decisive' improved model fit (Kass & Raftery, 1995). To determine the stability of APSQ scores between the calibration and validation samples, ANOVA evaluated any sample group differences for the APSQ subscales and APSQ Total Score. Differential item functioning, using likelihood ratios, was undertaken to assess for potential differences in responding to APSQ items based on level of education (i.e., potential bias that may occur in differences for those with/without a university degree; Teresi & Fleishman, 2007) and region of birth (e.g., Australian born versus non-Australian born). Receiver operator characteristic (ROC) curve analysis was undertaken to determine the sensitivity and specificity of the APSQ at identifying high psychological distress as assessed by the K-10. The area under curve (AUC) value was used to examine how well the APSQ correctly identified athletes reporting high distress. The Youden Index was employed to identify a cut-off score for the APSQ Total Score that would balance sensitivity and specificity. This procedure maximises the vertical distance from the line of equality to the point [x, y] and determines the point at which sensitivity (i.e., the true positive rate; correctly identifying condition) and specificity (i.e., false positive rate; correctly identifying absence of condition) are considered equally important. Convergent and divergent validity was determined through examining patterns of statistically significant correlations with the K-10 (convergent validity evidenced by significant positive associations) and the WEMWBS (divergent validity evidenced by significant negative associations). Finally, construct validity was assessed using multivariate analysis of covariance (MANCOVA) to determine group differences on APSQ domains according to athlete injury status. The three-APSQ domains were dependent variables, and in-season status was entered as a covariate.

Results

Sample ages ranged from 18 to 39 years ($M = 23.67$, $SD = 4.16$, $Median = 23$). Most of the sample reported being partnered, and the majority reported moving from home for their respective sport. Respondents were most likely to be living in rental accommodation, although a small percentage owned their home outright. Relative to the general population, there was a relatively high proportion of the sample reporting an Aboriginal or Torres Strait Island

TABLE 5.1 Sample demographics

Variables	*n (%)*
Currently studying	431 (42.8)
Completed a university degree	65 (6.5)
Marital status	
Partnered/de-facto	512 (50.9)
Single	332 (33.0)
Married	161 (16.0)
Separated	2 (0.2)
Moved from home to play sport	468 (69)
Another region within state	134 (13.3)
Another state within Australia	451 (44.8)
Another country	65 (6.5)
Living situation	
Renting	464 (46.1)
My own home with mortgage	277 (27.5)
Living with a host family	56 (5.6)
My own home outright	43 (4.3)
Family home	152 (15.1)
Other	14 (1.4)
Cultural background	
Born in Australia	916 (91.1)
Aboriginal or Torres Strait Islander	69 (6.9)
Maori	3 (0.3)
Time in current elite competition	
<1 year	108 (10.7)
1–5 years	500 (49.7)
>5 years	399 (39.6)
Currently injured/on adapted training programme	288 (28.6)

cultural background (6.9%). Most of the samples were within the first five years of elite competition, and just over a quarter (28.6%) reported being injured or on an adapted training programme at the time of the survey. Most of the sample (88.3%) were not currently in their competitive season at time of data collection. Demographic details are presented in Table 5.1.

Exploratory Factor Analysis

Prior to conducting principal axis factoring, correlations were inspected, Bartlett's test of sphericity was performed, and the Kaiser-Meyer-Olkin (KMO) Measure of Sampling Adequacy evaluated. The correlation matrix indicated most observed items were correlated (i.e., $r > 0.35$), Bartlett's test of sphericity was significant ($p < 0.001$), and the KMO value was > 0.6 (KMO = .921), indicating that factor analysis was appropriate for the present dataset

(Field, 2009). Following recommendations, the exploratory analyses were iteratively re-run after item deletion to ensure the factor structure did not change with omission of items.

Parallel analysis was undertaken using the rawpar.sps procedure (O'Connor, 2000) undertaken in SPSS 22.0, using 5,000 parallel datasets, $\alpha = .01$, principal axis factoring and permutations of the raw data set. Parallel analysis indicated a three-factor solution. Subsequently, principal axis factoring resulted in three factors, accounting for 50.16% of total variance. One item ('*My sleep was worse than usual*') cross-loaded > 0.32, and was omitted. The subsequent analysis (KMO = .913, Bartlett's test of sphericity $p < .001$) resulted in three factors, accounting for 51.08% of total variance, though there was another cross-loading item ('*I covered up my difficulties*'). The analysis was re-run (KMO = .890, Bartlett's test of sphericity $p < .001$), resulting in three factors accounting for 50.44% of total variance, with convergence in six iterations, suggesting good factor stability. Factor loadings are presented in Table 5.2. There were no cross-loading items > 0.32 as part of the final 10 items, three-factor solution. A final parallel analysis was undertaken using these 10 items, which further confirmed the three-factor solution.

The first factor comprised four items and was labelled Self-Regulation (calibration sample $\alpha = 0.79$; validation sample $\alpha = 0.84$, eigenvalue = 4.57), the second factor comprised four items and was termed Performance (calibration sample $\alpha = 0.75$; validation sample $\alpha = 0.73$, eigenvalue = 1.03), while the third factor comprised two items and was labelled External Coping (calibration sample $\alpha = 0.64$; validation sample $\alpha = 0.72$, eigenvalue = 0.87). Carpenter (2018) recommends that two-item factors should only be retained when the subscale reports internal consistency, is theoretically valid, and items are well correlated, each of which were the case in the present data (calibration sample $r = 0.484$, $p < .001$; validation sample $r = 0.576$, $p < .001$).

Confirmatory Factor Analysis

In order to validate the three-factor solution, data from the unanalysed validation dataset ($n = 507$) was subjected to CFA. Maximum likelihood estimation was undertaken yielding a significant p-value ($\chi^2 = 81.22(32)$, $p < .001$). Fit indices supported model fit; CFI = 0.976, TLI = 0.966, RMSEA = 0.055, SRMR = 0.032, sample size adjusted BIC = 9995.97 although the RMSEA was marginally above the suggested cut-off. A subsequent second-order factor model was evaluated, with the three APSQ factors loading on a higher-order 'Athlete Psychological Strain' factor (see Figure 5.1). The second-order factor model was also judged a good fit to the data, with improved SRMR and BIC values ($\chi^2 = 81.22(32)$, $p < .001$), CFI = 0.976, TLI = 0.966, RMSEA = 0.055, SRMR = 0.029, sample size

TABLE 5.2 APSQ response frequencies, descriptive and factor loadings

Scale Items	*Response Frequency %(n)* N = *497*					*Descriptive* N = *497*			*EFA Factor Loadings* N = *497*		
	1 None of the time	*2 A little of the time*	*3 Some of the time*	*4 Most of the time*	*5 All of the time*	*Mean*	*Median*	*SD*	*Factor 1 - Self-Regulation*[a]	*Factor 2 - Performance*[b]	*Factor 3 - External Coping*[c]
Self-Regulation	–	–	–	–	–	5.79	5.0	2.32	–	–	–
It was difficult to be around teammates	75.4 (371)	16.7 (82)	5.7 (28)	2.2 (11)	0 (0)	1.35	1.0	0.69	.783	.015	−.054
I found it difficult to do what I needed to do	73.4 (362)	19.5 (96)	6.1 (30)	1.0 (5)	0 (0)	1.35	1.0	0.64	.649	.052	.040
I was less motivated	60.0 (296)	25.6 (126)	11.0 (54)	2.4 (12)	1.0 (5)	1.59	1.0	0.85	.610	.193	−.030
I was irritable, angry or aggressive	64.0 (315)	25.4 (125)	8.7 (43)	1.0 (4)	0.8 (4)	1.50	1.0	0.77	.511	−.048	.260
Performance	–	–	–	–	–	6.51	6.0	2.80	–	–	–
I could not stop worrying about injury or my performance	58.6 (289)	25.4 (125)	8.9 (44)	6.3 (31)	0.8 (4)	1.65	1.0	0.93	−.114	.782	.081
I found training more stressful	58.9 (290)	26.2 (129)	10.0 (49)	4.3 (21)	0.6 (3)	1.61	1.0	0.87	.166	.743	−.114
I found it hard to cope with selection pressures	80.9 (397)	11.6 (57)	4.1 (20)	2.6 (13)	0.8 (4)	1.32	1.0	0.75	.119	.510	.041
I worried about life after sport	46.7 (230)	27.6 (136)	14.8 (73)	7.7 (38)	3.2 (16)	1.93	2.0	1.10	.122	.373	.145
External Coping	–	–	–	–	–	2.48	2.0	1.09	–	–	–
I needed alcohol or other substances to relax	82.0 (402)	10.8 (53)	4.5 (22)	2.0 (10)	0.6 (3)	1.29	1.0	0.71	−.128	.196	.727
I took unusual risks off-field	86.9 (425)	8.2 (40)	3.9 (19)	0.8 (4)	0.2 (1)	1.19	1.0	0.56	.279	−.143	.570

Note. Factors determined by principal axis factoring, [a]eigenvalue = 4.57, [b]eigenvalue = 1.03, [c]eigenvalue = 0.87, [d]standardised factor loadings.

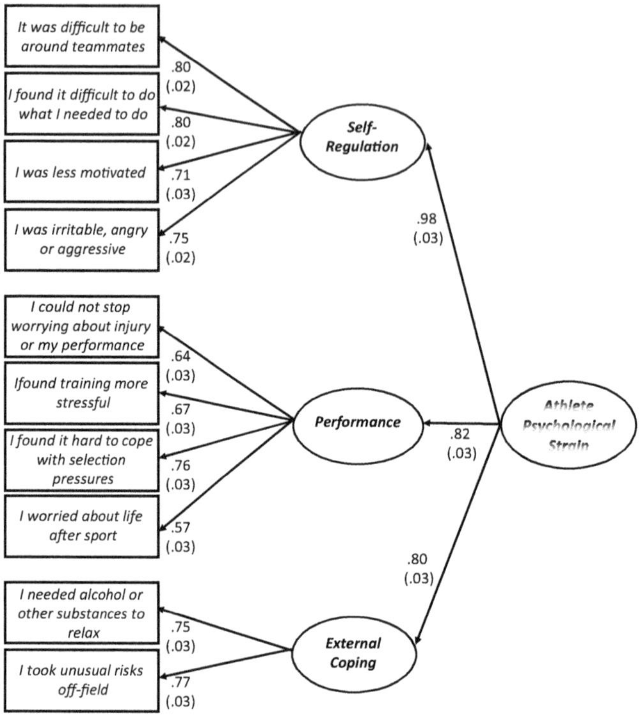

FIGURE 5.1 Standardised regression weights (with standard error values) for the second-order APSQ factor structure.

adjusted BIC = 9965.49 (Δ SSA BIC = 30.48). Standardised CFA factor loadings and standard error values for the second-order model are presented in Figure 5.1. Means were equivalent across the calibration and validation sub-samples for scale domains; APSQ Self-Regulation (calibration M = 5.79, SD = 2.32; validation M = 5.74, SD = 2.61; p = .784), APSQ Performance (calibration M = 6.51, SD = 2.80; validation M = 6.32, SD = 2.71; p = .281), APSQ External Coping (calibration M = 2.48, SD = 1.09; validation M = 2.52, SD = 1.16; p = .649), and APSQ Total Score (calibration M = 14.78, SD = 5.31; validation M = 14.58, SD = 5.62; p = .567).

Differential Item Functioning

Differential item functioning (DIF) was undertaken using the SPSS script DIFLRT to compute likelihood-ratio tests, including uniform and non-uniform DIF for differences according to education level (comparing those with and without degrees) and ethnicity (comparing those born in Australia and those born outside Australia). Uniform DIF exists when there is no interaction between ability level and group membership while non-uniform

DIF exists where there is an interaction (i.e., differences in probabilities of item endorsement are not the same over education level) (Swaminathan & Rogers, 1990). All DIF tests were non-significant, indicating consistency of responses over the 10 APSQ items (i.e., no evident bias) according to level of participant education and ethnicity (see Table 5.3).

Sensitivity and Specificity

ROC curve analysis was undertaken using the full sample (i.e., N = 1,007). The ROC curve state variable was selected as cases meeting the criteria of high distress on the K-10 (i.e., a K-10 score of ≥ 22), which included a total of 77 cases (i.e., the highest 7.6% of the distribution on K-10 scores). The area under curve (AUC) value for the APSQ was 0.955 [95% CI 0.938–0.972], SE = .009, p < .001. This AUC value indicates the APSQ is 'excellent' at correctly identifying athletes experiencing high psychological distress. The Youden Index indicated the optimal cut-off score on the APSQ as 21,[2] which reflected the uppermost 10.5% of the total sample. Based on use of the APSQ Total Score cut-off score of 21, the scale was able to accurately detect high psychological distress with a sensitivity of 93.5% and a specificity of 79.2%.

Convergent and Divergent Validity

The three domains of the APSQ demonstrated convergent validity with K-10 scores (see Table 5.4 for correlation coefficients). Robust moderate Pearson correlations (p's < .001) were observed separately for the calibration and validation samples for the APSQ Self-Regulation, Performance and External Coping subscales. Divergent validity was observed with significant negative correlations (p's < .001) between WEMWBS wellbeing scores and the three APSQ domains for the calibration and validation samples, respectively.

Construct Validity

A MANCOVA was used to determine differences for those injured or on an adapted programme versus those on standard training programmes. Injured athletes were hypothesised to be experiencing elevated role-related strain and were thus expected to reported higher scores on the APSQ domains. As expected, there was a significant multivariate effect observed for current injury $\Lambda = .992$, $F(3, 983) = 2.80$, $p = .040$, $\eta^2 = .008$, with the in-season variable a significant multivariate covariate $\Lambda = .989$, $F(3, 983) = 3.78$, $p = .010$, $\eta^2 = .011$ (see Table 5.5 for means and SDs). At the univariate level, in season status was a significant covariate for all APSQ domains (p's < .05). APSQ domain scores were higher for injured athletes on the Performance subscale (small effect size), with a non-significant trend for Self-Regulation subscale, and no difference for the External Coping subscale (see Table 5.5).

TABLE 5.3 Differential item functioning values for education and cultural background

APSQ Items	*Education*						*Cultural Background*					
	Omnibus Test, DIF		*Uniform DIF*		*Non-Uniform DIF*		*Omnibus Test, DIF*		*Uniform DIF*		*Non-Uniform DIF*	
	χ^2, *df*	p	χ^2, *df*	p	χ^2, *df*	p	χ^2, *df*	p	χ^2, *df*	p	χ^2, *df*	p
Self-Regulation												
It was difficult to be around teammates	0.022, 2	.989	0.022, 1	.882	0.000, 1	.987	3.569, 2	.168	0.169, 1	.681	3.400, 1	.065
I found it difficult to do what I needed to do	1.073, 2	.585	0.935, 1	.334	0.138, 1	.711	0.103, 2	.950	0.045, 1	.831	0.058, 1	.810
I was less motivated	1.493, 2	.474	0.118, 1	.731	1.375, 1	.241	0.556, 2	.757	0.004, 1	.949	0.552, 1	.457
I was irritable, angry or aggressive	0.454, 2	.797	0.407, 1	.524	0.047, 1	.828	1.120, 2	.571	0.058, 1	.810	1.062, 1	.303
Performance												
I could not stop worrying about injury or my performance	4.051, 2	.132	0.616, 1	.432	3.434, 1	.064	0.510, 2	.775	0.242, 1	.623	0.268, 1	.605
I found training more stressful	0.556, 2	.757	0.283, 1	.595	0.273, 1	.601	0.553, 2	.758	0.492, 1	.483	0.061, 1	.805
I found it hard to cope with selection pressures	3.146, 2	.207	2.647, 1	.104	0.499, 1	.480	1.065, 2	.587	0.005, 1	.942	1.059, 1	.303
I worried about life after sport	3.114, 2	.211	0.082, 1	.774	3.032, 1	.082	1.372, 2	.504	.376, 1	.540	0.995, 1	.318
External Coping												
I needed alcohol or other substances to relax	0.505, 2	.777	0.288, 1	.591	0.217, 1	.641	1.680, 2	.432	1.674, 1	.196	0.006, 1	.938
I took unusual risks off-field	1.601, 2	.449	0.492, 1	.483	1.110, 1	.292	3.984, 2	.136	3.531, 1	.060	0.453, 1	.501

TABLE 5.4 Zero-order correlations for study variables

	APSQ – Self-Regulation	*APSQ – Performance*	*APSQ – External Coping*	*APSQ – Total*
APSQ – Self-Regulation	–	.61***	.55***	.87***
APSQ – Performance	.66***	–	.50***	.90***
APSQ – External Coping	.61***	.50***	–	.71***
APSQ – Total	.91***	.89***	.73***	–

Note: *** = $p < .001$; calibration sample ($n = 497$) values above diagonal; validation sample ($n = 507$) values below diagonal.

Discussion

Findings from this representative sample of elite male athletes support the validity, reliability, factor structure, item functioning, and sensitivity/specificity of the APSQ. As a brief, three-factor screening tool, the APSQ may be a useful component within a broader assessment battery examining athlete performance and wellbeing. Since initial publication of the APSQ outcome paper in 2019, the scale has been adopted as part of the International Olympic Committee's Sports Mental Health Assessment Tool – 1 (SMHAT-1; Gouttebarge et al., 2021), with the APSQ now being used internationally (Lima et al., 2022; Ojio et al., 2021).

Aspects of convergent and divergent validity indicated that higher APSQ scores were associated with lower wellbeing and greater psychological distress. The APSQ demonstrated both high sensitivity (i.e., hit rate) and high specificity (i.e., correct rejection rate) relative to those experiencing elevated distress as identified by the K-10. An independent sample, using CFA, is needed to confirm the dimensionality of the APSQ. Nonetheless, findings are noteworthy given that APSQ items tap into domains specific to athletes that are distinct from those assessed by the K-10, and that the K-10 is a well-regarded scale widely used in major population health studies (Kessler et al., 2002; Slade et al., 2011). An advantage of using the APSQ with athlete populations may be that APSQ items are perceived by athletes as less 'intrusive' relative to those presented in general psychological distress measures (including the K-10), while simultaneously providing important information related to athlete mental health and adjustment.

The APSQ factors of Self-Regulation and External Coping are consistent with recent research suggesting that externalising symptoms may be early indicators of psychological strain (Genuchi & Valdez, 2015; Rice et al., 2015). In particular, Brownhill's 'big build' model identified externalising symptoms as part of a trajectory of distress (Brownhill et al., 2005), and population-based research (Martin et al., 2013) supports the notion that risk-taking, anger or aggression, and substance misuse may be associated with psychological strain or distress, especially in men (Cavanagh et al., 2017;

TABLE 5.5 Group comparisons on study outcome measures

APSQ Domain	*Full Sample* (*n = 1,003*) M (SD)	*Injured/Adapted Training* (n = *288*) M (SD)	*Uninjured* (n = *715*) M (SD)	df	F	p	*Effect Size* (*Partial* η^2)
Self-Regulation	5.76 (2.47)	5.97 (2.76)	5.68 (2.34)	1, 985	2.85	.092	.003
Performance	6.42 (2.75)	6.81 (3.00)	6.26 (2.63)	1, 985	8.32	.004	.008
External coping	2.50 (1.12)	2.58 (1.29)	2.46 (1.05)	1, 985	2.07	.151	.002
APSQ total	14.67 (5.47)	15.36 (6.10)	14.40 (5.18)	1, 988	3.38	.007	.007
K-10 total	14.16 (4.80)	14.08 (4.74)	14.19 (4.82)	1, 1000	0.09	.760	.000
WEMWEBS	51.39 (8.91)	50.84 (9.10)	51.61 (8.83)	1, 986	1.86	.173	.002

Seidler et al., 2016), but also in women (Möller-Leimkühler & Yücel, 2010). Whereas the Self-Regulation factor assesses a combination of low motivation and interpersonal difficulties, the two-item External Coping factor assesses substance-related coping and risk-taking outside the sports context. These types of behaviours or coping responses are likely to impede athlete achievement and increase the likelihood of athletes experiencing subsequent mental health or physical health problems (Conway et al., 2016; Rao & Hong, 2016).

Though beyond the scope of the present study, use of the APSQ alongside athlete-specific wellbeing interventions (e.g., Donohue et al., 2015, 2018) may assist in determining the influence of scale domains on psychosocial and athletic functioning. If problems related to Self-Regulation and External Coping are associated with higher levels of psychological strain in athletes, it stands to reason that currently injured athletes would report higher scores on these factors, in addition to the athlete-specific Performance factor. In the current study, this was true at the multivariate level, and more specifically on the Performance factor. These effects were relatively small, and there were no group differences according to injured and uninjured athletes for the Self-Regulation and External Coping factors. That said, the APSQ may be more effective than athlete non-specific measures in identifying psychological strain experienced by injured athletes, as there was no group difference observed for injured athletes on either the K-10 or WEMWBS.

While the APSQ total score was sufficiently sensitive in identifying athletes reporting high psychological distress (as defined by the K-10), larger studies are needed to determine correlates of the APSQ domains, and their relationship to psychological strain. As highlighted above, CFA outcomes should be replicated in another sample and more work undertaken to validate the APSQ cut-off score. The results of this research support the potential utility of the APSQ, although prospective studies are needed to establish the longer-term predictive validity of the APSQ relative to broader aspects of performance and health. Doing so may see measures such as the APSQ become useful in the early identification of elite athlete distress, and thus, enable effective, early intervention for emerging mental ill-health. This may be especially relevant if the APSQ is utilised by sporting codes during periods that are associated with heightened athlete distress, such as injury and retirement (Gouttebarge et al., 2014, 2015). Research into the utility of the APSQ is also warranted given that the peak years of elite athlete development and competition closely overlap with the peak ages for the onset of mental ill-health (12–25 years), and more specifically mental disorders (Rice et al., 2016).

There are a number of limitations that must be considered and addressed in future work related to the APSQ. The present validation samples were entirely male. The decision to use male-only samples in the present study was pragmatic, based on the data available to the researchers. However, since initial publication, the APSQ has been validated in female athletes (Rice et al., 2020a). We suggest that large, combined samples be collected, enabling a broadening of the differential item functioning analysis, testing for possible gender bias (or true gender differences) in APSQ items. Given the cross-sectional nature of the present study, the test-retest stability of the APSQ could not be determined. Future longitudinal work should address this, and ideally examine trajectories over time. Such work should include additional outcome measures to examine associations of the APSQ factors with broader symptom domains such as disordered eating behaviours (Petrie et al., 2008), or sleep problems (Sargent et al., 2014). Additional work should focus on the convergent and divergent validity of the scale, including assessment at key phases of risk, such as periods of injury or transition out of competitive sport, as well as exploring predictive relationships between relevant physical aspects (i.e., acute injury) and neuropsychological outcomes such as concussion which are implicated in athlete mental health outcomes (Rice et al., 2018). Other psychosocial pressures (i.e., social media abuse) unique to this population should also be examined. This would ideally include baseline (i.e., pre-season) screening, and periodic re-assessment to enable early detection and monitoring of change over time. It is also noted that the majority of participants were not currently in their main competitive season at the time of data collection. Future research should explore the impact of season timing on athlete mental health. Finally, the External Coping factor comprised only two items. While these two items were well correlated, future studies are required to verify the validity and reliability of this factor.

Recent work suggests that the APSQ demonstrates good reliability in athlete populations (e.g., Alhowimel et al., 2023; Taylor et al., 2023); however, current APSQ cut-offs may misidentify some cases (Anderson et al., 2023). As a brief screening tool, it is not possible for the APSQ to identify all cases of potential psychopathology. Consequently, clinician judgement is recommended when using the APSQ and subsequent assessment and intervention planning. Examination of APSQ subscale (or item-level) scores may assist clinicians in planning next steps. For example, elevated scores on the External Coping domain (i.e., impulsivity, occasional or frequent alcohol/drug use to relax) may be weighted as 'higher-risk' items deserving follow-up regardless of the cut-off score achieved. Future studies should examine the predictive validity of the APSQ cut-off scores in identifying psychopathology and determine whether a separate suicide risk screening item should be added.

Conclusion

The field of athlete mental health is gaining momentum, with specific athlete-centric models of care being developed and implemented (Moesch et al., 2018;

Purcell et al., 2019; Rice et al., 2020b). As greater clinical and research attention follows, the need for brief, targeted, athlete-specific measures will grow. The APSQ is a progression in the assessment of psychological strain in elite athletes and conversely, the absence of wellbeing. Use of the scale may assist in early identification and provision of support, corresponding to improved mental health and wellbeing for this cohort.

Declaration of Interest Statement

The authors report no conflicts of interest.

Acknowledgements & Funding

The authors thank the participating sporting codes and competitors for taking part in the study. Simon Rice was supported by the Mary Elizabeth Watson Early Career Fellowship in Allied Health from Royal Melbourne Hospital. This study was, in part, made possible from funding from several sporting bodies, all of whom requested anonymity.

Notes

1 The APSQ has also been validated in female athletes; see Rice et al., 2020a.
2 Subsequent validation of the APSQ in both male and female athletes yielded a range of cut-off scores (10–14 = low; 15–16 = moderate; 17–19 = high; ≥20 = very high); see Rice et al., 2020a.

References

Agnew, R. (1992). Foundation for a general strain theory of crime and delinquency. *Criminology*, *30*, 47–87. 10.1111/j.1745-9125.1992.tb01093.x

Alhowimel, A. S., Alenazi, A. M., Alshehri, M. M., Alqahtani, B. A., Aljaman, A., Alzahrani, H., ... & Rice, S. M. (2023). Translation and validation of the Arabic version of the Athlete Psychological Strain Questionnaire. *Journal of Sport Rehabilitation*, *32*, 709–712. 10.1123/jsr.2022-0311

Anderson, T., Adams, W. M., Bartley, J. D., Brutus, A. L., Donaldson, A. T., & Finnoff, J. T. (2023). Analysis of the Sport Mental Health Assessment Tool 1 (SMHAT-1) in Team USA athletes. *British Journal of Sports Medicine*, *57*(18), 1187–1194. 10.1136/bjsports-2022-106495

Bartram, D. J., Yadegarfar, G., Sinclair, J. M., & Baldwin, D. S. (2011). Validation of the Warwick–Edinburgh Mental Well-being Scale (WEMWBS) as an overall indicator of population mental health and well-being in the UK veterinary profession. *The Veterinary Journal*, *187*(3), 397–398. 10.1016/j.tvjl.2010.02.010

Beedie, C. J., Terry, P. C., & Lane, A. M. (2000). The profile of mood states and athletic performance: Two meta-analyses. *Journal of Applied Sport Psychology*, *12*(1), 49–68. 10.1080/10413200008404213

Bhagat, R. S., Krishnan, B., Nelson, T. A., Moustafa Leonard, K., Ford, D. L., & Billing, T. K. (2010). Organizational stress, psychological strain, and work outcomes in six national contexts. *Cross Cultural Management: An International Journal*, *17*(1), 10–29.

Boswell, W. R., Olson-Buchanan, J. B., & LePine, M. A. (2004). Relations between stress and work outcomes: The role of felt challenge, job control, and psychological strain. *Journal of Vocational Behavior*, *64*(1), 165–181.

Breslin, G., Shannon, S., Haughey, T., Donnelly, P., & Leavey, G. (2017). A systematic review of interventions to increase awareness of mental health and well-being in athletes, coaches and officials. *Systematic Reviews*, *6*(1), 1–15. 10.1186/s13643-017-0568-6

Brownhill, S., Harris, P., Harris, J., & Wilhelm, K. (2006). Depression: What should the doctor ask? *Australian Family Physician*, *35*(3), 163. 10.3316/informit.364635282355871

Brownhill, S., Wilhelm, K., Barclay, L., & Schmied, V. (2005). 'Big build': Hidden depression in men. *Australian and New Zealand Journal of Psychiatry*, *39*(10), 921–931. 10.1080/j.1440-1614.2005.01665.x

Byrne, B. M. (2001). Structural equation modeling with AMOS, EQS, and LISREL: Comparative approaches to testing for the factorial validity of a measuring instrument. *International Journal of Testing*, *1*(1), 55–86. 10.1207/S15327574IJT0101_4

Carpenter, S. (2018). Ten steps in scale development and reporting: A guide for researchers. *Communication Methods and Measures*, 12(1), 25–44. 10.1080/19312458.2017.1396583

Cavanagh, A., Wilson, C. J., Kavanagh, D. J., & Caputi, P. (2017). Differences in the expression of symptoms in men versus women with depression: A systematic review and meta-analysis. *Harvard Review of Psychiatry*, *25*(1), 29–38.

Clarke, A., Friede, T., Putz, R., Ashdown, J., Martin, S., Blake, A., … & Stewart-Brown, S. (2011). Warwick-Edinburgh Mental Well-being Scale (WEMWBS): Validated for teenage school students in England and Scotland. A mixed methods assessment. *BMC Public Health*, *11*(1), 487. 10.1186/1471-2458-11-487

Conway, K. P., Swendsen, J., Husky, M. M., He, J. P., & Merikangas, K. R. (2016). Association of lifetime mental disorders and subsequent alcohol and illicit drug use: results from the National Comorbidity Survey–Adolescent Supplement. *Journal of the American Academy of Child & Adolescent Psychiatry*, *55*(4), 280–288. 10.1016/j.jaac.2016.01.006

DeVellis, R. F. (2016). *Scale development: Theory and applications* (Vol. 26). Sage Publishing.

Doherty, S., Hannigan, B., & Campbell, M. J. (2016). The experience of depression during the careers of elite male athletes. *Frontiers in Psychology*, *7*, 1069. 10.3389/fpsyg.2016.01069

Donohue, B., Chow, G. M., Pitts, M., Loughran, T., Schubert, K. N., Gavrilova, Y., & Allen, D. N. (2015). Piloting a family-supported approach to concurrently optimize mental health and sport performance in athletes. *Clinical Case Studies*, *14*(3), 159–177. 10.1177/1534650114548311

Donohue, B., Galante, M., Hussey, J., Lee, B., Paul, N., Corey, A., & Allen, D. N. (2019). Empirical development of a screening method to assist mental health referrals in collegiate athletes. *Journal of Clinical Sport Psychology*, *13*(4), 561–579. 10.1123/jcsp.2018-0070

Donohue, B., Gavrilova, Y., Galante, M., Gavrilova, E., Loughran, T., Scott, J., ... & Allen, D. N. (2018). Controlled evaluation of an optimization approach to mental health and sport performance. *Journal of Clinical Sport Psychology*, 1–42. 10.1123/jcsp.2017-0054

Donohue, B., Michelle, P., Yulia G., Ashley A., & Cintron, K. (2013). A culturally sensitive approach to treating substance abuse in athletes using evidence-supported methods. *Journal of Clinical Sport Psychology*, *7*(2), 98–119. 10.1123/jcsp.7.2.98

Dunn, M., & Thomas, J. O. (2012). A risk profile of elite Australian athletes who use illicit drugs. *Addictive Behaviors, 37*(1), 144–147. 10.1016/j.addbeh.2011.09.008

Eitle, T. M., Eitle, D., & Johnson-Jennings, M. (2012). General strain theory and substance use among American Indian adolescents. *Race and Justice*, *3*(1), 3–30.

Fava, M., Hwang, I., Rush, A. J., Sampson, N., Walters, E. E., & Kessler, R. C. (2010). The importance of irritability as a symptom of major depressive disorder: Results from the National Comorbidity Survey Replication. *Molecular Psychiatry*, *15*(8), 856. 10.1038/mp.2009.20

Ferguson, H. L., Swann, C., Liddle, S. K., & Vella, S. A. (2018). Investigating youth sports coaches' perceptions of their role in adolescent mental health. *Journal of Applied Sport Psychology*. 10.1080/10413200.2018.1466839

Field, A. (2009). *Discovering statistics using SPSS*. Sage Publishing.

Filo, K., Lock, D., & Karg, A. (2015). Sport and social media research: A review. *Sport Management Review*, *18*(2), 166–181. 10.1016/j.smr.2014.11.001

Genuchi, M. C., & Valdez, J. N. (2015). The role of anger as a component of a masculine variation of depression. *Psychology of Men & Masculinity*, *16*(2), 149. 10.1037/a0036155

Gillan, C. M., Kosinski, M., Whelan, R., Phelps, E. A., & Daw, N. D. (2016). Characterizing a psychiatric symptom dimension related to deficits in goal-directed control. *Elife*, *5*, e11305. 10.7554/eLife.11305

Glaesmer, H., Romppel, M., Brähler, E., Hinz, A., & Maercker, A. (2015). Adjustment disorder as proposed for ICD-11: Dimensionality and symptom differentiation. *Psychiatry Research*, *229*(3), 940–948. 10.1016/j.psychres.2015.07.010

Gorczynski, P. F., Coyle, M., & Gibson, K. (2017). Depressive symptoms in high-performance athletes and non-athletes: A comparative meta-analysis. *British Journal of Sports Medicine*, *51*(18), 1348–1354. 10.1136/bjsports-2016-096455

Gouttebarge, V., Backx, F. J., Aoki, H., & Kerkhoffs, G. M. (2015). Symptoms of common mental disorders in professional football (soccer) across five European countries. *Journal of Sports Science and Medicine*, *14*(4), 811–818. https://pubmed.ncbi.nlm.nih.gov/26664278/

Gouttebarge, V., Bindra, A., Blauwet, C., Campriani, N., Currie, A., Engebretsen, L., ... & Budgett, R. (2021). International Olympic Committee (IOC) sport mental health assessment tool 1 (SMHAT-1) and sport mental health recognition tool 1 (SMHRT-1): Towards better support of athletes' mental health. *British Journal of Sports Medicine*, *55*(1), 30–37. 10.1136/bjsports-2020-102411

Gouttebarge, V., Hopley, P., Kerkhoffs, G., Verhagen, E., Viljoen, W., Wylleman, P., & Lambert, M. (2018). A 12-month prospective cohort study of symptoms of common mental disorders among professional rugby players. *European Journal of Sport Science*, *18*(7), 1004–1012. 10.1080/17461391.2018.1466914

Gouttebarge, V., Inklaar, H., & Frings-Dresen, M. (2014). Risk and consequences of osteoarthritis after a professional football career: A systematic review of the recent literature. *Journal of Sports Medicine and Physical Fitness*, *54*(4), 494–504. https://europepmc.org/article/med/25034551

Grove, J. R., Lavallee, D., & Gordon, S. (1997). Coping with retirement from sport: The influence of athletic identity. *Journal of Applied Sport Psychology*, *9*(2), 191–203. 10.1080/10413209708406481

Grove, J. R., & Prapavessis, H. (1992). Preliminary evidence for the reliability and validity of an abbreviated Profile of Mood States. *International Journal of Sport Psychology*. https://psycnet.apa.org/record/1993-15924-001

Hajebi, A., Motevalian, A., Amin-Esmaeili, M., Rahimi-Movaghar, A., Sharifi, V., Hoseini, L., ... & Mojtabai, R. (2018). Adaptation and validation of short scales for assessment of psychological distress in Iran: The Persian K10 and K6. *International Journal of Methods in Psychiatric Research*, *27*(3), e1726. 10.1002/mpr.1726

Henriksen, K., Schinke, R., Moesch, K., McCann, S., Parham, W. D., Larsen, C. H., & Terry, P. (2019). Consensus statement on improving the mental health of high performance athletes. *International Journal of Sport and Exercise Psychology*, *18*(5), 553–560. 10.1080/1612197X.2019.1570473

Hughes, L., & Leavey, G. (2012). Setting the bar: Athletes and vulnerability to mental illness. *British Journal of Psychiatry*, *200*(2), 95–96. 10.1192/bjp.bp.111.095976

Hussey, J., Donohue, B., Barchard, K., & Allen, D. N. (2019). Family contributions to sport performance and their utility in predicting appropriate referrals to mental health optimization programs. *European Journal of Sport Science*. 10.1080/17461391.2019.1574906

Jones, C. M., & Tenenbaum, G. (2009). Adjustment disorder: A new way of conceptualizing the overtraining syndrome. *International Review of Sport and Exercise Psychology*, *2*(2), 181–197. 10.1080/17509840903110962

Kass, R. E., & Raftery, A. E. (1995). Bayes factors. *Journal of the American Statistical Association*, *90*(430), 773–795. 10.1080/01621459.1995.10476572

Kellmann, M., & Kallus, K. W. (2001). *Recovery-Stress Questionnaire for athletes: User manual* (Vol. 1). Human Kinetics.

Kallus, K. W., & Kellmann, M., (Eds.). (2016).*The Recovery-Stress Questionnaires: User Manual*. Pearson.

Kerr, Z. Y., Register-Mihalik, J. K., Kroshus, E., Baugh, C. M., & Marshall, S. W. (2016). Motivations associated with nondisclosure of self-reported concussions in former collegiate athletes. *The American Journal of Sports Medicine*, *44*(1), 220–225. 10.1177/0363546515612082

Kessler, R. C., Andrews, G., Colpe, L. J., Hiripi, E., Mroczek, D. K., Normand, S.-L., ... & Zaslavsky, A. M. (2002). Short screening scales to monitor population prevalences and trends in non-specific psychological distress. *Psychological Medicine*, *32*(06), 959–976. 10.1017/S0033291702006074

King, B. S., & Beehr, T. A. (2017). Working with the stress of errors: Error management strategies as coping. *International Journal of Stress Management*, *24*(1), 18–33. 10.1037/str0000022.

Kroenke, K., Spitzer, R. L., & Williams, J. B. (2001). The PHQ-9: Validity of a brief depression severity measure. *Journal of General Internal Medicine*, *16*(9), 606–613. 10.1046/j.1525-1497.2001.016009606.x

Lai, H. M. X., Cleary, M., Sitharthan, T., & Hunt, G. E. (2015). Prevalence of comorbid substance use, anxiety and mood disorders in epidemiological surveys, 1990–2014: A systematic review and meta-analysis. *Drug and Alcohol Dependence*, *154*, 1–13.

Lima, Y., Öz, N. D., Denerel, N., Özkaya, Ö., Senışık, S., & Rice, S. (2022). Validity and reliability of the Turkish version of Athlete Psychological Strain Questionnaire (APSQ). *Turkish Journal of Sports Medicine*, *57*(3), 147–154. 10.47447/tjsm.0637

Lloyd, K., & Devine, P. (2012). Psychometric properties of the Warwick–Edinburgh mental well-being scale (WEMWBS) in Northern Ireland. *Journal of Mental Health*, *21*(3), 257–263. 10.3109/09638237.2012.670883

Martin, L. A., Neighbors, H. W., & Griffith, D. M. (2013). The experience of symptoms of depression in men vs women: Analysis of the National Comorbidity Survey Replication. *JAMA Psychiatry*, *70*(10), 1100–1106. 10.1001/jamapsychiatry.2013.1985

Massimiliano, O., Perret, L. C., Turecki, G., & Geoffroy, M. C. (2018). Association between irritability and suicide-related outcomes across the life-course: Systematic review of both community and clinical studies. *Journal of Affective Disorders*, *239*, 220–233. 10.1016/j.jad.2018.07.010

McNair, D. M. (1971). *Manual for the profile of mood states*. San Diego: Educational & Industrial Testing Service.

Mellalieu, S. D., Neil, R., Hanton, S., & Fletcher, D. (2009). Competition stress in sport performers: Stressors experienced in the competition environment. *Journal of Sports Sciences*, *27*(7), 729–744. 10.1080/02640410902889834

Moen, F., Myhre, K., Klöckner, C. A., Gausen, K., & Sandbakk, Ø. (2017). Physical, affective and psychological determinants of athlete burnout. *Sport Journal*, *1*, 1–14. https://hdl.handle.net/11250/2726055

Moesch, K., Kenttä, G., Kleinert, J., Quignon-Fleuret, C., Cecil, S., & Bertollo, M. (2018). FEPSAC position statement: Mental health disorders in elite athletes and models of service provision. *Psychology of Sport and Exercise*. 10.1016/j.psychsport.2018.05.013

Möller-Leimkühler, A. M., & Yücel, M. (2010). Male depression in females? *Journal of Affective Disorders*, *121*, 22–29. 10.1016/j.jad.2009.05.007

Mountjoy, M., Junge, A., Bindra, A., Blauwet, C., Budgett, R., Currie, A., … & Gouttebarge, V. (2023). Surveillance of athlete mental health symptoms and disorders: A supplement to the International Olympic Committee's consensus statement on injury and illness surveillance. *British Journal of Sports Medicine*. 10.1136/bjsports-2022-106687

O'Brien, K. S., Blackie, J. M., & Hunter, J. A. (2005). Hazardous drinking in elite New Zealand sportspeople. *Alcohol and Alcoholism*, *40*(3), 239–241. 10.1093/alcalc/agh145

O'Connor, B. P. (2000). SPSS and SAS programs for determining the number of components using parallel analysis and Velicer's MAP test. *Behavior Research Methods, Instrumentation, and Computers*, *32*, 396–402. 10.3758/BF03200807

Ojio, Y., Matsunaga, A., Kawamura, S., Horiguchi, M., Yoshitani, G., Hatakeyama, K., … & Fujii, C. (2021). Validating a Japanese version of the athlete psychological strain questionnaire. *Sports Medicine-Open*, *7*(1), 1–8. 10.1186/s40798-021-00385-9

Peluso, M. A. M., & Andrade, L. H. S. G. d. (2005). Physical activity and mental health: The association between exercise and mood. *Clinics*, *60*(1), 61–70. 10.1590/S1807-59322005000100012

Petrie, T. A., Greenleaf, C., Reel, J., & Carter, J. (2008). Prevalence of eating disorders and disordered eating behaviors among male collegiate athletes. *Psychology of Men & Masculinity*, *9*(4), 267–277. 10.1037/a0013178

Purcell, R., Gwyther, K., & Rice, S. M. (2019). Mental health in elite athletes: Increased awareness requires an early intervention framework to respond to athlete needs. *Sports Medicine Open*, *5*(1), 46. 10.1186/s40798-019-0220-1

Raedeke, T. D., & Smith, A. L. (2004). Coping resources and athlete burnout: An examination of stress mediated and moderation hypotheses. *Journal of Sport and Exercise Psychology*, *26*(4), 525–541.

Rao, A. L., & Hong, E. S. (2016). Understanding depression and suicide in college athletes: Emerging concepts and future directions. *British Journal of Sports Medicine*, *50*(3), 136–137. 10.1136/bjsports-2015-095658

Reardon, C., Hainline, B., Miller Aron, C., Baron, D., Baum, A., Bindra, A., … & Engebretsen, L. (2019). International Olympic Committee consensus statement on mental health in elite athletes. *Submitted to British Journal of Sports Medicine*, *53*(11), 667–699. 10.1136/bjsports-2019-100715

Rice, S., Butterworth, M., Clements, M., Josifovski, D., Arnold, S., Schwab, C., … & Purcell, R. (2020b). Development and implementation of the national mental health referral network for elite athletes: A case study of the Australian Institute of Sport. *Case Studies in Sport and Exercise Psychology*, *4*(S1), S1–S27. 10.1123/cssep.2019-0016

Rice, S. M., Fallon, B. J., Aucote, H. M., & Möller-Leimkühler, A. M. (2013). Development and preliminary validation of the Male Depression Risk Scale: Furthering the assessment of depression in men. *Journal of Affective Disorders*, *151*(3), 950–958. 10.1016/j.jad.2013.08.013

Rice, S. M., Fallon, B. J., Aucote, H. M., Möller-Leimkühler, A., Treeby, M. S., & Amminger, G. P. (2015). Longitudinal sex differences of externalising and internalising depression symptom trajectories: Implications for assessment of depression in men from an online study. *International Journal of Social Psychiatry*, *61*(3), 236–240. 10.1177/0020764014540149

Rice, S. M., Parker, A. G., Rosenbaum, S., Bailey, A., Mawren, D., & Purcell, R. (2018). Sport-related concussion and mental health outcomes in elite athletes: A systematic review. *Sports Medicine*, *48*(2), 447–465. 10.1007/s40279-017-0810-3

Rice, S., Olive, L., Gouttebarge, V., Parker, A. G., Clifton, P., Harcourt, P., … & Purcell, R. (2020a). Mental health screening: Severity and cut-off point sensitivity of the athlete psychological strain questionnaire in male and female elite athletes. *BMJ Open Sport & Exercise Medicine*, *6*(1), e000712. 10.1136/bmjsem-2019-000712

Rice, S. M., Purcell, R., De Silva, S., Mawren, D., McGorry, P. D., & Parker, A. G. (2016). The mental health of elite athletes: A narrative systematic review. *Sports Medicine*, *46*(9), 1333–1353. 10.1007/s40279-016-0492-2

Robertson, S., Bartlett, J. D., & Gastin, P. B. (2017). Red, amber, or green? Athlete monitoring in team sport: The need for decision-support systems. *International Journal of Sports Physiology and Performance*, *12*, S2–S73. 10.1123/ijspp.2016-0541

Sampasa-Kanyinga, H., Zamorski, M. A., & Colman, I. (2018). The psychometric properties of the 10-item Kessler Psychological Distress Scale (K10) in Canadian military personnel. *PLoS One*, *13*(4), e0196562. 10.1371/journal.pone.0196562

Sanderson, J., Snyder, E., Hull, D., & Gramlich, K. (2015). Social media policies within NCAA member institutions: Evolving technology and its impact on policy. *Journal of Issues in Intercollegiate Athletics*, *8*, 50–73. http://csri-jiia.org/old/documents/publications/research_articles/2015/JIIA_2015_8_3_Policies.pdf

Sargent, C., Lastella, M., Halson, S. L., & Roach, G. D. (2014). The impact of training schedules on the sleep and fatigue of elite athletes. *Chronobiology International*, *31*(10), 1160–1168. 10.3109/07420528.2014.957306

Sarkar, M., & Fletcher, D. (2014). Psychological resilience in sport performers: A review of stressors and protective factors. *Journal of Sports Sciences*, *32*(15), 1419–1434. 10.1080/02640414.2014.901551

Schuring, N., Kerkhoffs, G., Gray, J., & Gouttebarge, V. (2017). The mental wellbeing of current and retired professional cricketers: An observational prospective cohort study. *The Physician and Sportsmedicine*, *45*(4), 463–469. 10.1080/00913847.2017.1386069

Sebbens, J., Hassmén, P., Crisp, D., & Wensley, K. (2016). Mental health in sport (MHS): Improving the early intervention knowledge and confidence of elite sport staff. *Frontiers in Psychology*, *7*, 911. 10.3389/fpsyg.2016.00911

Seidler, Z. E., Dawes, A. J., Rice, S. M., Oliffe, J. L., & Dhillon, H. M. (2016). The role of masculinity in men's help-seeking for depression: A systematic review. *Clinical Psychology Review*, *49*, 106–118. 10.1016/j.cpr.2016.09.002

Slade, T., Grove, R., & Burgess, P. (2011). Kessler Psychological Distress Scale: Normative data from the 2007 Australian National Survey of Mental Health and Wellbeing. *Australian and New Zealand Journal of Psychiatry*, *45*(4), 308–316. 10.3109/00048674.2010.543653

Sliter, K. A., & Zickar, M. J. (2014). An IRT examination of the psychometric functioning of negatively worded personality items. *Educational and Psychological Measurement*, *74*(2), 214–226. 10.1177/0013164413504584

Smith, O. R., Alves, D. E., Knapstad, M., Haug, E., & Aarø, L. E. (2017). Measuring mental well-being in Norway: Validation of the Warwick-Edinburgh Mental Well-being Scale (WEMWBS). *BMC Psychiatry*, *17*(1), 182. 10.1186/s12888-017-1343-x

Stewart-Brown, S., Tennant, A., Tennant, R., Platt, S., Parkinson, J., & Weich, S. (2009). Internal construct validity of the Warwick-Edinburgh Mental Well-being Scale (WEMWBS): A Rasch analysis using data from the Scottish health education population survey. *Health and Quality of Life Outcomes*, *7*(1), 15. 10.1186/1477-7525-7-15

Sunderland, M., Mahoney, A., & Andrews, G. (2012). Investigating the factor structure of the Kessler Psychological Distress Scale in community and clinical samples of the Australian population. *Journal of Psychopathology and Behavioral Assessment*, *34*(2), 253–259. 10.1007/s10862-012-9276-7

Swaminathan, H., & Rogers, H. J. (1990). Detecting differential item functioning using logistic regression procedures. *Journal of Educational Measurement*, *27*(4), 361–370. 10.1111/j.1745-3984.1990.tb00754.x

Taggart, F., Friede, T., Weich, S., Clarke, A., Johnson, M., & Stewart-Brown, S. (2013). Cross cultural evaluation of the Warwick-Edinburgh Mental Well-being Scale (WEMWBS): A mixed methods study. *Health and Quality of Life Outcomes*, *11*(1), 27. 10.1186/1477-7525-11-27

Taylor, K., Chapman, D., Cronin, J., Newton, M. J., & Gill, N. (2012). Fatigue monitoring in high performance sport: A survey of current trends. *Journal of Australian Strength and Conditioning*, *20*(1), 12–23. https://www.academia.edu/download/39203240/54b9af6d0cf24e50e93dc960.pdf

Taylor, D. J., Huskey, A., Kim, K. N., Emert, S. E., Wardle-Pinkston, S., Auerbach, A., … & Milord, T. (2023). Internal consistency reliability of mental health questionnaires in college student athletes. *British Journal of Sports Medicine*, *57*(10), 595–601. 10.1136/bjsports-2021-105136

Teresi, J. A., & Fleishman, J. A. (2007). Differential item functioning and health assessment. *Quality of Life Research*, *16*(1), 33–42. 10.1007/s11136-007-9184-6

Terry, P. C., Lane, A. M., Lane, H. J., & Keohane, L. (1999). Development and validation of a mood measure for adolescents. *Journal of Sports Sciences*, *17*(11), 861–872. 10.1080/026404199365425

Thompson, B. (2004). *Exploratory and confirmatory analysis: Understanding concepts and applications*. Washington, DC: American Psychological Association.

Torregrosa, M., Boixadós, M., Valiente, L., & Cruz, J. (2004). Elite athletes' image of retirement: The way to relocation in sport. *Psychology of Sport and Exercise*, *5*(1), 35–43. 10.1016/S1469-0292(02)00052-3

Torregrosa, M., Ramis, Y., Pallarés, S., Azócar, F., & Selva, C. (2015). Olympic athletes back to retirement: A qualitative longitudinal study. *Psychology of Sport and Exercise*, *21*, 50–56. 10.1016/j.psychsport.2015.03.003

Trousselard, M., Steiler, D., Dutheil, F., Claverie, D., Canini, F., Fenouillet, F., … & Franck, N. (2016). Validation of the Warwick-Edinburgh Mental Well-being Scale (WEMWBS) in French psychiatric and general populations. *Psychiatry Research*, *245*, 282–290. 10.1016/j.psychres.2016.08.050

Worthington, R. L., & Whittaker, T. A. (2006). Scale development research: A content analysis and recommendations for best practices. *The Counseling Psychologist*, *34*(6), 806–838. 10.1177/0011000006288127

6

ELITE ATHLETES' ACHIEVEMENT GOALS, BURNOUT LEVELS, PSYCHOSOMATIC STRESS SYMPTOMS, AND COPING STRATEGIES

Martin Daumiller, Raven Rinas, and Jennifer Breithecker

Elite athletes, distinguished from regular athletes by outstanding performance in their competitive sport, constitute a critical population dedicated to achieving athletic excellence. Throughout their athletic journey, elite athletes undergo rigorous training and face intense competitive pressure, which can contribute to burnout and psychosomatic stress symptoms. Understanding relevant factors that may explain differences in and help mitigate these adverse experiences, such as athletes' individual motivations or their use of adaptive coping strategies, is thereby an important research avenue for prevention and intervention.

Athletes' motivation, central to their thoughts, feelings, and behaviors (Ryan & Deci, 2000), is a compelling research area for understanding individual differences in burnout levels, psychosomatic stress symptoms, and coping strategies. Contemporary perspectives on motivation emphasize not only how strongly an individual is motivated (i.e., quantity), but also the configuration of their motivations (i.e., quality; Pintrich, 2000). To elucidate qualitative motivational differences in athletes, the achievement goal approach has emerged as a promising motivational framework (e.g., Fernández-Rio et al., 2014; Isoard-Gautheur et al., 2013; Mascret et al., 2015; Van Yperen et al., 2014). According to this approach, the different goals that individuals pursue guide their interpretations, behaviors, and reactions (including patterns of coping and emotion) in achievement situations (Daumiller et al., 2021). Thus, elite athletes may respond to stressors differently depending on the personal goals they pursue. These goals may directly impact burnout and psychosomatic stress, while also indirectly influencing these factors through adaptive coping strategies (see Ntoumanis et al., 1999).

DOI: 10.4324/9781003459750-6

Despite the established relevance of achievement goals for the athlete context, there is limited research on how these goals relate to burnout and psychosomatic stress. This research gap extends beyond athletes to other populations, leaving limited insights into potential underlying mechanisms linking these constructs, such as coping strategies. While existing literature suggests that athletes' achievement goals matter for their experiences of strain, more research is needed, particularly focused on elite athletes who exhibit distinct motivations when compared to non-elite athletes (Kavussanu et al., 2011) and may be at risk for negative outcomes (e.g., Brand et al., 2012; Rice et al., 2016). Investigations that incorporate relevant mediators such as the use of coping strategies to better explain these relationships are highly valuable (Ntoumanis et al., 1999). As such, the aim of this study was to examine the relationships between elite athletes' achievement goals, burnout levels, and psychosomatic stress symptoms, as well as the role of coping strategies as a potential mediator therein.

Achievement Goals in the Athlete Context

Achievement goals represent competence-based end states that individuals strive to approach or avoid in achievement contexts. Four types of goals are contemporarily distinguished (Conroy et al., 2003; Elliot & McGregor, 2001; Jaitner et al., 2019; Van Yperen et al., 2014): mastery approach, mastery avoidance, performance approach, and performance avoidance goals.

Mastery approach goals involve a focus on improving competencies, skills, and knowledge, while *mastery avoidance* goals are centered around preventing their stagnation or loss. Within the athlete context, mastery approach goals are particularly adaptive, having positive associations with increased positive affect, self-esteem (Adie et al., 2008, 2010), enjoyment (Morris & Kavussanu, 2009), self-determined situational motivation, competence (Fernández-Rio et al., 2014), and adaptive perfection striving (Stoeber et al., 2008). Conversely, mastery avoidance goals are infrequently investigated and their findings remain unclear, often showing no significant or unfavorable associations. These goals are also criticized as being counter-intuitive and uncommon in sport domains (see Ciani & Sheldon, 2010), a topic of ongoing debate in achievement goal literature (Murayama et al., 2012). However, in our study, we considered mastery avoidance goals relevant, as elite athletes set and maintain high standards and may worry about not meeting them (e.g., "I don't want to lose my specialized sport skills"), especially as they approach the peak of their competitive careers (Larson et al., 2019), where skill retention becomes critical.

Performance goals in athlete settings are typically defined in line with Elliot and McGregor (2001) as striving to perform better than others (*performance approach*) or to avoid doing worse than others (*performance avoidance*). Findings on performance approach goals in the athlete context are mixed: On one hand, they have been associated with increased athlete performance (Stoeber et al., 2009) and intrinsic motivation in sports students (Cury et al., 2002). On the other hand, strong endorsement of performance approach goals has been linked to fear of failure (Conroy et al., 2003) and a disregard for social conventions, opponents, rules, and officials (Stornes & Ommundsen, 2004). Some studies have found no significant associations of this goal type, for example with well-being (Adie et al., 2008, 2010) or intrinsic motivation (Conroy et al., 2006). Performance avoidance goals, however, consistently show maladaptive patterns in the athlete context. These goals are linked with negative reactions to imperfections (Stoeber et al., 2008), concentration disruption, and worry (Morris & Kavussanu, 2009). They also have negative links with positive affect (Adie et al., 2010), intrinsic motivation (Conroy et al., 2006), as well as incremental beliefs about sport ability and physical education competence (Cury et al., 2002).

Aside from the above definitions, the literature also discusses other goal types (e.g., task goals, appearance goals, see Hulleman et al., 2010; Mascret et al., 2015; Wang et al., 2017). To be conceptually precise, in our study, we focus mastery goals solely on intrapersonal standards (e.g., striving to develop one's skills and to be better than in the past), and performance goals solely on normative standards (e.g., striving to be better than others) in line with Daumiller et al.'s (2019) overview model. These various achievement goals are expected to differentially matter for elite athletes' experiences and behaviors, specifically related to their burnout levels, psychosomatic stress symptoms, and coping strategies.

Achievement Goals and Elite Athletes' Burnout Levels and Psychosomatic Stress Symptoms

Athlete burnout, as outlined by Raedeke and Smith (2001), refers to (1) physical and emotional exhaustion, (2) reduced sense of accomplishment, and (3) sport devaluation. Despite similar training and competition regimes, athletes vary in their experiences of burnout (Cresswell & Eklund, 2007). Studies suggest that motivational factors, like achievement goals, can play a crucial role in explaining these differences (e.g., Lemyre et al., 2008). Mastery approach goals, focused on competence development, promote athletes to view challenging situations as learning opportunities, potentially lowering burnout levels. Conversely, individuals pursuing avoidance goals may see such situations as threats, contributing to stress and burnout. Those with performance goals may be more likely to base their self-worth on demonstrating ability, which can increase stress and burnout symptoms when facing competitive challenges.

Studies on athlete burnout and achievement goals reveal the potential of this motivational approach for explaining individual differences in burnout levels. High-level student athletes with strong mastery goals may experience lower burnout compared to those focused on performance goals (Sorkkila et al., 2018). In a longitudinal study on student athletes, Ingrell et al. (2018) found that mastery goal orientation was negatively associated with sport devaluation and reduced sense of accomplishment, while performance goal orientation did not show significant associations. Similar relationships were reported for Norwegian elite winter sport athletes (Lemyre et al., 2008).

A limitation of the aforementioned studies is that they did not distinguish between approach and avoidance goals, possibly contributing to null findings. This limitation was overcome in a study including 309 elite French handball players, where mastery approach goals were associated with reduced sport devaluation, while mastery avoidance goals were linked to a reduced sense of accomplishment (Isoard-Gautheur et al., 2013). Regarding performance goals, performance approach goals were linked to emotional and physical exhaustion, while no significant relationships emerged for performance avoidance goals (Isoard-Gautheur et al., 2013). These findings highlight the usefulness of achievement goals in explaining burnout in athletes and highlight the importance of differentiating approach and avoidance goals. However, more research is needed, especially as it is not clear if the findings by Isoard-Gautheur et al. (2013) can be generalized to elite athletes.

Psychosomatic Stress Symptoms

Aside from burnout, elite athletes experience psychosomatic stress symptoms, which manifest as physical issues rooted in psychological stress, such as abdominal pain, sleep loss, headaches, or weight loss. These symptoms pose particular challenges for elite athletes as their performance heavily relies on physical health. Empirical evidence also indicates that psychosomatic stress symptoms are prevalent and maladaptive for elite athletes. In a review on stress and sleep in elite soccer athletes, Nédélec et al. (2015) reported that different psychological, sociological, and physiological stressors can reduce sleep quality and quantity, leading to compromised psychological and physiological functioning (see also Asplund & Chang, 2020). Moreover, when comparing the mental health of German elite student-athletes with regular students, more frequent stress and somatoform symptoms were found for elite athletes (Brand et al., 2012).

Taken together, the aforementioned findings indicate that psychosomatic stress symptoms are prevalent and may hinder the performance and functioning of elite athletes. When considering the aims of our study, it is important to note that although psychosomatic stress symptoms and burnout experiences can both be viewed as adverse responses to stress, they are distinct constructs (see also Raedeke & Smith, 2004). Burnout pertains to subjective perceptions of reactions to stress regarding the athlete context (e.g., an athlete no longer seeing value in their sport after prolonged stress), while psychosomatic stress symptoms are direct and domain-unspecific symptoms of psychological and physical nature (e.g., an athlete having headaches and difficulties sleeping or eating as a result of stress). Throughout the literature, the distinction between stress (also psychosomatic stress) and burnout has been clearly indicated in terms of both constructs having different antecedents, correlates, and consequences (Bauer et al., 2005; Meeusen et al., 2010; Pines & Keinan, 2005). While studies suggest that achievement goals are an important factor to consider along with coping strategies and athlete well-being (Raedeke & Smith, 2004), to the best of our knowledge, research has yet to comprehensively consider the role of achievement goals for psychosomatic stress symptoms in elite athletes. However, some preliminary empirical evidence exists in support of this relationship. Throughout a concussion recovery process, athletes with mastery goal orientations experienced decreased psychological and physical symptoms compared to their performance goal-oriented counterparts (O'Rourke et al., 2017). This supports the potential importance of considering achievement goals to better understand elite athletes' psychosomatic stress. Similar to burnout, we expect that as the different goals that athletes pursue guide their assessments of achievement events (including patterns of coping and emotion), they should also matter for their psychosomatic stress symptoms.

Coping Strategies as a Mechanism between Achievement Goals and Strain

Concerning the link between achievement goals, burnout levels, and psychosomatic stress symptoms, the different methods that athletes use to handle stressors can be considered to be important (i.e., their use of coping strategies; Goodger et al., 2007; Lazarus, 2000; Nicholls & Polman, 2008; Williams, 2001). Coping strategies describe behaviors and relationships that help athletes to deal with "the problems, joys, disappointments, and stresses of life" (Williams, 2001, p. 774) and are thought to be influenced by individuals' pursuit of achievement goals (Kristiansen *et al.*, 2008). As described by Ntoumanis et al. (1999) goals are relevant for different levels of adaptive coping as they "bring to a particular situation different beliefs, commitments, and perceptions of what is at stake" (p. 318).

Researchers have extensively studied coping strategies, including positive thinking, active stress coping, and seeking social support, which have been classified as adaptive[1] across various populations (e.g., Hampel &

Petermann, 2006; Holton et al., 2016; Prati & Pietrantoni, 2009). Positive thinking involves reappraising stressful situations in a positive light; active stress coping entails using one's own psychological or behavioral resources to actively deal with stress; and seeking social support involves turning to friends, partners, or family for discussion and comfort during stressful times. The adaptive nature of these coping strategies has also been displayed in athlete-related research (Crocker & Graham, 1995; Gaudreau et al., 2002; Kristiansen & Roberts, 2010; Ntoumanis & Biddle, 1998). Given their positive role for maintaining athlete health, as well as their importance for dealing with burnout and stress (e.g., Shin et al., 2014), we focused on these strategies in our study as well. Specifically, we aimed to explore whether the use of adaptive coping, encompassing the aforementioned three strategies, would support athletes in dealing with burnout and psychosomatic stress, aligning with prior research that has combined individual coping strategies into a broader adaptive coping construct (e.g., Jonason et al., 2020; Sun et al., 2019).

When considering athletes' achievement goals, research indicates that mastery goals are more strongly and positively related to the use of adaptive coping strategies than performance goals (e.g., Kristiansen et al., 2008; Ntoumanis et al., 1999; Pensgaard & Roberts, 2003). While little is known regarding the approach and avoidance aspects of goals, these empirical findings, along with those previously mentioned, suggests that the use of adaptive coping strategies by elite athletes may serve as a mediating factor between their achievement goals and levels of burnout and psychosomatic stress.

Research Questions and Hypotheses

The primary objective of our study was to investigate the relationship between elite athletes' achievement goals and their burnout levels and psychosomatic stress symptoms, along with the role of adaptive coping strategies in these relationships. Drawing on the theorizing of the different types of goals and previous empirical findings, we hypothesized:

H1: Mastery approach goals are positively associated with use of adaptive coping strategies, and negatively associated with burnout levels and psychosomatic stress symptoms.

H2: Mastery avoidance goals are negatively associated with use of adaptive coping strategies, and positively associated with burnout levels and psychosomatic stress symptoms.

H3: Performance approach goals are positively associated with use of adaptive coping strategies, and negatively associated with burnout levels and psychosomatic stress symptoms.

H4: Performance avoidance goals are negatively associated with use of adaptive coping strategies, and positively associated with burnout levels and psychosomatic stress symptoms.

H5: The use of adaptive coping strategies mediates the effects of achievement goals on burnout levels and psychosomatic stress symptoms.

Method

Procedure

Elite athletes, operationalized as individuals who were part of the national or state squad in their sport, were asked to answer an online questionnaire assessing their achievement goals, adaptive coping strategies, burnout levels, and background variables. Prior to beginning the survey, participants were presented with the objectives of the study and the data protection policy before providing informed consent. There was no anticipated psychological harm associated with the survey for the participants.

Participants

We recruited participants by collaborating with athlete coordinators, who shared our survey invitation with athletes in their respective squads. Additionally, we sent personalized invitations to athletes for whom we had contact details. In total, 165 German elite athletes participated in the survey. We decided prior to conducting the study that we would only include those participants who filled out more than 1/3 of the survey. The final sample consisted of 125 athletes (97 males, 28 females) with an average age of 23.7 ($SD = 4.0$) years. These athletes dedicated an average of 12.2 hours a week ($SD = 8.5$) to training, and participated in an average of 28.1 competitions ($SD = 15.7$). The athletes were engaged in a variety of sports, including football, badminton, handball, gymnastics, ice hockey, skiing, basketball, volleyball, swimming, boxing, squash, and tennis, among others.

Measures

We asked the participants to report their achievement goals, burnout levels, psychosomatic symptoms, and adaptive coping strategies in relation to the past six months, focusing on the specific sport in which they were engaged.

Achievement Goals

Achievement goals were measured using a version of the achievement goal scale by Daumiller et al. (2019) adapted for the athlete context. We measured mastery approach (e.g., "I want to develop my sporting skills as much as possible"; α = .91), mastery avoidance (e.g., "I want to avoid not developing my competences further"; α = .70), performance approach (e.g., "It is my goal to perform better than other athletes"; α = .88), and performance avoidance (e.g., "I don't want to be worse than the other athletes"; α = .88) goals with four items each. Answers were recorded on a Likert-type scale ranging from 1 (*do not agree at all*) to 8 (*agree completely*).

Athlete Burnout Levels

We used the German version of the Athlete Burnout Questionnaire (ABQ-D) by Ziemainz et al. (2004) to measure participants' burnout levels in the context of their sport. The item stem read "How often do you feel this way?", followed by five items assessing emotional and physical exhaustion (e.g., "I feel excessively exhausted by my exercise"), five items assessing sport devaluation (e.g., "I am not as interested in my sport as I used to be"), and five items assessing reduced sense of accomplishment (e.g., "I achieve many desirable things in my sport", negatively coded item). Answers were recorded on a Likert-type scale ranging from 1 (*almost never*) to 8 (*very often*). As we were interested in burnout levels as a whole, we considered the construct on the overall scale level (see Brenninkmeijer & van Yperen, 2003) by averaging the three sub-aspects to a uniform indicator of burnout level (α = .88).

Psychosomatic Stress Symptoms

To measure psychosomatic symptoms of stress, we used the respective subscale of the validated Stress and Coping Inventory (SCI) by Satow (2012). This inventory has been used in numerous studies to measure psychosomatic stress symptoms as well as the use of coping strategies (e.g., Steinert & Haesner, 2018; Steiner-Hofbauer & Holzinger, 2020). The item stem read "Stress and pressure can cause physical symptoms. Which of the following statements have you observed in the last six months?" followed by 13 items listing psychosomatic symptoms (e.g., "I don't sleep well", "I often suffer from headaches"; α = .80) answered on a Likert-type scale ranging from 1 (*do not agree*) to 8 (*agree completely*).

Adaptive Coping Strategies

We again used a subscale of the Stress and Coping Inventory (SCI) by Satow (2012) to measure athletes' use of adaptive coping strategies. The item stem read "How do you deal with stress?" and included four items about positive thinking (e.g., "When confronted with stress and pressure, I concentrate on the bright side"), four items about active stress management (e.g., "I actively think about how I can avoid time pressures"), and four items about social support (e.g., "When I am under pressure, I have people to help me"). Answers were recorded on a Likert-type scale ranging from 1 (*do not agree*) to 8 (*agree completely*). As we were interested in participants' use of coping as a general mechanism, we considered the construct on the overall scale level ($\alpha = .92$; in line with prior literature, e.g., Jonason et al., 2020; Sun et al., 2019, and justified by large correlations between the three different strategies: $\rho = .70$–$.87$).

Analyses

Analyses were conducted with Mplus 8.1 (Muthén & Muthén, 2017) using MLR as an estimator to control for the fact that not all variables were normally distributed. To test our hypotheses, we conducted path modeling. Indirect effects were tested using the "model indirect" command in Mplus, which uses the delta method to calculate standard errors (MacKinnon, 2008). Missing values (< 10.4% for each item) were dealt with using the FIML estimator and the EM-algorithm for all analyses (Peugh & Enders, 2004). Power analyses based on multiple regression analyses indicated that a sample size of 116 participants was required to detect medium effects (Faul et al., 2009). Monte Carlo power analyses revealed that this was also sufficiently large to detect small-to-medium indirect effects (Schoemann et al., 2017).

Results

Preliminary Results

Descriptive statistics for the achievement goals, the use of adaptive coping strategies, burnout levels, and psychosomatic stress symptoms are presented in Table 6.1. Elite athletes reported rather strong mastery approach and performance goals, moderate levels of burnout levels and psychosomatic stress symptoms, and relatively high levels of adaptive coping strategies. Importantly, there were strong interindividual differences between the athletes, which were particularly strong for mastery avoidance goals.

Effects of Achievement Goals on Burnout Levels, Psychosomatic Stress Symptoms, and Use of Coping Strategies

Through path modeling, we investigated the direct effects of achievement goals on burnout levels, psychosomatic stress symptoms, and use of adaptive coping strategies, and examined how use of these coping strategies mediated the effects of achievement goals on burnout levels and psychosomatic stress symptoms (see Figure 6.1).

TABLE 6.1 Descriptive statistics and bivariate correlations for achievement goals, coping strategies, burnout levels, and psychosomatic stress symptoms

	Descriptive Statistics						*Bivariate Correlations*						
	M	*SD*	Min.	Max.	Skew	α	MAP	MAV	PAP	PAV	C	B	S
Achievement goals													
[MAP] Mastery approach	7.18	0.98	3.50	8.00	−1.49	.91							
[MAV] Mastery avoidance	5.46	1.77	1.00	8.00	−0.39	.70	**.22**						
[PAP] Performance approach	6.58	1.31	2.25	8.00	−1.07	.88	**.44**	.16					
[PAV] Performance avoidance	6.13	1.58	1.00	8.00	−1.08	.88	**.20**	**.34**	**.66**				
Athlete strain and coping													
[C] Adaptive coping strategies	6.24	1.36	1.00	8.00	−2.09	.92	**.23**	−.10	.10	−.03			
[B] Burnout levels	3.22	1.13	1.00	6.60	0.54	.88	**−.20**	**.22**	.10	**.20**	**−.32**		
[S] Stress symptoms	3.13	1.34	1.00	7.38	0.75	.80	−.08	**.34**	.05	.14	**−.27**	**.53**	
Background variables													
Age	23.70	4.04	12	39	0.61		−.01	−.17	.07	.03	**.21**	.03	−.04
Training hours per week	12.26	8.48	4	50	1.63		.30	−.09	**.31**	.11	−.03	.11	−.04
Sex (percentage of males)	78%				−0.34		−.03	−.07	−.02	−.01	.03	−.01	−.08

Note: $N = 125$. All bolded correlations are statistically significant at $p < .05$.

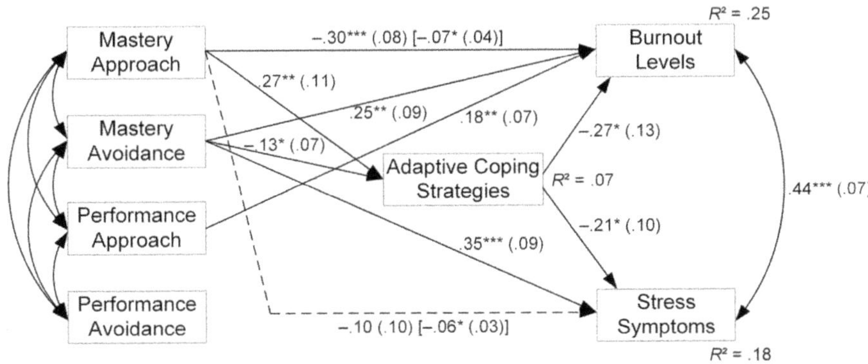

FIGURE 6.1 Path modeling and testing of the mediation effects between achievement goals, adaptive coping strategies, burnout levels, and psychosomatic stress symptoms. Presented are standardized regression coefficients with standard errors in round brackets. In square brackets, indirect effects are reported. Correlations between achievement goals were modeled but not presented for reasons of clarity. As the model is fully saturated, it perfectly fits the data with zero degrees of freedom. As such, this model does not provide a test of alternative models but allows for testing the statistical significance of all hypothesized paths in the model. Only statistically significant parameters at $p < .05$ are displayed (all parameter estimates are presented in Daumiller et al., 2022).

We found that mastery approach goals were negatively associated with burnout levels (but not psychosomatic stress symptoms; in terms of direct effects), and positively associated with use of coping strategies. Conversely, strong mastery avoidance goals were associated with increased burnout levels and increased psychosomatic stress symptoms as well as reduced use of coping strategies. Performance approach goals were positively associated with burnout levels, however, neither with coping strategies nor with stress symptoms. Finally, we did not observe any statistically significant effects for performance avoidance goals. Regarding the mediation effects, we found statistically significant indirect effects from mastery approach goals on burnout levels and psychosomatic stress symptoms, mediated by use of coping strategies, however for the other types of goals, no significant mediating effects were found.

Altogether, we found that substantial amounts of variance in participants' psychosomatic stress symptoms ($R^2 = .18$) and burnout levels ($R^2 = .25$) were explained. Further, these two aspects were not very strongly correlated and were differentially associated with the achievement goals.

Discussion

Our study aimed to expand our knowledge about the relevance of achievement goals for how elite athletes experience and deal with sport stressors. We adopted a motivational perspective to explain why some elite athletes may handle these adverse consequences more effectively than others. While previous research has successfully used the achievement goal approach to describe the motivations of this understudied population, it often overlooked the valence of these goals (i.e., their approach or avoidance components)—a limitation we addressed with our work. Moreover, our study advanced current research by incorporating the use of adaptive coping strategies in explaining how goals matter for individuals dealing with sport stressors. Regarding the latter, we included two important aspects—burnout levels and psychosomatic stress symptoms. The substantial variance explained in both of these aspects, as well as their interconnectedness, highlights the importance of investigating them simultaneously and the relevance of achievement goals for explaining differences within them.

Our hypotheses were partially supported in that achievement goals differentially predicted burnout levels, psychosomatic stress symptoms, and use of coping strategies in elite athletes. Notably, mastery approach goals were particularly beneficial, while mastery avoidance goals were associated with maladaptive outcomes. Moreover, consistent with previous literature on athletes, our study revealed high mean levels of mastery approach and performance goals as well as high levels of coping strategies, and moderate levels of burnout levels and psychosomatic stress symptoms with substantial interindividual differences (Fernández-Rio et al., 2014, 2017). This supports the relevance of achievement goals for understanding elite athletes' stress experiences and coping strategies, and suggests the importance of conducting further research focused on replicating and expanding upon these effects.

Mastery approach goals were positively related to adaptive coping strategies and negatively related to burnout levels (Hypothesis 1). Besides these direct effects, they were indirectly negatively related to psychosomatic stress symptoms. These results speak to the beneficial nature of mastery approach goals found in previous literature on athletes (e.g., Adie et al., 2008; Fernández-Rio et al., 2013). Specifically, athletes who strongly focus on developing their competencies and embrace intrapersonal challenges might exhibit greater conviction and coherence in their actions, resulting in increased resistance and resilience against burnout and psychosomatic stress (Ingrell et al., 2018; Isoard-Gautheur et al., 2013; Lemyre et al., 2008; Vitali et al., 2015).

Furthermore, we identified adverse associations between mastery avoidance goals and how elite athletes experienced and dealt with sport stressors (Hypothesis 2). These findings hold particular significance given the ongoing debate about the usefulness of mastery avoidance goals (see Ciani & Sheldon, 2010; Murayama et al., 2012). While it should be mentioned that the reliability of the mastery avoidance goal subscale was lower than that of the other goals (albeit still satisfactory), our findings suggest that individuals within the elite athlete context differ substantially in their pursuit of such goals, which is in turn meaningfully associated with their use of coping strategies, burnout levels, and psychosomatic stress symptoms. Athletes who prioritize avoiding the loss of existing skills rather than acquiring and enhancing new ones may struggle in improving both personal and athletic skills. This could lead to a reduced sense of accomplishment in sports and an increase in sport devaluation, a problematic combination in terms of early dropout of high-performance sports (Isoard-Gautheur et al., 2013; Le Bars et al., 2009; Raedeke & Smith, 2001).

Regarding Hypothesis 3, we found that performance approach goals were positively related to burnout levels, while no other significant relationships were observed. Athletes who consistently try to outperform others may experience difficulties in finding enjoyment in their sports participation and emphasize output and winning. Consequently, this motivational orientation might matter primarily for how individuals interpret their achievement situations and stressors therein. This may explain why we found statistically significant associations for burnout levels but not for psychosomatic stress symptoms. Furthermore, the fact that elite athletes striving to perform better than others reported higher burnout levels may point to negative effects of emphasizing competitive attitudes and performance climate in high performance sports training groups (Alvarez et al., 2012; Isoard-Gautheur et al., 2013; Rice et al., 2016).

We did not find significant associations between performance avoidance goals and use of adaptive coping strategies, psychosomatic stress, or burnout levels, contrary to Hypothesis 4. This finding was surprising, as we expected higher burnout levels and more psychosomatic stress symptoms in athletes in fear of performing worse than others. Our findings imply that such reactions might be more strongly associated with mastery avoidance goals than with performance avoidance goals. This is also supported by the findings of Isoard-Gautheur et al. (2013), who did not identify significant associations for performance avoidance goals and found unfavorable associations for mastery avoidance goals. To elaborate, elite athletes can be expected to have achieved high levels of mastery within their sport and to identify with their sport on a personal and intimate level. Given these high standards, they may be more affected by the prospect of losing their skills or not developing them further than performing worse than others. In line with this, Allen and Hopkins (2015) describe in their systematic review that elite athletes have a fleeting period of peak competitive performance in their lifetime. Thus, elite athletes may be especially affected by concerns about having already peaked in their sport, and worries about having a lack of improvement or regressing (see also Larson et al., 2019). To date, most research has not investigated achievement goals with burnout and stress in athletes by distinguishing between approach and avoidance goals, making this finding a valuable step toward gathering a comprehensive understanding of the role of achievement goals for athletes' cognitions and behaviors.

Finally, we found that the use of adaptive coping strategies mediated mastery approach goals and burnout levels/psychosomatic stress symptoms, while for the other goals, no significant mediating effects were found (partial support for Hypothesis 5). This implies that elite athletes with a high level of mastery goals also used these coping strategies to greater extent, which likely helps in reducing burnout levels and psychosomatic stress symptoms (Kristiansen et al., 2008; Ntoumanis et al., 1999; Pensgaard & Roberts, 2003). An important finding in this regard was that the use of coping strategies only partially mediated these relationships, with substantial direct effects between goals and burnout levels as well as psychosomatic stress symptoms remaining. This might imply that athletes also differ in their thought processes about successes and failures, and as a result of this, differ in their stress experiences—beyond differences in their coping behaviors.

In sum, elite athletes with weak mastery approach goals and/or strong mastery avoidance goal pursuit encompass a group that is more likely to suffer from suboptimal handling of stressors and more pronounced experiences of stress. This increased burden is particularly evident if they use few adaptive coping strategies. As a result, these athletes may require support in the form of mental training and coaching (Alvarez et al., 2012). As the coach-athlete relationship is a key factor for elite athletes who suffer from high burnout levels (McGee & DeFreese, 2019), coaches should support athletes in pursuing adaptive goals (i.e., mastery approach as opposed to mastery avoidance goals) and using adaptive coping strategies. Specifically, not only individual, but also organizational or combined efforts in the form of psychosocial support measures that consider motivational aspects may be effective in mitigating and preventing athlete burnout and drop out (Eklund & DeFreese, 2015). Furthermore, various intervention suggestions and programs have been developed to help young elite athletes cope with chronic stress when balancing school and sports commitments (Gledhill et al., 2018; Sallen et al., 2017). The literature also reflects an increasing focus on the beneficial effects of mindfulness training (Gustafsson et al., 2017). Lastly, athletes' perceptions of a mastery team climate predicting mastery approach goals (Morris & Kavussanu, 2008) and sportsmanship behaviors (Laparidis et al., 2003) speak to the importance of combined-person efforts for supporting athletes. Thus, incorporating reflections on athletes' goal pursuit into the aforementioned strategies can be seen as a promising avenue for better supporting elite athletes.

Limitations and Future Directions

When considering the implications of our study within the elite athlete literature on burnout, psychosomatic stress, and coping, several limitations should be acknowledged. First, we focused on coping strategies that are generally perceived as adaptive within the literature. However, it is important to note that what is considered adaptive may vary among individuals and across different situations. Future research could profit from exploring a wider array of coping strategies and potential moderators that may influence whether certain coping strategies are adaptive or maladaptive. Additionally, investigating coping strategies typically regarded as maladaptive and their associations with avoidance goals could be insightful. Secondly, our study design was correlational and thus, causal explanations cannot be drawn. While it is theoretically sensible that depending on the pursued achievement goals, individuals may perceive and react to stressors differently, reciprocal effects from burnout and stress experiences on changes in motivations cannot be ruled out (see Martinent et al., 2014). Future research should investigate how these variables function over time using longitudinal designs, which would allow for the testing of the proposed mediation effects beyond mere associations (see Maxwell & Cole, 2007 for a review of cross-sectional mediation models). To better understand how athletes with different levels and combinations of achievement goals function over time in terms of their coping strategies, burnout levels, and psychosomatic stress symptoms, incorporating a goal profile approach may also be an interesting research avenue, as also suggested by Harwood and Chan (2010). Moreover, the measures used in the current study were self-reported. While self-report measures are suitable for gauging motivations and subjective responses to stressors, future research could enhance our understanding by incorporating more objective indicators, especially concerning clinically relevant symptoms or implicit measures (see Gerber et al., 2018, 2019).

Note

1 When discussing coping strategies in the present study, we refer to strategies that have been empirically supported as adaptive within the athlete context. However, particularly for idiographic research (opposed to the nomothetic approach of the present work), it is important to acknowledge that what is adaptive for one person in a particular context may not be adaptive for another. Thus, despite our focus on adaptive strategies, individual and contextual differences are important to consider (see Folkman & Moskowitz, 2004; Pensgaard & Roberts, 2003).

References

Adie, J. W., Duda, J. L., & Ntoumanis, N. (2008). Achievement goals, competition appraisals, and the psychological and emotional welfare of sport participants. *Journal of Sport and Exercise Psychology*, *30*, 302–322. 10.1123/jsep.30.3.302

Adie, J. W., Duda, J. L., & Ntoumanis, N. (2010). Achievement goals, competition appraisals, and the well- and ill-being of elite youth soccer players over two competitive seasons. *Journal of Sport and Exercise Psychology*, *32*, 555–579. https://doi.org/10/d4j9

Allen, S. V., & Hopkins, W. G. (2015). Age of peak competitive performance of elite athletes. *Sports Medicine*, *45*, 1431–1441. https://doi.org/10/f7x4rq

Alvarez, M. S., Balaguer, I., Castillo, I., & Duda, J. L. (2012). The coach-created motivational climate, young athletes' well-being, and intentions to continue participation. *Journal of Clinical Sport Psychology*, *6*, 166–179. 10.1123/jcsp.6.2.166

Asplund, C., & Chang, C. J. (2020) The role of sleep in psychological well-being in athletes. In E. Hong & A. Rao (Eds.), *Mental health in the athlete*. Springer. 10.1007/978-3-030-44754-0_23

Bauer, J., Stamm, A., Virnich, K., Wissing, K., Müller, U., Wirsching, M., & Schaarschmidt, U. (2005). Correlation between burnout syndrome and psychological and psychosomatic symptoms among teachers. *International Archives of Occupational and Environmental Health*, *79*, 199–204. 10.1007/s00420-005-0050-y

Brand, R., Wolff, W., & Hoyer, J. (2012). Psychological symptoms and chronic mood in representative samples of elite student-athletes, deselected student-athletes and comparison students. *School Mental Health*, *5*, 166–174. https://doi.org/10/f5szbn

Brenninkmeijer, V., & van Yperen, N. (2003). How to conduct research on burnout. *Occupational and Environmental Medicine*, *60*, 16–20. 10.1136/oem.60.suppl_1.i16

Ciani, K. D., & Sheldon, K. M. (2010). Evaluating the mastery-avoidance goal construct. *Psychology of Sport and Exercise*, *11*, 127–132. 10.1016/j.psychsport.2009.04.005

Conroy, D. E., Elliot, A. J., & Hofer, S. M. (2003). A 2x2 achievement goals questionnaire for sport. *Journal of Sport & Exercise Psychology*, *25*, 456–476. 10.1123/jsep.25.4.456

Conroy, D. E., Kaye, M. P., & Coatsworth, J. D. (2006). Coaching climates and the destructive effects of mastery avoidance achievement goals on situational motivation. *Journal of Sport and Exercise Psychology*, *28*, 69–92. 10.1123/jsep.28.1.69

Cresswell, S., & Eklund, R. (2007). Athlete burnout. *Sport Psychologist*, *21*, 1–20. https://doi.org/10/ggcrk4

Crocker, P., & Graham, T. (1995). Coping by competitive athletes with performance stress. *The Sport Psychologist*, *9*, 325–338. 10.1123/tsp.9.3.325

Cury, F., Elliot, A. J., Sarrazin, P., Da Fonseca, D., & Rufo, M. (2002). The trichotomous achievement goal model and intrinsic motivation. *Journal of Experimental Social Psychology*, *38*, 473–481. 10.1016/S0022-1031(02)00017-3

Daumiller, M., Dickhäuser, O., & Dresel, M. (2019). University instructors' achievement goals for teaching. *Journal of Educational Psychology*, *111*, 131–148. 10.1037/edu0000271

Daumiller, M., Rinas, R., & Breithecker, J. (2022). Elite athletes' achievement goals, burnout levels, psychosomatic stress symptoms, and coping strategies. *International Journal of Sport and Exercise Psychology*, *20*(2), 416–435. 10.1080/1612197X.2021.1877326

Daumiller, M., Rinas, R., & Jaitner, D. (2021). The relevance of stability and change of achievement goals for self-regulated motor learning processes and outcomes. *Sport, Exercise, and Performance Psychology*, *10*(4), 519–535. 10.1037/spy0000260

Eklund, R., & DeFreese, J. (2015). Athlete burnout. *International Journal of Applied Sports Sciences*, *27*, 63–75. 10.24985/ijass.2015.27.2.63

Elliot, A. J., & McGregor, H. A. (2001). A 2x2 achievement goal framework. *Journal of Personality and Social Psychology*, *80*, 501–519. 10.1037/0022-3514.80.3.501

Faul, F., Erdfelder, E., Buchner, A., & Lang, A.-G. (2009). Statistical power analyses using G*Power 3.1. *Behavior Research Methods*, *41*, 1149–1160. 10.3758/BRM.41.4.1149

Fernández-Rio, J., Cecchini Estrada, J. A., & Méndez-Giménez, A. (2017). Does context, practice or competition affect female athletes' achievement goal dominance, goal pursuit, burnout and motivation? *Journal of Human Kinetics*, *59*, 91–105. 10.1515/hukin-2017-0150

Fernández-Rio, J., Cecchini Estrada, J. A., Mendez-Gimenez, A., Fernández-Garcia, B., & Saavedra, P. (2014). 2 × 2 dominant achievement goal profiles in high-level swimmers. *European Journal of Sport Science*, *14*, 265–272. https://doi.org/10/d4kc

Fernández-Río, J., Méndez-Giménez, A., & Méndez-Alonso, D. (2013). Effects of three instructional approaches in adolescents' physical self-concept. *Cultura y Educación*, *25*(4), 509–521.

Folkman, S., & Moskowitz, J. T. (2004). Coping: Pitfalls and promise. *Annual Review of Psychology*, *55*, 745–774. 10.1146/annurev.psych.55.090902.141456

Gaudreau, P., Blondin, J., & Lapierre, A. (2002). Athletes' coping during a competition. *Psychology of Sport and Exercise*, *3*, 125–150. https://doi.org/10/frjvdx

Gerber, M., Brand, R., Antoniewicz, F., & Isoard-Gautheur, S. (2019). Implicit and explicit attitudes towards sport among young elite athletes with high versus low burnout symptoms. *Journal of Sports Sciences*, *37*, 1–8. https://doi.org/10/d4kd

Gerber, M., Gustafsson, H., Kellmann, M., & Ludyga, S. (2018). Usefulness of the ABQ as a screening tool for the detection of clinically relevant burnout symptoms among young elite athletes. *Psychology of Sport and Exercise*, *39*, 104–113. https://doi.org/10/gd8pxw

Gledhill, A., Forsdyke, D., & Murray, E. (2018). Psychological interventions used to reduce sports injuries. *British Journal of Sports Medicine*, *52*, 967–971. https://doi.org/10/gc2tn6

Goodger, K., Gorely, T., Lavallee, D., & Harwood, C. (2007). Burnout in sport: A systematic review. *The Sport Psychologist*, *21*, 127–151. 10.1123/tsp.21.2.127

Gustafsson, H., DeFreese, J., & Madigan, D. J. (2017). Athlete burnout. *Current Opinion in Psychology*, *16*, 109–113. 10.1016/j.copsyc.2017.05.002

Hampel, P., & Petermann, F. (2006). Perceived stress, coping, and adjustment in adolescents. *Journal of Adolescent Health*, *38*, 409–415. 10.1016/j.jadohealth.2005.02.01

Harwood. C. , & Chan, D. K. C. (2010). Achievement goals and coping in sport. In A. R. Nicholls (Ed.), *Coping in sport: Theory, methods, and related constructs* (pp. 195–215). Nova Science Publisher.

Holton, M. K., Barry, A. E., & Chaney, J. D. (2016). Employee stress management. *Work*, *53*, 299–305. 10.3233/WOR-152145

Hulleman, C., Schrager, S., Bodmann, S., & Harackiewicz, J. (2010). A meta-analytic review of achievement goal measures. *Psychological Bulletin*, *136*, 422–449. https://doi.org/10/dkdjkc

Ingrell, J., Johnson, U., & Ivarsson, A. (2018). Developmental changes in burnout perceptions among student-athletes. *International Journal of Sport and Exercise Psychology*, *17*, 509–520. 10.1080/1612197x.2017.1421679

Isoard-Gautheur, S., Guillet-Descas, E., & Duda, J. L. (2013). How to achieve in elite training centers without burning out. *Psychology of Sport and Exercise*, *14*, 72–83. https://doi.org/10/f4h2z4

Jaitner, D., Rinas, R., Becker, C., Niermann, C., Breithecker, J., & Mess, F. (2019). A systematic review of achievement goal motivation in school physical education. *Frontiers in Education*, *4*. 10.3389/feduc.2019.00070

Jonason, P. K., Talbot, D., Cunningham, M. L., & Chonody, J. (2020). Higher-order coping strategies. *Personality and Individual Differences*, *155*. 10.1016/j.paid.2019.109755

Kavussanu, M., White, S. A., Jowett, S., & England, S. (2011). Elite and non-elite male footballers differ in goal orientation and perceptions of parental climate. *International Journal of Sport and Exercise Psychology*, *9*, 284–290. https://doi.org/10/ccbzn8

Kristiansen, E., & Roberts, G. C. (2010). Young elite athletes and social support. *Scandinavian Journal of Medicine & Science in Sports*, *20*, 686–695. https://doi.org/10/bm5qjr

Kristiansen, E., Roberts, G. C., & Abrahamsen, F. E. (2008). Achievement involvement and stress coping in elite wrestling. *Scandinavian Journal of Medicine & Science in Sports*, *18*, 526–538. 10.1111/j.1600-0838.2007.00646.x

Laparidis, K., Papaioannou, A., Vretakou, V., & Morou, A. (2003). Motivational climate, beliefs about the bases of success, and sportsmanship behaviors of professional basketball athletes. *Perceptual and Motor Skills*, *96*, 1141–1151. https://doi.org/10/c6bjxs

Larson, H. K., McHugh, T.-L. F., Young, B. W., & Rodgers, W. M. (2019). Pathways from youth to masters swimming: Exploring long-term influences of youth swimming experiences. *Psychology of Sport and Exercise*, *41*, 12–20. https://doi.org/10/d4kf

Lazarus, R. S. (2000). Toward better research on stress and coping. *American Psychologist*, *55*, 665–673. 10.1037/0003-066x.55.6.665

Le Bars, H., Gernigon, C., & Ninot, G. (2009). Personal and contextual determinants of elite young athletes' persistence or dropping out over time. *Scandinavian Journal of Medicine & Science in Sports*, *19*, 274–285. https://doi.org/10/b3ch4g

Lemyre, P. N., Hall, H., & Roberts, G. (2008). A social cognitive approach to burnout in elite athletes. *Scandinavian Journal of Medicine & Science in Sports*, *18*, 221–234. https://doi.org/10/bvmc95

MacKinnon, D. (2008). *Introduction to statistical mediation analysis*. Taylor and Francis.

Martinent, G., Decret, J.-C., Guillet-Descas, E., & Isoard-Gautheur, S. (2014). A reciprocal effects model of the temporal ordering of motivation and burnout among youth table tennis players in intensive training settings. *Journal of Sports Sciences*, *32*, 1648–1658. https://doi.org/10/dhq8

Mascret, N., Elliot, A. J., & Cury, F. (2015). Extending the 3×2 achievement goal model to the sport domain. *Psychology of Sport and Exercise*, *17*, 7–14. https://doi.org/10/f62px6

Maxwell, S. E., & Cole, D. A. (2007). Bias in cross-sectional analyses of longitudinal mediation. *Psychological Methods*, *12*, 23–44. 10.1037/1082-989x.12.1.23

McGee, V., & DeFreese, J. D. (2019). The coach-athlete relationship and athlete psychological outcomes. *Journal of Clinical Sport Psychology*, *13*, 152–174. https://doi.org/10/dhq5

Meeusen, V., Van Dam, K., Brown-Mahoney, C., Van Zundert, A., & Knape, H. (2010). Burnout, psychosomatic symptoms and job satisfaction among Dutch nurse anaesthetists. *Acta Anaesthesiologica Scandinavica*, *54*, 616–621. https://doi.org/10/fs9sfj

Morris, R. L., & Kavussanu, M. (2008). Antecedents of approach-avoidance goals in sport. Journal of Sports Sciences, *26*, 465–476. 10.1080/02640410701579388

Morris, R. L., & Kavussanu, M. (2009). The role of approach-avoidance versus task and ego goals in enjoyment and cognitive anxiety in youth sport. *International Journal of Sport and Exercise Psychology*, *7*, 185–202. 10.1080/1612197x.2009.9671899

Murayama, K., Elliot, A. J., & Friedman, R. (2012). Achievement goals. In R. Ryan (Ed.), *The Oxford handbook of human motivation* (pp. 191–207). Oxford University.

Muthén, L., & Muthén, B. (2017). *Mplus (version 8.1)*. Muthén & Muthén.

Nédélec, M., Halson, S., Abaidia, A., Ahmaidi, S., & Dupont, G. (2015). Stress, sleep and recovery in elite soccer. *Sports Medicine*, *45*, 1387–1400. https://doi.org/10/gdgzh2

Nicholls, A. R., & Polman, R. C. J. (2008). Think aloud. *Anxiety, Stress, & Coping*, *21*, 283–294. https://doi.org/10/cn7p9t

Ntoumanis, N., & Biddle, S. (1998). The relationship between competitive anxiety, achievement goals, and motivational climates. *Research Quarterly for Exercise and Sport*, *69*, 176–187. 10.1080/02701367.1998.10607682

Ntoumanis, N., Biddle, S. J. H., & Haddock, G. (1999). The mediating role of coping mechanisms on the relationship between achievement motivation and affect in sport. *Anxiety, Stress & Coping*, *12*, 299–327. 10.1080/10615809908250480

O'Rourke, D. J., Smith, R. E., Punt, S., Coppel, D. B., & Breiger, D. (2017). Psychosocial correlates of young athletes' self-reported concussion symptoms during the course of recovery. *Sport, Exercise, and Performance Psychology*, *6*, 262–276. https://doi.org/10/gbthfg

Pensgaard, A. M., & Roberts, G. C. (2003). Achievement goal orientations and the use of coping strategies among Winter Olympians. *Psychology of Sport and Exercise*, *4*, 101–116. 10.1016/S1469-0292(01)00031-0

Peugh, J. L., & Enders, C. K. (2004). Missing data in educational research. *Review of Educational Research*, *74*, 525–556. 10.3102/00346543074004525

Pines, A. M., & Keinan, G. (2005). Stress and burnout. *Personality and Individual Differences*, *39*, 625–635. 10.1016/j.paid.2005.02.009

Pintrich, P. R. (2000). Multiple goals, multiple pathways. *Journal of Educational Psychology*, *92*, 544–555. 10.1037/0022-0663.92.3.544

Prati, G., & Pietrantoni, L. (2009). Optimism, social support, and coping strategies as factors contributing to posttraumatic growth. *Journal of Loss & Trauma*, *14*, 364–388. 10.1080/15325020902724271

Raedeke, T. D., & Smith, A. L. (2004). Coping resources and athlete burnout. *Journal of Sport and Exercise Psychology*, *26*, 525–541. 10.1123/jsep.26.4.525

Raedeke, T. D., & Smith, A. L. (2001). Development and preliminary validation of an athlete burnout measure. *Journal of Sport and Exercise Psychology*, *23*(4), 281–306.

Rice, S., Purcell, R., De Silva, S., Mawren, D., McGorry, P., & Parker, A. G. (2016). The mental health of elite athletes. *Sports Medicine*, *46*, 1333–1353. https://doi.org/10/f9bvq9

Ryan, R. M., & Deci, E. L. (2000). Intrinsic and extrinsic motivations. *Contemporary Educational Psychology*, *25*, 54–67. 10.1006/ceps.1999.1020

Sallen, J., Hemming, K., & Richartz, A. (2017). Facilitating dual careers by improving resistance to chronic stress. *European Journal of Sport Science*, *18*, 112–122. https://doi.org/10/dhq6

Satow, L. (2012). Stress-und Coping-Inventar (SCI)[Stress and coping inventory] [PSYNDEX Tests-Nr. 9006508]. Elektronisches Testarchiv. ZPID.

Schoemann, A. M., Boulton, A. J., & Short, S. D. (2017). Determining power and sample size for simple and complex mediation models. *Social Psychological and Personality Science*, *8*(4), 379–386. 10.1177/1948550617715068

Shin, H., Park, Y. M., Ying, J. Y., Kim, B., Noh, H., & Lee, S. M. (2014). Relationships between coping strategies and burnout symptoms. *Professional Psychology: Research and Practice*, *45*, 44–56. 10.1037/a0035220

Sorkkila, M., Aunola, K., Salmela-Aro, K., Tolvanen, A., & Ryba, T. V. (2018). The co-developmental dynamic of sport and school burnout among student-athletes. *Scandinavian Journal of Medicine & Science in Sports*, *28*, 1731–1742. https://doi.org/10/dhq7

Steiner-Hofbauer, V., & Holzinger, A. (2020). How to cope with the challenges of medical education. *Academic Psychiatry*. 10.1007/s40596-020-01193-1

Steinert, A., & Haesner, M. (2018). Stress in retired adults – stressors, symptoms and coping strategies. *Ageing International*, *44*, 129–140. 10.1007/s12126-018-9327-9

Stoeber, J., Stoll, O., Pescheck, E., & Otto, K. (2008). Perfectionism and achievement goals in athletes. *Psychology of Sport and Exercise*, *9*, 102–121. https://doi.org/10/btfnch

Stoeber, J., Uphill, M. A., & Hotham, S. (2009). Predicting race performance in triathlon. *Journal of Sport and Exercise Psychology*, *31*, 211–245. 10.1123/jsep.31.2.211

Stornes, T., & Ommundsen, Y. (2004). Achievement goals, motivational climate and sportspersonship. *Scandinavian Journal of Educational Research*, *48*, 205–221. 10.1080/0031383042000198512

Sun, R., Vuillier, L., Hui, B. P. H., & Kogan, A. (2019). Caring helps. *PloS ONE*, *14*, e0213142. 10.1371/journal.pone.0213142

Van Yperen, N. W., Blaga, M., & Postmes, T. (2014). A meta-analysis of self-reported achievement goals and nonself-report performance across three achievement domains (work, sports, and education). *PLoS ONE*, *9*. https://doi.org/10/f5382v

Vitali, F., Bortoli, L., Bertinato, L., Robazza, C., & Schena, F. (2015). Motivational climate, resilience, and burnout in youth sport. *Sport Sciences for Health*, *11*, 103–108. 10.1007/s11332-014-0214-9

Wang, C. K. J., Liu, W. C., Sun, Y., & Chua, L. L. (2017). Psychometric properties of the 3 x 2 achievement goal questionnaire for sport. *International Journal of Sport and Exercise Psychology*, *15*, 460–474. 10.1080/1612197X.2016.1142458

Williams, J. M. (2001). Psychology of injury risk and prevention. In R. N. Singer, H. A. Hausenblas, & C. M. Janelle (Eds.), *Handbook of sport psychology* (2nd ed., pp. 766–786). Wiley.

Ziemainz, H., Abu-Omar, K., Raedeke, T., & Krause, K. (2004). Burnout im Sport [Burnout in sport]. *Leistungssport*, *2004*(6), 12–18.

7

SWEDISH ATHLETES' ADJUSTMENT PATTERNS IN THE JUNIOR-TO-SENIOR TRANSITION

Viewing the Study from Today's Perspective

Alina Franck, Natalia B. Stambulova, and Andreas Ivarsson

We are grateful to the ISSP for the opportunity to revisit the previously published manuscript (Franck et al., 2016b) and reflect on it from today's perspective. Below the chapter is presented as it was, followed by new reflections.

Athletes view the junior-to-senior transition (JST) as the most difficult transition of an athletic career (Stambulova, 2009), and many internal and external factors contribute to the transition outcome (e.g., Baron-Thiene & Alfermann, 2015; Gould et al., 2002; Poczwardowski et al., 2014; Rosier et al., 2015; Stambulova et al., 2012). During the athletic career, which is defined as 'a multiyear sport activity, voluntarily chosen by the person aimed at achieving his or her individual peak in athletic performance in one or several sport events' (Alfermann & Stambulova, 2007, p. 713), athletes must face both normative (e.g., the junior-to-senior transition, the sport career retirement) and non-normative transitions (e.g., injury). Authors of review papers on athletes' career transitions (Alfermann & Stambulova, 2007; Petitpas et al., 2009; Stambulova et al., 2009; Stambulova & Johnson, 2013; Stambulova & Wylleman, 2014; Wylleman et al., 2004), noticed a shift in the researchers' focus from transitioning out of sport to studies of within-career transitions, such as the JST. The interest in the JST stems from its particular importance for athletes and their lifestyle when trying to achieve an elite/professional level in their sports (Stambulova, 2009). According to the Swedish Sport Confederation (the Swedish abbreviation for Riksidrottsförbundet, RF will be used further), the most talented junior athletes motivated to reach the senior elite level in their sports should be given a chance to do so (Riksidrottsförbundet, 2009). One way to assist these athletes is through the national elite sport high schools, where athletes

DOI: 10.4324/9781003459750-7

can combine sport and studies. But, according to RF, only a part of the athletes who want to reach the senior level can be given this opportunity; most athletes have to find their own paths and the balance between sport, studies, and private life in their local sport clubs. The aim of this longitudinal project was to investigate the JST process (demands, coping strategies, support, pressure, personal resources, stress, need for additional help, and adjustment to the senior level) for club-based Swedish athletes. Treatment of the data from the five consecutive measurements has generated two foci for further analysis that are not built on each other but viewed as complementary. The first focus was on identifying profiles of athletes in the JST based on their personal characteristics (athletic identity, goal orientation, and self-esteem) and to describe the athletes' relevant pathways in the JST (Franck et al., 2016a). This analysis resulted in three personal characteristics profiles. Athletic identity appeared to be a key personal characteristic, and different styles of coping strategies were associated with different JST pathways. In the current study, we shifted the focus to the athletes' adjustment patterns in the JST (i.e., dynamics, over time, in their total perceived adjustment on the senior level comprising sport practice, competitions, non-sport activities, relationships, and life-style), and related demographic, personal, and transitional characteristics at the beginning of the JST.

Theoretical Frameworks

We selected two theoretical frameworks as the basis for this study. The holistic athletic career model (Wylleman et al., 2013) provides a comprehensive view of athletes' development, considering them not only as athletic performers, but also as people who engage in sports and in other areas of life. The athletic career transition model (Stambulova, 2003, 2009) provides an insight into the transition process, its outcomes, and the factors involved.

The holistic athletic career model by Wylleman et al. (2013) interweaves five concurrent domains of an athlete's lifelong development (i.e., athletic, psychological, psychosocial, academic/vocational, and financial) roughly aligned with chronological ages. In the athletic domain, the JST is similar to the transition from the developmental to the mastery stage. In the psychological domain, the JST coincides with the transition from adolescence to adulthood. In the psychosocial area, an example could be moving from living at home with parents to living independently. In the academic/vocational domain, they usually make a transition from the upper secondary school to college, university, or employment. In the financial domain, athletes experience a shift from primarily family to sponsors or federation support.

Stambulova's (2003, 2009) athletic career transition model outlines the transition process (i.e., demands/challenges, resources, barriers, coping strategies, and outcomes). According to this model, a transition is a process of coping with a set of transition demands. Coping strategies used and the dynamic balance between the athletes' resources and barriers are predictive of the transition outcomes. The resources that facilitate the transition can be both internal (e.g., personal characteristics) and external factors (e.g., social support), and barriers are the various internal (e.g., low levels of confidence/motivation) and external (e.g., limited financial support) factors that interfere with the coping process. The transition outcomes depend on the effectiveness of coping, and the model predicts two primary outcomes. A successful transition occurs when an athlete copes effectively due to a good fit between the transition demands and the athlete's resources and strategies. A crisis transition occurs when the athlete is not coping effectively, and/or has limited resources and faces too many barriers. Further, a crisis transition can have two secondary outcomes: delayed successful transition (in the case of effective intervention) and unsuccessful transition (in the case of no/or ineffective intervention). The latter is often associated with negative long-term consequences of not coping with a crisis (e.g., dropout, neuroses, eating disorders, substance abuse).

The JST Research Overview

The JST was first outlined in the analytic sports career model (Stambulova, 1994). This transition usually happens during athletes' adolescent years, but it is difficult to identify the exact timing because of gender, individual and sport differences, and the sociocultural context (Stambulova, 2009; Stambulova & Ryba, 2014). Previous studies showed that the JST lasts for between one and four years and is initiated by a set of demands related to athletic and non-athletic development. Several Swedish studies (e.g., Stambulova et al., 2012) and international investigations (e.g., Bruner et al., 2008; Tekavc et al., 2015) have been conducted on the JST and athletes' entry into elite sport.

Individual athletes begin the JST process when they start (or in the near future, going to start) to participate in senior competitions in their sports, and team sports athletes start the process when they begin (or in the near future, will begin) practicing with a senior team and play for at least some time in senior games (Stambulova, 1994, 2009; Stambulova et al., 2015). As revealed in several studies (Debois et al., 2012; Ekengren, 2002; Hollings et al., 2014; Lundell Olsson & Pehrson, 2014; Rosier et al., 2015; Stambulova et al., 2012; Stambulova et al., 2017), athletes recognised the JST as challenging, both physically (e.g., higher standards of both practice and performance than previously experienced) and mentally (e.g., high expectations but low awareness of the demands on the senior level) in terms of sport. Another challenging aspect for athletes is to be able to combine sport with other activities, such as studies and social life (e.g., Bruner et al., 2008; Lorenzo Calvo et al., 2009; Van Yperen, 2009; Wylleman & Reints, 2010). The JST process is not in any way a linear path to success; athletes face both ups and downs and need both internal and external resources to go through the transition successfully (e.g., Baron-Thiene & Alfermann, 2015; Morris et al., 2014; Pummell et al., 2008). Athletes' internal resources are personal characteristics (e.g., athletic identity, motivation, optimism, competitiveness, self-confidence) that coupled with the abilities to successfully achieve their goals will influence the JST outcome (Poczwardowski et al., 2014). One of the resources, suggested to have a strong relationship with JST outcome, is athletic identity (Stambulova et al., 2012). More specifically, when athletes are still in sport and expect their careers to progress to a higher level (like in the JST), athletic identity is an important resource stimulating athletes to prioritise sport and invest substantial efforts into their athletic development (Stambulova, 2009; Stambulova et al., 2015). However, as athletic retirement literature shows high and exclusive athletic identity might be a barrier for successful post-sport career adjustment (Park et al., 2013). External resources helping to deal with the JST demands are as follows: support from coaches, parents, and friends, along with a solid financial situation (e.g., Salmela et al., 2000). During the JST process athletes must overcome internal barriers, such as, athletes' ambitions to succeed in the JST together with uncertainty about success, high level of stress, limited confidence, low motivation, and injury (Stambulova, 2009). Athletes also face external barriers: too high expectations of others, limited support, and an insecure financial situation. To meet the challenges in the JST process and find a balance between resources and barriers, athletes must use coping strategies (Finn & McKenna, 2010). Examples of successful coping in the JST are the following: focusing on the task and block out distractions, working towards achieving goals, prioritising sport goals, having a strong work ethics, solving problems, accepting responsibility, having self-control, and making positive reappraisal. Morris (2013) identified different groups of athletes based on their dominant coping strategies in the JST: (a) athletes who did not rely on support from others even though it was offered to them (the avoidance group), (b) athletes who actively sought out support from others during and after the transition (the reactive coping group), and (c) athletes who actively searched for help when they felt they required it prior to, and throughout the transition process (the proactive coping group). The authors reflected that they could not completely distinguish these groups, but they concluded that the avoidance group appeared to cope less effectively with the transition than the other two (e.g., the reactive coping group and the proactive coping group).

Outcome of the JST

The JST is known for its high dropout rate. In Lindner and Johns (2004) study one-third of adolescent athletes' dropout of sport. In a study by Vanden Auweele et al. (2004) only 17% of elite junior athletes made a successful transition to senior elite sports during five years of observation. Talented young athletes who demonstrate quicker progress than their peers and receive social recognition being juniors most often find this transition especially difficult (Stambulova, 2009). Talented juniors and their supporters (e.g., coaches, parents) develop high expectations about smooth adjustment on the senior level, but typically this is not the case, and even a successful transition path is not a linier one (Debois et al., 2015; Finn & McKenna, 2010; Pummell et al., 2008; Stambulova, 2009).

There can be several criteria for a successful transition, for example, adaptive entry, perceived adjustment in- and outside of sport, life satisfaction, and athletic performance (Bruner et al., 2008; Morris et al., 2014; Pummell et al., 2008; Rosier et al., 2015; Stambulova et al., 2012). As shown in previous studies (Debois et al., 2015; Tekavc et al., 2015), it is important to view an athlete from the holistic lifespan perspective and, therefore, to assess the outcome of the transition not only based on athletic performance but on the athlete's overall adjustment in several areas of life. In this study, we asked for the transitional athletes' subjective feeling of adjustment in relation to sport practice and competitions on the senior level, goodness of balance between sport and non-sport activities, relationships, and lifestyle as a senior athlete.

Objectives of the Study

The review of the literature confirmed the importance of investigating the JST process. One potential limitation in previous research is the focus on cross-sectional designs. In this study, we used the longitudinal design to investigate the dynamics in the athletes' JST adjustment from the holistic lifespan perspective. Objectives of this study were (a) to identify adjustment patterns in the JST based on athletes' dynamics of adjustment during a two-and-a-half-year period, and (b) to describe the athletes' demographic, personal and transitional characteristics at the beginning of the JST that were related to the different adjustment patterns.

Method

Participants

Participants in the study were 101 club-based Swedish athletes at measurement one (74 males and 27 females); with the mean age 16.51 (SD = 1.32). Of these 20 were individual athletes (table tennis, tennis, and swimming) with the mean age of 16.85 (SD = 1.32) and 81 were team sports athletes (basketball and soccer) with the mean age of 16.43 (SD = 0.93). Two criteria were used to select the participants. First, the sport clubs the athletes belonged to had to have both junior and senior elite programs. The reason is that the athletes could develop and reach the senior level within their current sport club. Second, individual sports athletes had to have started (or were, in the near future, going to start) competing at the senior level in their sport, and the team sports athletes had to have started (or were, in the near future, going to start) practicing with a senior team. These inclusion criteria have also been used in previous studies (e.g., Stambulova et al., 2012). The dynamics of participants was characterised by an increasing dropout rate with 101, 68, 52, 55, and 37 participants from the first to the fifth measurement correspondingly. The dropout refers to participants' discontinuation in the study, but not compulsory to their discontinuation in sports.

Instruments

The four instruments used in this study and described below were selected based on previous JST research and availability of relevant validated instruments in Swedish language. The transition monitoring survey (TMS): The TMS (Stambulovaet al., 2012) was designed for studying athletes in the JST longitudinally. The TMS was developed based on the developmental model of transitions faced by athletes (Wylleman & Lavallee, 2004), the athletic career transition model (Stambulova, 2003, 2009), and previous Swedish JST research (e.g., Alge, 2008; Ekengren, 2002; Franck, 2009; Jorlén, 2007; Mavroidis, 2005). The survey had a three-part structure. The first part, the Introduction, contained a set of questions about personal and athletic background (e.g., age, gender, type of sport, level of competition, number of training hours, etc.), and a question about their motivation to reach the senior level in their sport (a scale 1–10; 1 = low motivated and 10 = highly motivated). The second part, the current situation in sport and life, explored the athlete's perception of different spheres of sport and life in regard of their importance and satisfaction. The third part, the Transition Process, included seven subscales exploring the transition process (demands, coping strategies, support, pressure, personal resources, stress, need for additional help, and adjustment to the senior level). The TMS has been used in previous studies and has been showed psychometric properties (e.g., Stambulova et al., 2012). In this study, Cronbach's alpha values for each TMS subscale were calculated based on the data from measurement one. In the second part, the Current Situation in Sport and Life, the alpha values ranged from 0.34 to 0.74 and in the third part, the Transition Process, the alpha values ranged from 0.58 to 0.95.

The athletic identity measurement scale (AIMS): The AIMS (Brewer et al., 1993) measured a person's identification with the role of athlete. Swedish version of the AIMS has been used in several studies (e.g., Stambulova et al., 2015) and exhibited acceptable psychometric properties. In this study, Cronbach's alpha from measurement one was 0.84.

The task and ego orientation in sport questionnaire (TEOSQ): The TEOSQ (Duda, 1989) consists of 13 items. Six of the items indicated ego orientation and seven items indicated task orientation. The Swedish version of TEOSQ was used in several studies (e.g., Gestranius, 2006) and showed acceptable psychometric properties. In this study, Cronbach's alpha from measurement one, were 0.70 for ego orientation and 0.82 for task orientation.

The physical self-perception profile – revised (PSPP-R): The PSPP-R (Lindwall et al., 2007) consists of 74 items that measured five factors (sport competence, strength, physical condition, body attractiveness, and self-esteem). For this study, only the self-esteem subscale was used to reduce an amount of variables included into the (further) latent profile analysis (LPA). The self-esteem subscale contained six items, which athletes rated from one to four, depending on how true the item was for them. The PSPP-R was used in previous Swedish studies (e.g., Gestranius, 2006) and exhibited acceptable psychometric properties. In this study, Cronbach's alpha for the self-esteem subscale was 0.88.

Procedure

This study was approved by (Lund) university ethical board. The study was designed as a quantitative longitudinal examination of the JST process with five measurements conducted approximately every six months, over a period of two-and-a-half-years.

The first organisational step was to reach the participants. Different sport clubs in Sweden were contacted and provided with information about the study. The clubs which showed an interest provided contact information of coaches. The coaches were then contacted, and if their interest was confirmed, they received more detailed information about the content of the study. Before the data collection occurred, informed consent forms were signed by coaches responsible for the participants. The next step was to arrange dates and time to meet the athletes (potential participants). The athletes were informed about the study and the related ethical issues (e.g., voluntary participation, confidentiality, and the right to drop out at any time). The authors also explained the selection criteria and asked for informed consent from the participants who met the criteria and were interested in taking part. The data collection was conducted in small groups before or after the athletes' training sessions at their clubs. One of the research group members was always present and available to help if needed. Athletes who were not present were contacted by post with two reminders.

Data Analysis

Descriptive statistics were obtained using SPSS version 20. An LPA, using Mplus 7.3 (Muthén & Muthén, 1998–2012) was performed with the robust maximum likelihood estimator. LPA can be used to identify subgroups that have similar patterns of change in longitudinal studies such as athletes' dynamic of adjustment in JST. Based on previous research, a non-linear model was used (e.g., Debois et al., 2015). We decided to set a cut-off point at the third measurement, to get a pattern of adjustment instead of merely a direction. The third measurement was chosen because it was the middle measurement, and one could assume that the athletes should have come a halfway in the JST (nevertheless all five measurements were included into the statistical model). A sequence of nested models, starting with one profile, was compared to examine if more complex models (i.e., a model containing one more profile) fitted the data better than more parsimonious models. In the present study, models with between one and four profiles were tested to identify the optimal model based on statistical criteria and substantive meaning. Several criteria were used to determinate the best model. First, the sample-size adjusted BIC (SSA-BIC; Yang, 2006) was inspected, with lower values indicating better model fit. Second, the Lo-Mendell- Rubin likelihood ratio test was used to compare the fit of two competing models. Statistically significant tests ($p < .05$) indicated that the current model solution fits the data better than a model solution with one less profile. Third, the entropy criterion was examined, which indicated how accurately people were classified into their respective profile (Aldridge & Roesch, 2008). Values closer to 1 indicated better accuracy (Berlin et al., 2014). Fourth, an expert evaluation was done by the authors to select the solution that was most meaningful from a theoretical perspective.

When the best model was determined, descriptive statistics on demographic, personal, and transitional characteristics for the identified profiles were calculated based on the first measurement data. Descriptive statistics for athletes' adjustment in specific areas were also calculated. These calculations could only be performed for the third, fourth, and fifth measurements since this specific part of the TMS was added after the second measurement (see Stambulova et al., 2012). Last, Cohen's d effect sizes were calculated to estimate the magnitude of difference between the profiles regarding their relationship with different transition process variables.

Results

The findings of the first measurement for the whole sample can be summarised as follows. The athletes were competing at different levels: local (n = 7), national (n = 16), and international (n = 76). They were highly motivated (M = 9.20, SD = 1.46) to reach the senior level in their sports,

TABLE 7.1 Model fit indices for the 2, 3, and 4 class solutions

	2 Profiles	*3 Profiles*	*4 Profiles*
Sample adjusted BIC	2647.30	2616.53	2625.92
Lo-Mendell-Rubin likelihood ratio test	$p = .002$	$p = .02$	$p = .58$
Entropy	.69	.75	.64

though the amount of training hours per week (e.g., sport-specific training, physical training) varied among the athletes. Ten athletes trained for fewer than 10 hours per week, 46 athletes trained for between 10 and 14 hours, 30 athletes trained for 15–18 hours, and 15 athletes spent more than 18 hours per week on training. A majority of the participants were student athletes. Eight of the 101 athletes had part-time work commitments in addition to school and sport, and five athletes were not students.

The results from the LPA indicated that the model with a three-profile solution was the one that showed the best fit to the data (see Table 7.1 for the model fit indices).

The three profiles contained 11 (Profile 1), 10 (Profile 2), and 80 (Profile 3) athletes, respectively. All three profiles had different trajectories in JST (see Figure 7.1). Profile 1, labelled 'Progressive adjustment pattern' had a steep positive growth, especially between the first and the third measurement waves. In Profile 2, labelled 'Regressive adjustment pattern', the slope was steep and decreasing. In Profile 3, labelled 'Sustainable adjustment pattern',

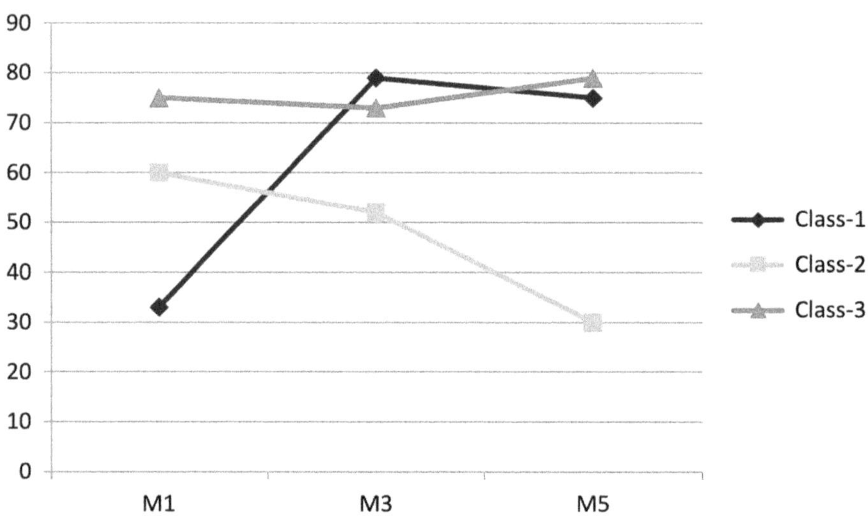

FIGURE 7.1 The 3-class model for athletes perceived adjustment to the senior level based on the LCA.

TABLE 7.2 Athletes perceived adjustment in different spheres of sport and life at measurement 3 (M3), measurement 4 (M4), and measurement 5 (M5)

	Class.1 M (SD)	*Class.2 M (SD)*	*Class.3 M (SD)*
M3 Adjusted in:			
Practice	8.00 (1.41)	5.57 (2.70)	7.73 (1.90)
Competition	7.17 (1.25)	5.43 (2.76)	7.32 (1.84)
Combining sport and other activities	8.43 (1.34)	5.57 (2.30)	7.32 (1.73)
Relationships	8.43 (1.51)	5.29 (3.35)	7.62 (1.57)
Lifestyle	8.57 (1.81)	6.14 (2.41)	7.32 (1.67)
M4 Adjusted in:			
Practice	7.57 (2.07)	4.67 (2.88)	7.79 (1.86)
Competition	7.57 (1.81)	4.00 (3.35)	7.13 (2.09)
Combining sport and other activities	7.57 (2.07)	4.50 (1.97)	6.84 (2.30)
Relationships	8.14 (1.78)	5.00 (2.53)	7.66 (1.72)
Lifestyle	8.14 (1.35)	4.67 (2.07)	7.45 (1.93)
M5 Adjusted in:			
Practice	7.33 (2.42)	4.00 (2.24)	7.90 (1.78)
Competition	7.50 (1.05)	3.00 (2.81)	7.66 (1.82)
Combining sport and other activities	7.00 (1.79)	1.50 (0.71)	7.93 (1.49)
Relationships	7.50 (2.51)	1.50 (0.71)	7.79 (1.63)
Lifestyle	7.50 (2.26)	1.50 (0.71)	7.93 (1.79)

the slope was stable throughout the measurements. Variances for all the variables in all profiles were statistically significant ($ps < .05$).

The three profiles are described in more detail below. The descriptive statistics for domain specific adjustments (e.g., practice, competition, combining sport with other activities, relationships, and lifestyle) can be viewed in Table 7.2. The demographic, personal, and transitional characteristics as well as the perceived importance of different spheres of life and sport are presented in Table 7.3.

Profile 1: Progressive Adjustment Pattern

The athletes in Profile 1 perceived themselves to be 33% adjusted to the senior level when entering the study. They increased their adjustment to 79% at the third measurement and then had a slight decrease at the fifth measurement, where they perceived themselves to be 75% adjusted to the senior level. If we look at the athletes' perceived adjustment across different spheres of life, we can see that they decreased their perceived adjustment in the domains of practice, combining sport with other activities, relationships and lifestyle, but increased their adjustment in competition between the third and the fifth measurements. At the end of the study, 55% of the athletes in this class remained in the study.

There were 11 athletes (males = 7, females = 4) in Profile 1. All of them were students and no one was working at the time of the first measurement.

TABLE 7.3 Descriptive statistics (n and M (SD)) for each class at the first measurement on demographic, personal and transitional characteristics as well as athletes overall perceived importance and satisfaction with sport and life

	Class 1 (n = *11*)	*Class 2* (n = *10*)	*Class 3* (n = *80*)
Demographic characteristics:			
Age	16.10 (0.70)	16.20 (1.32)	16.61 (1.38)
Male	n = 7	n = 6	n = 61
Female	n = 4	n = 4	n = 19
Individual athletes	n = 0	n = 4	n = 16
Team athletes	n = 11	n = 6	n = 64
Competition level Local	n = 2	n = 1	n = 4
Competition level National	n = 3	n = 1	n = 12
Competition level International	n = 6	n = 8	n = 62
School	n = 11	n = 10	n = 75
	n = 0	n = 0	n = 8
Personal characteristics:			
Motivation to reach the senior level	9.46 (0.93)	8.40 (1.43)	9.26 (1.50)
Athletic identity	5.73 (0.92)	5.19 (0.81)	5.79 (0.92)
Ego orientation	3.71 (0.56)	3.45 (0.60)	3.52 (0.67)
Task orientation	4.32 (0.32)	4.34 (0.38)	4.18 (0.52)
Self-esteem	3.48 (0.47)	3.55 (0.42)	3.77 (0.91)
Transitional characteristics:			
Transition demands	6.23 (0.67)	5.11 (0.41)	5.42 (0.20)
Coping strategies	7.33 (0.33)	6.82 (0.27)	7.14 (0.13)
Social support	7.65 (0.29)	7.92 (0.36)	7.63 (0.14)
Social pressure	6.69 (0.45)	5.40 (0.47)	6.45 (0.19)
Personal resources	6.94 (0.44)	6.94 (0.35)	7.48 (0.12)
Stress	5.27 (0.44)	4.19 (0.44)	4.38 (0.19)
Need for additional help	4.08 (0.60)	3.78 (0.50)	4.05 (0.22)
Importance different spheres of life	8.63 (0.98)	8.84 (1.05)	8.55 (1.11)
Satisfaction different spheres of life	8.22 (0.74)	8.05 (1.51)	7.84 (1.12)
Importance different spheres of sport	9.14 (0.79)	8.95 (0.96)	8.89 (1.13)
Satisfaction different spheres of sport	8.57 (1.57)	7.97 (0.75)	8.35 (1.59)

There were only team sport athletes represented in this class, and six out of the 11 athletes competed at the international level. The athletes' motivation to reach the senior level in their sport was high (M = 9.46, SD = 0.93), and they also had high athletic identity (M = 5.73, SD = 0.92). The athletes were more task oriented than ego and had relatively high self-esteem. They perceived different spheres of life to be important, but they perceived different spheres of sport to be more important, and the same was about their perceived satisfaction with both sport and life.

Profile 2: Regressive Adjustment Pattern

The athletes in Profile 2 perceived themselves to be 60% adjusted when entering the study. These athletes had a negative progression, evaluating themselves to be 52% adjusted to the senior level at the third measurement and only 30% at the fifth. Their perceived adjustment in different spheres (practice, competition, combining sports with other activities, relationships, and lifestyle) decreased in all of them from the third to the fifth measurement. In the end of the study, only 20% of the athletes in this class remained.

At the start of the study, there were 10 athletes (males = 6, females = 4) in Profile 2. All of them were students and no one was working. This class had both individual (n = 4) and team (n = 6) sport athletes, and 8 out of the 10 athletes competed at international level. Their motivation to reach the senior level was moderately high (M = 8.40, SD = 1.43), and they had athletic identity (M = 5.19, SD = 0.81) lower than Profile 1 athletes. Similar to the athletes in Profile 1, these athletes had higher task orientation than ego and relatively high self-esteem, but in contrast they perceived different spheres of life and sport to be almost equally important and satisfying.

Profile 3: Sustainable Adjustment Pattern

The athletes in Profile 3 perceived themselves to be 75% adjusted to senior level at the first measurement. We then see a minor decrease to 73% at the third measurement followed by a positive progression to the fifth measurement where they perceived themselves to be 79% adjusted to the senior level of sport. The athletes' perceived adjustment increased in all different spheres (practice, competition, combining sport with other activities, relationships, and lifestyle) between the third and the fifth measurements. By the end of the study 36% of athletes in this class remained.

There were 80 athletes (males = 61, females = 19) in Profile 3, of them 75 were also studying and 8 were working. This profile contained both individual (n = 16) and team (n = 64) sport athletes, and 62 of the athletes competed at international level. The athletes' motivation to reach senior level was high (M = 9.26, SD = 1.50) and they also had high athletic identity (M = 9.79, SD = 0.92). These athletes were more task oriented than ego and had high self-esteem. They perceived different spheres of life to be important, but they perceived different spheres of sport to be more important, the same was for their perceived satisfaction for the two spheres (e.g., life and sport).

Differences and Similarities between the Profiles

The descriptive statistics of the transitional characteristics relevant to each profile at the first measurement can be seen in Table 7.4. The results from the calculated Cohen's d (effect size) showed that there were large magnitudes

TABLE 7.4 Calculated effect size (Cohen's d) to compare the three classes transition variables

	1 vs. 2		*1 vs. 3*		*2 vs. 3*	
	d	*95% CI*	*d*	*95% CI*	*d*	*95% CI*
Demands	1.99	[0.88, 2.95]	2.76	[1.99, 3.48]	−1.35	[−2,02, −0.65]
Coping strategies	1.68	[0.63, 2.60]	1.15	[0.49, 1.79]	−2.13	[−2.83, −1.38]
Social support	−0.83	[−1.69, 0.09]	0.12	[−0.51, 0.75]	1.65	[0.94, 2.34]
Social pressure	2.81	[1.51, 3.88]	1.03	[0.37, 1.66]	−4.48	[−5.36, −3.51]
Personal resources	0.00	[−0.86, 0.86]	−2.91	[−3.64, −2.12]	−3.38	[−4.17, −2.53]
Stress level	2.45	[1.24, 3.47]	3.84	[2.97, 4.64]	−0.83	[−1.49, −0.16]
Perceived need for help/	0.54	[−0.35, 1.39]	0.10	[−0.53, 0.73]	−1.03	[−1.69, −0.34]

Note. 1 = Class 1; 2 = Class 2; 3 = Class 3.

between the three profiles for some of the variables of interest (see Table 7.4). A high magnitude of the effect was shown between Profile 1 and Profile 2 in terms of their experience of demands, pressure, support, stress levels, and coping strategies. However, a smaller magnitude can be seen for the differences between Profiles 1 and 2 in terms of personal resources and perceived need for additional help/support. Comparing Profile 1 and Profile 3, a higher magnitude of effect size was shown in terms of demands, coping strategies, stress, and pressure. Smaller magnitude was found between Profiles 1 and 3 in terms of the athletes' support and need for additional help/support. If we compare Profiles 2 and 3, there were examples of high magnitude, in terms of demands, coping strategies, support, and pressure.

Discussion

The objectives of the current study were (a) to identify adjustment patterns in the JST based on athletes' dynamics of adjustment during a two-and-a-half-year period, and (b) to describe the athletes' demographic, personal, and transitional characteristics at the beginning of the JST that were related to the different adjustment patterns. The LPA on athletes' perceived degree of adjustment to the senior level in their sports identified three profiles with different adjustment patterns. The descriptive statistics revealed different characteristics of the athletes in the three profiles, and Cohen's d indicated that there were differences (with variation in magnitude) between the profiles at the first measurement in terms of how athletes perceived different transitional characteristics.

Positioning the Study within the Longitudinal JST Project

There has been a call for longitudinal studies of athletes' transitions (e.g., Alfermann & Stambulova, 2007). In response, the current study was designed as a longitudinal project to provide a better understanding of the JST process (e.g., demands, coping, support, pressure, personal resources, stress, need for additional help, and adjustment to the senior level). Because the majority of junior athletes who want to reach the senior elite level are in different sports clubs, this project focused on these Swedish club-based athletes and not on the athletes who have got the opportunity to attend national elite sport high schools.

The project generated two foci for the data analysis: (a) to identify profiles of athletes in the JST based on their personal characteristics (athletic identity, goal orientation, and self-esteem) and to describe the athletes' relevant pathways in the JST, and (b) to investigate athletes' perceived degree of adjustment (in training, competition, combining sport with other activities, relationships, and lifestyle) in the JST. These two foci are seen as complementing each other to provide deeper understanding of the JST. The second focus taken in this chapter resulted in three different adjustment patterns (one progressive, one regressive, and one sustainable) based on the dynamics of athletes' perceived degree of adjustment.

The Adjustment Patterns in Relation to Previous Research

No previous research on the JST has used a longitudinal design, and a majority of studies on the JST were qualitative (e.g., Bruner et al., 2008; Debois et al., 2012; Lundell Olsson & Pehrson, 2014). The longitudinal design has provided new findings and also confirmed already existing knowledge about the JST, such as the importance of athletic identity (e.g., Alfermann & Stambulova, 2007; Stephen & Brewer, 2007), non-linear pathways in the transition process (e.g., Debois et al., 2015), and the high dropout rate in the JST (e.g., Lindner & Johns, 2004; Vanden Auweele et al., 2004). In terms of the new findings, the LCA in this study provided three profiles with different trajectories in JST. The first profile had a progressive adjustment pattern, while the second profile had a regressive adjustment pattern, and the third profile had a sustainable adjustment pattern.

The first profile, labelled 'Progressive adjustment pattern', showed a steep positive growth, especially between the first and third measurement waves. The perceived adjustment in this class increased from 33% to 75% during the study. At the end of the study, 55% of the athletes in this profile remained in the study. The athletes in Profile 1 decreased their perceived adjustment in several spheres of sport and life (practice, combining sport with other activities, relationships, and lifestyles). An exception was their adjustment in competition, which can be seen as a key sphere of the adjustment in the JST. The athletes in Profile 1 were the youngest when comparing the profiles, and as mentioned above, the athletes' perceived to be 33% adjusted at measurement one. Most probably they were at the beginning of the transition. The athletes in Profile 1 experienced higher demands compared to the other two profiles; however, they used coping strategies more than the other athletes. So, even if they experienced higher demands, they could meet those demands effectively by actively using coping strategies. In a previous study by Morris (2013), three groups (the avoidance coping group, the reactive coping group, and the proactive coping group) were identified in the JST. Athletes in Profile 1, who were at the beginning of the transition and actively used coping strategies, were most similar to the athletes in the proactive group Morris' study. The athletes in Profile 1 not only used coping strategies intensively, but they also had high athletic identity and high motivation to reach the senior level of their sport, being combined these factors contributed to the progressive adjustment pattern.

In the second profile, labelled 'Regressive adjustment pattern', the slope was steep and decreasing, the adjustment decreased from 60% to 30% during the study. These athletes decreased their perceived adjustment in all spheres of sport and life (practice, competition, combining sport with other activities, relationships, and lifestyle). In the end of the study only 20% of the athletes in this profile remained. The athletes in this profile had the lowest athletic identity and the lowest motivation to reach the senior level of sport in the beginning of the study, in contrast to previous research that indicated the importance of having strong athletic identity and high motivation to make the JST (e.g., Baron-Thiene & Alfermann, 2015; Poczwardowski et al., 2014; Stambulova, 2009). The athletes used coping strategies the least compared to the athletes in Profiles 1 and 3, which could indicate that they were similar to the athletes in the avoidance coping group in Morris' study (2013). Social support, especially from coaches, is the important external resource in the JST (e.g., Bruner et al., 2008). Athletes in Profile 2 experienced the most social support compared to the other profiles. But the amount of support may not have compensated for the lack of internal resources (e.g., lower athletic identity and motivation), and therefore the athletes experienced the regressive adjustment pattern during the JST.

The slope of the third profile, labelled 'Sustainable adjustment pattern', was stable over all five measurement waves, and the adjustment increased from 75% to 79% during the study. These athletes may have overestimated their adjustment or were already in the middle of the JST when entering the study. Athletes in this profile had the highest mean age of the three profiles, and therefore in measurement one, they were already further in the transition process compared to the other profiles. The athletes increased their perceived adjustment in all spheres of sport and life (practice, competition, combining sport with other activities, relationships, and lifestyle). Previous research has emphasised the importance for athletes to adjust in several areas of sport and life adopting the whole person perspective (e.g., Debois et al., 2015; Tekavc et al., 2015). Personal resources have been shown in previous research to be important for athletes to reach the senior level (Gould et al., 2002; Stambulova et al., 2015; Stephen & Brewer, 2007). The athletes in Profile 3 had the strongest personal resources (e.g., sport motivation, self-confidence, health condition, physical form, mental skills, etc.) compared to the other athletes; their athletic identity was high, and they were highly motivated to settle themselves on the senior sport level. The results indicated that key factors to a sustainable adjustment pattern were strong internal resources and adjustment covering several spheres of sport and life.

The Adjustment Patterns Related to Theoretical Frameworks

According to the holistic athletic career model by Wylleman et al. (2013) athletes should be considered not only as athletic performers, but also as people who engage in sports as well as in other activities and life domains. The three profiles differ in terms of how the athletes perceived the importance of, and satisfaction with different spheres of life and sport. The athletes in Profile 1 and Profile 3 perceived different spheres of life (e.g., family, friends, partner, studies) to be important but they perceived different spheres of sport (e.g., training, competition, recovery) to be more important, the same was true for their perceived satisfaction. Athletes in Profile 2 perceived different spheres of life and sport to be almost equally important and satisfying. However, to make a successful JST it seems that focusing on sport is a facilitating factor that contributes to both progressive and sustainable patterns of adjustment.

The athletic career transition model (Stambulova, 2003, 2009) outlines three transition outcomes: a successful transition, a delayed successful transition, and an unsuccessful transition (crisis transition). In this chapter, three patterns of adjustment were identified. The progressive and sustainable adjustment patterns can be viewed as two forms of successful transition (although reached in different ways). In both successful adjustment patterns athletes prioritised sport, were highly motivated, and had high athletic identity, confirming the role of these factors in the JST (Poczwardowski et al., 2014; Stambulova et al., 2012). The dropout rate (higher in Profile 3) was not the main indicator of the transition success or failure because we reported dropout rate from the study (but athletes could be still in sport). For example, 64 athletes from Profile 3 (n = 80) were from team sports and 62 competed internationally. So, we might guess that a good part of them relocated to play in other Swedish clubs or abroad, and we just could not keep them in our study. The regressive pattern is an unsuccessful JST outcome. Athletes in Profile 2 did not perceive themselves properly settled as senior athletes, and they paid more attention to other spheres of life (e.g., studies) and had lower athletic identity. Athletes in Profile 2 were less at risk in terms of athletic retirement compared to the athletes from Profiles 1 and 3, who can be more vulnerable in the case of unexpected career termination (e.g., injury).

Methodological Reflections

This study was designed as a quantitative longitudinal study, making it possible to follow a large number of athletes in the JST during the long time period. The LPA was an adequate tool to identify the JST adjustments patterns. The study has, however, some limitations.

First, when selecting the participants, our inclusion criteria were that the individual sports athletes had to have started or were, in the near future, going to start competing at the senior level in their sport; also, team sports athletes had to have started or were, in the near future, going to start practicing with a senior team. Based on the inclusion criteria it was still difficult to find athletes who were at the same point in the transition process at the start of the study. The athletes also represented different sports (table tennis, tennis, swimming, basketball, and soccer) which made the sample more diverse and, hence, more complicated to study.

Second, a major challenge when conducting a longitudinal study is a dropout, which most often is high. In this current study, 37% of the participants were still in the study and active as athletes at the fifth measurement. This high dropout percentage is considered as a major limitation of the study; however, the dropout refers to athletes' discontinuation in the study, and we could not follow whether the study dropouts continued in sport or not. Although the dropout rate was high, it is in line with previous research on the JST, which indicated that only one-third of the athletes during this period of the athletic career remained active in elite sport (e.g., Lindner & Johns, 2004; Vanden Auweele et al., 2004). In line with the recommendations from, for example, Newman (2014), a sensitivity analysis was conducted. More specifically, an independent sample t-test was used to investigate if there were any differences in JST at baseline between the two groups (i.e., full set of measurements, non-completed set of measurements). No statistically significant differences between the groups were discovered (Cohen's d effect size = .23). The missing data were, therefore, treated as missing at random.

Third, the Cronbach's alpha values for the instruments/subscales used were overall good, except for the second part (the Current Situation in Sport and Life) of the TMS. Although the Cronbach's alpha is a common method used to assess internal consistency, there have been discussions about how to use and interpret it correctly (Cortina, 1993; Schmitt, 1996). Research has showed that the alpha value is heavily influenced by the number of items: more items are related to a higher Cronbach's alpha value (Cortina, 1993). Because the alpha value only indicates to which extent one item correlates with at least one other item in the scale the alpha level does not indicate meaningfulness (Cortina, 1993). Therefore, questionnaires with low alphas can still be useful (Schmitt, 1996).

Fourth, after using the LPA three profiles were identified; however, one profile was substantially larger in number of athletes compared to the other two profiles. This imbalance made it difficult to analyse, and the reader should beware that this limitation could affect the results. For future quantitative longitudinal studies, it is important to reflect on the aforementioned limitations.

Conclusion

This longitudinal project has revealed the complexity of the JST by demonstrating athletes' different adjustment patterns. This chapter, along with the other paper (Franck et al., 2016a), has shown that internal resources, especially athletic identity and high motivation, play important roles in the JST process together with the athletes' ability to use adequate coping strategies. This indicates that even though external resources (e.g., support) are important and needed, the internal resources that the athletes possess are more crucial in adjusting to the senior level of sport. The results from the LPA in this study provided three unique profiles of athletes who indicated different adjustment patterns. This result demonstrated variations in how athletes move through the JST. The descriptive statistics and Cohen's d indicated that there were differences between the three profiles at the first measurement in terms of how athletes perceived different transitional characteristics. The progressive and sustainable patterns were interpreted as associated with successful transition outcomes, and the regressive pattern was seen as indicating unsuccessful transition.

In Sweden, there are more than 20,000 different sports clubs, with more than 600,000 non-profit leaders. National elite sports schools have employed practitioners who most often have an educational background related to sport compared to the non-profit club leaders with high variations in sport-related knowledge. It is therefore important to include the knowledge about the JST process and factors involved in different education programmes for club stakeholders. In the future research, quantitative measurements should be combined with in-depth interviews to create a mixed-method approach to provide an even more detailed picture of different pathways as well as athletes' sport and life experiences in the JST.

Reflections on the Study from Today's Perspective

Still today there are approximately 20,000 different sport clubs in Sweden, and it is within these clubs that most athletes go through the different stages and transitions during their athletic career. The concept of dual careers (Stambulova & Wylleman, 2015) and its implementation in the Swedish sport system is evolving (Linnér, 2021; Riksidrottsförbundet, 2018). During the JST there is an opportunity for selected junior athletes to attend the national elite sport schools which support athletes in finding an optimal balance between sport, studies, and private life (Stambulova et al., 2015). Most junior athletes, however, are still spending most of their time in the sport club environment. These athletes might not have the athletic level required to attend a national elite sport school or the interest or resources to do so.

This longitudinal study was part of a PhD dissertation (Franck, 2018) with the overall focus on exploring the JST in Swedish sport club athletes based on holistic developmental and ecological approaches. The results from the longitudinal project (Franck et al., 2016a, 2016b) were complemented by two qualitative narrative-type studies which resulted in two separate articles. The first article (Franck & Stambulova, 2019) examined the JST transition pathways of two individual sport athletes (a male swimmer and a female tennis player) and focused on the psychosocial factors that were seen as assisting or hindering the transition process. The study provided a major storyline – *a performance narrative* –that was shared by both athletes as well as two unique side stories: one for the tennis player's, the *injury and reorientation narrative,* and one for the swimmer's, the *effort and relationships narrative.* Both athletes faced a variety of crossroads and had similar views of the facilitating factors that helped them to cope (e.g., family, coaches, and the environment of an elite sports club), but their perception of the debilitating factors were more diverse. The second article (Franck & Stambulova, 2020) focused on two team sport athletes' JST pathways in male football and female basketball. The basketball player's reflections on the transition process generated an *enjoyment and relationship narrative*, whereas the football player's JST journey evolved into a *performance and family narrative.* The JST paths of the athletes included several crossroads, and throughout the transitions they perceived key facilitators to be their family (e.g., parents, grandparents, and siblings) and teammates, whereas some of the coaches' behaviours were perceived as debilitating factors. The overall PhD project (Franck, 2018) contributed to (a) considering the JST (longitudinally) as a process involving dynamics and interactions of the transition demands, coping strategies, personal and environmental resources, and barriers influencing the JST outcome; (b) supporting the athletic career transition model in combination with the holistic developmental and ecological perspectives as adequate frameworks to study the JST; and (c) demonstrating significant variations in the JST pathways and adjustment patterns on the subgroup and individual levels.

Since this study was published, there has been several new studies on the JST that have developed the topic (e.g., Andronikos et al., 2021;

Drew et al., 2019; Pehrson et al., 2017; Swainston et al., 2020; Tang & Wang, 2022). Drew et al.'s (2019) meta-study on existing qualitative research on JST resulted in 60 factors that were perceived to impact the quality of athletes' transitions. They were then categorised into 13 themes, such as perceptions of the transition, psychological factors, personal development factors, performance development factors, social support, motivation, sources of stress, physical factors, organisational culture and values, youth culture and values, coping strategies, mentoring and modelling, and educational programmes. Andronikos et al. (2021) investigated which factors contribute to the athletes' quality of the JST. The participants completed a Greek version of the Transition Monitoring Survey (TMS; Stambulova et al., 2012). The results revealed that personal resources, transition demands, and environmental support (e.g., teammates and family) were significant predictors of the JST adjustment. There has been a longitudinal study on the JST in professional football (Swainston et al., 2020) that identified different phases (e.g., academy phase and first team phase) with challenges and coping strategies used during each phase. Another study (Stambulova et al., 2017) targeting different phases in the JST for Swedish ice hockey players resulted in an empirical model titled Phases in the junior-to-senior transition of Swedish ice hockey players. The model outlined the players' transition experiences (i.e., perceived demands, resources, barriers, coping strategies, and outcomes) within each of the four JST phases (i.e., preparation, orientation, adaptation, and stabilisation). In a follow-up study, Pehrson et al. (2017) continued to explore the JST process in Swedish ice hockey by validating the empirical model. The results supported the JST phases (i.e., preparation, orientation, adaptation, and stabilisation), as well as the duration of the JST which can last up to four seasons, as outlined by the empirical model. As was shown in Franck (2018) foci on related contexts and environments are important for understanding the JST. This is confirmed in the recent Henriksen et al. (2023) paper where athletes' development is described as a journey through different environments and contexts.

At the time of the study (Franck et al., 2016b), we selected the holistic athletic career model (Wylleman et al., 2013) and the athletic career transition model (Stambulova, 2003, 2009) as theoretical frameworks, and since then the models have evolved. The holistic athletic career model by Wylleman (2019) interweaves six concurrent levels of an athlete's lifelong development (i.e., athletic, psychological, psychosocial, academic/vocational, financial, and legal) roughly aligned with chronological ages. The new legal level reflects how the legal rights and obligations of athletes may gradually converge with those of legal adults. Note that the legal level has not been explored in the study but is something to consider in future research since athletes in the JST also make the transition from minors to legal adults which is an important threshold in a person's life. In Stambulova et al. (2020), the transition process is seen as an interplay between the transition demands (i.e., what athletes want to achieve), resources and barriers (i.e., internal and external factors facilitating or debilitating coping), and coping strategies. The coping process leads to the primary transition outcomes: a successful or crisis-transition. Further, the crisis might have two secondary outcomes: an unsuccessful transition most often related to dropout and/or negative consequences (e.g., mental health issues) or a delayed successful transition facilitated by an effective intervention.

Most athletes are not able to make a successful transition to higher elite levels and must move to recreational sports or drop out during the JST (Franck, 2018). Career exploration and planning services should be available to help athletes before, during, and after their JST transition (Tang & Wang, 2022). A special focus on assisting athletes to combine sport with other life areas (e.g., higher education, social life) may help athletes develop well-balanced identities. For athletes to have a successful JST there are several key facilitating actors, such as sport federations, sport clubs, coach(es), and family members. It may be helpful to assist these key stakeholders in understanding their complex roles in the athletes' transition process with shifts between different environments that the athletes face (Henriksen et al., 2023).

More research and comprehensive reviews of the JST are needed. When searching for new studies since 2016, we realised that the number of publications were lower compared to the period before 2016. The area of career development and transitions for athletes is developing rapidly, and lately the emerging trends are dual career and cultural transitions (Stambulova et al., 2021). The JST is, however, still the most complex and challenging transition during the athletic career, and therefore it is important to continue with more longitudinal studies and contextualised studies to understand the uniqueness of different sports and cultures that influence the JST. More research on JST pathways for women and men is also of interest because the preconditions are still unequal.

Acknowledgements

The authors want to express their gratitude to the sports clubs, coaches, and participants that have taken time to participate in this longitudinal study. And finally, express gratitude to the ISSP for giving us the opportunity to revisit and reflect on this study retrospectively.

References

Aldridge, A. A., & Roesch, S. C. (2008). Developing coping typologies of minority adolescents: A latent profile analysis. *Journal of Adolescence*, *31*(4), 499–517. 10.1016/j.adolescence.2007.08.005

Alfermann, D., & Stambulova, N. B. (2007). Career transitions and career termination. In G. Tenenbaum & R. C. Eklund (Eds.), *Handbook of sport psychology* (pp. 712–736). Wiley.

Alge, E. (2008). Successful career transition from junior to senior level in equestrian sport (Unpublished master's thesis, Halmstad University).

Andronikos, G., Westbury, T., Brazo-Sayavera, J., Olivares, P. R., & Martindale, R. J. J. (2021). Factors contributing to the quality of the junior-to-senior transition in Greek athletes. *International Journal of Sport and Exercise Psychology*. 10.1080/1612197X.2021.1891116

Baron-Thiene, A., & Alfermann, D. (2015). Personal characteristics as predictors for dual career dropout versus continuation – A prospective study of adolescent athletes from German elite sport schools. *Psychology of Sport and Exercise*, *21*, 42–49. 10.1016/j.psychsport.2015.04.006

Berlin, K. S., Williams, N. A., & Parra, G. R. (2014). An introduction to latent variable mixture modeling (part 1): Overview and cross-sectional latent class and latent profile analyses. *Journal of Pediatric Psychology*, *39*(2), 174–187. 10.1093/jpepsy/jst084

Brewer, B. W., Van Raalte, J. L., & Linder, D. E. (1993). Athletic identity: Hercules' muscles or Achilles' heel? *International Journal of Sport Psychology*, *24*(2), 237–254. 10.1080/10413200701867745

Bruner, M. W., Munroe-Chandler, K. J., & Spink, K. S. (2008). Entry into elite sport: A preliminary investigation into the transition experiences of rookie athletes. *Journal of Applied Sport Psychology*, *20*(2), 236–252. 10.1080/10413200701867745

Cortina, J. M. (1993). What is coefficient alpha? An examination of theory and applications. *Journal of Applied Psychology*, *78*(1), 98–104. 10.1037/0021-9010.78.1.98

Debois, N., Ledon, A., Argiolas, C., & Rosnert, E. (2012). A lifespan perspective on transitions during a top sports career: A case of an elite female fencer. *Psychology of Sport and Exercise*, *13*(5), 660–668. 10.1016/j.psychsport.2012.04.010

Debois, N., Ledon, A., & Wylleman, P. (2015). A lifespan perspective on the dual career of elite male athletes. *Psychology of Sport and Exercise*, *21*, 15–26. 10.1016/j.psychsport.2014.07.011

Drew, K., Morris, R., Tod, D., & Eubank, M. (2019). A meta-study of qualitative research on the junior-to-senior transition in sport. *Psychology of Sport and Exercise*, *45*. 10.1016/j.psychsport.2019.101556

Duda, J. L. (1989). The relationship between task and ego orientation and the perceived purpose of sport among male and female high school athletes. *Journal of Sport and Exercise Psychology*, *11*(3), 318–335.

Ekengren, J. (2002). "Att gå från dröm till verklighet"—steget från handbollens u-landslag till a-landslag [Making dreams true: From-junior-to-elite junior team transition in handball] (Unpublished master's thesis, Halmstad University).

Finn, J., & McKenna, J. (2010). Coping with academy-to-first-team transitions in elite English male team sports: The coaches' perspective. *International Journal of Sports Science and Coaching*, *5*(2), 257–279. 10.1260/1747-9541.5.2.257

Franck, A. (2009). Individual and team sports athletes in the transition from junior to senior sports (Unpublished master's thesis, Halmstad University).

Franck, A. (2018). The junior-to-senior transition in Swedish athletes: A longitudinal study (Unpublished doctoral thesis, Linnaeus University).

Franck, A., & Stambulova, N. B. (2019). The junior to senior transition: A narrative analysis of the pathways of two Swedish athletes. *Qualitative Research in Sport, Exercise and Health, 11*(3), 284–298. 10.1080/2159676X.2018.1479979

Franck, A., & Stambulova, N. B. (2020). Individual pathways through the junior-to-senior transition: Narratives of two Swedish team sport athletes. *Journal of Applied Sport Psychology, 32*(2), 168–185. 10.1080/10413200.2018.1525625

Franck, A., Stambulova, N. B., & Ivarsson, A. (2016b). Swedish athletes' adjustment patterns in the junior-to-senior transition. *International Journal of Sport and Exercise Psychology, 16*(4), 398–414. 10.1080/1612197X.2016.1256339

Franck, A., Stambulova, N. B., & Weibull, F. (2016a). Profiles of personal characteristics and relevant pathways in the junior-to-senior transition: A longitudinal study of Swedish athletes. *International Journal of Sport Psychology, 47*(6), 483–507. 10.7352/IJSP.2016.47.483

Gestranius, J. (2006). Factors influencing athletes' tendencies towards healthy vs. unhealthy sport participation (Unpublished bachelor's thesis, Halmstad University).

Gould, D., Dieffenbach, K., & Moffett, A. (2002). Psychological characteristics and their development in Olympic champions. *Journal of Applied Sport Psychology, 14*(3), 172–204. 10.1080/10413200290103482

Henriksen, K., Stambulova, N., Kamuk Storm, L., & Schinke, R. (2023). Towards an ecology of athletes' career transitions: conceptualization and working models. *International Journal of Sport and Exercise Psychology*. 10.1080/1612197X.2023.2213105

Hollings, S. C., Mallett, C. J., & Hume, P. A. (2014). The world junior athletics championships: New Zealand athletes' lived experiences. *International Journal of Sports Science and Coaching, 9*(6), 1357–1374. 10.1260/1747-9541.9.6.1357

Jorlén, D. (2007). Career transitions for Swedish golf juniors: From regional to national junior elite competitions (Unpublished bachelor's thesis, Halmstad University).

Lindner, K. J., & Johns, D. P. (2004). Factors in withdrawal from youth sport: A proposed model. *Journal of Sports Behavior, 14*(1), 3–16.

Lindwall, M., Hagger, M., & Asci, H. (2007). Introducing the physical self-perception profile – revised: Psychometric examination in three samples from Great Britain, Sweden and Turkey. In Y. Theodorakis, M. Goudas, & A. Papaioannou (Eds.), *Book of abstracts of the 12th European congress of sport psychology* (p. 228). Halkidiki, Greece: FEPSAC.

Linnér, L. (2021). Dual careers of Swedish University student-athletes: A synthesis of holistic developmental and ecological approaches (Unpublished doctoral thesis, Halmstad University).

Lorenzo Calvo, A., Borrás, P. J., Sánchez, J. M., Jiménez Sáis, S. L., & Sampedro, J. (2009). Career transition from junior to senior in basketball players. *Revista de Psicología del Deporte, 18*, 309–312. https://ddd.uab.cat/record/62654

Lundell Olsson, K., & Pehrson, S. (2014). Exploratory study – outlining the temporal structure of the junior-to-senior transition in Swedish ice hockey: Phases in the junior-to-senior transition (Unpublished bachelor's thesis, Halmstad University).

Mavroidis, D. (2005). Coaches' perception of the transition from junior elite football to professional (Unpublished master's thesis, Halmstad University).

Morris, R. (2013). Investigating the youth to senior transition in sport: From theory to practice (Unpublished doctoral dissertation, Aberystwyth University).

Morris, R., Tod, D., & Oliver, E. (2014). An analysis of organizational structure and transition outcomes in the youth-to-senior professional soccer transition. *Journal of Applied Sport Psychology*, *27*(2), 216–234. 10.1080/10413200.2014.980015

Muthén, L. K., & Muthén, B. O. (1998–2012). *Mplus user's guide* (7th ed.). Muthén & Muthén.

Newman, D. A. (2014). Missing data: Five practical guidelines. *Organizational Research Methods*, *17*(4), 372–411. 10.1177/1094428114548590

Park, S., Lavallee, D., & Tod, D. (2013). Athletes' career transition out of sport: A systematic review. *International Review of Sport and Exercise Psychology*, *6*(1), 22–53. 10.1080/1750984X.2012.687053

Pehrson, S., Stambulova, N. B., & Olsson, K. (2017). Revisiting the empirical model 'Phases in the junior-to-senior transition of Swedish ice hockey players': External validation through focus groups and interviews. *International Journal of Sports Science & Coaching*, *12*(6), 747–761. 10.1177/1747954117738897

Petitpas, A. J., Brewer, B. W., & Van Raalte, J. L. (2009). Transitions of the student-athlete: Theoretical, empirical, and practical perspectives. In E. F. Etzel (Ed.), *Counseling and psychological services for college student-athletes* (pp. 283–302). Fitness Information Technology.

Poczwardowski, A., Diehl, B., ÓNeil, A., Cote, T., & Haberl, P. (2014). Successful transitions to the Olympic training center, Colorado Springs: A mixed-method exploration with six resident-athletes. *Journal of Applied Sport Psychology*, *26*(1), 33–51. 10.1080/10413200.2013.773950

Pummell, B., Harwood, C., & Lavallee, D. (2008). Jumping to the next level: A qualitative examination of within-career transition in adolescent event riders. *Psychology of Sport and Exercise*, *9*(4), 427–447. 10.1016/j.psychsport.2007.07.004

Riksidrottsförbundet [Swedish Sport Confederation]. (2009). Idrotten vill: Idrottsrörelsens idéprogram [The Swedish Sport Confederation vision document]. Retrieved from: Idrotten Vill – Idrottsrörelsens idéprogram.pdf (rf.se).

Riksidrottsförbundet. (2018). Swedish national guidelines for elite athletes' dual careers. Recommended actions for the combination of high-performance sports and university education at Swedish national sports universities (RIUs) and elite sports-friendly universities (EVLs). Retrieved from: swedish-national-guidelines-dual-careers.pdf (rf.se).

Rosier, N., Wylleman, P., De Bosscher, V., & Van Hoecke, J. (2015). The transition from junior to senior elite athlete. In O. Schmid & R. Seiler (Eds.), *Proceedings 14th European congress of sport psychology* (p. 162). Bern: FEPSAC.

Salmela, J. H., Young, B. W., & Kallio, J. (2000). Within-career transitions of the athlete-coach-parent triad. In D. Lavallee & P. Wylleman (Eds.), *Career transitions in sport: International perspectives* (pp. 181– 193). Fitness Information Technology.

Schmitt, N. (1996). Uses and abuses of coefficient alpha. *Psychological Assessment*, *8*(4), 350–353. 10.1037/1040-3590.8.4.350

Stambulova, N. B. (1994). Developmental sports career investigations in Russia: A post-perestroika analysis. *The Sport Psychologist*, *8*(4), 221–237. 10.1123/tsp.8.3.221

Stambulova, N. B. (2003). Symptoms of a crisis-transition: A grounded theory study. In N. Hassmen (Ed.), *SIPF yearbook 2003* (pp. 97–109). Örebro University Press.

Stambulova, N. B. (2009). Talent development in sport: A career transitions perspective. In E. Tsung-Min Hung, R. Lidor, & D. Hackfort (Eds.), *Psychology of sport excellence* (pp. 63–74). Fitness Information Technology.

Stambulova, N. B., Alfermann, D., Statler, T., & Côté, J. (2009). ISSP position stand: Career development and transitions of athletes. *International Journal of Sport and Exercise Psychology*, *7*(4), 395–412. 10.1080/1612197X.2009.9671916

Stambulova, N. B., Engström, C., Franck, A., Linnér, L., & Lindahl, K. (2015). Searching for an optimal balance: Dual career experiences of Swedish adolescent athletes. *Psychology of Sport and Exercise*, *21*, 4–14. 10.1016/j.psychsport.2014.08.009

Stambulova, N. B., Franck, A., & Weibull, F. (2012). Assessment of the transition from junior to senior sports in Swedish athletes. *International Journal of Sport and Exercise Psychology*, *10*(2), 1–17. 10.1080/1612197X.2012.645136

Stambulova, N. B., & Johnson, U. (2013). Athletes' careers in Sweden: Facilitating socialization into sports and re-socialization upon retirement. In N. B. Stambulova & T. V. Ryba (Eds.), *Athletes' careers across cultures* (pp. 197–208). Routledge.

Stambulova, N., Pehrson, S., & Olsson, K. (2017). Phases in the junior-to-senior transition of Swedish ice- hockey players: From a conceptual framework to an empirical model. *International Journal of Sport Science and Coaching*, *12*(2), 231–244. 10.1177/1747954117694928

Stambulova, N. B., & Ryba, T. V. (2014). A critical review of career research and assistance through the cultural lens: Towards cultural praxis of athletes' careers. *International Review of Sport and Exercise Psychology*, *7*(1), 1–17. 10.1080/1750984X.2013.851727

Stambulova, N. B., Ryba, T. V., & Henriksen, K. (2021). Career development and transitions of athletes: The International Society of Sport Psychology Position Stand Revisited. *International Journal of Sport and Exercise Psychology*, *19*(4), 524–550. 10.1080/1612197X.2020.1737836

Stambulova, N. B., Schinke, R. J., Lavallee, D., & Wylleman, P. (2020). The COVID-19 pandemic and Olympic/Paralympic athletes' developmental challenges and possibilities in times of a global crisis-transition. *International Journal of Sport and Exercise Psychology*, *20*(1), 92–101. 10.1080/1612197X.2020.1810865

Stambulova, N., & Wylleman, P. (2014). Athletes' career development and transitions. In A. Papaioannou & D. Hackfort (Eds.), *Routledge companion to sport and exercise psychology* (pp. 605–621). Routledge.

Stambulova, N., & Wylleman, P. (2015). Dual career development and transitions (editorial). *Psychology of Sport and Exercise*, *21*, 1–3. 10.1016/j.psychsport.2015.05003

Stephen, Y., & Brewer, B. W. (2007). Perceived determinants of identification with the athlete role among elite competitors. *Journal of Applied Sport Psychology*, *19*(1), 67–79. 10.1080/10413200600944090

Swainston, S. C., Wilson, M. R., & Jones, M. I. (2020). Players experiences during the junior to senior transition in professional football: A longitudinal case study. *Frontiers in Psychology*, *11*, 1672. 10.3389/fpsyg.2020.01672

Tang, Q., & Wang, P. (2022). Facilitating the junior-to-senior transition: A stress-coping training program for young rugby players.*Journal of Sport Psychology in Action*. 10.1080/21520704.2022.2152513

Tekavc, J., Wylleman, P., & Cecić Erpič, S. (2015). Perceptions of dual career development among elite level swimmers and basketball players. *Psychology of Sport and Exercise*, *21*, 27–41. 10.1016/j.psychsport.2015.03.002

Van Yperen, N. W. (2009). Why some make it and other do not: Identifying psychological factors that predict career success in professional adult soccer. *The Sport Psychologist*, *23*(3), 317–329. 10.1123/tsp.23.3.317

Vanden Auweele, Y., De Martelaer, K., Rzewnicki, R., De Knop, & Wylleman, P. (2004). Parents and coaches: A help or a harm? Affective outcome for children in sport. In Y. Vanden Auweele (Ed.), *Ethics in youth sport*(pp. 179–193). Lannoocampus.

Wylleman, P. (2019). A developmental and holistic perspective on transitioning out of elite sport. In M. H. Anshel (Ed.), *APA handbook of sport and exercise psychology: Vol. 1. Sport psychology* (pp. 201–216). American Psychological Association.

Wylleman, P., Alfermann, D., & Lavallee, D. (2004). Career transitions in sport: European perspectives. *Psychology of Sport and Exercise*, *5*(1), 7–20. 10.1016/S1469-0292(02)00049-3

Wylleman, P., & Lavallee, D. (2004). A developmental perspective on transitions faced by athletes. In M. Weiss (Ed.), *Developmental sport and exercise psychology: A lifespan perspective* (pp. 507–527). Fitness Information Technology.

Wylleman, P., & Reints, A. (2010). A lifespan perspective on the career of talented and elite athletes: Perspectives on high-intensity sports. *Scandinavian Journal of Medicine & Science in Sport*, *20*, 88–94. 10.1111/j.1600-0838.2010.01194.x

Wylleman, P., Reints, A., & De Knop, P. (2013). A developmental and holistic perspective on athletic career development. In P. Sotiaradou & V. De Bosscher (Eds.), *Managing high performance sport* (pp. 159– 182). Routledge.

Yang, C.-C. (2006). Evaluating latent class analyses in qualitative phenotype identification. *Computational Statistics & Data Analysis*, *50*, 1090–1104. 10.1016/j.csda.2004.11.004

8

CUMULATIVE LIFETIME STRESSOR EXPOSURE AND HEALTH IN ELITE ATHLETES

The Moderating Role of Perfectionism

Ella McLoughlin, David Fletcher, Hannah L. Graham, Rachel Arnold, Daniel J. Madigan, George M. Slavich, and Lee J. Moore

Research suggests that lifetime stressor exposure is an important predictor of a variety of health-related outcomes (Burani et al., 2022; McLoughlin et al., 2022a; Slavich & Shields, 2018). Recent work on this topic has used the Stress and Adversity Inventory for Adults (STRAIN) to assess exposure to major stressors occurring over the entire life course. The STRAIN systematically enquires about a stressor's type (e.g., acute life events vs. chronic difficulties), exposure timing (e.g., early life vs. adulthood), primary life domain (e.g., education, work), and social-psychological characteristic (e.g., interpersonal loss, physical danger), and thus provides a comprehensive picture of stressor exposure. Since its initial development, the STRAIN has been used to examine how lifetime stressor exposure predicts numerous biological, behavioural, and clinical outcomes (e.g., Klatzkin et al., 2023). Broadly speaking, this research demonstrates that as lifetime stressor exposure increases, so too does the vulnerability for future psychological problems (e.g., depression, anxiety; Parra et al., 2023), as well as physical health complaints (e.g., colds; Cazassa et al., 2020). Moreover, experiencing more severe stressors over the life course has been identified as a relatively stronger predictor of ill health as compared to the total count of such stressors (Shields et al., 2022). As a result, it is relatively well established that greater lifetime stressor exposure contributes to various health problems in the general population (Slavich, 2016). However, research on this topic is limited among elite athletes who experience high levels of stress-related burden (c.f. McLoughlin et al., 2021, 2023a).

DOI: 10.4324/9781003459750-8

Initial research within a sporting context has suggested that elite athletes who have experienced greater lifetime stressors report more symptoms of depression and anxiety, as well as poorer psychological well-being (McLoughlin et al., 2021). Additionally, the qualitative findings reported by McLoughlin et al. (2021) suggested that relatively high lifetime stressor exposure fostered poorer health and well-being by promoting greater use of maladaptive long-term coping strategies (e.g., denial), increased susceptibility to future stress, and limiting interpersonal relationships (i.e., social support; McLoughlin et al., 2021). More recently, these qualitative results were extended by McLoughlin et al. (2023b) who used semi-structured interviews, complemented by timelining, to explore *how* lifetime stressor exposure influenced sport performers' health, well-being, and performance. Results revealed the psychological (e.g., maladaptive coping strategies), social (e.g., difficulties in building and maintaining relationships), and behavioural (e.g., risky behaviours) factors that further explain how lifetime stressor exposure influences sport performers' health, well-being, and performance. Furthermore, McLoughlin et al. (2022a) found that greater lifetime stressor exposure was associated with more mental and physical health problems (e.g., depression, respiratory infections). The results revealed that sport performers who experienced more severe lifetime stressors were more likely to appraise potentially stressful situations as a threat (vs. a challenge; McLoughlin et al., 2022a). To further understand the potential mechanisms underlying the stressor-health relationship, McLoughlin et al. (2022b) found that exposure to a moderate number of lifetime stressors was associated with adaptive cardiovascular reactivity, whereas very low or very high stressor exposure was related to maladaptive reactivity. Turning to performance-related outcomes, McLoughlin et al. (2023a) explored male elite athletes' experiences of lifetime stressor exposure and performance in their sport. Results revealed that the athletes viewed their sport as a form of escape from the stressors they experienced in their daily lives (e.g., parental divorce). It was, however, when stressors occurred in the sporting environment (e.g., selection) that the symptoms of mental ill-health were intensified and resulted in performance decrements.

Although this body of work has improved our understanding of the stressor-health relationship, this research has not explored any potential moderating factors such as personality. This is surprising given the prominent role that personality is proposed to play in stress-health theories such as the integrative model of stress and health (Epel et al., 2018). While there is an abundance of moderators that could be examined, one characteristic that has received growing attention is perfectionism (Curran & Hill, 2019; Hill, 2023; Hill et al., 2018). At its broadest, perfectionism is a multidimensional personality trait that is characterised by a combination of striving for flawlessness and overly critical evaluations of behaviour (Frost et al., 1990). One of the most utilised models of perfectionism was proposed by Hewitt and Flett (1991a), which differentiates between three dimensions of perfectionism based upon the direction of perfectionistic thoughts, feelings, and behaviours. The first dimension, self-oriented perfectionism, is the demand of perfection from the self. The second dimension, socially prescribed perfectionism, is the belief that others expect one to be perfect. And the final dimension, other-oriented perfectionism, is the demand of perfection from others (Hewitt & Flett, 1991a). Importantly, these different dimensions are thought to have varying effects on outcomes such as performance and health (Molnar et al., 2012).

Some investigators have suggested that perfectionism is essential to obtain success in sport (e.g., Hardy et al., 2017). However, research has also examined perfectionism in relation to health in both general and clinical populations (Flett et al., 2022; Sirois & Molnar, 2016; Smith et al., 2021). In this regard, there is evidence that the direction, size, and strength of associations differ based on which dimension is examined. Generally, socially prescribed perfectionism has shown the strongest positive associations with mental (e.g., depression; Limburg et al., 2016) and physical (e.g., migraines; Flett et al., 2016) health outcomes. Similarly, other-oriented perfectionism is positively related to health outcomes, but the effects are typically smaller in size (e.g., Saboonchi & Lundh, 2003). Finally, the association between self-oriented perfectionism and health is more ambiguous, with some studies showing positive associations and others revealing negative associations (e.g., Molnar et al., 2012).

Beyond this, perfectionism has also been linked to psychological stress (Hewitt & Dyck, 1986). In this regard, Flett and Hewitt (2002) proposed several theoretical pathways through which perfectionism may affect stress. Two pathways are particularly relevant for the present study. The first pathway, stress perpetuation, refers to the tendency for those high in perfectionism to maintain a stressful episode via the use of maladaptive coping techniques (e.g., rumination over mistakes). The second pathway, stress enhancement, refers to the tendency for those high in perfectionism to adopt self-defeating cognitive appraisals (e.g., threat, harm, loss) resulting in the magnification of stress (e.g., over-emphasising the importance of minor mistakes). These pathways may help explain why perfectionism, and particularly high levels of socially prescribed and other-oriented perfectionism, predict ill health. However, in contrast to socially prescribed and other-oriented perfectionism, self-oriented perfectionism may buffer stress (e.g., via problem-focused coping). Despite some research supporting these pathways in athletic populations (e.g., Hill et al., 2018), no study has investigated whether perfectionism moderates the association between lifetime stressor exposure and health in elite athletes.

To address this, we examined (a) how lifetime stressor exposure was associated with general physical and mental health complaints among elite athletes, and (b) the extent to which these associations were moderated by perfectionism (socially prescribed, self-oriented, or other-oriented). Based on the research described above, we first hypothesised that greater lifetime stressor exposure (count and severity) would be related to poorer mental and physical health among elite athletes. Second, we hypothesised that perfectionism would moderate the relationship between elite athletes' lifetime stressor exposure and health, such that higher self-oriented perfectionism would attenuate, and greater socially prescribed and other-oriented perfectionism would strengthen these stress-health associations.

Method

Participants

Participants were 110 elite athletes (64 females, 45 males, 1 preferred to self-describe) aged between 18 and 59 years old (M_{age} = 29.98 years, SD_{age} = 10.54), from a variety of sports (e.g., swimming, rugby). All participants were classified as elite because they had competed, or were currently competing, at an international or professional level (Swann et al., 2015). An *a priori* power calculation using G*Power software revealed that a minimum sample of 64 participants was required given a medium effect of 0.30, an alpha of 0.05, and power of 0.80. The effect size was based on prior research linking lifetime stressor exposure to symptoms of depression (McLoughlin et al., 2021).

Study Design and Procedure

This study used a cross-sectional design. Following institutional ethical approval, participants were recruited through the researchers' existing contacts and social media. Prior to taking part, participants read an information sheet that described the study's aim and informed them of their ethical rights. After participants had provided consent, data was collected through an online survey which took approximately 45 minutes to complete.

Measures

Cumulative Lifetime Stressor Exposure

Lifetime stressor exposure was assessed using the Adult STRAIN (Slavich & Shields, 2018). The STRAIN is an online interview assessing 55 major life stressors (e.g., job loss). For every stressor that is endorsed, follow-up questions are asked assessing severity (1 = *not at all* to 5 = *extremely*), frequency (*1* to *5 or more* times), timing (1 = *ongoing* to 7 = *over 5 years*), and duration (years and/or months; Slavich & Shields, 2018). The STRAIN assesses stressors across two types (acute life events vs. chronic difficulties) and time periods (early life vs. adulthood), as well as 12 life domains (housing, education, work, health, marital/partner, reproduction, financial, legal, other relationships, death, life-threatening situations, and possessions) and five social-psychological characteristics (interpersonal loss, physical danger, humiliation, entrapment, and role change/disruption). This study focused on STRAIN's two main outcomes: (1) total count of lifetime stressors experienced (range = 0–166), and (2) total severity of lifetime stressors experienced (range = 0–265). The STRAIN has very good concurrent (*r*s = 0.15–0.62) and discriminant validity, with excellent test-retest reliability (*r*s = 0.90–0.95; Cazassa et al., 2020). Furthermore, the STRAIN has demonstrated good predictive validity in relation to various health-related outcomes (Moseley et al., 2021).

Physical Health Complaints

The Physical Health Questionnaire (PHQ; Schat et al., 2005) measured physical health complaints (headaches, upset stomachs, colds) over the past month via 14 items. Eleven items (e.g., "How often have you experienced headaches?") were scored on a 7-point Likert scale ranging from 1 (*not at all*) to 7 (*all the time*), two items (e.g., "How many times have you had minor colds that made you feel uncomfortable but did not keep you sick in bed or make you miss work?") were scored on a 7-point Likert scale ranging from *0 times* to *7+ times*, and one item ("When you had a bad cold or flu, how long did it typically last?") was scored on a 7-point Likert scale ranging from *1 day* to *7+ days*. All items were summed (range = 12–98), with higher scores indicating greater physical health complaints. The PHQ has demonstrated acceptable factorial validity and excellent convergent and divergent validity (Schat et al., 2005), and in this study, it had good internal consistency ($\alpha = .85$).

Mental Health Complaints

The Kessler 6-Item Psychological Distress Inventory (K-6; Kessler et al., 2002) measured general mental health complaints over the past month via six items (e.g., "How often did you feel so depressed that nothing could cheer you up?"), with each item scored on a 5-point Likert scale ranging from 1 (*never*) to 5 (*very often*). All items were summed (range = 6–30), with higher scores indicating greater mental health complaints. The K-6 has shown excellent factorial validity and strong predictive validity in relation to mental health (e.g., depression; Kessler et al., 2002). In this study, it had excellent internal consistency ($\alpha = .92$).

Perfectionism

The Multidimensional Perfectionism 15-Item Scale (MPS-15; Hewitt & Flett, 1991b) measured perfectionism. The MPS-15 has three subscales: self-oriented perfectionism (e.g., "One of my goals is to be perfect in everything I do"), other-oriented perfectionism (e.g., "It doesn't matter to me when someone close to me does not do their absolute best"), and socially prescribed perfectionism (e.g., "Anything that I do that is less than excellent will be seen as poor work by those around me"). Each item was scored on a 7-point Likert scale ranging from 1 (*strongly disagree*) to 7 (*strongly agree*). The five items for each subscale were summed (range = 5–35), with higher scores indicating greater perfectionism. The MPS-15 has shown good reliability and validity (Hewitt & Flett, 1991b; Stoeber, 2018), and, in this study, it had good internal consistency for self-oriented perfectionism ($\alpha = .85$), and acceptable internal consistency for other-oriented ($\alpha = .71$) and socially prescribed ($\alpha = .79$) perfectionism.

Data Analysis

Data were analysed using SPSS version 27.0. Prior to any analyses, 17 outliers (z-scores ≥ 3.29) were detected and removed from the dataset. Following these outlier analyses, visual inspection confirmed all data were normally distributed. Additional checks for other assumptions of linear regression analyses were conducted, with visual inspection of bivariate scatterplots confirming all data were linearly related and homoscedastic.

To examine if total lifetime stressor count or severity predicted mental and physical health complaints, hierarchical linear multiple regression analyses were run. Specifically, physical and mental health complaints were entered into separate models as dependent variables, while in each model, independent variables were entered at step 1 (i.e., total lifetime stressor count or severity), and *a priori* covariates were entered at step 2 (i.e., age and gender). Next, hierarchical linear regression analyses were run to examine if different stressor types (i.e., acute life events vs. chronic difficulties), exposure times (i.e., early-life vs. adulthood), life domains (e.g., work), or social-psychological characteristics (e.g., physical danger) predicted general physical and mental health complaints, above and beyond covariates.

Moderation analyses were then conducted via the PROCESS SPSS custom dialogue (Hayes, 2017) to examine if self-oriented, other-oriented, or socially prescribed perfectionism moderated the relationship between lifetime stressor exposure (i.e., total count or severity) and physical and mental health complaints. Lifetime stressors count or severity [X] were entered as independent variables, physical and mental health complaints [Y] as dependent variables, and the perfectionism dimensions [W] were entered as moderating variables. A moderation model was deemed statistically significant if the 95% confidence intervals did not cross zero.

Results

Descriptive Statistics

All descriptive statistics including the means and standard deviations for, and correlations between, the main study variables are shown in Table 8.1.

Lifetime Stressor Count and Health

Cumulative lifetime stressor count was associated with physical ($\beta = .34, p < .001$) and mental ($\beta = .49, p < .001$) health complaints, above and beyond age and gender (Table 8.2). Moreover, total count of acute life events was associated with physical ($\beta = .23, p = .024$) and mental ($\beta = .24, p = .018$) health complaints, above and beyond age and gender. Similarly, total count of chronic difficulties was associated with physical ($\beta = .24, p = .020$) and mental ($\beta = .36, p < .001$) health complaints, above and beyond age and gender. Furthermore, total count of early-life adversity was associated with mental health complaints ($\beta = .24, p = .019$), above and beyond age and gender, but not physical health complaints ($\beta = -18, p = .084$). In contrast, total count of adulthood stressors was associated with physical ($\beta = .24, p = .023$) and mental ($\beta = .30, p = .003$) health complaints, above and beyond age and gender.

In terms of count, the lifetime stressor characteristics that were associated with physical health complaints, while controlling for age and gender,

TABLE 8.1 Means, standard deviations, and intercorrelations for the main study variables

Variable	Mean	SD	*1*	*2*	*3*	*4*	*5*
1 Mental Health Complaints	14.12	5.97	–				
2 Physical Health Complaints	33.13	11.78	.61***	–			
3 Self-Oriented Perfectionism	28.69	4.47	−.10	−.07	–		
4 Other-Oriented Perfectionism	15.56	4.62	.10	.07	−.04	–	
5 Socially Prescribed Perfectionism	17.03	6.54	.06	.10	.32***	−.07	–
6 Total Count of Lifetime Stressors	17.68	11.01	.40***	.33***	−.01	−.15	.05
7 Total Severity of Lifetime Stressors	40.02	25.95	.47***	.36***	−.12	−.03	−.03
8 Count of Acute Life Events	10.40	7.17	.28**	.26**	.04	−.16	.06
9 Count of Chronic Difficulties	7.28	5.07	.48***	.36***	−.09	−.11	.02
10 Count of Early Stressors	4.70	4.45	.40***	.24*	−.12	−.01	−.01
11 Count of Adulthood Stressors	12.28	8.62	.28**	.28**	.03	.18	.06
12 Severity of Acute Life Events	19.35	12.08	.35***	.32***	−.09	−.06	−.02
13 Severity of Chronic Difficulties	20.80	16.03	.51***	.35***	−.12	−.01	−.03
14 Severity of Early Stressors	12.54	11.72	.44***	.28**	−.16	−.00	−.02
15 Severity of Adulthood Stressors	27.62	19.81	.36***	.31***	−.07	−.04	−.02

TABLE 8.2 Hierarchical regression models examining if lifetime stressor (LTS) count and severity were significantly associated with physical (a) and mental (b) health complaints, both before (model 1) and after adjusting for age and gender (model 2)

(a) ***Physical Health Complaints***

	Model 1			*Model 2*				*Model 1*			*Model 2*		
	B	*SE B*	β	*B*	*SE B*	β		*B*	*SE B*	β	*B*	*SE B*	β
LTS Count	0.36 (0.16, 0.56)	0.10	0.33**	0.37 (0.17, 0.57)	0.10	0.34***	LTS Severity	0.17 (0.09, 0.26)	0.04	.037***	0.18 (0.09, 0.26)	0.04	0.38***
Age				−0.18 (−0.41, 0.04)	0.11	−0.15	Age				−0.23 (−0.45, −0.03)	0.11	−0.18*
Gender				−5.11 (−9.35, −0.88)	2.13	−0.22*	Gender				−4.14 (−8.36, 0.81)	2.13	−0.18

(b) ***Mental Health Complaints***

	Model 1			*Model 2*				*Model 1*			*Model 2*		
	B	*SE B*	β	*B*	*SE B*	β		*B*	*SE B*	β	*B*	*SE B*	β
LTS Count	0.25 (0.16, 0.35)	0.05	0.47***	0.27 (0.18, 0.36)	0.05	0.49***	LTS Severity	0.12 (0.08, 0.16)	0.02	.051***	0.13 (0.09, 0.17)	0.02	0.56***
Age				−0.19 (−0.29, −0.09)	0.05	−0.31***	Age				−0.22 (−0.31, −0.12)	0.05	-.0.36***
Gender				−1.50 (−3.40 to 0.40)	0.96	−0.13	Gender				−0.78 (−2.61 to 1.05)	0.92	−0.67

* $p < .05$; ** $p < .01$, *** $p < .001$, two-tailed.

included health ($\beta = .26$, $p = .006$), marital/partner ($\beta = .28$, $p = .003$), life-threatening situations ($\beta = .20$, $p = .040$), physical danger ($\beta = .32$, $p = .001$), entrapment ($\beta = .22$, $p = .022$), and role change ($\beta = .23$, $p = .019$). Housing, work, financial, other relationships, death, possessions, interpersonal loss, and humiliation were not significantly associated with physical health complaints (Figure 8.1a). The characteristics that were associated with mental health complaints, while controlling for age and gender, included health ($\beta = .28$, $p = .004$), marital/partner ($\beta = .19$, $p = .043$), financial ($\beta = .19$, $p = .043$), other relationships ($\beta = .20$, $p = .037$), interpersonal loss ($\beta = .32$, $p = .001$), physical danger ($\beta = .21$, $p = .033$), humiliation ($\beta = .25$, $p = .008$), and entrapment ($\beta = .36$, $p < .001$). Housing, work, death, life-threatening situations, possessions, and role change were not significantly associated with mental health complaints (Figure 8.1b).

Lifetime Stressor Severity and Health

Cumulative lifetime stressor severity was associated with physical ($\beta = .38$, $p < .001$) and mental ($\beta = .57$, $p < .001$) health complaints, above and beyond age and gender (Table 8.2). Moreover, total severity of acute life events was associated with physical ($\beta = .35$, $p = .001$) and mental ($\beta = .42$, $p < .001$) health complaints, above and beyond age and gender. Similarly, total severity of chronic difficulties was associated with physical ($\beta = .26$, $p = .013$) and mental ($\beta = .40$, $p < .001$) health complaints, above and beyond age and gender. Furthermore, total severity of early-life adversity was associated with physical ($\beta = .21$, $p = .040$) and mental ($\beta = .27$, $p = .008$) health complaints, above and beyond age and gender. Comparably, total severity of adulthood stressors was associated with physical ($\beta = .30$, $p = .005$) and mental ($\beta = .42$, $p < .001$) health complaints, above and beyond age and gender.

In terms of severity, the lifetime stressor characteristics that were associated with physical health complaints, while controlling for age and gender, included health ($\beta = .38$, $p < .001$), marital/partner ($\beta = .29$, $p = .002$), other relationships ($\beta = .24$, $p = .015$), life-threatening situations ($\beta = .25$, $p = .011$), interpersonal loss ($\beta = .28$, $p = .005$), physical danger ($\beta = .40$, $p < .001$), humiliation ($\beta = .27$, $p = .005$), entrapment ($\beta = .24$, $p = .010$), and role change ($\beta = .31$, $p = .001$). Housing, work, financial, death, and possessions were not significantly associated with physical health complaints (Figure 8.1a). The characteristics that were associated with mental health complaints, while controlling for age and gender, included housing ($\beta = .20$, $p = .037$), health ($\beta = .45$, $p < .001$), marital/partner ($\beta = .27$, $p = .004$), financial ($\beta = .25$, $p = .008$), other relationships ($\beta = .21$, $p = .036$), death ($\beta = .25$, $p = .013$), life-threatening situations ($\beta = .29$, $p = .003$), interpersonal loss ($\beta = .42$, $p < .001$), physical danger ($\beta = .41$, $p < .001$), humiliation ($\beta = .30$, $p = .002$), entrapment ($\beta = .39$, $p <.001$), and role change ($\beta = .33$, $p = .001$).

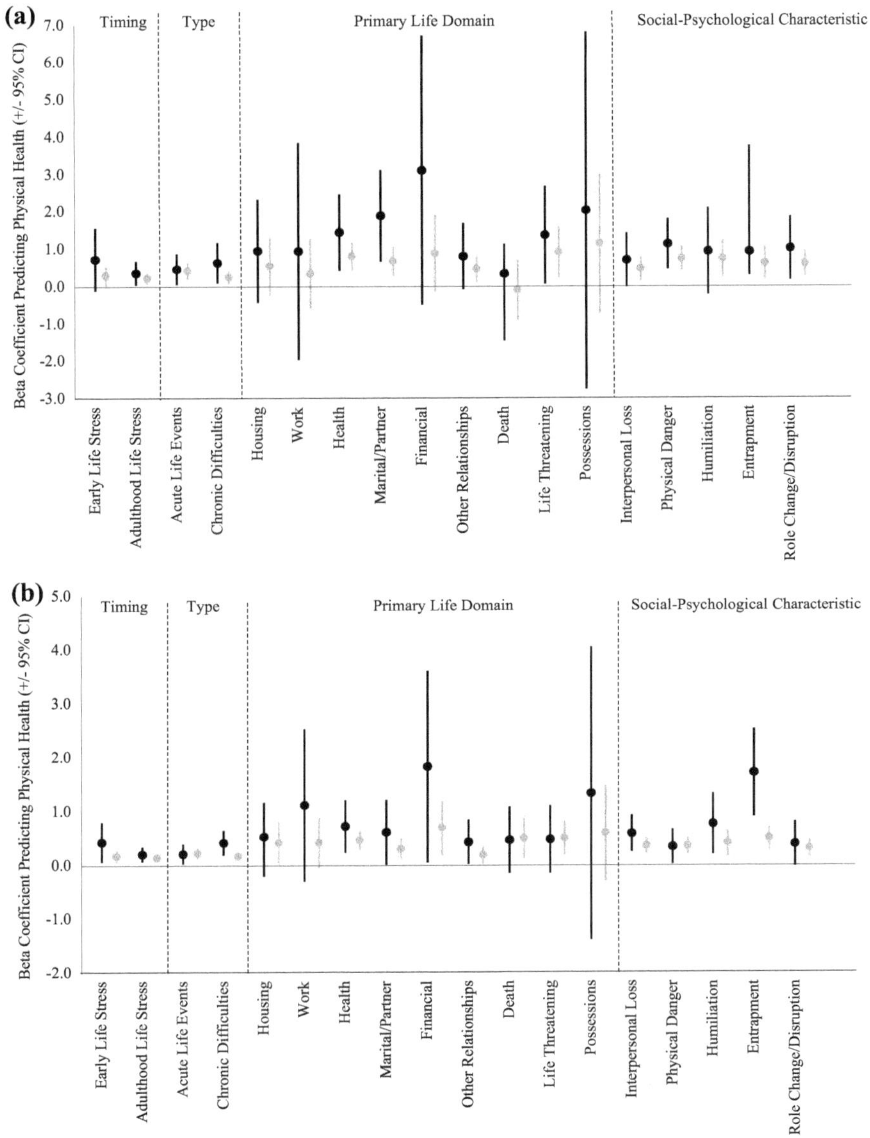

FIGURE 8.1 Associations between total count and severity of lifetime stress exposure and (a) physical health complaints and (b) mental health complaints, categorised by stressor timing, type, primary life domain, and social-psychological characteristic. Error bars represent 95% confidence intervals.

Work and possessions were not significantly associated with mental health complaints (Figure 8.1b).

Moderation Analyses

No significant moderation effects were found with mental health complaints as the dependent variable, or when socially prescribed or other-oriented perfectionism were entered as moderators (Table 8.3). However, self-oriented perfectionism moderated the lifetime stressor exposure and physical health complaints relationship (Table 8.3). To illustrate these significant interaction effects, the associations between lifetime stressor exposure, self-oriented perfectionism, and physical health complaints are depicted in Figures 8.2a and 8.2b.

Self-oriented perfectionism moderated the relationship between lifetime stressor count and physical health complaints ($F_{(3,\ 89)} = 6.16$, $p < .001$, $R^2 = 0.17$). Specifically, when self-oriented perfectionism was low, a positive association was observed between lifetime stressor count and physical health complaints ($b = 0.76$, 95% CI [0.40, 1.12], $t = 4.21$, $p < .001$). Yet, at the mean value of self-oriented perfectionism ($b = 0.18$, 95% CI [−0.09, 0.45], $t = 1.35$, $p = .180$), and when self-oriented perfectionism was high ($b = -0.20$, 95% CI [−0.60, 0.20], $t = -0.98$, $p = .329$), the lifetime stressor count and physical health relationship was not significant. The Johnson-Neyman method illustrated that lifetime stressor count was associated with physical health complaints when self-oriented perfectionism was ≤ 29.21. When self-oriented perfectionism exceeded 29.21, the association was no longer significant.

Self-oriented perfectionism also moderated the relationship between lifetime stressor severity and physical health complaints ($F_{(3,\ 89)} = 5.97$, $p < .001$, $R^2 = 0.17$). Specifically, when self-oriented perfectionism was low ($b = 0.30$, 95% CI [0.16, 0.44], $t = 4.17$, $p < .001$), and at the mean value of self-oriented perfectionism ($b = 0.12$, 95% CI [0.01, 0.24], $t = 2.14$, $p < .035$), a positive association was found between lifetime stressor severity and physical health complaints. However, when self-oriented perfectionism was high, the lifetime stressor severity and physical health association was not significant ($b = 0.01$, 95% CI [−0.16, 0.18], $t = 0.09$, $p = 0.931$). The Johnson-Neyman method illustrated that lifetime stressor severity was associated with physical health complaints when self-oriented perfectionism was ≤ 30.23. When self-oriented perfectionism exceeded 30.23, the association was no longer significant.

Discussion

Although greater lifetime stressor exposure has been associated with physical and mental health issues in the general population (Shields et al., 2022),

TABLE 8.3 Linear models of predictors of (a) physical and (b) mental health complaints. Lifetime stressor (LTS) count (model 1) and severity (model 2), moderated by self-oriented perfectionism (SOP)

(a)	***Physical Health Complaints***						
	Model 1				*Model 2*		
	B	*SE B*	t		*B*	*SE B*	t
Constant	−19.50 (−48.21, 9.21)	14.45	−1.35	Constant	−8.98 (36.59, 18.62)	13.90	−0.65
LTS Count	3.06 (1.44, 4.68)	0.82	3.75***	LTS Severity	1.00 (0.34, 1.66)	0.33	3.03**
SOP	1.64 (0.65, 2.62)	0.49	3.30**	SOP	1.24 (0.28, 2.19)	0.48	2.58*
LTS Count X SOP	−0.10 (−0.15, −0.04)	0.03	−3.39**	LTS Severity X SOP	−0.03 (−0.05, −0.01)	0.01	−2.53*

(b)	***Mental Health Complaints***						
	Model 1				*Model 2*		
	B	*SE B*	t		*B*	*SE B*	t
Constant	−1.65 (−14.91, 11.61)	6.67	−0.25	Constant	5.39 (−6.99, 17.78)	6.23	0.87
LTS Count	0.76 (0.01, 1.51)	0.38	2.02*	LTS Severity	0.12 (−0.18, 0.41)	0.15	0.80
SOP	0.44 (−0.02, 0.89)	0.23	1.91	SOP	0.17 (−0.26, 0.59)	0.22	0.77
LTS Count X SOP	−0.02 (−0.05, 0.01)	0.01	−1.56	LTS Severity X SOP	−0.001 (−0.01, 0.01)	0.01	−0.16

Note. $R^2 = 0.17$, * $p < .05$; ** $p < .01$, *** $p < .001$, two-tailed.

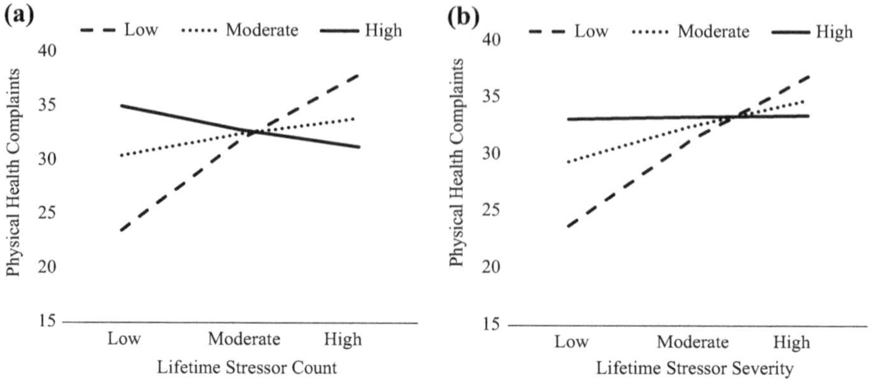

FIGURE 8.2 A simple slopes equation of the regression of lifetime stressor (a) count and (b) severity on physical health complaints at three levels of self-oriented perfectionism low (1 SD below the mean), moderate (mean), and high (1 SD above the mean).

relatively little is known about how lifetime stressors impact the physical and mental health of elite athletes, or the factors moderating this association. To address these issues, we examined how cumulative lifetime stressor exposure was associated with general physical and mental health complaints among elite athletes, and the extent to which this association was moderated by perfectionism. We found that greater lifetime stressor exposure was associated with more general physical and mental health complaints, with exposure to more severe lifetime stressors increasing the likelihood of general physical and mental health complaints. These associations were robust while controlling for age and gender, which are known predictors of poorer health (e.g., Droogenbroeck et al., 2018). Furthermore, self-oriented perfectionism was found to moderate the relationship between lifetime stressor exposure (count and severity) and physical health.

With respect to stressor timing, the results revealed that total count and severity of adulthood stressors were marginally stronger predictors of elite athletes' health than early life stressors. This finding is consistent with prior research (e.g., McLoughlin et al., 2022a), which has suggested that exposure to greater and more severe recent life stressors is more predictive of ill health. Interestingly, the data also revealed that whereas total count of early-life adversity only predicted mental health complaints, total severity of early-life adversity predicted both mental and physical health complaints. Therefore, these results suggest that, for the first time, it is the severity of early life adversities that predicts physical health complaints in elite athletes, rather than the total lifetime stressor count.

Turning to stressor type, total count of chronic difficulties was more strongly related to health compared to acute life events. This finding is consistent with prior research (e.g., Slavich et al., 2019), which has often found that chronic difficulties are particularly detrimental to health. Despite this, however, we also found that total severity of acute life events was a relatively stronger predictor of physical and mental health complaints than the total severity of chronic difficulties. The use of qualitative research may be able to provide a more in-depth exploration of these contrasting findings, which are particularly important given that ill-health can interfere with social and occupational functioning (Wahlbeck, 2015). Taken together, these findings imply that stressors may have varying effects on health depending on their timing (e.g., adulthood vs. early life) and type (e.g., acute life events vs. chronic difficulties).

Stressors from diverse life domains and with unique social-psychological characteristics were found to be differentially associated with physical and mental health complaints. Most notably, the lifetime stressor count and severity indices most consistently and significantly associated with health were physical danger (e.g., being robbed at gunpoint), health (e.g., ongoing health problems), and interpersonal loss (e.g., close friend moves away). These results partially support prior research with elite athletes (e.g., McLoughlin et al., 2021), which found that interpersonal loss and physical danger were relatively consistent predictors of poorer mental health. These findings also advance prior research (e.g., McLoughlin et al., 2021), demonstrating that health-related stressors can be harmful for health outcomes.

This study examined whether perfectionism moderated the association between lifetime stressor exposure and health among elite athletes. As hypothesised, self-oriented perfectionism moderated the relationship between lifetime stressor exposure (both count and severity) and physical health complaints. Thus, these results suggest that self-oriented perfectionism may attenuate the positive association between lifetime stressor exposure and physical health complaints. This finding supports prior research suggesting that this dimension of perfectionism is highly complex and can sometimes be associated with adaptive functioning (e.g., Hill et al., 2018). In contrast, no moderation effects were found for self-oriented perfectionism and mental health complaints. One potential explanation for this finding could be that to portray themselves as "perfect," the athletes may have masked symptoms of mental ill-health to hide "negative" aspects of themselves (Hewitt et al., 2003). Indeed, the desire to appear perfect has been associated with greater stigma and negative attitudes towards help seeking for mental health difficulties (e.g., Watson et al., 2021). Furthermore, there were no moderation effects for other-oriented or socially prescribed perfectionism and health complaints. One potential explanation for this null finding could be that the sample did not have high enough levels of other-oriented (M = 15.56, Range = 7–30) or socially prescribed (M = 17.03, Range = 6–33) perfectionism for any moderating effects to emerge.

From an applied perspective, the findings might be useful in helping practitioners and sporting organisations better identify elite athletes who may be at elevated risk of physical and mental health problems (Rice et al., 2021). Indeed, by assessing elite athletes' lifetime stressor exposure using the STRAIN, practitioners could identify athletes who have been exposed to a large amount and severe personal stressors across their lives, and particularly stressors that are chronic or have occurred recently. Furthermore, although self-oriented perfectionism moderated the relationship between lifetime stressor exposure and physical health complaints, caution is required from a practical standpoint given that this dimension of perfectionism has also been linked to burnout, psychological difficulties, and performance decrements (Hill & Curran, 2015). However, given that many elite-level athletes exhibit perfectionism (e.g., Gould et al., 2002), and attribute this to their success (Madigan, 2019), practitioners should be aware of the complex role of some types of perfectionism (e.g., self-oriented) and consider tailored support for those displaying high levels of perfectionism (James & Rimes, 2018).

Despite the important implications arising from this study, it is not without its limitations. First, the study design was cross-sectional, and thus causality cannot be inferred. To facilitate a better understanding of how lifetime stress, perfectionism, and health affect athletes across time, future longitudinal research is recommended (Morgado et al., 2018). Second, the study used self-report measures, which could have been influenced by bias (e.g., social desirability). Future research could assess objective (e.g., salivary biomarkers) indices of psychological stress. Third, this study only assessed general physical and mental health complaints (e.g., headaches, sadness). Therefore, future research could use alternative measures that may more accurately and reliably screen for mental disorders among athletes (e.g., Sport Mental Health Assessment Tool 1; Gouttebarge et al., 2022), and should account for confounding factors that may interact with perfectionism towards sporting performance (e.g., physical fitness, injury; Madigan et al., 2017). Finally, this study only measured non-sport stressors and did not assess stressors experienced specifically in the sporting context (e.g., underperformance). Indeed, while the STRAIN is a valid and reliable measure of lifetime stressor exposure, athletes encounter additional stressors to those experienced in everyday life (e.g., organisational and competitive stressors such as coach-athlete relationship difficulties and underperformance; Arnold & Fletcher, 2021). Therefore, future research should assess sport-related stressors as well as personal stressors to improve our understanding of how lifetime stressor exposure, perfectionism, and health interact (see McLoughlin et al., 2022a).

In conclusion, the present data demonstrate that exposure to greater and more severe lifetime stressors was associated with poorer health among elite athletes, but that these effects differed depending on the specific types of stressors experienced and when they occurred. Moreover, self-oriented perfectionism attenuated the relationship between lifetime stressor exposure and physical health complaints, suggesting that modifying such beliefs may represent a potentially useful strategy for mitigating the negative effects of lifetime stress on health. Looking forward, practitioners may benefit from being more aware of the stressors that elite athletes experience and how their perfectionistic tendencies may be affecting their health.

References

Arnold, R., & Fletcher, D. (2021). Stressors, hassles, and adversities. In R. Arnold & D. Fletcher (Eds.), *Stress, well-being, and performance in sport* (pp. 31–62). Routledge.

Burani, K., Brush, C. J., Shields, G. S., Klein, D. N., Nelson, B., Slavich, G. M., & Hajcak, G. (2022). Cumulative lifetime acute stressor exposure interacts with reward responsiveness to predict longitudinal increases in depression severity in adolescence. *Psychological Medicine*, *53*(10), 4507–4516. doi: 10.1017/s0033291722 001386

Cazassa, M. J., Oliveira, M. D. S., Spahr, C. M., Shields, G. S., & Slavich, G. M. (2020). The Stress and Adversity Inventory for Adults (Adult STRAIN) in Brazilian Portuguese: Initial validation and links with executive function, sleep, and mental and physical health. *Frontiers in Psychology*, 10, 30383. 10.3389/fpsyg. 2019.03083

Curran, T., & Hill, A. (2019). Perfectionism is increasing over time: A meta-analysis of birth cohort differences from 1989 to 2016. *Psychological Bulletin, 145*(4), 410–429. 10.1037/bul0000138

Droogenbroeck, F. V., Spruyt, B., & Keppens, G. (2018). Gender differences in mental health problems among adolescents and the role of social support: Results from the Belgian health interview surveys 2008 and 2013. *BMC Psychiatry*, *18*(6). 10.1186/s12888-018-1591-4

Epel, E. S., Croswell, A. D., Mayer, S. E., Prather, A. A., Slavich, G. M., Puterman, E., & Mendes, W. B. (2018). More than a feeling: A unified view of stress measurement for population science. *Frontiers in Neuroendocrinology*, *49*, 149–169. 10.1016/j.yfrne.2018.03.001

Flett, G. L., Hewitt, P. L., Nepon, T., Sherry, S. B., & Smith, M. (2022). The destructiveness and public health significance of socially prescribed perfectionism: A review, analysis, and conceptual extension. *Clinical Psychology Review, 93*, 102130. 10.1016/j.cpr.2022.102130

Flett, G. L., & Hewitt, P. L. (2002). Perfectionism and maladjustment: An overview of theoretical, definitional, and treatment issues. In G. L. Flett & P. L. Hewitt (Eds.), *Perfectionism: Theory, research, and treatment* (pp. 5–31). American Psychological Association. 10.1037/10458-001

Flett, G. L., Hewitt, P. L., & Molnar, D. S. (2016). Perfectionism in health and illness from a person-focused, historical perspective. In F. M. Sirois & D. M. Molnar (Eds.), *Perfectionism, health, and well-being* (pp. 25–44). Springer.

Frost, R. O., Marten, P., Lahart, C., & Rosenblate, R. (1990). The dimensions of perfectionism. *Cognitive Therapy and Research, 14*(5), 449–468.

Gould, D., Dieffenbach, K., & Moffett, A. (2002). Psychological characteristics and their development in Olympic champions. *Journal of Applied Sport Psychology,* 14(3), 172–204. 10.1080/10413200290103482

Gouttebarge, V., Bindra, A., Drezner, J. A., Mkumbuzi, N., Patricios, J., Rao, A., Thornton, J. S., Watson, A., & Reardon, C. L. (2022). Minds matter: How COVID-19 highlighted a growing need to protect and promote athlete mental health. *British Journal of Sports Medicine*, *56*(17), 953–955. 10.1136/bjsports-2022-106017.

Hardy, L., Barlow, M., Evans, L., Rees, T., Woodman, T., & Warr, C. (2017). Great British medallists. *Progress in Brain Research,* 1–119. 10.1016/bs.pbr.2017.03.004

Hayes, A. F. (2017). *Introduction to mediation, moderation, and conditional process analysis: A regression-based approach.* Guilford Publications.

Hewitt, P. L., & Dyck, D. G. (1986). Perfectionism, stress, and vulnerability to depression. *Cognitive Therapy and Research, 10*(1), 137–142. 10.1007/BF01173389

Hewitt, P. L., & Flett, G. L. (1991a). Perfectionism in the self and social contexts: Conceptualization, assessment, and association with psychopathology. *Journal of Personality and Social Psychology*, 60(3), 456–470. 10.1037//0022-3514.60.3.456.

Hewitt, P. L., & Flett, G. L. (1991b). The Multidimensional Perfectionism Scale: Reliability, validity, and psychometric properties in psychiatric samples. *Psychological Assessment*, *3*(3), 464–468. 10.1037/1040-3590.3.3.464

Hewitt, P. L., Flett, G. L., Sherry, S. B., Habke, M., Parkin, M., Lam, R. W., ... & Stein, M. B. (2003). The interpersonal expression of perfection: Perfectionistic self-presentation and psychological distress. *Journal of Personality and Social Psychology*, *84*(6), 1303–1325. 10.1037/0022-3514.84.6.1303.

Hill, A. P. (2023). *The psychology of perfectionism in sport, dance, and exercise.* Taylor & Francis.

Hill, A. P., & Curran, T. (2015). Multidimensional perfectionism and burnout: A meta-analysis. *Personality and Social Psychology Review, 20*(3), 269–288. 10.1177/1088868315596286

Hill, A. P., Mallinson-Howard, S. H., & Jowett, G. E. (2018). Multidimensional perfectionism in sport: A meta-analytical review. *Sport, Exercise, and Performance Psychology, 7*(3), 235–270. 10.1037/spy0000125

James, K., & Rimes, K. A. (2018). Mindfulness-based cognitive therapy versus pure cognitive behavioural self-help for perfectionism: A pilot randomised study. *Mindfulness*, *9*, 801–814. 10.1007/s12671-017-0817-8

Kessler, R., Andrews, G., Colpe, L., Hiripi, E., Mroczek, D., Normand, S., ... & Zaslavsky, A. M. (2002). Short screening scales to monitor population prevalences and trends in non-specific psychological distress. *Psychological Medicine*, *32*(6), 959–976.

Klatzkin, R. R., Nadel, T., Wilkinson, L. L., Gaffney, K., Files, H., Gray, Z. J., & Slavich, G. M. (2023). Lifetime stressor exposure, eating expectancy, and acute social stress-related eating behavior: A pre-registered study of the emotional eating cycle. *Appetite*, *185*, 106494. 10.1016/j.appet.2023.106494

Limburg, K., Watson, H., Hagger, M., & Egan, S. (2016). The relationship between perfectionism and psychopathology: A meta-analysis. *Journal of Clinical Psychology*, *73*(10), 1301–1326. 10.1002/jclp.22435

Madigan, D. (2019). A meta-analysis of perfectionism and academic achievement. *Educational Psychology Review, 31*(4), 967–989. 10.1007/s10648-019-09484-2

Madigan, D., Stoeber, J., Forsdyke, D., Dayson, M., & Passfield, L. (2017). Perfectionism predicts injury in junior athletes: Preliminary evidence from a prospective study. *Journal of Sports Sciences, 36*(5), 545–550. 10.1080/02640414.2017.1322709

McLoughlin, E., Arnold, R., Cavallerio, F., Fletcher, D., & Moore, L. J. (2023a). A creative nonfiction story of male elite athletes' experiences of lifetime stressor exposure, performance, and help-seeking behaviors. *Sport, Exercise, and Performance Psychology, 12*(3), 189–204. 10.1037/spy0000319

McLoughlin, E., Arnold, R., Fletcher, D., Spahr, C. M., Slavich, G. M., & Moore, L. M. (2022a). Assessing lifetime stressor exposure in sport performers: Associations with trait stress appraisals, health, well-being, and performance. *Psychology of Sport and Exercise, 58.* 10.1016/j.psychsport.2021.102078

McLoughlin, E., Arnold, R., Freeman, P., Turner, J. E., Roberts, G. A., Fletcher, D., Slavich, G. M., & Moore, L. J. (2022b). Lifetime stressor exposure and psychophysiological reactivity and habituation to repeated acute social stressors. *Journal of Sport and Exercise Psychology, 44*(6), 427–438. 10.1123/jsep.2022-0196

McLoughlin, E., Arnold, R., Moore, L. J., Slavich, G. M., & Fletcher, D. (2023b). A qualitative exploration of how lifetime stressor exposure influences sport performers' health, well-being, and performance. *Anxiety, Stress, & Coping*, 1–18. 10.1080/10615806.2023.2246023

McLoughlin, E., Fletcher, D., Slavich, G. M., Arnold, R., & Moore, L. J. (2021). Cumulative lifetime stress exposure, depression, anxiety, and well-being in elite athletes: A mixed-method study. *Psychology of Sport and Exercise, 52.* 10.1016/j.psychsport.2020.101823

Molnar, D., Sadava, S., Flett, G., & Colautti, J. (2012). Perfectionism and health: A mediational analysis of the roles of stress, social support and health-related behaviours. *Psychology and Health, 27*(7), 846–864. 10.1080/08870446.2011.630466

Moseley, R. L., Turner-Cobb, J. M., Spahr, C. M., Shields, G. S., & Slavich, G. M. (2021). Lifetime and perceived stress, social support, loneliness, and health in autistic adults. *Health Psychology, 40*, 556–568. 10.1037/hea0001108

Morgado, F. F. R., Meireles, J. F. F., Neves, C. M., Amaral, A. C. S., & Ferreria, M. E. C. (2018). Scale development: Ten main limitations and recommendations to improve future research practices. *Psicologia: Reflexão e Crítica, 30*, 3. 10.1186/s41155-016-0057-1

Parra, L. A., Spahr, C. M., Goldbach, J. T., Bray, B. C., Kipke, M. D., & Slavich, G. M. (2023). Greater lifetime stressor exposure is associated with poorer mental health among sexual minority people of color. *Journal of Clinical Psychology, 79*(4), 1130–1155. 10.1002/jclp.23463

Rice, S., Walton, C. C., Gwyther, K., & Purcell, R. (2021). Mental health. In R. Arnold & D. Fletcher (Eds.), *Stress, well-being, and performance in sport* (pp. 167–187). Oxford, UK: Taylor & Francis.

Saboonchi, F., & Lundh, L. G. (2003). Perfectionism, anger, somatic health, and positive affect. *Personality and Individual Differences, 35*(7), 1585–1599. 10.1016/S0191-8869(02)00382-3

Schat, A., Kelloway, E., & Desmarais, S. (2005). The Physical Health Questionnaire (PHQ): Construct validation of a self-report scale of somatic symptoms. *Journal of Occupational Health Psychology*, *10*(4), 363–381.

Shields, G. S., Fassett-Carman, A., Gray, Z. J., Gonzales, J. E., Snyder, H. R., & Slavich, G. M. (2022). Why is subjective stress severity a stronger predictor of health than stressor exposure? A preregistered two-study test of two hypotheses. *Stress and Health*. 10.1002/smi.3165

Sirois, F. M., & Molnar, D. S. (Eds.). (2016). *Perfectionism, health, and well-being* (p. 45). Cham: Springer International Publishing.

Slavich, G. (2016). Life stress and health: A review of conceptual issues and recent findings. *Teaching of Psychology*, *43*(4), 346–355. 10.1177/0098628316662768

Slavich, G. M., & Shields, G. S. (2018). Assessing lifetime stress exposure using the Stress and Adversity Inventory for Adults (Adult STRAIN). *Psychosomatic Medicine*, *80*(1), 17–27. 10.1097/PSY.0000000000000534

Slavich, G. M., Stewart, J. G., Esposito, E. C., Shields, G. S., & Auerbach, R. P. (2019). The Stress Adversity Inventory for Adolescents (Adolescent STRAIN): Associations with mental and physical health, risky behaviour, and psychiatric diagnoses in youth seeking treatment. *Journal of Child Psychology and Psychiatry*, *60*(9), 998–1009. 10.1111/jcpp.13038.

Smith, M. M., Sherry, S. B., Ray, C., Hewitt, P. L., & Flett, G. L. (2021). Is perfectionism a vulnerability factor for depressive symptoms, a complication of depressive symptoms, or both? A meta-analytic test of 67 longitudinal studies. *Clinical Psychology Review, 84*, 101982. 10.1016/j.cpr.2021.101982

Stoeber, J. (2018). Comparing two short forms of the Hewitt-Flett Multidimensional Perfectionism Scale. *Assessment*, *25*(5), 578–588. 10.1177/1073191116659740

Swann, C., Moran, A., & Piggott, D. (2015). Defining elite athletes: Issues in the study of expert performance in sport psychology. *Psychology of Sport and Exercise*, *16*, 3–14. 10.1016/j.psychsport.2014.07.004

Wahlbeck, K. (2015). Public mental health: The time is ripe for translation of evidence into practice. *World Psychiatry*, *14*, 36–42. 10.1002/wps.20178

Watson, D. R., Hill, A. P., & Madigan, D. J. (2021). Perfectionism and attitudes toward sport psychology support and mental health support in athletes. *Journal of Clinical Sport Psychology*,*17*(1), 11–26.

9

BODY SHAMING AS A FORM OF EMOTIONAL ABUSE IN SPORT

Erin Willson and Gretchen Kerr

Introduction

Research on experiences of athlete maltreatment has increased substantially in response to high-profile cases across numerous countries and sports. Emotional abuse, which has been defined as "a pattern of deliberate non-contact behaviours by a person within a critical relationship role that have the potential to be harmful" (Stirling & Kerr, 2008, p. 178), is consistently reported as the most frequently experienced form of maltreatment (Hartill et al., 2021; Ohlert et al., 2021; Willson et al., 2022). Emotional abuse in sport comprises three types of behaviours: (i) negative verbal comments that are degrading, humiliating, demeaning, and threatening (Stirling & Kerr, 2008); (ii) physical behaviours such as throwing objects out of anger or frustration (without striking another individual); and (iii) the denial of attention and support; for example, when a coach deliberately withdraws attention or feedback in response to an athlete's poor performance (Stirling & Kerr, 2008). In addition to emotional abuse being the most frequently reported form of athlete maltreatment, research indicates that it is also normalised as an expected and even necessary method of producing top athletic performance (Stafford et al., 2015; Stirling & Kerr, 2013).

Research on the effects of emotional abuse on young people and athletes includes reports of decreased self-esteem, depression, psychiatric treatment, eating disorders and suicide (Humphreys et al., 2020; Norman et al., 2012; Parent et al., 2022; Willson et al., 2023). The normalisation of emotionally abusive practices in sport and a subsequent failure to label these practices as harmful may contribute to the lack of research attention to its effects; however, preliminary research on sport-specific outcomes including decreased

DOI: 10.4324/9781003459750-9

motivation and enjoyment (Stirling & Kerr, 2013; Yabe et al., 2019). A recent qualitative study exploring the long-term effects of emotionally abusive coaching practices found that elite female athletes report feelings of anxiety, depression, and symptoms akin to post-traumatic stress disorder (Kerr et al., 2020). Moreover, all eight of the participating athletes in this study required professional mental health support post-retirement (Kerr et al., 2020). In these athletes' disclosures of their experiences and effects of emotionally abusive coaching practices, frequent references to negative perceptions of their bodies and harmful strategies of managing their weight were made. As such, we engaged in a pluralistic data analysis process to explore the experiences and impact of emotionally abusive coaching practices focusing specifically on the athletes' comments pertaining to the body.

Substantial research exists on body image, disordered eating and eating disorders in athletes (Bratland-Sanda & Sundgot-Borgen, 2013; Huellemann et al., 2023; Reel et al., 2013; Vani et al., 2020), highlighting that aesthetic sports, which focus on appearance and leanness, present an additional risk factor for the development of eating disorders (Bratland-Sanda & Sundgot-Borgen, 2013; Krentz & Warschburger, 2011). Aesthetic sports typically include a combination of athletic ability and artistic flair, and performances are subjectively evaluated by judges (Robertson & Mountjoy, 2018). While physical appearance is not an explicit criterion for performance evaluation, there is an expectation for a specific physical appearance that coincides with the artistic component of the evaluation (Robertson & Mountjoy, 2018). Barker-Ruchti (2009) claimed that the "ideal body" in aesthetic sports is influenced by cultural beauty standards and believed requirements for performance success. For example, those in the aesthetic sport of artistic swimming value the look of long, straight lines in the performance of technical skills, a look that is associated with being tall, lean, and a pre-pubescent figure. Despite the expansive research on disordered eating and eating disorders in aesthetic sports athletes, these have not been explored in relation to emotional abuse. As such, in this study, we sought to further explore the relationship between experiences of emotionally abusive coaching practices and body-related challenges.

Methodology

Methodological Perspective

We adopted a constructivist approach for this study, which is grounded in the assumption that reality is constructed based on an individual's interpretations (Green & Thorogood, 2009). This paradigm follows a relativist ontology, meaning that realities are subjective and based on an individual's own experience, and subjective epistemology, in which knowledge is created between the participants and the researcher (Guba & Lincoln, 1994).

Participants

Eight retired female athletes participated in this study; all had been members of a Canadian National Team, including five athletes who competed at the Olympic Games. Female participants were purposively recruited from the aesthetic sports of artistic gymnastics, rhythmic gymnastics, and artistic swimming as previous researchers have shown that female athletes from aesthetic sports experience emotional abuse (Kerr et al., 2020), female athletes experience more emotional abuse than male athletes (Willson et al., 2021) and female athletes disproportionately experience eating disorders (Bratland-Sanda & Sundgot-Borgen, 2013). Retired athletes were selected because of existing evidence indicating that athletes normalise harmful behaviours while in their sports careers and become more reflexive and critical about their experiences once removed from the environment (Kerr & Dacyshyn, 2000). Athletes in the current study were between 24 and 29 years of age and had been retired for two to six years (mean of 4.5 years) at the time of their interviews.

Methods

The first author conducted a single semi-structured interview with each athlete. The researcher asked athletes to "describe their experiences as an elite athlete" and "can you tell me some positive and negative aspects of your sports experience?" The questions then focused on potential experiences of emotionally abusive coaching practices, such as "Please tell me about some of behaviours that your coach used that made you feel badly about yourself/ were hurtful." As many of the responses to this question referenced coaching comments and behaviours that addressed the athletes' bodies, the researcher probed with, "Please tell me more about what you did to meet the coaches' expectations for your appearance/weight?" The questions also addressed athletes' responses to emotionally abusive coaching practices such as, "How did these experiences make you feel?" and "Have there been longer-term impacts of those experiences?"

Procedure

Following University human ethics approval, athletes were recruited through social media platforms and snowball sampling. A recruitment message was distributed asking to participate in a study of the potential effects of harmful coaching practices on athletes who had retired from elite-level aesthetic sports. Interested participants were asked to respond directly to the first author to set a date and time for the interview. Prior to the interview, a signed letter of consent was required. The interviews took place over the phone, lasted between 40 and 80 minutes and, with consent from the participants, were audio-recorded.

The interviews were transcribed verbatim and anonymised using pseudonyms. Transcriptions and analyses occurred following each interview and were reviewed by the authors, noting emerging themes and comparing these with the interview guide to make any needed refinements. For example, the participants were unexpectedly eager to speak in detail about their experiences with disordered eating, which resulted in generating more prompts about these experiences.

Data Analysis

We used a pluralistic approach to analyse the interview data. In the previously published paper (Kerr et al., 2020), the approach to data analysis reflected a reflexive thematic analysis (Braun & Clarke, 2019) to elicit themes based on the explicit meanings in the athletes' disclosures about the general effects of emotionally abusive coaching practices. In this initial analysis, we identified that the athletes reported negative effects of emotionally abusive coaching practices on their psychological well-being, their relationships with others and with sport, with these effects differing across the time periods of pre-retirement, during the retirement transition and post-retirement. However, it became apparent through this previous data analysis process that the participants made references to the ways in which their coaches' practices influenced the athletes' perceptions of their bodies and eating behaviours. As a result, the first analysis informed the second, which involved analysing the same dataset with a latent focus on the disclosures about the body that wove through the explicit messages about the effects of emotionally abusive coaching practices. This sequential pluralistic approach enabled us to take a different perspective to the data to elicit alternative findings and insights (Clarke et al., 2016; Frost et al., 2010). We conducted a reflexive thematic analysis for this study (Braun & Clarke, 2019).

Enhancing Rigour

Rigour in this study was approached from a non-foundational approach, meaning that criteria were not static, but rather open-ended throughout the research process (Smith & McGannon, 2018). Criteria for rigour were adopted to align with our objectives, specifically: sincerity, credibility, and worthiness of the topic, resonance of the research, meaningful coherence, and ethical considerations (Tracy, 2010). The sincerity of this research is demonstrated by the reflexivity of the authors, particularly due to the co-construction of information between the researchers and participants (Guba & Lincoln, 1994). The first author was an Olympic athlete, who experienced body shaming during most of her seven years on the national team. The first author also had to be reflexive of her experience during the interview to ensure that the participants' stories and perspectives were being told by asking them to elaborate or provide examples, particularly when the respondents would say "You know what I mean?" The strong rapport built between the interviewer and the participants, given their similarities in experiences, allowed for rich data to be elicited, with thick descriptions and concrete details, both of which have been identified as important aspects of credibility (Tracy, 2010).

Other measures to ensure rigour included choosing a topic that was relevant and significant (Tracy, 2010). As body image concerns in sports continue to arise in media and in research (Ingle, 2020; Weiss & Mohr, 2018), we believe this is a worthy topic. To ensure resonance, we were conscious of highlighting quotes from participants that were detailed but also accessible to all readers and provided suggestions for practical application. This was done with the intent that these findings could be transferable to the athletic environment. In line with Tracy's (2010) suggestions, the methods and procedures fit the goals and achieved the established purpose and in doing so established a "meaningful coherence." Finally, there were several measures taken to ensure the highest ethical standards of research were upheld.

Ethical Considerations

The sensitive nature of this study required additional ethical considerations to ensure the safety of our participants. To demonstrate a caring approach to the participants, the researcher told each participant at the start of the interview that they did not have to answer any questions they were not comfortable with, and that they could pause, take a break, reschedule, or stop the interview at any time. Additionally, the researcher who conducted the interviews was highly attentive during the interview to cues of discomfort, including long pauses, a shaking voice, and any indicators of crying. Trust and rapport were built with the participants by engaging in active listening and demonstrating interest in their stories with the use of affirming body language, probes such as "if you're comfortable, please tell me more" and by inviting questions. The interviews were conducted in a sensitive manner and questions were communicated in an empathic manner. For example, if a participant raised the topic of an eating disorder, the researcher followed up with "Is this something you would like to talk about more or elaborate on? Or would you like to move on?" Following the interview, participants were sent a list of mental health resources and counselling services.

Results

Setting the Stage: "Our Bodies Are Judged"

Athletes acknowledged that pressures to look a certain way were very common in their sports, particularly due to the aesthetic nature of their disciplines.

Athletes prefaced many of their discussions about emotionally abusive experiences with statements such as "one of the big things in our sport is aesthetics, the way we look. Our bodies are judged, literally, we are in [revealing outfits]." Similarly, Carly discussed:

> So [physical appearance] is very important, especially for us doing the team event. And, it was important for us to look all the same, which is super thin and tall. Which is hard for 6 girls to look the same. So, there's a few girls on my team that were naturally thin and I was not so I was getting in trouble for not being as thin as they were. So, it just, took a toll.

Many of the athletes reportedly understood that their appearance took priority over technical aspects of their sport, as Hilary said:

> We had to be at that weight on the scale on that day, and if it wasn't, if we were too heavy, it was like all those other aspects - the physical aspects, it didn't matter if you were flexible or if you worked hard, if you weren't the weight you were supposed to be, all of that didn't matter. You were screwed because you weren't doing it on the scale.

The following section will address the major themes and sub-themes reported by the athletes including the body-related practices that athletes perceived as abusive, followed by the reported effects of these experiences.

Experiences of Body-Related Emotionally Abusive Practices

Athletes reported harmful practices experienced relative to their bodies, including negative comments about their bodies, monitoring of their bodies, being reprimanded for their appearance, seeing their teammates' bodies being criticised, and being removed or threatened to be removed from the team. Each of these sub-themes will be discussed in turn.

Negative Verbal Comments: "She Was Just Saying How Big My Legs Were"

All of the athletes recalled specific negative comments made about their bodies. For example, Hilary reflected,

> The coach put so much pressure on my weight. Like it's one of those examples where weight was so much of a big issue that nothing else mattered. And she wasn't even coaching me [in training], she was just saying how big my legs were.

Many of the negative comments about bodies were made in public and around their teammates, as Amy described:

> [my coach] put people on the spot … When it has to do with weight, to me, that's not something you do. She would call it out in a way that would make you seem like you were stupid and question why you were on the team.

Athletes' bodies continued to be scrutinised by coaches even after retirement. Carly reflected that she had lost weight once she had retired, reportedly due to being out of the stressful environment and becoming healthier; when she visited to watch her old teammates, her coach expressed: "Oh Carly, you look so much healthier and so much better … I wasn't surprised that was their first comment was about my body because that's something they cared about the most."

Body Monitoring: "I Felt Like Everyone Was Looking at Your Weight"

Athletes discussed both explicit and implicit forms of body monitoring such as regular weigh-ins and constant observations. Blair claimed: "We were often looked at in terms of making sure we were eating the proper food, or following the proper diets, so that we were always at our peak weight. Some bodies aren't made to be that thin so that was a very difficult situation."

Vanessa discussed the strict demands that were placed on her team to be at a specific weight:

> We had meetings about nutrition, they set goals of what they wanted our weight to be … I felt like they put a general standard on the team and did not consider that people are different heights, so someone who is 5'11 can't weigh as much as someone who is 5'4 but they would just look at a standard number and say this is the weight you need to be.

Additionally, many athletes reported being weighed by their coaching staff. Emma recalled:

> It's kind of scary going into like the BodPod and getting weighed all the time. I never thought it was like that important until I got [on the National Team] and was under those coaches' eyes. I felt like everyone was looking at your weight no matter which weight you were. So, I thought that was really hard, just mentally.

Food and Water Restrictions: "We Weren't Allowed to Drink Water during Training"

Food consumption was monitored and regulated by coaches. Carly expressed: "[my coach] would put me on ridiculous diets, like on weekends if we had Sundays off, I would only be allowed to eat watermelon for the Saturday and Sunday." Vanessa recalled a scenario where her coach had removed food from her:

> This is the moment where it kind of all hit me, it was like "oh my god, this stuff is intense." It was at a competition, we were eating dinner and I was having dessert, and I remember my coach just came up from behind me, grabbed my dessert out of my hand and pretty much threw it on the empty dirty dishes tray … later that evening we had a team meeting and she specifically called out me and one other person who didn't meet our competition goal weight. We got called out in front of the whole team and had to stay after the meeting … we got in trouble for being a bad example for the team and all this negative stuff. That's like the one memory that really sticks to me … but I know from that moment my health definitely declined for the next year and half that I was on the team.

Another athlete reported their coach would restrict their water intake: "We weren't allowed to drink water during training because it would make us heavier and that would be harder to jump during our routine," contradicting their nutritionist's advice.

Witnessing the Criticism of Teammates' Bodies

Many athletes reported that seeing other teammates chastised for their weight affected their own perceptions of their bodies as Blair described:

> It wasn't necessarily the comments directed at me personally, but it was to other people. And that would impact me because if you look at someone on your team who's very slim and slender and they are being told they are overweight, obviously then you look at yourself and go "okay, well clearly I'm not doing very well."

Alternatively, athletes also reflected on the public praise that was given to athletes who met the ideal body standards. Hilary recounted one such incident:

> One day my coach made us clap for my teammate who had hit her goal weight, but I just remember looking at [my teammate] and thinking about how skinny she was, her ribs were literally sticking out of her skin. It was

> hard to praise someone who looked so sick, and I know she wasn't eating properly, but that's what [my coach] wanted us to look like.

Punishment for Non-compliance

Athletes described consequences faced if they did not meet their coaches' weight and appearance standards, including, extra conditioning, threats of being removed from the team, or being removed from the team. Morgan reported that "if the teammate wasn't at that weight requirement, she would have to condition for the entire day and come back the next day to try to meet that weight requirement before she was allowed to work on the skills."

Many athletes faced threats of being removed from the team because of their physical appearance. Hilary recounted "[my coaches] were threatening me to not participate in the Olympics because I was too heavy, and I'm not but … ." Amy shared a distressing experience when one of her teammates was removed from her place on the team because of her weight:

> [my teammate] just showed up one day and all of a sudden wasn't on the team and when she was asked why, she was told, in front of the whole team, that it was because she was too fat and did not, you know, try hard enough or something along those lines. And I remember it crushed me. I couldn't believe it. In my eyes she was one of the best on the team and I couldn't understand why a coach would do such a thing to another athlete … it broke my heart, and I remember, god, just feeling crushed that day.

Athletes' Responses to Experiences of Body-Related Emotionally Abusive Practices

Athletes discussed their responses to experiences of body-related emotionally abusive practices, including normalisation, social comparisons, excessive food and weight control, negative health outcomes, a decline in performance, and decreased enjoyment in sports.

Normalisation: "It Was All I Really Knew"

Athletes reportedly did not initially recognise the weight and body-related comments and behaviours as abnormal. Carly explained, "At first, I thought it was normal, just because it was all I really knew." Athletes talked about accepting these behaviours and integrating them within their own belief systems as Vanessa recounted: "You kinda get brainwashed … you don't talk about it because to you, nothing's wrong. I think that's the biggest part, you never really accept what's going on."

Similarly, Blair recalled the pressures from her sport to obtain "perfection":

> You start to believe what people say to you, you start to believe that when someone looks you up and down, and tilt their head, they are basically implying that you ate too much cake this weekend and it shows, and you start to believe it. And you're not big, or you're not ugly and you're not too pale and look sick, but you start to believe it because you're told day in and day out that you should be like this, you should look like that. It's almost inherent in the sport, the sport is about achieving perfection and about being perfect, so anything below that standard you start to believe you weren't good enough.

Emma also described the process of accepting these behaviours as normal:

> Before I was on the National Team, training on my club team, the focus was improving your technical skills, getting stronger, … and not once did you ever think about body image. I don't think that thought ever came into my head until I went on the national team. I never thought about how much I weighed, if I should lose weight? I just thought about how do I look sport-wise, athletic wise? But when I was on the National Team, it definitely became something that was very normal when you compare yourself to others, and then compete body image wise and not only about what you can do in [your sport].

Social Comparisons: "A Competition of Body Image"

Athletes discussed comparing themselves to others and competing against their teammates regarding weight and weight control strategies: "You're always competing against everyone else, and it became a competition of body image rather than [skill] and what you can do in [your sport]" [Vanessa]. Similarly, Emma used her weight to secure her spot on the team:

> I was looking at other teammates and I was like okay, well they are all super skinny, so I have to be like that. And I think it was one practice and someone was like "well yea, we can throw her higher but she's like 15 pounds less than you" and I was like okay, then I have to change that because I want to be the person that's [thrown] … it was an alleyway that you could control aside from my ability or whether the coaches liked me or not, that I couldn't control. But I could control my weight, so I kinda went towards that.

Extreme Weight Control Methods: "I Got So Obsessed"

Several athletes claimed that weight control was a tactic they used because it was one thing within their power. Vanessa reflected on her state of mind:

> I got so obsessed with how much I weighed because it was something I could personally control. I can lose and gain weight when I want, that's something I can do ... And I got determined to make the coaches happy. I felt like that my purpose was to make them happy - I had to reach that goal weight. So, I almost became obsessed with losing weight and meeting my goal weight and not thinking about [my sport].

Athletes recalled controlling their weight through an obsession with food, food restriction, and increased conditioning. Hilary reflected on her limited food consumption:

> I remember just eating like an apple and banana for a lunch break for lunch and that was it. I was just putting myself through all that just for a number on the scale. So that my coach would just, you know, let me breathe a little.

Hilary also discussed forcing herself to do extra conditioning to maintain her weight "after training I would go upstairs on the rooftop and there was a little gym, and I would go running after 8 h of practice in the sun. I would go running on the treadmill for like an hour."

Negative Health Outcomes: "My Eating Disorder Is One of My Big Regrets"

Athletes reported negative health outcomes such as being diagnosed with eating disorders because of the emphasis on weight and appearance. Emma reflected on her health during one of her first major competitions on the National Team, after an altercation with her coach:

> That competition was the first time I acknowledged my health habits, my eating disorder. I remember trying to make myself puke after one dinner because I was so scared I ate too much. It was one of the first times I really had like, I felt like vomiting after dinner was a solution and it shouldn't be. So, yeah, that was one of the worst memories.

Even though Hilary had retired several years previously, her eating disorder continued to be a source of regret: "My eating disorder is one of my big regrets, because even though it's better now, it's taken me a long time to recover. I wish it didn't affect me as much when I was younger – all those coaches' comments."

Resulting from efforts to meet her coaches' weight standards, Carly shared: "No matter what I did, I couldn't be the size and weight [my coach] wanted me to be. Because of that, I ended up getting sick."

Declining Performance: "I Had No Energy to Give"

Performance effects were also discussed in relation to the athletes' extreme weight control methods as Vanessa recounted: "I couldn't eat but I had to train really hard. I had no energy to give into [training] because I was just starving all the time." Hilary also described the relationship between her coaches' pressures and her training:

> I was so nervous and there was so much pressure. [My coach] was telling me at the time how I was not good, too fat. I wasn't correcting my mistakes fast enough and I just couldn't. I was paralyzed in [training] trying to do my best but clearly it was worse. Like with no stress or pressure, I would have done it a million times better because I would have been free in my mind. I would be thinking about the movements and not just "how are my legs looking in the camera, is she going to tell me I look fat afterwards?"

Decreased Enjoyment in Sport

Athletes reported their experiences with body shaming led to decreased enjoyment in the sport which, in turn, influenced their decisions to retire. Vanessa shared:

> When I quit, I was still in that kind of brainwashed state about my body image so I'm still surprised that I quit. I quit because of that unhealthy environment but I didn't believe that it was unhealthy. I feel like something must have sparked in my head that said, "you got to get out of there" and I listened. Thank goodness I quit when I did is all I have to say.

According to Hilary, the effects of emotionally abusive practices persisted years after leaving the sport: "A lot of my memories of sport are tainted by the weight issue. As I look back, it's not necessarily good."

Discussion

In this study, we sought to explore female aesthetic sports athletes' experiences of emotional abuse with respect to their bodies and the effects of these experiences. We identified that emotionally abusive coaching practices reportedly centred on their bodies and had long-term negative effects. Emotionally abusive behaviours have been conceptualised in three forms: verbal behaviours, physical behaviours, and the denial of attention and support (Stirling & Kerr, 2008). Verbal behaviours may include yelling, humiliating, and degrading comments (Stirling & Kerr, 2008) and in the current study, athletes experienced these through having body parts critiqued as being too fat, being criticised for their weight publicly, and witnessing coaches' criticisms of teammates' bodies. Physical acts reportedly experienced by the current participants were through constant weigh-ins, especially in public spaces, having food taken away from them, having extra conditioning administered for not meeting weigh-in goals, and being prescribed restrictive diets. Finally, denial of attention and support was reportedly experienced by the athletes in this study through the removal or threat of removal of athletes from the team because of their weight and prohibiting the consolation of distressed teammates. Although body-related comments and behaviours were not referenced in previous conceptualisations of emotional abuse (Stirling & Kerr, 2008), we recommend, based upon the current findings, that body-related experiences be included.

We also posit that the coaches' behaviours with respect to the athletes' bodies should be interpreted as body shaming practices. Body shaming has become a common term in public discourse, typically used to describe negative or critical comments about another's appearance, body size, shape, or weight (Duncan et al., 2019; Lupton, 2017). Given that body shaming tends to focus on fat or obesity (Kyrölä, 2016), and athletes are not typically described by these characteristics, body shaming has not been explored in sports in depth. Recently, McMahon et al. (2021) also referred to body shaming of athletes by their entourage through ridicule and demeaning comments.

Braithwaite's theory of shaming and reintegration is useful in interpreting the current findings. According to Braithwaite (1989, p. 100), shaming is "the social process of expressing disapproval which can, intentionally or otherwise, invoke remorse." Braithwaite (1989, 2000) claims that shaming occurs when a person deviates from an established social norm and this results in expressions of disapproval from oneself or others. When an individual witnesses shaming, by direct confrontation or a general sense of disapproval from others, it can be internalised as "I would hate that to happen to me" and therefore people seek to avoid deviations from the norm (Ahmed et al., 2001, p. 31). Aligned with this theory, athletes in this study discussed engaging in food restrictions and/or excessive exercise following personal attacks of body shaming, witnessing others being reprimanded, or even after teammates engaged in body-related talk.

Fundamental to shaming is the focus on social processes; shaming processes are dependent upon our needs as social beings for belonging, relatedness, and connectedness, and when used appropriately, can promote a sense of consciousness in individuals and encourage adherence to established social norms (Murphy & Harris, 2007). Shaming is more impactful when close relationships exist and membership in the social group is very important to the individual (Braithwaite, 1989). The well-documented closeness that develops between teammates, and between coaches and athletes (Jowett, 2007), and the importance of team membership for athletes, fulfils the requirement of a close social circle, and since critical relationships and group membership are at stake, shaming may be particularly impactful in sport. The participants in the current study clearly understood that the community-specific norm and expectation was to be extremely thin and they used exceptional measures to adhere to this norm, including disordered eating behaviours. Evidence of internalisation of the social norm of thinness included athletes discussing weight and food restrictions with their teammates, engaging in social comparisons with respect to weight, and normalisation of unhealthy practices.

Athletes in this study reported practices that can be interpreted as body shaming, including being publicly criticised or humiliated for their weight; regular, and at times public, weigh-ins; diet monitoring and restrictions; additional training as punishment for failure to meet prescribed weight goals; observing teammates being criticised, or being ostracised due to weight or appearance. Many of these practices have been previously documented in the literature in relation to body image concerns, disordered eating and eating disorders (Anderson et al., 2012; Reel et al., 2013). The current study's findings add to these practices with the inclusion of public body shaming behaviours such as having food taken away from athletes, threatening to remove or removing athletes from the team based on weight, observing criticisms of teammates' bodies, and prohibiting athletes from supporting teammates who have experienced body-related criticisms. These findings also contribute to the existing literature by emphasising social influences; specifically, through shaming, relationships were used to modify and/or control behaviour through public displays of body disparagement, threats of removal or removal from the team.

Braithwaite (1989) claims that shaming can be used in positive ways to encourage expected normative conduct if directed at the behaviour rather than the individual and if the individual is subsequently welcomed, treated with respect and empathy, and re-integrated into the group. This positive approach of re-integration was not expressed in the participants' disclosures. The only time attempts to re-integrate an athlete occurred was after an athlete had retired and lost weight and the coaches conveyed they would be happy to have her back. This example reinforces the participants' experiences that the only way to be accepted within this group is to fit the prescribed appearance and doing whatever is necessary to achieve this outcome. Instead, we interpret the shaming behaviours experienced by the athletes as consistent with Brathwaite's concept of stigmatisation (1989, 2000), the negative form of shaming in which an individual is treated with disrespect, criticised as a person, and ostracised from the group. The athletes in the current study were not only publicly shamed through public weigh-ins and criticisms but were marginalised from teammates by being removed from training to engage in extra conditioning or being removed from the team entirely. Ostracisation was reinforced by prohibiting athletes from consoling the teammate who had experienced the shaming. Again, we see the disruption of athletes' needs for social inclusion and approval used by coaches to modify the athletes' behaviours and appearances.

Psychological outcomes were reported from the athletes' experiences of body shaming such as feeling anxious, preoccupation with their bodies, and eating disorders. Performance decrements were also experienced, reportedly due to low energy, and more errors as attention shifted from the technical requirements of performance to increased anxiety about coaches' comments about their appearances. These effects are consistent with previous findings on the effects of emotional abuse, including negative performance and mental health detriments (Stirling & Kerr, 2013; Yabe et al., 2019).

This study contributes to the substantial body of research on body dysmorphia, disordered eating and eating disorders in athletes by identifying the occurrence of body shaming, a concept previously reserved for those criticised for being overweight or obese and not applied to athletes. The importance of social influences that contribute to disordered eating and eating disorders in sports, specifically context-specific norms and expectations that guide behaviours, and social exclusion for those who deviate from these norms and expectations, are highlighted. Further, the ways in which body shaming occurs – through verbal comments, physical acts, and the denial of attention and support – match the previously documented forms of emotional abuse. The negative physical and mental health outcomes associated with body-related emotionally abusive experiences (i.e., body shaming) are significant and consistent with the documented outcomes of emotional abuse outside of sport.

From an applied perspective, body shaming is important for coaches and athletes to understand because it goes beyond the current understanding that coaches' comments can lead to unhealthy practices by athletes and highlights the use of social processes to cause harm. This study's findings could be an important component of coach education programs, specifically to promote an understanding that body shaming practices can constitute emotional abuse, and to emphasise the harmful effects of body shaming.

Limitations

This study's findings are limited by the small sample of adult, women-only athletes in aesthetic sports, its retrospective design and potential for recall bias. While previous research has shown that retired athletes can provide a more reflective perspective of their experiences (Kerr & Dacyshyn, 2000), it would also be informative to gather data on the lived experiences of body shaming from current athletes. As this study explored body shaming from the athlete's perspective, future research could incorporate views from coaches and other sports personnel (e.g., trainers, sports administrators).

Conclusions

The athletes in this study reported body shaming practices in sports including constant body monitoring, regular weigh-ins, negative comments about the body, food and water restrictions, witnessing criticisms of teammates' bodies, and punishments for failing to meet the ideal body standards of the sport, practices that often occurred publicly. The behaviours associated with body shaming are congruent with the forms of emotional abuse including verbal comments, physical acts, and denial of attention and support. The importance of context-specific norms was highlighted as athletes were aware of the appearance-related norms, and whether they were directly shamed or witnessed shaming, they regulated their bodies to fit the established norms to avoid future shaming. The normalisation of these behaviours is concerning given the impacts of body shaming on the athletes' physical and mental health outcomes, sports performance and enjoyment. Future recommendations include expanding populations of athletes, exploration of ways to change the culture of aesthetic sports in which body shaming is seemingly engrained.

References

Ahmed, E., Harris, N., Braithwaite, J., & Braithwaite, V. (2001). *Shame management through reintegration*. Cambridge University Press.

Anderson, C. M., Petrie, T. A., & Neumann, C. S. (2012). Effects of sport pressures on female collegiate athletes: A preliminary longitudinal investigation. *Sport, Exercise, and Performance Psychology*, *1*(2), 120. 10.1037/a0026587

Barker-Ruchti, N. (2009). Ballerinas and pixies: A genealogy of the changing female gymnastics body. *The International Journal of the History of Sport, 26*(1), 45–62. 10.1080/ 09523360802500089

Braithwaite, J. (1989). *Crime, shame and reintegration*. Cambridge University Press.

Braithwaite, J. (2000). Reintegrative shaming. In R. Paternoster, & R. Bachman (Eds.), *Explaining criminals and crime: Essays in contemporary criminological theory* (pp. 1–20). Roxbury.

Bratland-Sanda, S., & Sundgot-Borgen, J. (2013). Eating disorders in athletes: overview of prevalence, risk factors and recommendations for prevention and treatment.*European Journal of Sport Science*, *13*(5), 499–508. 10.1080/17461391.2012.740504

Braun, V., & Clarke, V. (2019). Reflecting on reflexive thematic analysis. *Qualitative Research in Sport, Exercise and Health, 11*(4), 589–597. 10.1080/2159676X.2019.1628806

Clarke, N. J., Caddick, N., & Frost, N. (2016). Pluralistic data analysis: Theory and practice. In B. Smith, & A. Sparkes (Eds.), *Routledge handbook of qualitative research in sport and exercise* (pp. 390–403). Routledge.

Duncan, N., Zimmer-Gembeck, M. J., & Furman, W. (2019). Sexual harassment and appearance-based peer victimization: Unique associations with emotional adjustment by gender and age. *Journal of Adolescence, 75*, 12–21. 10.1016/j.adolescence.2019.06.016

Frost, N., Nolas, S.-M., Brooks-Gordon, B., Esin, C., Holt, A., Mehdizadeh, L., & Shinebourne, P. (2010). Pluralism in qualitative research: The impact of different researchers and qualitative approaches on the analysis of qualitative data. *Qualitative Research, 10*(4), 441–460. 10.1177%2F1468794110366802

Green, J., & Thorogood, N. (2009). Qualitative methods for health research. In J. Green, & N. Thorogood (Eds.), *Qualitative methods for health research* (pp. 3–34). Sage.

Guba, E. G., & Lincoln, Y. S. (1994). Competing paradigms in qualitative research. In N. Denzin, & Y. Lincoln (Eds.), *Handbook of qualitative research* (pp. 105–117). Thousand Oaks, CA: Sage.

Hartill, M., Rulofs, B., Lang, M., Vertommen, T., Allroggen, M., Cirera, E., Diketmüller, R., Kampen, J., Kohl, A., & Martin, M. (2021). *Cases: General report. The prevalence and characteristics of interpersonal violence against children (IVAC) inside and outside sport in six European countries.* Ormskirk (United Kingdom): Edge Hill University. https://fis.dshs-koeln.de/en/publications/cases-general-report-the-prevalence-and-characteristics-of-interp

Humphreys, K. L., LeMoult, J., Wear, J. G., Piersiak, H. A., Lee, A., & Gotlib, I. H. (2020). Child maltreatment and depression: A meta-analysis of studies using the Childhood Trauma Questionnaire. *Child Abuse & Neglect, 102*, 104361. 10.1016/j.chiabu.2020.104361

Huellemann, K., Ens, G., Gray, E., Osa, M., & Pila, E. (2023). "If I talk about it, I'm weak, and I'm supposed to be strong": Experiences of body-related shame in women athletes. *International Journal of Sport and Exercise Psychology.* 10.1080/1612197X.2023.2238277

Ingle, S. (2020, July 7).*British Gymnastics to investigate alleged abuse of elite athletes.* The Guardian. https://www.theguardian.com/sport/2020/jul/07/uk-sport-to-investigate-shocking-and-upsetting-claims-of-gymnastics-abuse?utm_term=RWRpdG9yaWFsX0d1YXJkaWFuVG9kYXlVS19XZWVrZGF5cy0yMDA3MDg%3D&utm_source= esp&utm_medium=Email&CMP=GTUK_email&utm_campaign=GuardianTodayUK

Jowett, S. (2007). Interdependence analysis and the 3 + 1Cs in the coach-athlete relationship. In S. Jowett & D. Lavallee (Eds.), *Social psychology in sport* (pp. 15–27). Human Kinetics.

Kerr, G., & Dacyshyn, A. (2000). The retirement experiences of elite, female gymnasts.*Journal of Applied Sport Psychology, 12*(2), 115–133. 10.1080/10413200008404218

Kerr, G., Willson, E., & Stirling, A. (2020). "It Was the Worst Time in My Life": The effects of emotionally abusive coaching on female Canadian national team athletes. *Women in Sport and Physical Activity Journal, 28*(1), 81–89. 10.1123/wspaj.2019-0054

Krentz, E. M., & Warschburger, P. (2011). Sports-related correlates of disordered eating in aesthetic sports. *Psychology of Sport and Exercise, 12*(4), 375–382. 10.1016/j.psychsport.2011.03.004

Kyrölä, K. (2016). *The weight of images: Affect, body image and fat in the media.* Routledge.

Lupton, D. (2017). Digital media and body weight, shape, and size: An introduction and review. *Fat Studies*, *6*(2), 119–134. 10.1080/21604851.2017.1243392

McMahon, J., McGannon, K. R., & Palmer, C. (2021). Body shaming and associated practices as abuse: Athlete entourage as perpetrators of abuse. *Sport, Education and Society*, 1–14. 10.1080/13573322.2021.1890571

Murphy, K., & Harris, N. (2007). Shaming, shame and recidivism: A test of reintegrative shaming theory in the white-collar crime context. *The British Journal of Criminology, 47*(6), 900–917. 10.1093/bjc/azm037

Norman, R. E., Byambaa, M., De, R., Butchart, A., Scott, J., & Vos, T. (2012). The long-term health consequences of child physical abuse, emotional abuse, and neglect: A systematic review and meta-analysis. *PLoS Medicine*, *9*(11), e1001349. 10.1371/journal.pmed.1001349

Ohlert, J., Vertommen, T., Rulofs, B., Rau, T., & Allroggen, M. (2021). Elite athletes' experiences of interpersonal violence in organized sport in Germany, the Netherlands, and Belgium. *European Journal of Sport Science, 21*(4), 604–613.

Parent, S., Vaillancourt-Morel, M.-P., & Gillard, A. (2022). Interpersonal violence (IV) in sport and mental health outcomes in teenagers. *Journal of Sport and Social Issues*, *46*(4), 323–337.

Reel, J. J., Petrie, T. A., SooHoo, S., & Anderson, C. M. (2013). Weight pressures in sport: Examining the factor structure and incremental validity of the weight pressures in sport – females. *Eating Behaviors, 14*(2), 137–144. 10.1016/j.eatbeh.2013.01.003

Robertson, S., & Mountjoy, M. (2018). A review of prevention, diagnosis, and treatment of relative energy deficiency in sport in artistic (synchronized) swimming. *International Journal of Sport Nutrition and Exercise Metabolism, 28*(4), 375–384. 10.1123/ijsnem.2017-0329

Smith, B., & McGannon, K. R. (2018). Developing rigor in qualitative research: Problems and opportunities within sport and exercise psychology. *International Review of Sport and Exercise Psychology*, *11*(1), 101–121. 10.1080/1750984X.2017.1317357

Stafford, A., Alexander, K., & Fry, D. (2015). "There was something that wasn't right because that was the only place I ever got treated like that": Children and young people's experiences of emotional harm in sport. *Childhood*, *22*(1), 121–137. 10.1177/0907568213505625

Stirling, A., & Kerr, G. A. (2013). The perceived effects of elite athletes' experiences of emotional abuse in the coach-athlete relationship.*International Journal of Sport and Exercise Psychology, 11*(1), 87–100. 10.1080/1612197X.2013.752173

Stirling, A. E., & Kerr, G. A. (2008). Defining and categorizing emotional abuse in sport. *European Journal of Sport Science*, *8*(4), 173–181. 10.1080/17461390802086281

Tracy, S. J. (2010). Qualitative quality: Eight "big-tent" criteria for excellent qualitative research. *Qualitative Inquiry*, *16*(10), 837–851. 10.1177/1077800410383121

Vani, M. F., Pila, E., de Jonge, M., Solomon-Krakus, S., & Sabiston, C. M. (2020). "Can you move your fat ass off the baseline?" Exploring the sport experiences of adolescent girls with body image concerns. *Qualitative Research in Sport, Exercise and Health*, 1–19. 10.1080/2159676X.2020.1771409

Weiss, M., & Mohr, H. (2018, February 24). *U.S. gymnasts speak of eating disorders, emotional abuse, training on broken bones*. Global News. https://globalnews.ca/news/4045312/usa-gymnastics-abuse-victims/

Willson, E., Buono, S., Kerr, G., & Stirling, A. (2023). Maltreatment experiences and mental health indicators among elite athletes. *Psychology of Sport and Exercise*, *69*, 102493.

Willson, E., Kerr, G., Stirling, A., & Buono, S. (2021). Prevalence of maltreatment among Canadian national team athletes. *Journal of Interpersonal Violence*. 10.1177/08862605211045096

Willson, E., Kerr, G., Stirling, A., & Buono, S. (2022). Prevalence of maltreatment among Canadian national team athletes. *Journal of Interpersonal Violence*, *37*(21–22), NP19857–NP19879.

Yabe, Y., Hagiwara, Y., Sekiguchi, T., Momma, H., Tsuchiya, M., Kuroki, K., Kanazawa, K., Koide, M., Itaya, N., Yoshida, S., Sogi, Y., Yano, T., Itoi, E., & Nagatomi, R. (2019). Verbal abuse from coaches is associated with loss of motivation for the present sport in young athletes: A cross-sectional study in Miyagi prefecture. *The Tohoku Journal of Experimental Medicine*, *248*(2), 107–113. 10.1620/tjem.248.107

10

LIFESTYLE CHALLENGES AND MENTAL HEALTH OF PROFESSIONAL TENNIS PLAYERS

An Exploratory Case Study

Saul Shrom, Jennifer Cumming, and Sarah-Jane Fenton

Each year, thousands of tennis players from around the world compete against each other on the professional tennis circuit (International Tennis Federation (ITF), 2020). However, as the most recent ITF Pro Circuit Review has highlighted (ITF, 2017), their pursuit of success is not without obstacles. Most notably, there is a considerable financial imbalance on tour, with the top 1% of players having earned 60% and 51% of the prize money distributed on the men's and women's tours in 2013, respectively, and only 1.8% of male and 3.1% of female players earning a profit (ITF, 2017). This leaves most professional players in varying degrees of financial debt and in danger of prematurely ending their professional pursuits due to an inability to fund the extensive costs. Further, the time taken from earning one's first professional ranking to reaching the world's Top 100 has increased from 3.7 to 4.8 years (men) and 3.4 to 4.1 years (women) from 2000 to 2013 (ITF, 2017), and even further to 5 years (men) and 4.9 years (women) by 2017 (ITF Global Tennis Report, 2019), suggesting that additional challenges are at play making the professional tour an increasingly difficult environment to thrive in. While research has identified lifestyle challenges of professional athletes in other sports (Battochio et al., 2009; 2016; Gordin, 2016; Moore, 2016; Schinke et al., 2012), we do not yet sufficiently understand the specific challenges (in addition to the identified financial ones) faced by tennis players in their lifestyle on the professional tour, nor how these potentially impact their mental health and well-being. Whilst there is existing literature into players' transitions into professional tennis (Jensen, 2012; Pummell, 2008), the knowledge base around lifestyle challenges from these studies is minimal and would benefit from more diverse samples, involving players of both sexes and from a range of nationalities. With regards to mental health and

DOI: 10.4324/9781003459750-10

well-being, although there has been increased attention in mainstream media through the voices of Naomi Osaka (Osaka, 2021), retired player Mardy Fish in the Netflix series "Untold" (Way & Way, 2021) and several players in the new Netflix series "Break Point" (Webb, 2023), there is limited academic research to date exploring mental health in professional tennis (Sievert, 2022). In addition to adding depth to the academic literature, investigating players' lifestyle challenges and their impact on mental health and well-being can help to inform aspiring players' preparations for a professional career from both a performance and mental health standpoint.

The developmental period in which tennis players, and athletes in most disciplines, generally reach their peak performance overlaps with the peak onset of mental health disorders in the general population (Jones, 2013). It is estimated that 75% of mental health disorders are established by the age of 24 (Kessler et al., 2005). When this sensitive developmental period is combined with the unique stressors (i.e., competitive, organisational, and personal) that athletes experience in high-performance environments (Sarkar & Fletcher, 2014), elite athletes may be at an increased vulnerability to mental ill-health compared to the general population (Gucciardi et al., 2017). To date, research on mental illness within elite sports has reported prevalence rates between 17% and 47% (Foskett & Longstaff, 2018; Gouttebarge et al., 2017; Gulliver et al., 2015; Schaal et al., 2011), which are comparable, and in some cases, higher than the general population rates for young adults estimated to range between 19% and 26% (Australian Bureau of Statistics, 2007; Education Policy Institute, 2018; Mental Health Foundation, 2016). While it has not been substantiated that elite athletes experience higher prevalence of mental illness than the general population, the environmental challenges and age-related risk factors they experience during their careers make mental ill-health within elite sports a cause for concern.

The increased focus on mental health within elite sports in recent years is also reflected in position and consensus statements published by major sporting organisations including the International Society of Sport Psychology (Henriksen et al., 2020a; 2020b; Schinke et al., 2018) and the International Olympic Committee (Reardon et al., 2019). With considerable research having been undertaken to attempt to quantify and classify the nature and prevalence of mental illness within sport (Gorczynski et al., 2017; Rice et al., 2016), Henriksen et al. (2020b) recently argued for the importance of focusing on mental health in addition to mental illness and conceptualising mental health as more than simply the absence of mental illness. This argument aligns with Keyes' (2005) definition of mental health as being free of mental illness and flourishing with high levels of emotional, psychological, and social well-being, as well as Keyes' (2002; 2005) dual continuum model which views mental health and mental illness as two distinct but related dimensions existing on two separate continua. The model provides a holistic understanding of mental health (Iasiello & Agteren, 2020; Uphill et al., 2016) by conceptualising flourishing (i.e., high levels of mental health) as being made up of three distinct types of well-being (i.e., emotional, psychological, and social), as well as demonstrating how athletes can experience high or low levels of mental health, while simultaneously experiencing either high or low levels of mental illness.

Theoretical Underpinning

To explore challenges experienced by professional tennis players, the present study adapted an established theory – Maslow's (1943) hierarchy of needs – and used it as an innovative theoretical framework and approach within the sports psychology discipline. The theory continues to be relevant decades after its inception, informing research and applied practice in diverse fields such as education, medicine, and business (e.g., Benson & Dundis, 2003; Hale et al., 2019; Jerome, 2013; Milheim, 2012). As a classic theory of motivation, Maslow (1943) posited that four basic sets of needs (i.e., physiological, safety, love and belonging, and esteem) must be satisfied for individuals to be motivated to reach maximum human potential (i.e., self-actualisation). While most often visually represented as a pyramid with higher-order needs dependent on lower-order needs, the importance of each level of needs varies from person to person and is not a rigid hierarchy as originally conceptualised (Maslow, 1987). Instead, these need levels are more flexible and dynamic, based on contextual factors and individual differences. Thus, this theory is more recently understood as a group of coexisting needs to be satisfied instead of as a hierarchy, with people able to experience higher needs even if the more basic ones are not met.

Only limited sport research has adopted Maslow's hierarchy of needs (1943) as a motivational framework (e.g., Andrew et al., 2016; Homan, 2021; Nikitina, 2021). But, we propose that it would enable a holistic view of the challenges faced on tour by professional players and be well-suited for exploring their mental health and well-being. In support, in their study analysing over 60,000 participants across 123 countries, Tay and Diener (2011) found universal needs aligned with Maslow's theory to increase subjective well-being regardless of cultural differences. Further, Crandall et al. (2020) found Maslow's theory to partially predict and explain baseline rates and changes in adolescent depressive symptoms. Despite this, Maslow's theory has not yet specifically been applied to understanding athlete mental health. Adopting this theory would provide an insightful look at how the satisfaction or lack thereof of basic human needs can impact players' progression on tour and their mental health and well-being. The hierarchy of needs also offers a guiding framework for developing interventions to support the well-being of professional players through a holistic consideration of their needs and by acknowledging multiple concurrent threats to them (Hale et al., 2019).

Study Aims

The present study aimed to provide a detailed, contextualised understanding of the lifestyle challenges that professional tennis players face on the professional tour and the potential impact these challenges have on their mental health. This was the first study to investigate the lifestyle challenges of the professional tennis tour within a diverse, international sample. Additionally, it makes a unique theoretical contribution by providing a novel application of Maslow's (1943) hierarchy of needs to the sports psychology discipline.

Methods

Design

This study was underpinned by an interpretivist approach consisting of a relativist ontology and a subjectivist epistemology (Sparkes & Smith, 2014). It adopted an exploratory case study methodology (Yin, 2017), an approach selected to gain rich insight (Cooper et al., 2019) into a previously under-studied area. The case study consisted of a single holistic case: Behind the Racquet (BTR) (2021), a social media platform aimed at raising awareness of the challenges that tennis players face on the professional tour. BTR as a case study offered unique opportunities for research into the voice of players, being an authentic, self-reported platform of players' professional experiences (Paulhus & Vazire, 2007). The case study was bound to understand the challenges that professional players face in their lifestyle on tour. The units of analysis were individual players who contributed to the BTR platform. Theoretically underpinned by Maslow's (1943) hierarchy of needs, the study looked to understand the extent to which players' basic needs were met amidst the challenges they faced on the professional tour. With the first researchers' background in tennis, a reflexive approach to the data analysis process was used (Braun & Clarke, 2019).

Data Collection

Self-reported narrative data was collected via blog posts from professional tennis players who contributed to BTR. Given the competitive nature of professional tennis, these types of vulnerable narratives are rarely shared, making them an invaluable data source, as well as the case study unique. The data provided an excellent opportunity to gain a self-reported understanding of professional tennis players' lifestyles, and as such, best answered the study's research questions of "What challenges do professional tennis players face in their lives on the professional tour?" and "What type of impact do these challenges have on players' mental health?"

Blogs provide access to hard-to-reach populations from which the researcher is either geographically or socially removed from (Mann & Stewart, 2000; Wilson et al., 2015), while offering a publicly available, low-cost, and instantaneous way of collecting a considerable amount of data with the transparency of a built-in audit trail (Hookway, 2008; Moravcsik, 2014). The use of blogs in academic research is becoming increasingly common (Kurtz et al., 2017; Wilkinson & Thelwall, 2011) with growing support for its use for data collection purposes in qualitative research in health (Wilson et al., 2015) and sport (Brown & Billings, 2013; Kavanagh et al., 2016). Ethical considerations of blog use, such as informed consent and the public or private nature of information, are increasingly important as they become a more common data source for academic research (Kurtz et al., 2017). In the present study, the Association of Internet Researchers (AoIR) recommendations (Ess et al., 2002; Markham et al., 2012) were followed, which consider blogs as public webpages that can be viewed by anyone and explained that "the greater the acknowledged publicity of the venue, the less obligation there may be to protect individual privacy, confidentiality, right to informed consent, etc." (Ess et al., 2002, p. 5). As informed consent does not apply to published material (e.g., newspapers) and sending participation requests to players who had already consented to sharing their narratives to a popular platform like BTR seen as potentially intrusive (Snee, 2013), it was not deemed necessary to obtain additional consent to use these blogs for research purposes. Nonetheless, consent to use the platform (whilst publicly available) was still sought from the founder of BTR (N. Rubin, personal communication, July 16, 2019). Additionally, to ensure trustworthiness of the posts, the first researcher liaised with the platform's creator to confirm validity checks were in place for the posts selected for inclusion.

Sample

Of the 115 posts uploaded between January 19, 2019 and March 31, 2020, 66 were selected for analysis according to the following inclusion criteria: (a) the post shared players' experiences unique to their professional career; and (b) the post illustrated experiences which had a psychological impact on the player. The dataset included experiences of 65 professional players (one player had two separate posts), of which 33 were male, and 32 were female. Further details of the sample are provided in Table 10.1. A wide range of achievement levels existed across the dataset, ranging from Grand Slam and Olympic champions to players within the Association of Tennis Professionals (ATP) and Women's Tennis Association (WTA) Top 10, and those within and outside of the ATP and WTA Top 100.

TABLE 10.1 Sample breakdown

Age and Sex Breakdown	*Age Descriptive Statistics*	*Nationalities*	*Playing Status*
< 21: N = 5 M: 1; F: 4 **21–25: N = 20** M: 10; F: 10 **26–30: N = 23** M: 11; F: 12 **31–35: N = 14** M: 8; F: 6 **36+: N = 3** M: 3; F: 0	Mean: 27.34 Range: 29 SD: 5.23	United States (20), Canada (4), France (4), Russia (4), Australia (3), Germany (3), Great Britain (3), Croatia (2), Czech Republic (2), South Africa (2), Argentina, Barbados, Belgium, Brazil, Colombia, Egypt, Hungary, Israel, Italy, Japan, Netherlands, New Zealand, Puerto Rico, Romania, Serbia, Slovakia, Switzerland, Taiwan	Active: 56 Retired: 9

Data Analysis

Data was analysed inductively using reflexive thematic analysis, a flexible process where researchers generate patterns of meaning within their dataset through reflexive and thoughtful consideration of their data (Braun & Clarke, 2019). This approach was adopted due to the exploratory nature of the case study, which aimed to gain a contextual understanding of the beliefs, thoughts, and experiences of professional players. In line with the phases of thematic analysis (Braun et al., 2016), the first author began the analysis process by familiarising themselves with the data before embarking on the initial coding process. NVivo 12 was used to organise and code the data. The entire dataset was coded before the codes were subsequently grouped into initial themes. The initial themes were presented to a group of researchers in the university's sport psychology department (including post-graduate students and post-doctoral research fellows) independent from the project where useful discussion on the analysis led to further adaptations to the themes. After this meeting, discussion amongst the authors of this chapter led to further adaptations leading to six themes that more clearly represented how players' challenges on tour impact their ability to meet their basic needs (Maslow, 1943). Involving outside researchers was a collaborative process to help "develop a richer more nuanced reading of the data, rather than seeking a consensus of meaning" (Braun & Clarke, 2019, p. 594). The steps taken throughout this reflexive thematic analysis led to prolonged engagement with the data and continual reflection and questioning of assumptions that were made in interpreting the data (Braun & Clarke, 2019). For increased trustworthiness of the data, a range of rich quotes were used to exhibit confirmability and authenticity in the report of the findings (Cope, 2014).

The analysis was underpinned by the modern discussion on rigour in qualitative research (e.g., Morse, 2015; Smith & McGannon, 2018). With the first author's extensive background as a tennis player, both at the collegiate and professional level, this offered the opportunity to harness reflexivity in the analysis to complement and enhance the process. Reflexivity was described by Berger (2015) as turning the researcher's lens to oneself to recognise and take responsibility for one's position within the research and the effect this could have on the research process and outcome. Specifically, the first researcher used "critical friends" who were post-doctorate researchers who had no background in tennis, but had expertise in qualitative research, and thematic analysis specifically, to provide a sounding board for ideas and encourage potential alternative explanations of the data throughout the analysis process.

Results

In line with the study's aims, data analysis led to a deeper and contextualised understanding of the challenges that players face in their lifestyle as professional tennis players. Six themes were developed in the analysis (i.e., Physical and Mental Fatigue, Financial Imbalance of the Professional System, The Social and Psychological Impact of Living a Nomadic Existence, The Weight of Expectation, Structural-Caused Instability and Mental Ill-Health), and these themes and their connection to the levels of Maslow's (1943) hierarchy are outlined below.

Physical and Mental Fatigue (Physiological Needs)

The weekly travel from one country to another, where players are confronted by different time zones, cultures, foods, and playing conditions, is a major challenge, which leads to physical and mental fatigue and impedes players' physiological need for rest (Maslow, 1943). As Player 1 (male, French), a veteran of the professional tour, explained:

> On one side I feel lucky to be able to travel around the world and see different cultures, and on the other side it was just tiring. From New York to Tokyo and then Moscow, in one month, it's three different worlds that you have to get used to.

The fatigue which Player 1 explains is exacerbated by the professional tennis calendar, which due to its short offseason, means players compete for 11 months of the year. The relentless nature of this lifestyle is illustrated by Player 2 (female, Russian), who explained:

> The long year of tennis is exhausting. Other sports have two to three months off to use as a break. I understand that other sports may push their players harder during the short seasons but there is no way they are put in the same amount of stressful situations as tennis players are.

Financial Imbalance of the Professional System (Safety Needs)

A financial imbalance exists in the professional system which represents a major barrier to its players. With players at the lower levels earning far less money than those at the top, yet still responsible for the substantial costs of a professional career, navigating a professional career becomes a monumental financial challenge. This impacts players' safety needs (Maslow, 1943) by challenging their financial and job security. Indeed, the financial stress professional players experience on tour hangs like a dark cloud over their professional existence, leading to doubt over the feasibility of their continued involvement on tour. With the endless expenses of travel, accommodation, equipment, and other playing essentials, players must earn as much prize money as possible to offset these costs. As illustrated by Player 3 (male, South African), the precarious nature of this funding is a significant source of stress and leads players to questioning: (a) can they afford to continue; and (b) is it worthwhile for them to do so:

> The question always came up, 'What am I doing?' I was going week to week, making two or three hundred dollars. Then after taxes it was basically nothing. What am I doing with my life? I am twenty nine now. I don't have a degree … Other people around my age, who I went to school with, have cars, house, etc. … living the less stressful life. They see me and think that I am living this glamorous lifestyle, playing at Wimbledon, but in actuality I was barely surviving paycheck to paycheck.

Despite considerable success at the entry-level of the professional tour and amassing a world singles ranking of 350, Player 3 was barely making ends meet and lacked the financial stability that his friends outside of tennis enjoyed in their chosen careers. His experiences exemplify the poor financial security that many professional players face (safety needs; Maslow, 1943). As a result, they may need to rely on family for financial support. It is not uncommon that the considerable financial resources needed to support a professional tennis career lead to stress and financial difficulties for the players' families. As Player 4 (male, American) explained "It took a major toll, forcing my family to take out multiple mortgages on the house … They sacrificed everything for us to play tennis." While the depths to which Player 4's family went to fund their son's professional tennis career may seem extraordinary, it is not unusual for professional players' families to make major financial and lifestyle sacrifices for their children's tennis careers. Player 5 (male, French) noted:

> My dad stopped working to travel with me full time. There was already pressure from not being too wealthy and now my father wasn't making money ... There was a lot of pressure on the whole family to also keep up with the expenses of travel ... My mom switched jobs and started to work at home so she had time to look after my brother by herself.

This example further magnifies the substantial sacrifices families make to help their children reach their tennis dreams, in addition to highlighting questions over the feasibility of such sacrifices. While Player 5 has reached the highest tier of the professional game and is financially stable, most players are not as fortunate, and like Player 4, leave the professional tour having spent much of their own and their family's financial resources.

The Social and Psychological Impact of Living a Nomadic Existence (Love and Belonging Needs)

The opportunities to play tournaments in all but one week of the calendar year and the fierce competition to earn ranking points and prize money to move up the ranking system and fund the costs of the professional tour are strong incentives for players to compete in different parts of the world throughout the year. The resulting nomadic existence challenges players' love and belonging needs (Maslow, 1943) by inhibiting their need for sense of connection and friendship. Humans are a social species which require social contact and support to survive and thrive (Seppala et al., 2013) and this contributes to their social well-being (Keyes, 2005). Not meeting these needs in young adulthood while embarking on a professional career can be particularly disorienting for players. As Player 6 (female, German) explains, the constant travelling and inability to settle in a geographical location for an extended period makes it difficult to maintain relationships and feel connected with others:

> It's hard to maintain relationships with a boy/girlfriend, with friends ... it's hard not to see your family for long periods because you are rarely home. You miss out on important things that happen in your friends' lives. It's your job to be on the road and play.

These relationship challenges affect players' ability to nurture key relationships that they would otherwise rely on for valuable emotional support to counteract the challenges they face on tour. While players at the highest level of the sport like Carlos Alcaraz and Iga Swiatek are able to cover the travelling costs of numerous members of their support networks to attend tournaments, most professional players cannot afford this luxury. Consequently, these players embark on a year's worth of travel, often without members of their support network. Feelings of loneliness were reported by a range of players, with some examples including: "traveling alone was exhausting" (Player 7; male, American), "(I) spent almost a year alone on the tour after that. I was so miserable" (Player 8; female, French), and "Most people can understand how alone you can feel on a tennis court, but as a tennis player there are moments when you feel just as isolated off court" (Player 9; male, American).

The Weight of Expectation (Esteem Needs)

The journey of becoming a professional tennis player is time-consuming, challenging and includes numerous sacrifices from the player and their families. It is unsurprising that when a player reaches the professional level, the weight of expectation to succeed can negatively impact their esteem needs of feelings of achievement, recognition, and status (Maslow, 1943). To remain on the professional tour, players must consistently achieve results and earn the necessary ranking points to maintain or increase their world ranking. This results-focused environment puts thousands of highly motivated and capable players head-to-head and under immense pressure to achieve. This is seen through the experiences of Player 10 (female, American), who broke into the Top 100 at the age of 20, and Player 11 (male, Canadian), who began a professional career after being the number 1 ranked junior player in the world:

> I broke into the top 100 for the first time and had some of my best results to date. Unfortunately, that season changed my expectations. I began to put a lot more pressure on myself … my focus was on all the wrong things. I was so worried about defending/recreating the previous year I had, that I barely had a single productive practice. (Player 10)

> Nobody truly expected me to be a contender for junior slams, so everyone was pretty surprised that I made four finals, winning two of them in just a year. That obviously changed peoples' perspectives. It was definitely a lot of pressure, having everyone expecting me to be top 100 right out of juniors. (Player 11)

Because of the extensive sacrifices made by players and their families, players internalise this pressure as a sense of responsibility to succeed, and it can be accompanied by a fear of failure. Player 12 (male, American) explained:

> To let down the people closest to me, my friends and family, is my most daunting fear. From an early age I was pretty aware about how many lives I affected. How many people had to sacrifice time, energy and money. The idea that it may not be worth it, or there might not be a way to repay them, haunts me at times.

This quote highlights the depth of responsibility Player 12 felt to succeed for those who had sacrificed so much for him. Player 13 (female, American) shared similar thoughts when explaining the fear associated with not meeting her professional career expectations:

> If I wasn't going to use my college degree to work towards financial independence, I needed to make this endeavor worth it. My family helped me financially and my coach agreed to be compensated with lunches after practice. There was constant fear on whether I would ever be good enough to make it all worthwhile.

Another negative feeling that comes with carrying this weight of expectation is a loss of enjoyment, which may lower emotional well-being (Keyes, 2005). This was seen with Player 14 (female, American), who explained "I felt absolutely no thrill being on the court. I didn't want to compete and didn't care if I practiced or not … I had no motivation, no real desire to play, and I hated anything tennis related." This is a powerful example of how the wear and tear of sustained expectation throughout Player 14's career led to a shift in their views about tennis. A similar experience was shared by Player 10 (female, American), who after struggling with the expectations she felt after reaching the Top 100, shared, "I wasn't enjoying any of the travel, training or competition. Tennis was becoming more stressful than enjoyable, and it was affecting my whole life. I was disappointed … for letting my results on the tennis court dictate my overall happiness."

Structural-Caused Instability (Esteem Needs)

The structure of the professional tour creates an environment of instability that also impacts on esteem needs. The lack of salaries or contracts on tour leaves players dependent on achieving results to earn money. Further, the 52-week rolling ranking system, where ranking points from more than 52 weeks prior are removed from players' point total, places a time-sensitive pressure on players to earn results and maintain their spot within the professional system. The uncertainty caused by the tour's structure is the catalyst for two challenges that players face on tour and inhibits their esteem needs (Maslow, 1943) of status and recognition. It also leads them to making choices that are not always in the best interest of their health and well-being.

While injuries are an unfortunate reality across professional sport, the unique structure of tennis makes time away from the sport a serious threat to one's ability to maintain a foothold within the system. Specifically, with no form of income, and the risk of ranking points disappearing, players feel pressure to avoid missing time from injury and an urgency to return to play as soon as possible. The experience of Player 15 exemplifies the difficult choices made to minimise the time away from the tour:

> I broke into the top 10 for the first time at St Petersburg in 2016. Then soon came Miami where I got my first injury, which led to many others. A severe wrist problem came and I tried to avoid surgery while playing for nine months. April 2017, I finally decided to get it done. I was out for about six months and my ranking dropped to 350. Tennis is super difficult because you never stay where you are. (Player 15; female, Swiss)

Player 15's decision to play through injury for nine months to maintain their hard-earned top 10 ranking illustrates the stress surrounding taking time away from tennis. In the Top 10, Player 15 has entry to the top tournaments in the world, earns substantial prize money and endorsement deals. However, lowering to 350 means significantly decreased prize money and ranking points, as well as a threat to their status (Maslow, 1943), which would require several weeks' worth of strong results to regain.

The instability caused by the professional structure also leads to players feeling underappreciated. With a tournament system where only one player is victorious each week, the regularity of losing becomes commonplace and recent success gains prominence, with past successes losing significance. These feelings were experienced by Player 12 (male, American), a former Wimbledon junior singles champion, who stated "the sport has a way of making you feel irrelevant ... with the likelihood of losing every week and the forever expanding field of players, chances are if you were once talk of the town, that will quickly diminish over time." These feelings of irrelevance and change in status relate to Player 16's (female, American) frustration regarding the status that is given to "winners," and lack of appreciation of "losers." Specifically, she explained: "Tennis puts this stigma on losing to the point that only winners receive the platform to speak. It's truly sad that losers are barely acknowledged in a sport where defeat is an every week occurrence."

Player 16's views point to further inequalities that exist on the tour; a small number of players at the top of the sport's structure are given the ability to shape the narrative of professional tennis through on-court interviews and increased media opportunities, compared to the many lower ranked players who are not given this opportunity. This leads to concern that a skewed image of the professional system is being portrayed to the public, one in which the experiences of the highest-ranked players with their financial security and other benefits are shared, and the realities of most players are not represented.

Mental Ill-Health (Self-Actualisation)

Symptoms of mental illness associated with tour lifestyle challenges were a consistent finding across the data. While there were many subclinical symptoms of mental illness, there were additionally over 15% of players who explicitly reported experiencing mental illness on the professional tour (e.g., anxiety, panic attacks, depression and eating disorders). An example of this is seen in a quotation from Player 17 (female, Puerto Rican):

> There is trauma after winning something that major that pushes you flat on your butt … As I became more upset I saw that depression was inevitable when it was tough to get out of bed. At one point you're on top of the world and all of a sudden it ends and you just don't know what just happened. It's like whiplash. I couldn't find ways to motivate myself to play. I just didn't know what to do with myself. There are many times when all I wanted to do was cry every day, in bed, in a dark room.

Another example is seen in Player 18 (male, American), who experienced panic attacks on tour, one of which came after experiencing expectation-related stress of reaching the world's Top 100 and feeling antsy to return to play after managing nagging injuries. They detailed their experience by describing:

> It is now two weeks before my first French Open main draw. It felt as if I had no control of my mind. I had a panic attack on my flight from Dallas to Paris. It was nine hours of some of the most agony and pain I have ever felt. I thought that every breath I took could be my last. After getting to Paris, I could barely practice. I would walk off the court immediately and hop into a car to get back to my hotel. I just couldn't function at all, not wanting to leave the hotel room.

Reflecting on the experience, Player 18 went on to say "I held it all in, not thinking much of it. Everyone has adversities … As athletes you are always told to push through it, not knowing what to deal with, until it's too late." Similar feelings were shared by Player 19 (female, American) who had experienced depression on tour for years and explained "it can be difficult to show vulnerability in such a competitive, high stakes profession."

These examples, as well as others from the dataset, highlight the powerful impact that mental illness has on professional players' lives both inside and outside of tennis. Mental illness inhibits players' ability to reach their full potential (i.e., self-actualisation; Maslow, 1943) on the professional tour.

Discussion

The present study aimed to gain a detailed, contextual understanding of the challenges that tennis players experience in their professional tour lifestyles and examine the impact these challenges have on their mental health. Analysis of a social media platform provided access to an extensive range of self-reported experiences of professional players and a deeper understanding of the professional tennis environment. The study's findings are in line with Sarkar and Fletcher's (2014) assertion that elite sporting environments consist of a range of competitive, organisational, and personal stressors. Specifically, on the professional tennis tour, these include the weight of expectation (competitive), financial imbalance of the professional system, the social and psychological impact of living a nomadic existence, and structural-caused instability (organisational) and physical and mental fatigue (personal). Collectively, these challenges represent barriers to the satisfaction of key human needs (Maslow, 1943) and pose a risk to players' mental health.

Challenges on the professional tour inhibit players' ability to satisfy their needs on each level of Maslow's (1943) hierarchy. At the physiological level, physical and mental fatigue hindered players' ability to meet their need for rest. At the safety needs level, the financial imbalance of the professional system led to employment uncertainty and financial stress impacting players' job and financial security. Players' love and belonging needs are impeded through their nomadic existence which threatens their need for sense of connection and friendship. At the esteem level, players' needs are impacted by both the weight of expectation and structural-caused instability of the tour challenging their needs for feelings of achievement, recognition, and status. Finally, players' self-actualisation is inhibited due to existing mental ill-health issues on tour. The impact of tour challenges on players' needs is illustrated in Figure 10.1.

Beyond impacting players' ability to progress on tour, inhibited needs have implications for mental health. Not only did 15% of players within the sample explicitly refer to experiencing mental illness, but the very challenges which players face on the professional tour have known links to decreased mental health. For example, fear of failure that players exhibited due to the weight of their expectations on tour is associated with anxiety, depression, and eating disorders (Lavallee et al., 2009; Sagar et al., 2007). Additionally, there are known links between financial stress and poorer mental health outcomes (Wadsworth, 2013), and research illustrating the impact of social support and

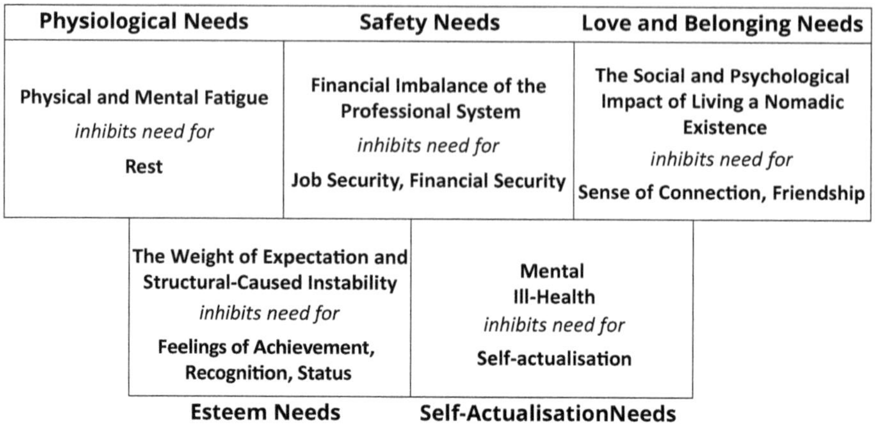

FIGURE 10.1 Impact of challenges on players' needs.

connectedness on managing sporting and non-sporting challenges and enhancing well-being (Bernat & Resnick, 2009; DeFreese & Smith, 2014; Sheridan et al., 2014).

The present study's findings illustrate a concerning picture. This is the first study to examine the mental health challenges on the professional tour, and further research is needed. A holistic approach to mental health like Keyes' (2002; 2005) dual continuum model can provide a more contextualised understanding of mental health and mental illness on tour by recognising the importance of acknowledging players' levels of both mental health and illness. In an environment where the identified challenges of this study exist, simply focusing on preventing mental illness prevalence will not do enough to promote players' emotional, psychological, and social well-being.

The study's findings also pose questions around the structural issues in professional tennis. Most notably, the financial challenges players experience, which was partially understood prior to this research (ITF, 2017), became increasingly apparent. Players' daily existence on tour was directly affected by the financial challenges in professional tennis. These findings beg the question: what steps can be taken by the ITF, ATP, and WTA to improve the financial situation on tour? After uncovering financial issues within tennis in the ITF Pro Circuit Review (2017), the ITF restructured entry-level tournaments so that $10,000 and $15,000 events became $15,000 and $25,000 events, respectively. However, adding $5,000 or $10,000 to be spread across an entire lower-level tournament may not be enough of a step in a sport where 1.8% and 3.1% of male and female players are earning a profit, respectively (ITF, 2017). With prize money increasing at the highest level of the sport (i.e., Grand Slam events) each year (Clarey, 2019), and the range of financial-related challenges identified throughout the professional structure, there are important questions to be asked about the distribution of prize money in the sport and the implications this has on the livelihood of players throughout the entire professional system. In the last two years, Novak Djokovic and Vasek Pospisil launched an alternative Professional Tennis Players' Association (PTPA) to advocate for the rights of male and female professional players by inspiring collective reform to ensure more players are able to earn sustainable livings from tennis and that players are fairly represented. It is too early to understand the impact this player-led project will have, but there is certainly reason for optimism with the rate of its growth in recent months (PTPA, 2023).

While structural-related challenges are not directly within the control of professional players, other challenges are within players' control and provide an opportunity to better manage on tour. One of these challenges is managing the weight of expectation that players experience. In line with achievement goal theory (Nicholls, 1989), working on shifting players' focus from a performance orientation emphasising outperforming others and results to a mastery orientation emphasising what is within players' control like continual improvement, decision-making, and effort can lead to decreased anxiety, increased intrinsic motivation, positive affect, and basic need satisfaction (Alvarez et al., 2012; Kipp & Weiss, 2013, Smith et al., 2007). This could be complemented by developing the players' ability to effectively self-regulate their thoughts, emotions, and behaviours through psychological skills training. Further, players can work to increase their ability to maintain relationships and connectedness amidst their nomadic existence, as well as increase their financial literacy and discover ways to generate alternative forms of income and sponsorships to increase their opportunities on tour. The ATP and WTA offer player development programs (i.e., ATP University, WTA Player Development Program) which cover topics like finances, tour lifestyle, and health and wellness to assist players adjust to the professional game. While these programs provide important opportunities for players to better prepare themselves for professional tour lifestyle challenges, they are only offered to players who have ATP/WTA player membership and meet certain ranking requirements (i.e., ATP Top 200 singles or Top 100 doubles, WTA Top 750 singles or Top 200 doubles) (ATP, 2021; WTA, 2021). Courses like these could be extended to all full-time professional players across the ATP, WTA, and ITF, as adjusting to tour challenges is not something that only top-ranked players require. Regardless of whether players enrol in official training courses or not, educating oneself on the challenges of professional tennis and ways to manage these challenges is crucial to players' development from performance and mental health standpoints.

Implications and Future Research

The findings of the present study have implications for players aspiring to play professional tennis. Prospective professional players and their coaches, families, and other support networks can gain insightful information about the professional tour which can assist in the familiarisation and preparation processes for their professional careers. These findings also strengthen the tennis literature by providing a contextualised understanding of the professional tennis lifestyle and challenges within the sport, which can be used to inform future tennis research.

Future research can build on this study's findings by investigating how players manage the professional tour lifestyle challenges identified in this study. This can be done through examining players' transitioning experiences into the sport. Ideally, this research would be longitudinal as a way to investigate players' experiences as they are occurring. Future studies should also look to better understand mental health in professional tennis, taking a holistic approach (Keyes, 2002; 2005) to better comprehend the complexity of the issue.

Limitations

While the present study offers important contributions to the literature, it is not without limitations. First, the data was collected at a single time point rather than at various points throughout the players' careers. A longitudinal design would allow for an understanding of whether identified challenges endured throughout players' careers or changed over time. Second, although there was even distribution in the sample between North Americans (n = 26) and Europeans (n = 26), a disproportionate amount of the sample (i.e., 30.8%) was from the United States. Finally, the nature of the dataset (i.e., blog posts) meant that it was not possible for the researchers to follow up with probing questions that may have helped to reveal connections between themes. For example, players discussed pressures experienced when injured as "structural-caused instability," which may also have implications for their physical and mental health. Future research could complement the findings of the present study via alternative qualitative methods like narrative research to provide rich insights into the lived experiences of professional tennis players. Whilst blog posts put players in the role of storyteller, narrative research can also explore the interactions between how the players' personal experiences unfold over time and within a particular socio-cultural context (Douglas & Carless, 2014).

Conclusion

This study provided evidence of the range of challenges that professional players face in their lifestyles on the professional tour, while highlighting the concern these challenges pose to players' mental health. Access to a hard-to-reach population for data collection was gained through the use of a social media platform and data was analysed through a novel application of Maslow's (1943) hierarchy of needs to the sport discipline. The findings demonstrated the model's relevance for understanding athletes' performance challenges and their implications on athletes' mental health. In doing so, the study adds empirical, theoretical, and methodological significance to the literature, in addition to its applied potential of informing aspiring professional players and their support networks with vital information to assist in their professional endeavours.

Disclosure Statement

No potential conflict of interest was reported by the authors.

Data Availability Statement

The data that support the findings of this study are available at https://behindtheracquet.com/, as well as on Instagram under the handle @behindtheracquet.

Acknowledgements

We would like to thank Noah Rubin for sharing with us his inspiration behind, and steps in, creating Behind the Racquet. His platform was invaluable for the completion of this study.

References

Alvarez, M. S., Balaguer, I., Castillo, I. & Duda, J. L. (2012). The coach-created motivational climate, young athletes' well-being, and intentions to continue participation. *Journal of Clinical Sport Psychology*, *6*(2), 166–179.

Andrew, D. P., Martinez, J. M., & Flavell, S. (2016). Examining college choice among NCAA student-athletes: An exploration of gender differences. *Journal of Contemporary Athletics*, *10*(3), 201–214.

ATP (2021). *The 2021 ATP official rulebook*. https://www.atptour.com/en/corporate/rulebook

Australian Bureau of Statistics (2007). *National survey of mental health and wellbeing: Summary of results.* https://www.abs.gov.au/AUSSTATS/abs@.nsf/Lookup/4326.0Main+Features32007?OpenDocument

Battochio, R. C., Schinke, R. J., Eys, M. A., Battochio, D. L., Halliwell, W., & Tenenbaum, G. (2009). An examination of the challenges experienced by Canadian ice-hockey players in the National Hockey League. *Journal of Clinical Sport Psychology, 3*(3), 267–285.

Battochio, R. C., Stambulova, N., & Schinke, R. J. (2016). Stages and demands in the careers of Canadian National Hockey League players. *Journal of Sports Sciences, 34*(3), 278–288.

Behind the Racquet. (2021, May 13). *Behind the Racquet.* https://behindtheracquet.com/

Benson, S. G., & Dundis, S. P. (2003). Understanding and motivating health care employees: integrating Maslow's hierarchy of needs, training and technology. *Journal of Nursing Management, 11*(5), 315–320.

Berger, R. (2015). Now I see it, now I don't: Researcher's position and reflexivity in qualitative research. *Qualitative Research, 15*(2), 219–234.

Bernat, D. H., & Resnick, M. D. (2009). Connectedness in the lives of adolescents. In R. J. DiClemente, J. S. Santelli, & R. A. Crosby (Eds.), *Adolescent health: Understanding and preventing risk behaviors* (pp. 375–389). Jossey-Bass.

Braun, V., & Clarke, V. (2019). Reflecting on reflexive thematic analysis. *Qualitative Research in Sport, Exercise and Health, 11*(4), 589–597.

Braun, V., Clarke, V., & Weate, P. (2016). Using thematic analysis in sport and exercise research. In B. Smith & A. C. Sparkes (Eds.), *Routledge handbook of qualitative research in sport and exercise* (pp. 213–227). Routledge.

Brown, N. A., & Billings, A. C. (2013). Sport fans as crisis communicators on social media websites. *Public Relations Review, 39*(1), 74–81.

Clarey, C. (2019). *In tennis, men and women are united in looming prize-money fight.* The New York Times. https://www.nytimes.com/2019/10/11/sports/tennis/grand-slam-prize-money.html

Cooper, K. B., Wilson, M., & Jones, M. I. (2019). An exploratory case study of mental toughness variability and potential influencers over 30 days. *Sports, 7*(7), 156.

Cope, D. G. (2014, January). Methods and meanings: Credibility and trustworthiness of qualitative research. *Oncology Nursing Forum, 41*(1), 89–91.

Crandall, A., Powell, E. A., Bradford, G. C., Magnusson, B. M., Hanson, C. L., Barnes, M. D., Novilla, M. L. B., & Bean, R. A. (2020). Maslow's hierarchy of needs as a framework for understanding adolescent depressive symptoms over time. *Journal of Child and Family Studies,29*(2), 273–281.

DeFreese, J. D., & Smith, A. L. (2014). Athlete social support, negative social interactions, and psychological health across a competitive sport season. *Journal of Sport and Exercise Psychology,36*(6), 619–630.

Douglas, K. , & Carless, D. (2014). *Life story research in sport: Understanding the experiences of elite and professional athletes through narrative.* Routledge.

Education Policy Institute (2018). *Prevalence of mental health issues within the student-aged population.* https://epi.org.uk/publications-and-research/prevalence-of-mental-health-issues-within-the-student-aged-population/

Ess, C. and the AoIR ethics working committee (2002). Ethical decision-making and Internet Research: Recommendations from the AoIR Ethics Working Committee. http://aoir.org/reports/ethics.pdf

Foskett, R. L., & Longstaff, F. (2018). The mental health of elite athletes in the United Kingdom. *Journal of Science and Medicine in Sport*, *21*(8), 765–770.
Gorczynski, P. F., Coyle, M., & Gibson, K. (2017). Depressive symptoms in high-performance athletes and non-athletes: A comparative meta-analysis. *British Journal of Sports Medicine*, *51*(18), 1348–1354.
Gordin, R. (2016). My consulting life on the PGA tour: A 25-year experience. In R. J. Schinke, & D. Hackfort (Eds.), *Psychology in professional sports and the performing arts* (pp. 107–115). Routledge.
Gouttebarge, V., Jonkers, R., Moen, M., Verhagen, E., Wylleman, P., & Kerkhoffs, G. (2017). The prevalence and risk indicators of symptoms of common mental disorders among current and former Dutch elite athletes. *Journal of Sports Sciences*, *35*(21), 2148–2156.
Gucciardi, D. F., Hanton, S., & Fleming, S. (2017). Are mental toughness and mental health contradictory concepts in elite sport? A narrative review of theory and evidence. *Journal of Science and Medicine in Sport*, *20*(3), 307–311.
Gulliver, A., Griffiths, K. M., Mackinnon, A., Batterham, P. J., & Stanimirovic, R. (2015). The mental health of Australian elite athletes. *Journal of Science and Medicine in Sport, 18*(3), 255–261.
Hale, A. J., Ricotta, D. N., Freed, J., Smith, C. C., & Huang, G. C. (2019). Adapting Maslow's hierarchy of needs as a framework for resident wellness. *Teaching and Learning in Medicine*, *31*(1), 109–118.
Henriksen, K., Schinke, R., McCann, S., Durand-Bush, N., Moesch, K., Parham, W. D., Larsen, C. H., Cogan, K., Donaldson, A., Poczwardowski, A., Noce, F., & Hunziker, J. (2020a). Athlete mental health in the Olympic/Paralympic quadrennium: a multi-societal consensus statement. *International Journal of Sport and Exercise Psychology*, *18*(3), 391–408.
Henriksen, K., Schinke, R., Moesch, K., McCann, S., Parham, W. D., Larsen, C. H., & Terry, P. (2020b). Consensus statement on improving the mental health of high performance athletes. *International Journal of Sport and Exercise Psychology*, *18*(5), 553–560.
Homan, A. G. (2021). *The needs of Virginia tech student athletes during the transfer process*. (Master's dissertation, Virginia Tech University).
Hookway, N. (2008). Entering the blogosphere': some strategies for using blogs in social research. *Qualitative Research*, *8*(1), 91–113.
Iasiello, M., & Van Agteren, J. (2020). Mental health and/or mental illness: A scoping review of the evidence and implications of the dual-continua model of mental health. *Evidence Base: A Journal of Evidence Reviews in Key Policy Areas*, *1*, 1–45.
International Tennis Federation. (2017, March 30). *ITF pro circuit review*. https://www.itftennis.com/procircuit/about-pro-circuit/player-pathway.aspx
International Tennis Federation. (2020, January 17). *ITF World Tennis Tour by the numbers*. https://www.itftennis.com/en/news-and-media/articles/itf-world-tennis-tour-by-the-numbers/
ITF Global Tennis Report (2019). *ITF global tennis report 2019: A report on tennis participation and performance worldwide*. ITF. http://itf.uberflip.com/i/1169625-itf-global-tennis-report-2019-overview/0
Jensen, J. C. (2012). *When are you going to get a real job?: An experiential sport ethnography of players' experiences on the men's pro tennis futures tour*. [Unpublished doctoral dissertation]. Knoxville: University of Tennessee.

Jerome, N. (2013). Application of the Maslow's hierarchy of need theory; impacts and implications on organizational culture, human resource and employee's performance. *International Journal of Business and Management Invention*, *2*(3), 39–45.

Jones, P. B. (2013). Adult mental health disorders and their age at onset. *The British Journal of Psychiatry*, *202*(54), 5–10.

Kavanagh, E., Jones, I., & Sheppard-Marks, L. (2016). Towards typologies of virtual maltreatment: sport, digital cultures & dark leisure. *Leisure Studies*, *35*(6), 783–796.

Kessler, R. C., Berglund, P., Demler, O., Jin, R., Merikangas, K. R., & Walters, E. E. (2005). Lifetime prevalence and age-of-onset distributions of DSM-IV disorders in the National Comorbidity Survey Replication. *Archives of General Psychiatry*, *62*(6), 593–602.

Keyes, C. L. (2002). The mental health continuum: From languishing to flourishing in life.*Journal of Health and Social Behavior, 43*(2), 207–222.

Keyes, C. L. (2005). Mental illness and/or mental health? Investigating axioms of the complete state model of health. *Journal of Consulting and Clinical Psychology*, *73*(3), 539.

Kipp, L. E., & Weiss, M. R. (2013). Social influences, psychological need satisfaction, and well-being among female adolescent gymnasts. *Sport, Exercise, and Performance Psychology*, *2*(1), 62.

Kurtz, L. C., Trainer, S., Beresford, M., Wutich, A., & Brewis, A. (2017). Blogs as elusive ethnographic texts: Methodological and ethical challenges in qualitative online research. *International Journal of Qualitative Methods*, *16*, 1–12.

Lavallee, D., Sagar., S. S., & Spray, C. M. (2009). Coping with the effects of fear of failure: A preliminary investigation of young elite athletes. *Journal of Clinical Sport Psychology*,*3*(1), 73–98.

Mann, C., & Stewart, F. (2000). *Internet communication and qualitative research: A handbook for researching online*. Sage.

Markham, A. N., Buchanan, E. A., and the AoIR ethics working committee (2012). Ethical decision-making and Internet Research (version 2.0): Recommendations from the AoIR Ethics Working Committee. Retrieved from: http://aoir.org/reports/ethics2.pdf

Maslow, A. H. (1943). A theory of human motivation. *Psychological Review*, *50*(4), 370–396.

Maslow, A. H. (1987). *Motivation and personality* (3rd ed.). Pearson Education.

Mental Health Foundation. (2016). *Fundamental facts about mental health 2016*. https://www.mentalhealth.org/uk/sites/deafult/files/fundamental-facts-about-mental-health-2016.pdf

Milheim, K. L. (2012). Towards a better experience: Examining student needs in the online classroom through Maslow's hierarchy of needs model. *Journal of Online Learning and Teaching*, *8*(2), 159.

Moore, Z. E. (2016). Working with transnational professional athletes. In R. J. Schinke, & D. Hackfort (Eds.), *Psychology in professional sports and the performing arts* (pp. 65–76). Routledge.

Moravcsik, A. (2014). Transparency: The revolution in qualitative research. *Political Science & Politics*, *47*(1), 48–53.

Morse, J. M. (2015). Critical analysis of strategies for determining rigor in qualitative inquiry. *Qualitative Health Research, 25*(9), 1212–1222.

Nicholls, J.G. (1989). *The competitive ethos and democratic education.* Harvard University Press.

Nikitina, T. K. (2021). *Determinate factors affecting the selection process of National Junior College Athletic Association (NJCAA) Institutions by student-athletes* (Doctoral dissertation, Cleveland State University).

Osaka, N. (2021, July 8). *Naomi Osaka: "It's O.K. not to be O.K." Time.* https://time.com/6077128/naomi-osaka-essay-tokyo-olympics/

Paulhus, D. L., & Vazire, S. (2007). The self-report method. In R. W. Robins, R. C. Fraley, & R. F. Krueger (Eds.), *Handbook of research methods in personality psychology* (pp. 224–239). Guilford.

PTPA (2023). *About PTPA.* Professional Tennis Players' Association. https://ptpaplayers.com/about/

Pummell, E. K. L. (2008). *Junior to senior transition: Understanding and facilitating the process.* [Unpublished doctoral dissertation]. Loughborough University.

Reardon, C. L., Hainline, B., Aron, C. M., Baron, D., Baum, A. L., Bindra, A., Budgett, R., Campriani, N., Castadelli-Maia, J. M., Currie, A., Derevensky, J. L., Glick, I., Gorczynski, P., Gouttebarge, V., Grandner, M. A., Han, D. H., McDuff, D., Mountjoy, M., Polat, A. … & Engebretsen, L. (2019). Mental health in elite athletes: International Olympic Committee consensus statement (2019). *British Journal of Sports Medicine, 53*(11), 677–699.

Rice, S. M., Purcell, R., De Silva, S., Mawren, D., McGorry, P. D., & Parker, A. G. (2016). The mental health of elite athletes: A narrative systematic review. *Sports Medicine, 46*(9), 1333–1353.

Sagar, S. S., Lavallee, D., & Spray, C. M. (2007). Why young elite athletes fear failure: Consequences of failure. *Journal of Sports Sciences, 25*(11), 1171–1184.

Sarkar, M., & Fletcher, D. (2014). Psychological resilience in sport performers: A review of stressors and protective factors. *Journal of Sports Sciences, 32*(15), 1419–1434.

Schaal, K., Tafflet, M., Nassif, H., Thibault, V., Pichard, C., Alcotte, M., Guillet, T., El Helou, N., Berthelot, G., Simon, S., & Toussaint, J. F. (2011). Psychological balance in high level athletes: Gender-based differences and sport-specific patterns. *PLoS ONE, 6*(5), e19007.

Schinke, R. J., Bonhomme, J., McGannon, K. R., & Cummings, J. (2012). The internal adaptation processes of professional boxers during the Showtime Super Six Boxing Classic: A qualitative thematic analysis. *Psychology of Sport and Exercise, 13*(6), 830–839.

Schinke, R. J., Stambulova, N. B., Si, G., & Moore, Z. (2018). International society of sport psychology position stand: Athletes' mental health, performance, and development. *International Journal of Sport and Exercise Psychology, 16*(6), 622–639.

Seppala, E., Rossomando, T., & Doty, J. R. (2013). Social connection and compassion: Important predictors of health and well-being. *Social Research: An International Quarterly, 80*(2), 411–430.

Sheridan, D., Coffee, P., & Lavallee, D. (2014). A systematic review of social support in youth sport. *International Review of Sport and Exercise Psychology, 7*(1), 198–228.

Sievert, E. (2022). *Mental health and performance: Narratives of Swedish elite tennis players.* (Master's dissertation, Halmstad University).

Smith, B., & McGannon, K. R. (2018). Developing rigor in qualitative research: Problems and opportunities within sport and exercise psychology. *International Review of Sport and Exercise Psychology*, *11*(1), 101–121.

Smith, R. E., Smoll, F. L., & Cumming, S. P. (2007). Effects of a motivational climate intervention for coaches on young athletes' sport performance anxiety. *Journal of Sport and Exercise Psychology*, *29*(1), 39–59.

Snee, H. (2013). Making ethical decisions in an online context: Reflections on using blogs to explore narratives of experience. *Methodological Innovations Online*, *8*(2), 52–67.

Sparkes, A. C., & Smith, B. (2014). *Qualitative research methods in sport, exercise and health: From process to product*. Routledge.

Tay, L., & Diener, E. (2011). Needs and subjective well-being around the world. *Journal of Personality and Social Psychology*, *101*(2), 354–365.

Uphill, M., Sly, D., & Swain, J. (2016). From mental health to mental wealth in athletes: Looking back and moving forward. *Frontiers in Psychology*, *7*, 935.

Wadsworth, M. E., Rindlaub, L., Hurwich-Reiss, E., Rienks, S., Bianco, H., & Markman, H. J. (2013). A longitudinal examination of the adaptation to poverty-related stress model: predicting child and adolescent adjustment over time. *Journal of Clinical Child & Adolescent Psychology*, *42*, 713–725.

Way, C., & Way, M. (Directors). (2021). *Untold: Breaking point.* [Film]. Netflix.

Webb, M. (Director). (2023). *Break Point* [Film]. Netflix.

Wilkinson, D., & Thelwall, M. (2011). Researching personal information on the public web: Methods and ethics. *Social Science Computer Review*, *29*(4), 387–401.

Wilson, E., Kenny, A., & Dickson-Swift, V. (2015). Using blogs as a qualitative health research tool: a scoping review.*International Journal of Qualitative Methods*, *14*(5), 1609406915618049.

WTA (2021). *WTA 2021 official rulebook*. https://photoresources.wtatennis.com/wta/document/2021/03/08/d6d2c650-e3b4-42e7-ab2b-e539d4586033/2021Rulebook.pdf

Yin, R. K. (2017). *Case study research and applications: Design and methods*. Sage.

11

THE ASSOCIATION AND MECHANISMS BETWEEN MINDFULNESS AND MENTAL HEALTH OUTCOMES IN ATHLETES

Testing Self-Determination Theory

Stephen Shannon, Donncha Hanna, Gerry Leavey, Tandy Haughey, Drew Neill, and Gavin Breslin

Background

Well-being is one dimension of a two continua model of mental health (Keyes, 2005), defined as a state of optimal functioning (Ryan & Deci, 2017) characterised by psychological (e.g., a sense of purpose, realising one's potential), emotional (i.e., positive affective states, reduced negative affect) and social (i.e., relationships) dimensions. High well-being reliably produces positive mental health states (e.g., flourishing) (Keyes, 2005) and reduces incidences of mental illness (Huppert, 2009). In contrast, stress arises when perceived demands on an individual exceed their personal resources and capacity to cope (Steptoe, 1997) and is inversely related to well-being (Gu et al., 2015). A recent systematic review (Kegelaers et al., 2022) established that the student-athlete (or collegiate athlete) populations are at risk of experiencing multiple, coexisting, sporting, academic and social stressors (discussed below), and subsequent mental health issues (Gavrilova et al., 2017). Indeed, student-athletes demonstrate a higher clinical and sub-clinical risk for behavioural issues than non-athletes (e.g., substance misuse, eating disorders, gambling; Moreland et al., 2017), and most data indicate that student-athletes are at least as likely as non-athletes, or in some cases more likely, to experience mood disorders (Donohue et al., 2018). As such, consensus statements have outlined that innovative approaches to mental health promotion are required for the athlete population (Breslin et al., 2019; Moesch et al., 2018; Schinke et al., 2018; Vella et al., 2021).

Student-athletes' experience of co-existing academic, social and sporting demands may relate to living away from home, undergoing academic assessment expectations, financial stressors and uncertain career prospects

DOI: 10.4324/9781003459750-11

(Pitt et al., 2017; Sudano et al., 2017), whilst concurrently managing the pressures of demanding sporting participation and employment. The mental health strain of managing such pressures was highlighted in a recent review focusing on Dual Careers (DC) in student-athletes (Kegelaers et al., 2022). Indeed, surveys indicate that sport competition demands (e.g., physical and technical preparation) negatively impact upon student-athletes' social life and relationships (Pritchard, 2005), with some equating sporting participation to working in two full-time jobs (Bennett, 2007). As such, through feeling pressure to perform in both academic and sporting pursuits, student-athletes report having a constrained social life and relationship difficulties (Abedalhafiz et al., 2010; Gavrilova et al., 2017). Furthermore, due to the physical and often aggressive nature of sport, student-athletes are likely to sustain injury, and experience emotional and physical fatigue from competition and over-training (Putukian, 2016). When not managed appropriately, the presence of such multifaceted stressors can result in impaired functioning and maladaptive coping (e.g., gambling, substance misuse) (Moreland et al., 2017). As such, a recommended framework for improving mental health care in student-athletes (see, Kegelaers et al., 2022) suggests mental health self-management strategies can partly help address the above concerning evidence.

Mental health self-management is a concept consistent with recent updated definitions of mental health literacy, shifting attention away from the disorder-focused model to a positive health asset model, emphasising personal understanding of how to obtain and maintain good mental health (Sampaio et al., 2022). Mental health self-management has been defined as an ability to self-monitor how one's mental health is impacting upon personal functioning, and use of strategies that protect and promote mental health (Shannon et al., 2019; Wolf, 1996). However, many student-athletes report that they do not have the awareness and knowledge required to self-manage mental health (Eisenberg et al., 2007; Hunt & Eisenberg, 2010). One self-management intervention that is receiving increasing cultural support among athletes is mindfulness (Noetel et al., 2017; Anderson et al., 2021). Mindfulness is defined by Brown and Ryan (2003) as being attentive to, and aware of, present events and experiences. The benefits of mindfulness to mental health are diverse (Creswell, 2017), with a variety of interventions helping individuals alleviate depression and anxiety symptoms, and improve emotional well-being (Chiesa & Serretti, 2011; Creswell, 2017; Keng et al., 2011). Mindfulness may also help individuals direct motivations and intentions into health behaviour change (Chatzisarantis & Hagger, 2007).

Mindfulness is increasingly being used in sport psychology (Noetel et al., 2017) largely on the basis that mindfulness may improve sport-related mental states among athletes (e.g., reducing performance anxiety, improving flow) (Sappington & Longshore, 2015), thereby improving skills and performance.

However, despite the advent of several recent position and consensus statements on athlete mental health (Breslin et al., 2019; Moesch et al., 2018; Reardon et al., 2019; Schinke et al., 2018), several systematic reviews with the exception of Prior et al. (2022) have established that mindfulness studies in sport have focused on performance-related outcomes, with fewer centred on mental health (Noetel et al., 2017; Sampaio et al., 2022). Furthermore, of the few mental health studies that have been conducted (e.g., Vidic et al., 2017; Mohammed et al., 2018), there has been limited attention to the precise mechanisms driving the effects of mindfulness on mental health outcomes.

To ascertain how mindfulness may relate to improved mental health, theoretical constructs can be modelled to study the indirect effect of a predictor variable (X) on an outcome (Y) through one or more mediating variables (M) (Kok et al., 2004). Through Self-Determination Theory (SDT), Ryan and Deci (2000) contend that satisfaction of one's innate psychological need for autonomy is an essential requirement for optimal well-being. Autonomy satisfaction is defined as experiencing volitional actions/beliefs that are self-endorsed (Ryan & Deci, 2000). Research indicates that autonomy satisfaction is related to mental health outcomes and self-management behaviours (Ryan & Deci, 2017). Whilst SDT's other core psychological needs of competence (i.e., sense of effectiveness) and relatedness (i.e., sense of belonging) needs satisfaction are relevant to mental health self-management (Wolf, 1996), autonomy satisfaction has particular theoretical alignment, such that when one's need for autonomy is satisfied, one may experience a sense of personal volition regarding their selection of mental health-related behaviours (e.g., help-seeking, relaxation), through to endorsing values (e.g., importance of mental health) at a high level of awareness (Ryan & Deci, 2017). From an SDT perspective, it is well established that socio-environmental support can facilitate psychological needs satisfaction. Yet, mindfulness is also viewed as an internal support mechanism that individuals can avail of to satisfy basic needs such as autonomy (Ryan & Deci, 2017; Weinstein & Ryan, 2011), yet such hypotheses lack comprehensive empirical inquiry.

In SDT it is proposed that autonomy satisfaction can be supported by mindfulness, insofar as mindful states provide individuals with a greater awareness of ongoing events and subsequent purposeful selection of need-satisfying experiences (Campbell et al., 2015, 2017) that is consistent with one's values, motives and interest (Brown & Ryan, 2003; Schultz et al., 2014). In contrast, less mindful individuals are assumed to have a reduced capacity to satisfy their need for autonomy and self-regulate their actions, making them more reactive or impulsive, especially under controlled environmental conditions, resulting in subsequent needs frustration (Brown et al., 2007). Scant research has examined the association with mindfulness and autonomy satisfaction, however (Parto & Besharat, 2011), with only one study to our knowledge among athletes (Chang et al., 2018). Both aforementioned studies supported the mechanism that autonomy satisfaction partially mediated the relationship between mindfulness with psychological well-being. However, with replication being a cornerstone of the scientific method in prevention science (Valentine et al., 2011), further research is required to determine sufficient rigour in the understanding of the mindfulness and mental health relationship. Furthermore, those studies included a sample of 717 seventeen-year-old at-risk students not involved in competitive sport (Parto & Besharat, 2011), or among Eastern athletes (Chang et al., 2018) which raises the methodological issue of extrapolation of the data to Western athletes (Schumacker, 2004), particularly given the cultural prevalence and relevance of meditative practices in Eastern populations, that is not as evident in Western populations (Creswell, 2017). Furthermore, stress which is a significant factor implicated in mental health (Gu et al., 2015; Huppert, 2009), particularly in student-athlete mental health (Kegelaers et al., 2022) has yet to be studied in current SDT research on mindfulness, suggesting a gap in current theoretical understanding.

Hence, in response to recent consensus statements (Breslin et al., 2019; Schinke et al., 2018) and systematic reviews (Breslin et al., 2022) that innovative and theoretically driven approaches are required for athlete mental health promotion, the present study sought to understand the role of mindfulness in promoting well-being and reducing stress among student-athletes, through the mediating role of autonomy satisfaction. The findings will contribute to theoretical advancement of SDT, and towards evidence-based recommendations for mental health promotion among the student-athlete population.

Study Hypotheses

In accordance with SDT hypotheses (Ryan & Deci, 2000; see Figure 11.1) and extant mindfulness research applying SDT (Chang et al., 2018), two models were tested assessing (1) well-being, and (2) stress as dependent variables (Y), with mindfulness as the independent variable (X) and autonomy satisfaction (M), as the mediating variable.

In Model 1, mindfulness was hypothesised to directly and positively predict well-being (Hypothesis 1; H1a) and autonomy satisfaction (Hypothesis 2; H2). Autonomy satisfaction was also hypothesised to directly and positively predict well-being (Hypothesis 3; H3). Given mindfulness may exert a direct and indirect link to well-being through a variety of biopsychosocial self-regulatory mechanisms (Brown et al., 2007; Brown & Ryan, 2003; Gu et al., 2015), the link between mindfulness and well-being was hypothesised to be partially, rather than fully mediated through autonomy satisfaction (Hypothesis 4; H4a). In Model 2, all of the above hypotheses were repeated (H1b, H2, H3, H4b), replacing well-being with stress as the dependent

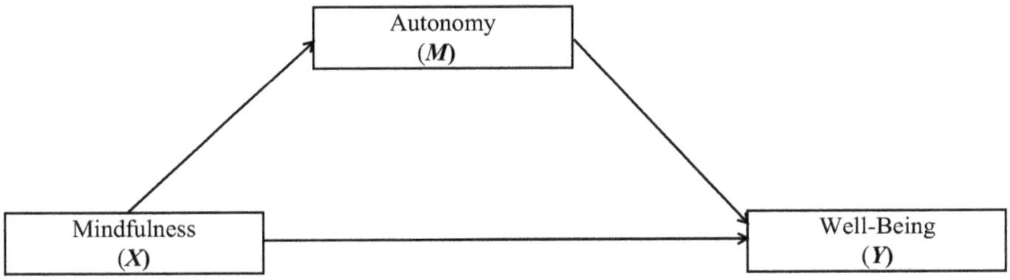

FIGURE 11.1 Multivariate regression model assessing direct and indirect effects of mindfulness (X) on well-being/stress (Y) through autonomy (M). Note: H4 refers to the indirect effect of mindfulness (X) on well-being/stress (Y) through autonomy (M); each relationship predicting stress is hypothesised to be negative.

variable, and each of the relationships predicting stress was hypothesised to be negative.

Method

Study Design, Size, Setting and Participants

The Strengthening the Reporting of Observational Studies in Epidemiology (STROBE) guidelines were adopted (see von Elm et al., 2007). Ethical approval was granted from Ulster University. Data collection was conducted through online Survey-Monkey software. Inclusion criteria were based on student-athletes reporting "yes" to the following question consistent with the definition of sport, "Are you an athlete involved in a structured, competitive physical activity?" (Rejeski & Brawley, 1988).

Variables and Measurement

Demographic Variables

Two hundred and forty student-athletes took part. The mean age of the sample was 20.50 years (SD = 3.29), 57.3% were males and 42.7% were females. A broad range of sports were represented in the sample, with the most common being Irish Gaelic Sports (42%), Football (soccer) (22.5%), Rugby (5.8%), Hockey (5.1%), Basketball (3.6%), Netball (2.9%), Irish Dancing (2.9%), and other sports (15.2%; e.g., Athletics, Combat, Rowing).

Mindfulness

The Mindfulness Attention Awareness Scale (MAAS; Brown & Ryan, 2003) was used to measure mindfulness disposition. The MAAS is a 15-item scale constructed through a uni-dimensional factor, designed to assess an individual's attention to, and awareness of, day-to-day internal and external experiences. An example item is "I could be experiencing some emotion and not be conscious of it until some-time later." A 6-point Likert scale scoring method ranging from "almost always" (1), to "almost never" (6) is used, wherein higher scores reflect higher mindfulness. Several studies have demonstrated the validity and reliability of the MAAS, including support for a unidimensional factor structure (Brown & Ryan, 2003; MacKillop & Anderson, 2007), including those in sport with athlete samples (Araya-Vargas et al., 2009). Cronbach's alpha within the present sample = .88.

Autonomy Satisfaction

The Perceived Choice and Awareness of Self Scale (PCASS), or as formerly labelled the "Self-Determination Scale" (Sheldon et al., 1996), was used to measure autonomy satisfaction, specifically to the degree of volition one experiences over their behaviour and sense of self. The PCASS is a 10-item measure with items scored on a 5-point Likert scale on a structured alternative format. Participants selected if "only A feels true" (1 point) through to "only B feels true" (5 points). PCASS is a valid and reliable measure of autonomy satisfaction (Sheldon et al., 1996; Thrash & Elliot, 2002). An example item includes: "A. I always feel like I choose the things I do," or "B. I sometimes feel that it's not really me choosing the things I do." The PCASS has been psychometrically tested with athletic populations (Mouratidis & Michou, 2011). Cronbach's alpha within the present sample = .82.

Well-Being

The Warwick-Edinburgh Mental Well-Being Scale (WEMWBS; Tennant et al., 2007) was used to assess student-athletes' levels of well-being. The WEMWBS is a valid and reliable tool for measuring well-being (Stewart-Brown et al., 2011; Tennant et al., 2007), and has been used extensively in athletic populations (Appelqvist-Schmidlechner et al., 2018). Cronbach's alpha analysis yielded .90 within the present sample. The measure comprises 14 items through a uni-dimensional factor structure, with statements designed to measure both hedonic (e.g., happiness and life satisfaction), social (i.e., relationships) and eudemonic (i.e., self-actualisation) well-being components. Each item is positively worded and scored on a 5-point Likert scale ranging from "none of the time" (1), to "all of the time" (5). Total scores can range from 14 through to 70, with higher scores indicating higher well-being. Previous research (Fat et al., 2017) has established three well-being profiles from the measure scores, including "low" (i.e., 14–42), "medium" (i.e., 43–60) and "high" (i.e., 61–70).

Stress

The Perceived Stress Scale (PSS; Cohen et al., 1994) was used to measure student-athlete's appraisal of stress in day-to-day experiences. The PCSS is constructed through a uni-dimensional factor, and includes 10 items, each scored on a 5-point Likert scale ranging from 0 "never" to 4 "very often." The PCSS demonstrates excellent psychometric properties across a range of samples including students (Lee, 2012; Roberti, Harrington, & Storch, 2006). The PSS has been tested in mindfulness intervention studies with athletes (Vidic et al., 2017), and Cronbach's alpha was high (.83) within the present sample. Scoring methodology for the PCSS (Cohen et al., 1994) indicates a uni-dimensional structure, with a total score reflecting stress levels, and lower scores indicate less stress.

Statistical Methods and Bias

Data Management

Raw scores were transferred into Statistical Package for Social Sciences (SPSS version 22). Two researchers inspected the data set for outliers. For each scale, Little's Missing Completely at Random (MCAR; Little, 1988) was conducted to determine if missing data were in random order. MCAR analyses revealed the data was indeed missing at random ($p > .05$), with missing responses ranging between 2% and 5%. Subsequently, the Expectation Maximisation (EM) algorithm was conducted on each individual scale, using inter-correlated items for estimating missing values (Field, 2013).

Data Analyses

Descriptive statistics were calculated for each scale, with total mean scores and standard deviations produced. A correlation matrix was produced for each of the outcome variables. Low, moderate and high well-being profiles were created based on the scoring methodology for the WEMWBS (Tennant et al., 2007).

Hayes et al.'s (2017) PROCESS macro for SPSS was used to test the study hypotheses (see Figure 11.1). To produce standardised beta coefficient (β) values, all variables were standardised as z-scores. In Model 1, mindfulness was specified as the independent variable (X), and regressed onto autonomy satisfaction (M) and well-being (dependent variable; Y). In Model 2, stress replaced well-being as the dependent variable (Y; depicted in Figure 11.1). To examine indirect relationships, a bootstrapping technique was conducted with 5000 samples to improve model accuracy and parameter estimate reliabilities (Byrne, 2001). Results show if the relationship between X and Y is (i) non-significant; (ii) direct with non-mediation (i.e mediator does not influence relationship); (iii) fully meditated (i.e., direct effect is no longer significant after controlling for mediators' effect); (iv) partially mediated (i.e., direct effect is

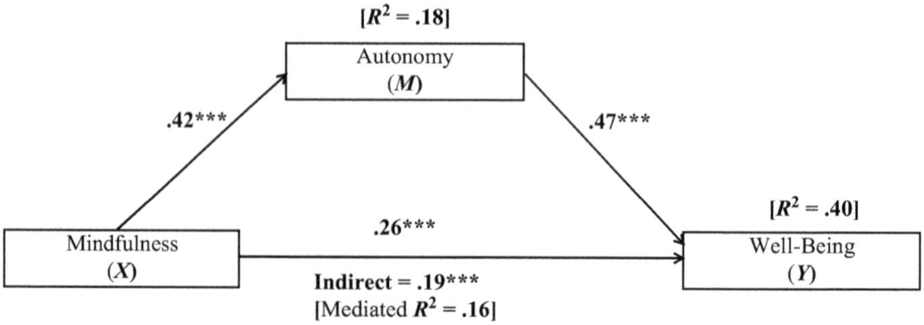

FIGURE 11.2 Model 1 showing the effect of mindfulness (X) on well-being (Y) through autonomy satisfaction (M). Note: *= p < .05; **= p < .01; ***= p < .001.

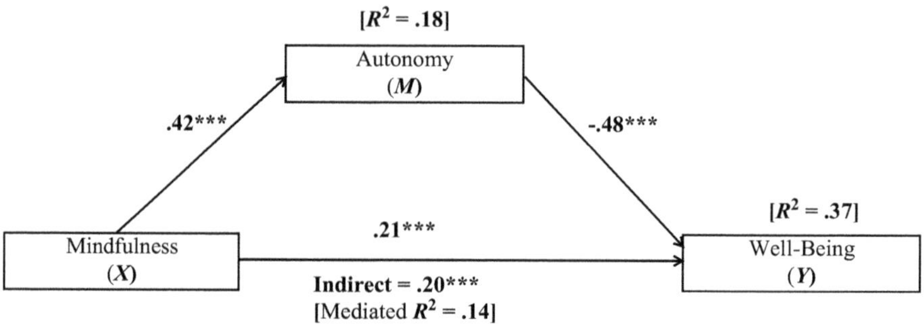

FIGURE 11.3 Model 2 showing the effect of mindfulness (X) on stress (Y), through autonomy satisfaction (M).

significant alongside an indirect effect) or, (v) indirect (i.e., no direct effect, but significant indirect effects: Hayes, 2009). Associations between the variables were determined statistically significant ($p < .05$) on the basis of confidence intervals not crossing zero (Field, 2013). Two figures were produced to visually illustrate Models 1 and 2 (see Figures 11.2 and 11.3 respectively), including completely standardised beta (β) coefficient values for each direct path, and R^2 values for proportion of total predicted variance in the model on the dependent variable, mediators and the R^2 mediated effect size.

Results

Outcome Data

Mean scores and standard deviations for psychometric scales are presented in Table 11.1. Categorisation of the sample based on well-being scores showed that 35% of student-athletes scored low, 62% medium and 3% high.

TABLE 11.1 Correlation matrix, Cronbach's alpha (α) internal consistency values, mean scores and standard deviations (SD) for the study outcomes

Variable				
Mindfulness	1			
Autonomy	.42*	1		
Well-being	.47*	.58*	1	
Stress	−.42*	−.57*	−.72*	1
Cronbach's α	.88	.82	.90	.83
Sample M (SD)	54.91 (11.95)	37.32 (7.31)	44.63 (7.73)	18.13 (.36)

Note: standard deviations in brackets.*Statistical significance at p <.001.

Main Results

Model 1: Well-Being as the Dependent Variable

Results from Model 1 indicated that mindfulness (X) significantly and directly predicted autonomy satisfaction (M; $\beta = .42$, $p< .001$, 95% CI's = [.304 to .506]; $R^2 = .18$), and well-being (Y; β = .26, p< .001, 95% CI's = [.158 to .377]), supporting H1a and H2. In support of H3, autonomy satisfaction also directly and positively predicted well-being (Y; β = .47, p< .001, 95% CI's = [.361 to .580]). When exploring the indirect relationship between mindfulness and well-being through autonomy satisfaction, analyses revealed that while the direct relationship remained significant, indirect associations were also present, suggesting partial mediation through autonomy satisfaction. Specifically, and in support for H4a, mindfulness (X) in sequence with autonomy satisfaction (M) resulted in a significant indirect association with well-being (Y; β = .19, 95% CI's = [.120 to .289]), and an R^2 mediated effect size of .16. Factoring in all of the variables in Model 1 resulted in a significant pro- portion of variance predicted for well-being ($R^2 = .40$). See Figure 11.2 for a visual description of Model 1, including specific β coefficients for significant paths.

Model 2: Stress as the Dependent Variable

Results from Model 2 were aligned with Model 1, to the extent that mindfulness (X) significantly and directly positively predicted autonomy satisfaction (M; β = .42, p < .001, 95% CI's = [.304 to .506]; $R^2 = .18$), and in this case, negatively predicted stress (Y; β =−.21, p< .001, 95% CI's = [−.330 to −.105]), supporting H1b and H2. Autonomy satisfaction also directly and negatively predicted stress (Y; β = −.48, p< .001, 95% CI's= −.594 to −.370), supporting H3. When exploring H4b, specifically regarding the indirect association between mindfulness and stress through autonomy satisfaction, analyses revealed partial mediation. Specifically, the direct path remained significant, but mindfulness (X) in sequence with autonomy satisfaction (M) resulted in a significant indirect association with stress ($\beta = -.20$, $p < .001$, 95% CI's = [−.282 to −.141]), and an R^2 mediated effect size of .14. Factoring in all of the variables in Model 2 resulted in a significant proportion of variance predicted for stress ($R^2 = .36$). See Figure 11.3 for a visual description of Model 2, including specific beta coefficients for significant paths.

Model 2: Stress as the Dependent Variable

Results from Model 2 were aligned with Model 1, to the extent that mindfulness (X) significantly and directly positively predicted autonomy satisfaction (M; $\beta = .42$, $p < .001$, 95% CI's = [.304 to .506]; $R^2 = .18$), and in this case, negatively predicted stress (Y; $\beta = -.21$, $p < .001$, 95% CI's = [−.330 to −.105]), supporting H1b and H2. Autonomy satisfaction also directly and negatively predicted stress (Y; $\beta = -.48$, $p < .001$, 95% CI's= −.594 to −.370), supporting H3. When exploring H4b, specifically regarding the indirect association between mindfulness and stress through autonomy satisfaction, analyses revealed partial mediation. Specifically, the direct path remained significant, but mindfulness (X) in sequence with autonomy satisfaction (M) resulted in a significant indirect association with stress ($\beta = -.20$, $p < .001$, 95% CI's = [−.282 to −.141]), and an R^2 mediated effect size of .14. Factoring in all of the variables in Model 2 resulted in a significant proportion of variance predicted for stress ($R^2 = .36$). See Figure 11.3 for a visual description of Model 2, including specific beta coefficients for significant paths.

Discussion

This study was in response to calls that theoretically driven research is needed for improved understanding of athlete mental health (Breslin & Leavey, 2019; Moesch et al., 2018; Schinke et al., 2018), with a focus on student-athletes who report high levels of stress and difficulty managing multiple co-existing sporting, academic and personal demands (Kegelaers et al., 2022). As such, mindfulness was examined as a predictor of mental health outcomes including stress and well-being, with autonomy satisfaction derived from SDT (Ryan & Deci, 2000) used as a theoretical lens to understand the underlying mechanisms between mindfulness and mental health.

As one of the pioneering mindfulness studies to incorporate SDT (Ryan & Deci, 2000) among a student-athlete population at risk of mental health challenges (Shannon, Hanna et al., 2019), our study makes a number of contributions to the literature, specifically through examining the indirect mechanisms driving the salutary associations between mindfulness and mental health (Creswell, 2017). Overall, a significant proportion of variance was explained in both models (Model 1: R^2 = .40; Model 2: R^2 = .37), with results supporting the study hypotheses. Specifically, mindfulness predicted well-being and stress (H1a,b), autonomy satisfaction (H2); autonomy satisfaction predicted well-being and stress (H3); and autonomy satisfaction partially mediated the association between mindfulness and the mental health outcomes of well-being and stress (H4a,b). Taken collectively, the findings are of theoretical value to understanding the mechanisms of mental health promotion through mindfulness and are now discussed in relation to practical and theoretical considerations in further work.

As well-being is a key dimension of mental health (Keyes, 2002), it was notable that descriptive statistics showed that just 3% of the sample scored high, in contrast to the 35% that scored low and 62% at medium in the WEMWBS (Tennant et al., 2007). To provide context to these figures, comparisons with a UK sample (n = 27,169) using the same measures (Fat et al., 2017), suggest lower well-being among student-athletes than the general population who scored 15% (low), 71% (medium), and 14% (high). The significant proportion of the student-athletes (35%) reporting low well-being is of concern, particularly given that low well-being increases likelihood of mental illnesses (Huppert, 2009; Keyes, 2005). Likewise, on average student-athletes reported higher stress levels (M: 18.13) than various demographic groups in a sample based in the United States (US; Cohen & Janicki-Deverts, 2012), including those in unemployment (M: 16.46). As such, it was of initial primary empirical value to test predictors of well-being and stress.

Results of Model 1 and Model 2 showed that mindfulness directly predicted well-being and stress (H1a,b). Given that the direct effects of mindfulness on well-being and stress remained significant in the model after accounting for the mediating influence of autonomy satisfaction, i.e., partial rather than full mediation (discussed below), mindfulness may have unique associations with mental health beyond psychological needs satisfaction. For example, there are proposals that mindfulness improves somatic experiences and reduces inflammatory markers which lead to greater positive effect, and less negative effect (Brown et al., 2007; Hölzel et al., 2011), and mindfulness results in better cognitive appraisal and reductions in rumination (Gu et al., 2015). Moreover, mindfulness may increase one's likelihood to convert intentions into health behaviours that promote well-being such as physical activity (Chatzisarantis & Hagger, 2007).

Most relevant to our findings however, as the mindfulness construct has been shown to mediate effects of mindfulness programmes on mental health outcomes (Gu et al., 2015), it is worth aiming to effectively engage athletes with regular mindfulness practices to improve mindfulness disposition. Such provision may be better received and deemed acceptable and attractive when athletes feel the mindfulness intervention is sensitive to the nuances of sports culture, and endorsed by athletes, coaches, and prominent providers (Gavrilova et al., 2017), and mindfulness is deemed a skill that is first learnt, then regularly practised, so the benefits accrue accumulatively over time (Myall et al., 2023). Examples can be seen in the Mindfulness-Acceptance-Commitment Programme (MACP; Gardner & Moore, 2004), which has been linked with both positive sporting-related performance and mental health outcomes (Gardner & Moore, 2007; Gross et al., 2018; Perry et al., 2017; Zhang et al., 2016). Beyond the aforesaid direct associations between mindfulness and mental health outcomes, the present study sought to delve further into the mechanisms driving the salutary role of mindfulness.

Specifically, results of Model 1 and Model 2 showed that mindfulness directly and positively predicted autonomy satisfaction (H2). These findings lend support to the view that beyond interpersonal factors, mindfulness can act as a mechanism from within which may satisfy one's innate psychological need for autonomy (Ryan & Deci, 2017; Schultz et al., 2014). Specifically, the data support the hypotheses that mindfulness may facilitate a mental state that is attentive to the present, which helps individuals remain reflective of ongoing internal (e.g., strong emotions) and external (e.g., demanding tasks) prompts. Subsequently, athletes may be able to make dispassionate, autonomy-satisfying decisions during demanding and stressful experiences (Campbell et al., 2015, 2017). For example, a coach may demand that their team behave unethically during a sporting competition in order to intimidate/distract other competitors, despite such behaviour being inconsistent with many of the individual team members' autonomous values. Importantly, Schultz et al. (2014) have outlined that in these cases, mindful and less mindful athletes within the team will experience similar levels of autonomy frustration, however, the more mindful athlete will be more resilient to the control over their autonomy and self-regulate their behaviours accordingly. Furthermore, and specific to the student-athlete population, a holistic developmental perspective suggests that stressors experienced in sporting, academic, social and employment domains often reciprocally influence functioning in other life domains (Wylleman & Rosier, 2016; Wylleman 2019). Therefore, cultivating mindfulness through meditative practices may have value in increasing the likelihood of adaptive responses to the multiple stressors faced by student-athletes (Gross et al., 2018).

Mindfulness can be enhanced during short (Rosenkranz et al., 2019) and longer-term (Cayoun, 2011; Creswell, 2017) interventions, and therefore basic to intensive intervention involvement with athletes is welcomed for improving autonomy fulfilment. However, while most SDT theorists propose that the mindfulness construct precedes autonomy satisfaction, in addition to competence and relatedness satisfaction (e.g., Brown et al., 2007; Schultz et al., 2014), it is worth raising the point that, in a temporal sense, the relationship between mindfulness and needs satisfaction has been mixed. For instance, some authors (Olafsen, 2017; Shannon, Hanna, et al., 2019) have found empirical support for needs satisfaction preceding the mindfulness construct, and thus may produce the energy to enable one to focus on the present. Whereas, others suggest that mindfulness is the precursor to needs satisfaction (Chang et al., 2018; Schultz et al., 2014). The cross-sectional nature of the present research study permits testing the temporal order of these events, and therefore, future longitudinal intervention studies may consider this open question, which is of theoretical value.

Models 1 and 2 demonstrated that autonomy satisfaction positively predicted well-being, and negatively predicted stress (H3). The data, therefore, supports SDT hypotheses (Ryan & Deci, 2000), and a cogent body of research that autonomy satisfaction is robustly related to positive mental health (Sheehan et al., 2018; Shannon et al., 2023). While the present study supports the view that mindfulness be explored as a potential facilitator of autonomy satisfaction (Ryan & Deci, 2017), the multitude of interpersonal factors influencing student-athletes' sense of autonomy satisfaction should not be discounted. For example, the provision of input into sporting, social and academic matters by coaches (Ntoumanis et al., 2017), peers (Moreland et al., 2017) and university tutors (Pitt et al., 2017) may be as significant, or indeed more so, as mindfulness to student-athletes basic needs fulfilment. Thus, both intra and interpersonal support mechanisms should be considered in the context of mental health provision for student-athletes.

The mediating role exerted by autonomy satisfaction in the mindfulness and well-being and stress relationship (H4a,b) supports the SDT perspective (Brown & Ryan, 2003; Weinstein & Ryan, 2011) and empirical evidence (Chang et al., 2018; Chang et al., 2015) that the fulfilment of basic psychological needs can mediate the effects of mindfulness on mental health outcomes. Examined through the lens of eudemonic (e.g., realising one's potential), emotional (i.e., positive affective states, reduced negative affect) and social (i.e., relationships) well-being dimensions, through mindfulness an athlete may be, for example, more capable of recognising injury and ill-being symptoms stemming from their sporting participation (Gustafsson et al., 2015). In this example, an athlete might experience ongoing pressures from their coaching staff to continue training and competing under injury. However, the more mindful athlete may understand such attempts to control their autonomy, and instead, decide to seek medical attention based upon the best interests of their mental and physical health, and sporting performance (Gross et al., 2018). Being better informed and reflective to such somatic information has been shown to prevent ill-being, and promote longer-term wellness (Creswell, 2017). In contrast, with acting without mindfulness, an athlete may continue competing through painful injury, and despite achieving short-term introjected approval, struggle with the negative long-term effects on their health and sporting participation, sometimes resulting in burnout and withdrawal from their sport (Gustafsson et al., 2015).

Lastly, the present study was the first among athletes to evidence that autonomy satisfaction mediated the relationship between mindfulness and stress (H4b). In a practical sense, when student-athletes develop improved awareness through mindfulness, this may reduce stress through self-regulation, such that attention can be directed to behaviours and coping mechanisms that fulfil their needs, values and interests (Brown & Ryan, 2003). For example, athletes could draw upon mindfulness to satisfy their autonomy in social contexts that are controlling and stressful in nature, wherein peers may provoke them to display values (e.g., hedonistic) and behaviours (e.g., drug use) inconsistent with their basic need for autonomy (Reb et al., 2015). Given mindfulness is characterised by a non-judgmental and open attention to the present, such athletes may be less likely to introject external values, or ruminate over whether to engage with approval-seeking behaviours (Creswell et al., 2007; Weinstein et al., 2009).

The key contribution of the current study was the integration of SDT (Ryan & Deci, 2000) into a predictive model of student-athletes mindfulness and mental health, who remain an understudied sporting population at-risk of mental health challenges (Shannon, Breslin, et al., 2019). The findings provide several theoretical and practical considerations. For instance, the link found between mindfulness and mental health outcomes indicates that practitioners may consider a proactive attempt to engage athletes with mindfulness interventions, whilst also paying attention to the remaining open questions regarding access and potential risks (see Creswell, 2017). Further, as autonomy satisfaction was found to mediate the association between mindfulness and well-being and stress, further research may consider integrating components of SDT into a mindfulness intervention to help determine the precise mechanisms of well-being promotion through mindfulness. Such work may consider assessing the temporal order of the mindfulness-needs satisfaction relationship, and be rigorously tested through a longitudinal, controlled study design. Despite these contributions, our study is not without its limitations. One limitation was that we could not infer causality from the data because of the cross-sectional design, and additional SDT components (i.e., competence and relatedness satisfaction) were absent from the models. A future recommendation is that studies adopt a longitudinal experimental design with additional SDT components that consider these limitations.

To conclude, recent position statements (Breslin et al., 2019; Moesch et al., 2018; Schinke et al., 2018) have indicated that theoretically-driven mental health research is needed among athletes. Therefore, the present study assessed the role of mindfulness in predicting well-being and stress in student-athletes through autonomy satisfaction, an innate psychological need according to SDT. Study hypotheses were supported, and the findings have led us to suggest that more mindful student-athletes may act with an awareness which may reduce stress and improve well-being through mechanisms reflective of autonomy satisfaction. To this end, mindful student-athletes may have a greater volitional capacity, in the sense that their attention can be directed to behaviours and coping mechanisms during times of stress, that can fulfil their needs, which may ultimately result in positive mental health (Brown & Ryan, 2003). As such, attempts to engage athletes with mindfulness interventions may be considered, with caution to be given to the remaining open questions regarding accessibility and adherence (Creswell, 2017) that in some cases the challenges of uptake and maintenance of mindfulness exercise (Shannon, Hanna et al., 2019). From a theoretical, practical and research standpoint, SDT may be considered in the design and evaluation of mindfulness interventions, in which researchers may consider employing a longitudinal controlled research design.

Disclosure Statement

All authors declare no conflict of interest. This research adhered to the ethical principles of the Declaration of Helsinki. All participants provided informed consent prior to their involvement in the study.

Acknowledgements

We would like to acknowledge the contribution of the student-athletes who participated in the study, and Caoimhín Ó Seanáin for his help in proofreading the chapter. We would also like to acknowledge the late Dr Martin Lawlor, co-founder of the State of Mind Ireland Programme and advocate for mental health.

References

Abedalhafiz, A., Altahayneh, Z., & Al-Haliq, M. (2010). Sources of stress and coping styles among student-athletes in Jordan universities. *Procedia-Social and Behavioral Sciences*, *5*, 1911–1917.

Appelqvist-Schmidlechner, K., Vaara, J., Häkkinen, A., Vasankari, T., Mäkinen, J., Mäntysaari, M., & Kyröläinen, H. (2018). Relationships between youth sports participation and mental health in young adulthood among Finnish males. *American Journal of Health Promotion, 32*(7), 1502–1509.

Anderson, S. A., Haraldsdottir, K., & Watson, D. (2021). Mindfulness in athletes. *Current Sports Medicine Reports*, *20*(12), 655–660.

Araya-Vargas, G. A., Gapper-Morrow, S., Moncada-Jiménez, J., & Buckworth, J. (2009). Translation and cross-cultural validation of the Spanish version of the mindful awareness attention scale (MAAS): An exploratory analysis and potential

applications to exercise psychology, sport and health. *International Journal of Applied Sports Sciences, 21*(1), 94–114.
Bennett, G. (2007). The role of a clinical psychologist in a Division I athletics program. *Journal of Clinical Sport Psychology*, *1*(3), 261–269.
Breslin, G., & Leavey, G. (2019). *Mental health and well-being interventions in sport: Research, theory and practice*. London: Routledge.
Breslin, G., Shannon, S., Cummings, M., & Leavey, G. (2022). An updated systematic review of interventions to increase awareness of mental health and well-being in athletes, coaches, officials and parents. *Systematic Reviews, 11*(1), 1–29.
Breslin, G., Smith, A., Donohue, B., Donnelly, P., Shannon, S., Haughey, T., & Leavey, G. (2019). Consensus statement on psychosocial and policy-related approaches to mental health awareness programmes in sport. *BMJ Open Sport and Exercise Medicine*, *5*(1), e000585. 10.1136/bmjsem-2019-000585.
Brown, K. W., & Ryan, R. M. (2003). The benefits of being present: Mindfulness and its role in psycho-logical well being. *Journal of Personality and Social Psychology*, *84*(4), 822.
Brown, K. W., Ryan, R. M., & Creswell, J. D. (2007). Mindfulness: Theoretical foundations and evidence for its salutary effects. *Psychological Inquiry, 18*(4), 211–237.
Byrne, B. M. (2001). Structural equation modeling with AMOS, EQS, and LISREL: Comparative approaches to testing for the factorial validity of a measuring instrument. *International Journal of Testing*, *1*(1), 55–86. 10.1207/S15327574 IJT0101_4.
Campbell, R., Tobback, E., Delesie, L., Vogelaers, D., Mariman, A., & Vansteenkiste, M. (2017). Basic psychological need experiences, fatigue, and sleep in individuals with unexplained chronic fatigue. *Stress and Health, 33*(5), 645–655.
Campbell, R., Vansteenkiste, M., Delesie, L. M., Mariman, A. N., Soenens, B., Tobback, E., & Vogelaers, D. P. (2015). Examining the role of psychological need satisfaction in sleep: A self-determination theory perspective. *Personality and Individual Differences*, *77*(12), 199–204.
Cayoun, B. A. (2011). *Mindfulness-integrated CBT: Principles and practice*. Oxford: John Wiley & Sons.
Chang, W. H., Chang, J. H., & Chen, L. H. (2018). Mindfulness enhances change in athletes' well-being: The mediating role of basic psychological needs fulfillment. *Mindfulness*, *9*(3), 815–823.
Chang, J. H., Huang, C. L., & Lin, Y. C. (2015). Mindfulness, basic psychological needs fulfillment, and well-being. *Journal of Happiness Studies*, *16*(5), 1149–1162.
Chatzisarantis, N. L. D., & Hagger, M. S. (2007). Mindfulness and the intention-behavior relationship within the theory of planned behavior. *Personality and Social Psychology Bulletin*, *33*(5), 663–676.
Chiesa, A., & Serretti, A. (2011). Mindfulness-based cognitive therapy for psychiatric disorders: A systematic review and meta-analysis. *Psychiatry Research, 187*(4), 441–453.
Cohen, S., & Janicki-Deverts, D. (2012). Who's stressed? Distributions of psychological stress in the United States in probability samples from 1983, 2006 and 2009. *Journal of Applied Social Psychology*, *42*(6), 1320–1334.
Cohen, S., Kamarck, T., & Mermelstein, R. (1994). Perceived stress scale. Measuring stress: A guide for health and social scientists. *Perspectives on Psychological Science*, *6*(4), 537–559.

Creswell, J. D. (2017). Mindfulness interventions. *Annual Review of Psychology, 68*(6), 491–516.
Creswell, J. D., Way, B. M., Eisenberger, N. I., & Lieberman, M. D. (2007). Neural correlates of dispositional mindfulness during affect labelling. *Psychosomatic Medicine, 69*(8), 560–565.
Donohue, B., Gavrilova, Y., Galante, M., Gavrilova, E., Loughran, T., Scott, J., … Allen, D. N. (2018). Controlled evaluation of an optimization approach to mental health and sport performance. *Journal of Clinical Sport Psychology, 12*(7), 1–42.
Eisenberg, D., Golberstein, E., & Gollust, S. E. (2007). Help-seeking and access to mental health care in a university student population. *Medical Care, 45*(7), 594–601.
Fat, L. N., Scholes, S., Boniface, S., Mindell, J., & Stewart-Brown, S. (2017). Evaluating and establishing national norms for mental wellbeing using the short Warwick–Edinburgh mental well-being scale (SWEMWBS): Findings from the health survey for England. *Quality of Life Research, 26*(5), 1129–1144.
Field, A. (2013). *Discovering statistics using IBM SPSS statistics.* London: Sage.
Gardner, F. L., & Moore, Z. E. (2004). A mindfulness-acceptance-commitment-based approach to athletic performance enhancement: Theoretical considerations. *Behavior Therapy, 35*(4), 707–723.
Gardner, F. L., & Moore, Z. E. (2007). *The psychology of enhancing human performance: The mindful-ness-acceptance-commitment (MAC) approach.* New York, NY: Springer.
Gavrilova, Y., Donohue, B., & Galante, M. (2017). Mental health and sport performance programming in athletes who present without pathology: A case examination supporting optimization. *Clinical Case Studies, 16*(3), 234–253.
Gross, M., Moore, Z. E., Gardner, F. L., Wolanin, A. T., Pess, R., & Marks, D. R. (2018). An empirical examination comparing the mindfulness-acceptance-commitment approach and psychological skills training for the mental health and sport performance of female student athletes. *International Journal of Sport and Exercise Psychology, 16*(4), 431–451.
Gu, J., Strauss, C., Bond, R., & Cavanagh, K. (2015). How do mindfulness-based cognitive therapy and mindfulness-based stress reduction improve mental health and wellbeing? A systematic review and meta-analysis of mediation studies. *Clinical Psychology Review, 37*, 1–12.
Gustafsson, H., Skoog, T., Davis, P., Kenttä, G., & Haberl, P. (2015). Mindfulness and its relationship with perceived stress, affect, and burnout in elite junior athletes. *Journal of Clinical Sport Psychology, 9*(3), 263–281.
Hayes, A. F. (2009). Beyond Baron and Kenny: Statistical mediation analysis in the new millennium. *Communication Monographs, 76*(4), 408–420.
Hayes, A. F., Montoya, A. K., & Rockwood, N. J. (2017). The analysis of mechanisms and their contingencies: PROCESS versus structural equation modelling. *Australasian Marketing Journal, 25*(1), 76–81.
Hölzel, B. K., Lazar, S. W., Gard, T., Schuman-Olivier, Z., Vago, D. R., & Ott, U. (2011). How does mindfulness meditation work? Proposing mechanisms of action from a conceptual and neural perspective. *Perspectives on Psychological Science, 6*(6), 537–559.

Hunt, J., & Eisenberg, D. (2010). Mental health problems and help-seeking behavior among college students. *Journal of Adolescent Health*, *46*(1), 3–10.

Huppert, F. A. (2009). Psychological well-being: Evidence regarding its causes and consequences. *Applied Psychology: Health and Well Being*, *1*(2), 137–164.

Kegelaers, J., Wylleman, P., Defruyt, S., Praet, L., Stambulova, N., Torregrossa, M., … & De Brandt, K. (2022). The mental health of student-athletes: A systematic scoping review. *International Review of Sport and Exercise Psychology,* (in press) 1–34. 10.1080/1750984X.2022.2095657.

Keng, S., Smoski, M., & Robins, C. (2011). Effects of mindfulness on psychological health: A review of empirical studies. *Clinical Psychology Review*, *31*, 1041–1056.

Keyes, C. L. (2002). The mental health continuum: From languishing to flourishing in life. *Journal of Health and Social Behavior, 43*(2), 207–222.

Keyes, C. L. (2005). Mental illness and/or mental health? Investigating axioms of the complete state model of health. *Journal of Consulting and Clinical Psychology, 73*(3), 539.

Kok, G., Schaalma, H., Ruiter, R. A., Van Empelen, P., & Brug, J. (2004). Intervention mapping: Protocol for applying health psychology theory to prevention programmes. *Journal of Health Psychology, 9*(1), 85–98.

Lee, E. H. (2012). Review of the psychometric evidence of the perceived stress scale. *Asian Nursing Research*, *6*(4), 121–127.

Little, R. J. (1988). A test of missing completely at random for multivariate data with missing values. *Journal of the American Statistical Association*, *83*(404), 1198–1202.

MacKillop, J., & Anderson, E. J. (2007). Further psychometric validation of the mindful attention awareness scale (MAAS). *Journal of Psychopathology and Behavioral Assessment, 29*(4), 289–293.

Moesch, K., Kenttä, G., Kleinert, J., Quignon-Fleuret, C., Cecil, S., & Bertollo, M. (2018). FEPSAC position statement: Mental health disorders in elite athletes and models of service provision. *Psychology of Sport and Exercise*, *38*, 61–71.

Mohammed, W. A., Pappous, A., & Sharma, D. (2018). Effect of mindfulness based stress reduction (MBSR) in increasing pain tolerance and improving the mental health of injured athletes. *Frontiers in Psychology*, *9*, 722. 10.3389/fpsyg.2018.00722.

Moreland, J. J., Coxe, K. A., & Yang, J. (2017). Collegiate athletes' mental health services utilization: A systematic review of conceptualizations, operationalizations, facilitators, and barriers. *Journal of Sport and Health Science*. 10.1016/j.jshs.2017.04.009

Mouratidis, A., & Michou, A. (2011). Perfectionism, self-determined motivation, and coping among adolescent athletes. *Psychology of Sport and Exercise*, *12*(4), 355–367.

Myall, K., Montero-Marin, J., Gorczynski, P., Kajee, N., Sheriff, R. S., Bernard, R., … & Kuyken, W. (2023). Effect of mindfulness-based programmes on elite athlete mental health: a systematic review and meta-analysis. *British Journal of Sports Medicine*, *57*(2), 99–108.

Noetel, M., Ciarrochi, J., Van Zanden, B., & Lonsdale, C. (2017). Mindfulness and acceptance approaches to sporting performance enhancement: A systematic review. *International Review of Sport and Exercise Psychology*, *12*, 1–37.

Ntoumanis, N., Quested, E., Reeve, J., & Cheon, S. H. (2017). Need supportive communication: Implications for motivation in sport, exercise, and physical activity. In B. Jackson, J. A. Dimmock & J. Compton (Eds.), *Persuasion and communication in sport, exercise, and physical activity* (1st edition, pp. 64–77). Abingdon, UK: Routledge.

Olafsen, A. H. (2017). The implications of need-satisfying work climates on state mindfulness in a longitudinal analysis of work outcomes. *Motivation and Emotion, 41*, 22–37.

Parto, M., & Besharat, M. A. (2011). Mindfulness, psychological well-being and psychological distress in adolescents: Assessing the mediating variables and mechanisms of autonomy and self-regulation. *Procedia - Social and Behavioral Sciences, 30*(4), 578–582.

Perry, J. E., Ross, M., Weinstock, J., & Weaver, T. (2017). Efficacy of a brief mindfulness intervention to prevent athletic task performance deterioration: A randomized controlled trial. *The Sport Psychologist, 31*(4), 410–421.

Pitt, A., Oprescu, F., Tapia, G., & Gray, M. (2017). An exploratory study of students' weekly stress levels and sources of stress during the semester. *Active Learning in Higher Education.* 10.1177/ 1469787417731194

Pritchard, M. (2005). Comparing sources of stress in college student athletes and non-athletes. *Athletic Insight: The Online Journal of Sports Psychology, 5*(1), 1–8.

Prior, E., Papathomas, A., & Rhind, D. (2022). A systematic scoping review of athlete mental health within competitive sport: interventions, recommendations, and policy. *International Review of Sport and Exercise Psychology* (in press), 1–23. 10.1080/1750984X.2022.2095659

Putukian, M. (2016). The psychological response to injury in student athletes: A narrative review with a focus on mental health. *British Journal of Sports Medicine, 50*(3), 145–148.

Reardon, C. L., Hainline, B., Aron, C. M., Baron, D., Baum, A. L., Bindra, A., … Derevensky, J. L. (2019). Mental health in elite athletes: International Olympic Committee consensus statement. *British Journal of Sports Medicine, 53*(11), 667–699.

Reb, J., Narayanan, J., & Ho, Z. W. (2015). Mindfulness at work: Antecedents and consequences of employee awareness and absent-mindedness. *Mindfulness, 6*(1), 111–122.

Rejeski, W. J., & Brawley, L. R. (1988). Defining the boundaries of sport psychology. *The Sport Psychologist, 2*(3), 231–242.

Roberti, J. W., Harrington, L. N., & Storch, E. A. (2006). Further psychometric support for the 10-item version of the perceived stress scale. *Journal of College Counselling, 9*(2), 135–147.

Rosenkranz, M. A., Dunne, J. D., & Davidson, R. J. (2019). The next generation of mindfulness-based intervention research: What have we learned and where are we headed? *Current Opinion in Psychology, 28*(6), 179–183.

Ryan, R. M., & Deci, E. L. (2000). Self-determination theory and the facilitation of intrinsic motivation, social development, and well-being. *American Psychologist, 55*(1), 68.

Ryan, R. M., & Deci, E. L. (2017). *Self-determination theory: Basic psychological needs in motivation, development, and wellness.* New York: Guilford Publications.

Sappington, R., & Longshore, K. (2015). Systematically reviewing the efficacy of mindfulness-based interventions for enhanced athletic performance. *Journal of Clinical Sport Psychology, 9*(3), 232–262.

Sampaio, F., Gonçalves, P., & Sequeira, C. (2022). Mental health literacy: it is now time to put knowledge into practice. *International Journal of Environmental Research and Public Health, 19*(12), 7030.

Schinke, R. J., Stambulova, N. B., Si, G., & Moore, Z. (2018). International society of sport psychology position stand: Athletes' mental health, performance, and development. *International Journal of Sport and Exercise Psychology, 16*(6), 622–639.

Schultz, P. P., Ryan, R. M., Niemiec, C. P., Legate, N., & Williams, G. C. (2014). Mindfulness, work climate, and psychological need satisfaction in employee well-being. *Mindfulness, 6*(5), 971–985.

Schumacker, R. L. R. (2004).*A beginner's guide to structural equation modelling* (pp. 88–89). New York: Psychology Press.

Shannon, S., Breslin, G., Haughey, T., Sarju, N., Neill, D., Lawlor, M., & Leavey, G. (2019). Predicting student-athlete and Non-athletes' intentions to self-manage mental health: Testing an Integrated behaviour change Model. *Mental Health & Prevention, 13*(12), 92–99.

Shannon, S, Brick, N., Prentice, G., & Breslin, G. (2023). The influence of athletes' psychological needs on motivation, burnout, and well-being: A test of self-determination theory. *Journal of Clinical Sport Psychology, 1*(aop), 1–20.

Shannon, S., Hanna, D., Haughey, T., Leavey, G., McGeown, C., & Breslin, G. (2019). Effects of a mental health intervention in athletes: Applying self-determination theory. *Frontiers in Psychology, 10*(1), 1875.

Sheehan, R. B., Herring, M. P., & Campbell, M. J. (2018). Associations between motivation and mental health in sport: A test of the hierarchical model of intrinsic and extrinsic motivation. *Frontiers in Psychology, 9*(4), 707.

Sheldon, K. M., Ryan, R. M., & Reis, H. (1996). What makes for a good day? Competence and autonomy in the day and in the person. *Personality and Social Psychology Bulletin, 22*, 1270–1279.

Steptoe, A. (1997). *Stress management*. Cambridge: Cambridge University Press.

Stewart-Brown, S. L., Platt, S., Tennant, A., Maheswaran, H., Parkinson, J., Weich, S., & Clarke, A. (2011). The Warwick-Edinburgh mental well-being scale (WEMWBS): A valid and reliable tool for measuring mental well-being in diverse populations and projects. *Journal of Epidemiology and Community Health, 65*(Suppl 2), A38–A39.

Sudano, L. E., Collins, G., & Miles, C. M. (2017). Reducing barriers to mental health care for student-athletes: An integrated care model. *Families, Systems, & Health, 35*(1), 77.

Tennant, R., Hiller, L., Fishwick, R., Platt, S., Joseph, S., Weich, S., & Stewart-Brown, S. (2007). The Warwick-Edinburgh mental well-being scale (WEMWBS): Development and UK validation. *Health and Quality of Life Outcomes, 5*(1), 63.

Thrash, T. M., & Elliot, A. J. (2002). Implicit and self-attributed achievement motives: Concordance and predictive validity. *Journal of Personality, 70*, 729–755.

Valentine, J. C., Biglan, A., Boruch, R. F., Castro, F. G., Collins, L. M., Flay, B. R., & Schinke, S. P. (2011). Replication in prevention science. *Prevention Science, 12*(2), 103.

Vidic, Z., Martin, M. S., & Oxhandler, R. (2017). Mindfulness Intervention with a US women's NCAA division I basketball team: Impact on stress, athletic coping skills and perceptions of intervention. *The Sport Psychologist, 31*(2), 147–159.

Vella, S. A., Schweickle, M. J., Sutcliffe, J. T., & Swann, C. (2021). A systematic review and meta-synthesis of mental health position statements in sport: Scope, quality, and future directions. *Psychology of Sport and Exercise*, *55*, 101946

von Elm, E., Altman, D. G., Egger, M., Pocock, S. J., Gøtzsche, P. C., Vandenbroucke, J. P., et al. (2007). The Strengthening the reporting of observational studies in epidemiology (STROBE) statement: Guidelines for reporting observational studies. *PLoS Medicine*, *4*(10), e296. 10.1371/journal.pmed.0040296

Weinstein, N., Brown, K. W., & Ryan, R. M. (2009). A multi-method examination of the effects of mindfulness on stress attribution, coping, and emotional well-being. *Journal of Research in Personality, 43*, 374–385.

Weinstein, N., & Ryan, R. M. (2011). A self-determination theory approach to understanding stress incursion and responses. *Stress and Health, 27*(1), 4–17.

Wolf, H. (2012). Self-management and mental health. In S. Bährer-Kohler (Ed.), *Social determinants and mental health.* New York: Nova Science.

Wylleman, P., & Rosier, N. (2016). Holistic perspective on the development of elite athletes. In M. Raab et al. (Eds.), *Sport and exercise psychology research* (pp. 269–288). Academic Press.

Wylleman, P. (2019). A developmental and holistic perspective on transiting out of elite sport. In M. H. Anshel, T. A. Petrie, & J. A. Steinfeldt (Eds.), *APA handbook of sport and exercise psychology, Vol. 1. Sport psychology* (pp. 201–216). American Psychological Association. 10.1037/0000123-011

Zhang, C. Q., Si, G., Chung, P. K., & Gucciardi, D. F. (2016). Mindfulness and burnout in elite junior athletes: The mediating role of experiential avoidance. *Journal of Applied Sport Psychology, 28*(4), 437–451.

12

REFLECTIONS ON THE EMPIRICAL EXAMINATION COMPARING THE MINDFULNESS-ACCEPTANCE COMMITMENT APPROACH AND PSYCHOLOGICAL SKILLS TRAINING FOR THE MENTAL HEALTH AND SPORT PERFORMANCE OF FEMALE STUDENT ATHLETES

Zella E. Moore, Frank L. Gardner, Mike Gross, Andrew T. Wolanin, Rachel Pess-Gross, and Donald R. Marks

Mental health issues and clinical disorders among university students are highly prevalent and represent an ongoing concern (Hunt & Eisneberg, 2010). In a survey conducted by the American College Health Association-National College Health Assessment (ACHA, 2015), it was found that roughly 35% of the American university students sampled reported feeling so depressed at some point within the past 12 months that it was difficult for them to function, and 57% of the respondents reported that they felt overwhelming anxiety at some point within the past 12 months. The prevalence of psychological distress among collegiate student-athletes is generally comparable to, and for some disorders, even greater than, that of the general non-athlete population (Wolanin et al., 2016). In fact, according to Wieland et al. (2018), student-athletes are at an increased risk for experiencing anxiety, depression, eating disorders, and substance abuse. Additionally, Drew and Matthews (2019) found that 31% of Irish collegiate student-athletes reported moderate to severe symptoms of depression and/or anxiety, and Sullivan et al. (2019) found that 20% of collegiate student-athletes experienced generalised psychological distress. As psychological problems and the number of students seeking psychological services across college campuses worldwide have increased, it is exceedingly important to

DOI: 10.4324/9781003459750-12

identify at-risk populations. The prevalence data noted above suggests that the supposition that sport participation buffers the development of psychopathological conditions is not supported.

According to Etzel et al. (2002), student-athletes are an at-risk population for the development of mental health concerns, in part because they face pressures and stressors that non-athletes do not typically confront. Consistent with this hypothesis, Humphrey et al. (2000) found that nearly half of male student-athletes and a just over half of female student-athletes reported that sport-related stressors significantly impacted their mental and emotional health, and Bennett (2007) contended that being a student-athlete is "inherently stressful" and, at least at the Division I level, is similar to working two full-time jobs. College is already a stressful time for young adults as they deal with issues related to academics, adjusting to a new environment, managing new interpersonal relationships, financial difficulties, transitioning to a new developmental stage, and establishing professional and personal identity (Hamaideh, 2011). Yet, student-athletes confront both the aforementioned stressors and also several other distinct sources of stress as they navigate their dual roles (Lopes Dos Santos et al., 2020), such as managing academic demands with minimal time, performing physically and emotionally demanding tasks, playing status, dealing with coaches and teammates, extensive training programs, coping with injuries, competitive schedules, and competing in high-pressure situations (Proctor & Boan-Lenzo, 2010).

Sport Psychology Service Provision

With National Collegiate Athletic Association (NCAA, 2023b) statistics reporting that over 520,000 student-athletes are competing on nearly 20,000 teams across the United States, athletic departments are likely to increasingly look to sport psychologists to improve student-athlete performance and well-being, both on and off the field. This includes providing services to the full range of student-athletes, including non-clinical, subclinical, and clinical populations. For a long time, however, there were no known evidence-based interventions employed by sport psychologists that could effectively and simultaneously target mental health and sport performance outcomes. According to Moore (2007):

> … Of major significance to the evolving discipline of sport psychology, there is a near complete absence of studies examining the impact that interventions for psychological health and athletic performance may have on each other. The potential interaction between these two areas (to date seen as separate and disconnected) is one of the guiding concepts in the promotion of the science and practice of clinical sport psychology. (p. 18)

Psychological Skills Training (PST)

The field of sport psychology long focused on providing psychosocial interventions for the enhancement of athletic performance. For several decades, the primary intervention for this purpose was PST, which frequently employs techniques such as imagery, positive self-talk, relaxation, arousal control procedures, and goal-setting. Often, PST involves a multimodal format, meaning that a combination of the aforementioned techniques is used in service delivery. PST was developed within the cognitive-behavioural tradition and was largely influenced by Meichenbaum's (1977) integrative approach to cognitive modification. Proponents of PST suggest that practitioners using this approach should have a solid foundational knowledge of the basic assumptions and theoretical underpinnings of cognitive-behavioural interventions (Claspell, 2010). The theoretical foundation of PST is that optimal performance occurs when athletes learn to control their internal processes such as cognitions and emotions in order to create an ideal performance state (Hardy et al., 1996). Proponents of PST contend that athletic performance can be disrupted due to "negative" cognitions, emotions, and bodily sensations (Weinberg & Gould, 2015). As such, the ultimate goal of PST has been the development of the athlete's capacity to monitor and manage his or her cognitions, emotions, and behaviours (Weinberg & Gould, 2015), and the aforementioned techniques are postulated to work through reducing negative thoughts, increasing confidence, and decreasing undesired emotional states such as anxiety (Hardy et al., 1996). Although this framework was widely adopted in the sport psychology community for decades, research on these interventions has not found a consistent relationship between the reduction of negative internal states and increases in competitive performance. In some reviews of the empirical literature, PST procedures have been shown to have limited efficacy based on systematic qualitative reviews of the empirical data on competitive athletes (Birrer & Morgan, 2010; Gardner & Moore, 2006; Moore, 2003). However, other reviews have concluded that the delivery of PST does result in positive performance effects. For example, Weinberg and Williams (2001) reviewed 45 studies in which some component of PST was used, and found that 85% demonstrated increased performance.

The Mindfulness-Acceptance-Commitment (MAC) Programme

Inspired by the mindfulness- and acceptance-based movement in clinical psychology (Hayes et al., 1999; Segal et al., 2002), in 2000, Gardner and Moore developed the first formal sport psychology intervention geared towards mindfulness, and the promotion of acceptance and non-judgmental present-moment awareness (Gardner & Moore, 2004, 2007). The MAC's approach to performance enhancement and optimisation of personal well-being is based upon the premise that neither optimal performance nor adaptive behavioural health necessarily results from anxiety reduction, increasing confidence, or minimising uncomfortable cognitions or other internal states. Rather, the MAC programme postulates that optimised performance and well-being outcomes are influenced by an athlete's ability to remain non-judgmentally present with his or her internal experiences, while persisting with the task-at-hand despite possible internal discomfort, and without losing present-moment focus on the environmental demands of a given performance.

The manualised MAC protocol employs a multitude of techniques and experiential exercises aimed at increasing mindful awareness and non-judgmental acceptance of in-the-moment cognitive, sensory, and affective experiences (see Gardner & Moore, 2007 for the entire MAC manual). The MAC also uses techniques to help individuals develop the willingness to remain in contact with the full range of internal experiences in order to engage in behaviours consistent with their personal values. These strategies include mindfulness training, cognitive defusion, promotion of experiential acceptance, and values clarification and pursuit. These techniques are primarily used to target the MAC's proposed mechanisms of change, which include enhanced attentional awareness, a non-judgmental task-relevant focus, improved emotion regulation, and greater psychological flexibility in the face of the full range of internal and external stimuli that individuals confront. Likewise, of particular relevance to the present RCT study, Gardner and Moore (2007) contend that MAC techniques are used not only to assist athletes with performance, but to also enhance overall psychosocial well-being as individuals navigate and deal with issues outside of sport.

Over the years since MAC was presented as a theoretical and intervention model, there have been extensive empirical examinations on MAC's influence on performance and personal well-being/mental health. To name a few, a number of randomised controlled trials (RCTs) have demonstrated that MAC enhances athletic performance across sports (Andersson & Nilsson, 2019; Josefsson et al., 2019; MacDougall et al., 2019; Robinson and Cedenblad, 2020), enhances personal well-being/reduces psychological distress (Ajilchi et al., 2022; Andersson & Nilsson, 2019; MacDougall et al., 2019; Mohebi et al., 2021; Ning et al., 2022), has been shown to be effective and readily adapted for use across cultures (Ajilchi et al., 2022; Mohebi et al., 2021; Su et al., 2019; Yau et al., 2021), has been shown to work via the theorised mechanisms of enhanced mindfulness, emotion regulation, and attention (Andersson & Nilsson, 2019; Josefsson et al., 2019; Goodman et al., 2014; Ning et al., 2022), and appears to be more effective than traditional PST (Gross et al., 2016; Josefsson *et al*, 2019).

The Present Study

Mindfulness- and acceptance-based interventions have been found to effectively help individuals with a number of issues, including but not limited to eating disorders (Kristeller et al., 2013), substance use (Bautista, James, & Amaro, 2019), recurrent depression (Schuling et al., 2020), chronic depression (Barnhofer et al., 2009), generalised anxiety (Hoge et al., 2013), and chronic pain (Trindade et al., 2021). And, MAC has been shown to be effective in enhancing performance and personal well-being in collegiate and elite-level athletes across the world and across sports, as noted earlier in this paper. The present paper, however, reflects on an enlightening RCT that compared MAC to traditional PST. The study reflected upon herein sought to determine whether mindfulness- and acceptance-based skills primarily taught through the lens of sport could translate into improvements in the overall psychosocial well-being of collegiate athletes more effectively than PST. The RCT compared the MAC programme with traditional PST interventions, to better understand their effectiveness in improving mental health and sport performance outcomes among a group of female collegiate athletes. The central purpose of the study was to examine whether the manualised MAC programme (Gardner & Moore, 2007) could meet the broad needs of athlete-clients, and provide sport psychologists with a single intervention that can target both athletic performance and mental health concerns. It was hypothesised that when compared to the traditional PST approach, MAC participants would demonstrate a greater reduction in behavioural issues, emotional distress, and psychological symptoms, while improving athletic performance as rated by coaches. It was also hypothesised that participants in the MAC group would demonstrate significantly greater increases in psychological flexibility, dispositional mindfulness, and emotion regulation when compared to participants in the PST group.

Method

Participants

Following Institutional Review Board (IRB) approval, 22 women's basketball players were recruited from an NCAA Division III university athletic department in the northeastern United States. Participants from the same athletic team were utilised in an effort to reduce extraneous variables (i.e., team-related stressors) that may impact the results of the study. Prior to the intervention, participants were randomly assigned into either the MAC or traditional PST group based upon matching of pre-intervention scores on the Counselling Centre Assessment of Psychological Symptoms-62 (CCAPS-62) overall distress scale (described below). Eleven participants were randomly assigned to the MAC group, and 11 participants were randomly assigned to the traditional PST group. The MAC group consisted of six freshmen, two sophomores, two juniors, and one senior, and the traditional PST group consisted of four freshmen, three sophomores, three juniors, and one senior. In terms of race and ethnicity, the MAC group was comprised of seven student-athletes identifying as African-American, two identifying as Caucasian, one identifying as American Indian, and one identifying as Hispanic. The PST group had nearly identical rates, with seven student-athletes identifying as African-American, two identifying as Caucasian, one identifying as American Indian, and one identifying as Asian.

Due to academic issues, two participants dropped out of the study (one from the MAC group and one from the PST group) prior to the post-intervention data collection. Another two participants (one from the MAC group and one from the PST group) did not complete measures at the one-month follow-up due to being cut from the team after post-intervention data collection. Participants received no compensation for their participation in the study. Prior to participation, each participant signed an informed consent form and the purpose of the study was reviewed.

Clinicians

The MAC group was led by the original first author (Dr. Mike Gross), who at the time was a fourth-year doctoral student with previous experience running MAC groups and providing services to athletes. The traditional PST group was led by a third-year doctoral student with training and experience using traditional PST techniques with athletes. These doctoral students were utilised because both had already obtained master's degrees in psychology, and additionally, recent studies have indicated that therapists' experience, whether examined as global amount of experience or targeted experience delivering a specific intervention protocol, was unrelated to intervention outcomes across a wide range of possible variables (Norton et al., 2014).

Procedure

Coaches from several athletic teams at the university were interested in recruiting their athletes for participation in the study. However, due to time constraints and scheduling conflicts, only the women's basketball team was able to commit to participation.

Following random assignment to the intervention groups, both intervention groups met once per week over the course of seven weeks, with each session lasting 60 minutes. Consistent with previous studies comparing acceptance-based interventions to cognitive-behavioural interventions, the present study did not include a no-treatment control group, particularly because PST had been the gold standard intervention in the sport domain for nearly 40 years at that point. According to Kazdin (2002), it is not necessary and potentially unethical to include a no-treatment control group when comparing a newer intervention to a long-standing intervention. Finally, given the previous assertion that PST is best delivered prior to a team's season (Weinberg & Gould, 2015), the intervention took place during the preseason (September–November).

The first meeting consisted solely of data collection, and therefore, the interventions themselves took place over the course of six weeks. Attendance in both intervention groups was very high. Only two participants missed one session each (one MAC and one PST), thereby suggesting that the interventions were fully delivered to participants. As an adherence check, participants in each group were given a three-question quiz following each session, which asked questions associated with the topic discussed in the session. In total, participants in the MAC group scored 93% on the quizzes, and participants in the PST group scored 91%, suggesting that each intervention was delivered and received as intended.

Assessment measures (described below) were completed pre- and post-intervention during weeks 1 and 7, respectively. The Acceptance and Action Questionnaire-II (AAQ-II; Bond et al., 2011) was given at the above time points, and prior to the third session. During week 3, participants completed the Working Alliance Inventory, Short Version (WAI-S; Tracey & Kokotovic, 1989) to determine whether outcomes could potentially be attributed to therapeutic rapport. Participants also completed assessment measures one-month post-intervention. The coach of the women's basketball team completed the Sport Performance Questionnaire (SPQ; Wolanin, 2005) both pre- and post-intervention.

MAC Group

The MAC intervention group followed the manualised protocol outlined in Gardner and Moore's (2007) text entitled "The Psychology of Enhancing Human Performance: The Mindfulness-Acceptance-Commitment (MAC) Approach." The protocol contains seven modules, including (1) psychoeducation; (2) mindfulness and cognitive defusion; (3) values and values-driven behaviour; (4) acceptance; (5) commitment; (6) skill consolidation and poise (which combines mindfulness, acceptance, and commitment); and (7) maintaining and enhancing mindfulness, acceptance, and commitment. Consistent with the MAC protocol, each session began with a mindfulness exercise known as the Brief Centering Exercise (BCE; Eifert & Forsyth, 2005). The BCE promotes mindfulness practice and provides participants with experiential exposure to the concepts discussed during the intervention. Further, the MAC protocol consists of several other experiential exercises and forms which were used throughout the intervention to maintain treatment integrity.

Descriptions of the experiential exercises and forms used in the present study can be found in the manualised MAC protocol outlined in the text (2007).

PST Group

The PST group followed the manualised protocol in Suinn's (1986) text entitled, "Seven Steps to Peak Performance: The Mental Training Manual for Athletes." The decision to use this intervention was based upon two primary factors. One, it was the only multicomponent intervention that demonstrated efficacy in Moore's (2003) systematic review of PST. Two, Suinn's (1986) intervention utilised a manualised protocol, which provided a direct guide for what was delivered in the PST group. According to Moore (2003), sport psychology studies often do not provide sufficient descriptions of the interventions utilised, and "in essence, it is meaningless to say that an intervention works without being able to accurately say what the interventions entails" (p. 60). The seven skills included in the Suinn manual are relaxation training, stress management, positive thought control, self-regulation, mental rehearsal, concentration, and energy control. Goal-setting and self-confidence, albeit common PST procedures/skills, were not directly addressed by this intervention. Skills training for each step was implemented in the order presented by the manual, and the second session included two steps (relaxation training and stress management) to enable an introductory session. Each step in the manual incorporates rationale for the skill, assessments of the skill, learning activities, and recommendations for practising the skill. These components were slightly modified for appropriate use in a group format. Each session began with an explanation of the purpose of the skill, discussion of the current use of the skill guided by the assessment in the manual, a training activity to learn the skill, and information about how to use a training log to monitor development of the skill. By way of example, the step of relaxation training began with an introduction to the purpose of relaxation training, followed by discussion of how muscle tension may influence performance. Next, the group participated in a progressive relaxation exercise. The step concluded with information on how a training log can be used for recording relaxation practices and effects, as well as how to use a "cue" to relax.

The mental skills taught in this particular PST intervention differ rather significantly from those in MAC. As one example, relaxation training in the PST group focused on reducing tension to help athletes feel loose during competition. In contrast, MAC participants were taught not to fight with or attempt to eliminate internal experiences (i.e., tension), but rather to develop a willingness to experience whatever arises – whether it be perceived as positive, negative, or neutral. This fundamental difference in control- versus acceptance-based strategies was represented in group exercises, such as using progressive muscle relaxation in PST and BCEs in MAC.

Measures

Counselling Centre Assessment of Psychological Symptoms-62 (CCAPS-62)

The CCAPS-62 (Locke et al., 2011) is a self-report questionnaire initially developed primarily for use within college counselling centres, which assesses psychological symptoms and distress in college students via eight distinct subscales: Depression, Generalised Anxiety, Social Anxiety, Academic Distress, Eating Concerns, Family Distress, Hostility, and Substance Abuse, and a Distress Index, which is a general measure of psychological distress. The CCAPS-62 has demonstrated adequate convergent and discriminant validity, with internal consistency reliabilities ranging from $\alpha = 0.82$ to 0.92, and one-week test–retest reliabilities ranging from $r = 0.78$ to 0.93 (Locke et al., 2011).

Acceptance and Action Questionnaire-II (AAQ-II)

The AAQ-II (Bond et al., 2011) is a 7-item measure that assesses an individual's psychological flexibility. The instrument is currently one of the most frequently used measures in both clinical psychology and mindfulness- and acceptance-based research. Each item consists of a statement that is rated on a Likert scale ranging from 1 (never true) to 7 (always true). Higher scores indicate that an individual has greater levels of psychological inflexibility. Reliability of the AAQ-II had a mean Cronbach's α coefficient of 0.84 (0.78–0.88), and adequate 3- and 12-month test–retest reliability of 0.81 and 0.79, respectively (Bond et al., 2011).

Difficulties with Emotion Regulation Scale (DERS)

The DERS (Gratz & Roemer, 2004) is a 36-item self-report measure that assesses overall difficulties with emotion regulation (total score) and other aspects of emotion regulation (subscale scores) on a 5-point Likert scale ranging from 1 (almost never) to 5 (almost always). The present study used the DERS total scale scores for analysis, as higher scores on the DERS total scale are indicative of increased difficulties with emotion regulation. DERS total scores exhibited adequate convergent and discriminant validity in the validation sample (Gratz & Roemer, 2004). Over a period of 4–8 weeks, test–retest reliability was 0.88 for the total score (Gratz & Roemer, 2004).

Mindful Awareness Attention Scale (MAAS)

The MAAS (Brown & Ryan, 2003) is a 15-item self-report measure that assesses core characteristics of dispositional mindfulness, particularly awareness and attention in the present moment. Items are rated on a 6-point Likert scale ranging from 1 (almost always) to 6 (almost never), with higher scores reflecting greater dispositional mindfulness. The MAAS has demonstrated adequate reliability and validity among college students, and internal consistency levels (Cronbach's alphas) generally range from 0.80 to 0.90 (Brown & Ryan, 2003).

Sport Performance Questionnaire (SPQ)

The SPQ (Wolanin, 2005) is a coach-completed measure that rates an athlete's performance on a 10-point Likert scale ranging from 1 (poor) to 10 (perfect). The SPQ assesses an athlete's ability in numerous domains including concentration, strength, competitiveness, motivation, quickness, fitness, endurance, mechanics, aggressiveness, and agility. The SPQ also contains an overall performance rating, which was used as the sport performance outcome in the present study. The decision to use overall performance as the primary outcome was decided prior to the study because the other variables are thought to potentially mediate performance outcomes (Wolanin, 2005). As such, the overall performance scale was thought to be the best indicator of athletic performance. The SPQ was completed by the head coach of the team both pre-intervention and post-intervention.

Marlowe–Crowne Social Desirability Scale – Short Form C (MC-C)

The MC-C (Reynolds, 1982) assesses for the presence of impression management. The MC-C is a self-report measure consisting of 13 dichotomous items, which were derived from the original 33-item Marlowe–Crowne Social Desirability Scale (MC; Crowne & Marlowe, 1960). Internal consistency estimates for the MC-C range from 0.62 to 0.76 (Loo & Thorpe, 2000; Reynolds, 1982; Zook & Sipps, 1985) and six-week test–retest correlation of 0.74 (Zook & Sipps, 1985).

Working Alliance Inventory-Short Version (WAI-S)

The WAI-S (Tracey & Kokotovic, 1989) is a 12-item self-report measure used to assess therapeutic alliance. The WAI-S measures one general alliance factor, as well as the three specific alliance factors of task, bond, and goal. The items are rated on a 7-point scale representing to what degree a statement is true, ranging from never to always. Cronbach's alpha estimates internal consistency to be in the range of 0.69–0.89.

Analyses

Prior to analysis, independent-sample t-tests were used to examine any differences between the intervention group and control group on the demographic variables. The groups did not significantly differ regarding age, race, year in school, or pre-intervention grade point average.

A mixed-model analysis of variance (ANOVA) was used to test within-group differences across time, between-group differences at each time point, and the Group × Time interaction effect. This analysis was conducted with each of the completed measures. The within-subjects factor was time, with three time points (i.e., pre-intervention, post-intervention, and one-month follow-up), and the between-subjects factor was group (i.e., MAC or PST). Bonferroni-corrected pairwise comparisons were examined to determine at which time points the significant differences, if any, occurred. Given the relatively small sample size, effect sizes were calculated using partial eta-squared estimates (included in Tables 12.1 and 12.2). Partial eta squared estimates were also utilised, given that this is the appropriate effect size estimate to report when analysing data using ANOVA (Cohen, 1992). The categorisation of these values into small, medium, and large differs from the classic classification system used for Cohen's d effect sizes. Based on a categorisation system established by Cohen (1992), for effect sizes calculated using partial eta squared estimates, 0.02 is indicative of a small effect, 0.15 is considered a medium effect, and 0.35 is indicative of a large effect.

After conducting the main analyses, scores on the Marlowe–Crowne Social Desirability Scale were examined to detect impression management. Scores of 10 or above were considered indicative of a participant engaging in impression management (Andrews & Meyer, 2003). Those participants who met criteria at all three time points were eliminated from the analysis ($n = 3$), and the statistical tests for each outcome and process measure were re-examined.

Results

The findings of the mixed-model ANOVA analyses are grouped by outcome measures, process measures, and sport-specific measures below (also see Tables 12.1 and 12.2).

Therapeutic Relationship

An independent-sample t-test was conducted to test for differences on the WAI-S, which measures the therapeutic relationship. Statistically significant differences were not found between the MAC and PST participants on this measure ($t = 0.29$, $p = .78$), suggesting that participants in each group had similar ratings of their relationship with their lead therapist. Additionally, the distribution of WAI-S scores was examined using a histogram and, a q–q plot. These scores were found to be normally distributed.

Although the WAI-S measures three specific alliance factors, according to Tracey and Kokotovic (1989), it "measures primarily" the general alliance factor. As such, this general alliance dimension was considered the optimal

TABLE 12.1 CCAPS-62 outcome measure across condition and time

	MAC Group Mean (SD)	*PST Group* Mean (SD)	*Within-Group Effect* (F, η_p^2)	*Between-Group Effect* (F, η_p^2)	*Interaction Effect* (F, η_p^2)
Depression			1.04, 0.06	0.02, 0.00	0.83, 0.05
Pre	0.66 (0.55)	0.56 (0.47)			
Post	0.56 (0.42)	0.45 (0.45)			
Follow-Up	0.40 (0.37)	0.53 (0.61)			
Eating Concerns			4.86*, 0.23	1.00, 0.06	1.38, 0.08
Pre	1.00 (0.97)	0.79 (0.32)			
Post	1.03 (0.93)	0.53 (0.34)			
Follow-Up	0.38 (0.28)	0.43 (0.38)			
Substance Use			4.55*, 0.22	1.06, 0.06	3.72*, 0.19
Pre	0.61 (0.61)	0.37 (0.37)			
Post	0.56 (0.60)	0.17 (0.22)			
Follow-Up	0.11 (0.14)	0.26 (0.31)			
Generalised Anxiety			5.24*, 0.25	0.00, 0.00	1.29, 0.08
Pre	0.84 (0.65)	0.90 (0.56)			
Post	1.10 (0.54)	0.90 (0.62)			
Follow-Up	0.57 (0.46)	0.72 (0.54)			
Hostility			5.05*, 0.24	2.17, 0.12	5.92**, 0.27
Pre	0.67 (0.50)	0.64 (0.57)			
Post	0.94 (0.57)	0.25 (0.24)			
Follow-Up	0.37 (0.35)	0.30 (0.42)			

(*Continued*)

TABLE 12.1 (Continued)

	MAC Group Mean *(SD)*	*PST Group* Mean *(SD)*	*Within-Group Effect* (F, η_p^2)	*Between-Group Effect* (F, η_p^2)	*Interaction Effect* (F, η_p^2)
Social Anxiety			0.70, 0.04	0.01, 0.00	0.27, 0.02
Pre	1.32 (0.67)	1.38 (0.77)			
Post	1.30 (0.55)	1.32 (0.62)			
Follow-Up	1.25 (0.46)	1.11 (0.33)			
Family Distress			2.82^{+}, 0.15	0.72, 0.04	2.63^{+}, 0.14
Pre	0.44 (0.51)	0.91 (0.65)			
Post	0.43 (0.31)	0.52 (0.41)			
Follow-Up	0.69 (0.39)	0.70 (0.82)			
Academic Distress			0.11, 0.01	0.02, 0.00	0.88, 0.05
Pre	1.00 (0.63)	1.07 (0.84)			
Post	1.18 (0.72)	1.00 (0.74)			
Follow-Up	0.91 (0.51)	1.13 (0.95)			
Distress Index			3.26*, 0.17	0.00, 0.00	1.21, 0.07
Pre	0.64 (0.50)	0.62 (0.42)			
Post	0.72 (0.43)	0.60 (0.30)			
Follow-Up	0.38 (0.30)	0.53 (0.34)			

Note: $^{+}p < .10$, $*p < .05$, $**p < .01$, For η_p^2: Small = 0.02, Moderate = 0.15, Large = 0.35.

TABLE 12.2 Process and sport-specific measures across condition and time

	MAC Group Mean *(SD)*	*PST Group* Mean *(SD)*	*Within-Group Effect (F, η_p^2)*	*Between-Group Effect (F, η_p^2)*	*Interaction Effect (F, η_p^2)*
AAQ-II			6.31*, 0.35	0.01, 0.00	0.35, 0.03
Pre	14.13 (9.45)	15.83 (6.56)			
Session 3	25.38 (11.78)	22.33 (9.18)			
Post	14.38 (9.91)	15.00 (5.93)			
Follow-Up	11.75 (8.01)	13.83 (8.42)			
MAAS			0.55, 0.03	4.69*, 0.23	0.11, 0.01
Pre	3.84 (0.65)	4.42 (0.61)			
Post	3.60 (0.97)	4.30 (0.76)			
Follow-Up	3.88 (0.68)	4.39 (0.85)			
DERS Total			2.21, 0.12	0.57, 0.03	4.32*, 0.21
Pre	79.44 (19.11)	70.56 (10.20)			
Post	84.78 (18.64)	71.67 (17.01)			
Follow-Up	67.56 (17.34)	74.11 (17.44)			
SPQ Overall Performance			5.77*, 0.23	0.41, 0.02	0.49, 0.03
Pre	6.91 (1.51)	7.50 (1.08)			
Post	8.00 (2.00)	8.10 (0.99)			

Note: $^+p < .10$, $*p < .05$, $**p < .01$, For η_p^2: Small = 0.02, Moderate = 0.15, Large = 0.35.

measure for assessing therapeutic relationship. Given that there was no statistically significant difference in WAI-S scores between the two groups, therapeutic relationship was not assessed in each subsequent analysis.

Outcome Measures

Mixed-model ANOVAs were conducted for each subscale of the CCAPS-62, and two statistically significant interaction effects were identified. The interaction of intervention group and time was significant for Substance Use (F (2, 32) = 3.72, p = .04, h^2p = .19) and Hostility (F (2, 32) = 5.92, p = .01, h^2p = .27) scores, demonstrating that the MAC intervention had a greater influence than the PST intervention on the decrease of Substance Use and Hostility over time (see Figure 12.1).

Results also revealed a statistically significant within-group main effect of time on the following subscale scores: Distress Index (F (2, 32) = 3.26, p = .05, h^2p = .17), Substance Use (F (2, 32) = 4.55, p = .02, h2p = .22), Generalised Anxiety (F (2, 32) = 5.24, p = .01, h^2p = .25), Hostility (F (2, 32) = 5.05, p = .01, h^2p = .24), and Eating Concerns (F (2, 32) = 4.86, p = .01, h^2p = .23), demonstrating that differences existed within one or both of the groups across time (see Figure 12.1).

Pairwise comparisons revealed that the MAC participants had statistically significant decreases from post-intervention to one-month follow-up on Distress

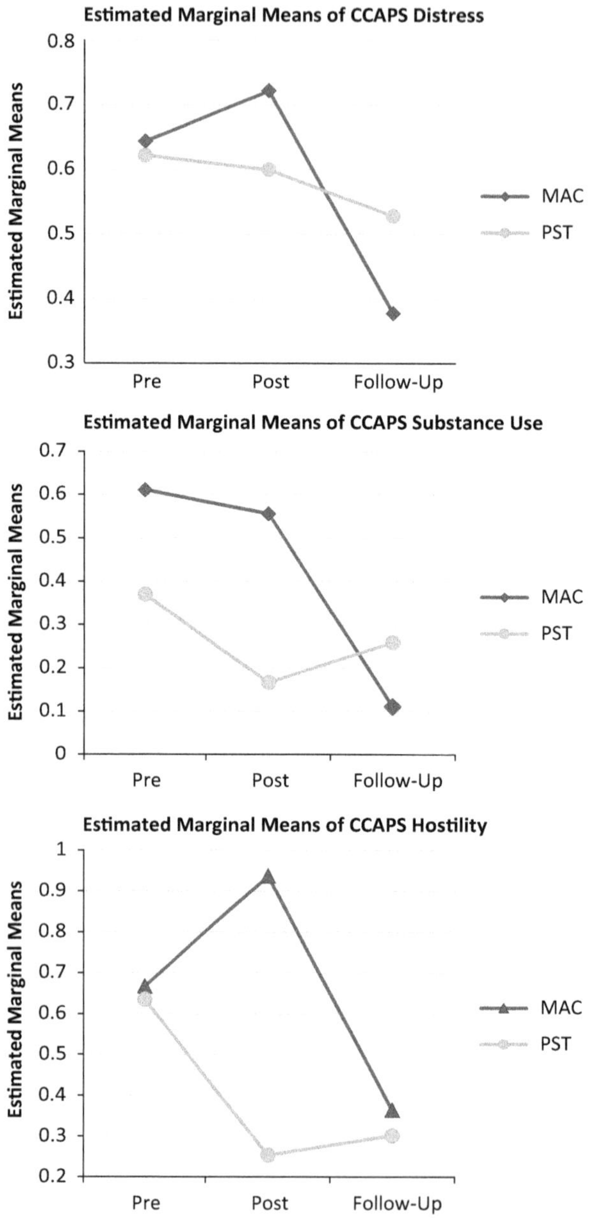

FIGURE 12.1 Estimated marginal means of CCAPS distress, substance use, and hostility scores by group across time.

Index (p = .01), Generalised Anxiety (p = .00), Substance Use (p = .01), and Hostility (p = .01) scores. Additionally, from pre-intervention to one-month follow-up, MAC participants had significant decreases in Substance Use scores (p = .01). From pre-intervention to post-intervention, the PST participants had statistically significant decreases on Family Distress scores (p = .03).

A within-group main effect of time was not found for the following subscales: Depression (F (2, 32) = 1.04, p = .37, h^2p = .06), Social Anxiety (F (2, 32) = 0.70, p = .50, h^2p = .04), and Academic Distress (F (2, 32) = 0.11, p = .90, h^2p = .01).

Process Measures

Mixed-model ANOVAs were conducted for each of the process measures, as well (AAQ-II, DERS, and MAAS scores). Consistent with our hypotheses, there was a statistically significant interaction of intervention group and time on the DERS (F (3, 32) = 4.32, p = .02, h^2p = .21), which suggests that the MAC intervention had a greater influence than the PST intervention on decreases in difficulties with emotion regulation over time (see Figure 12.2).

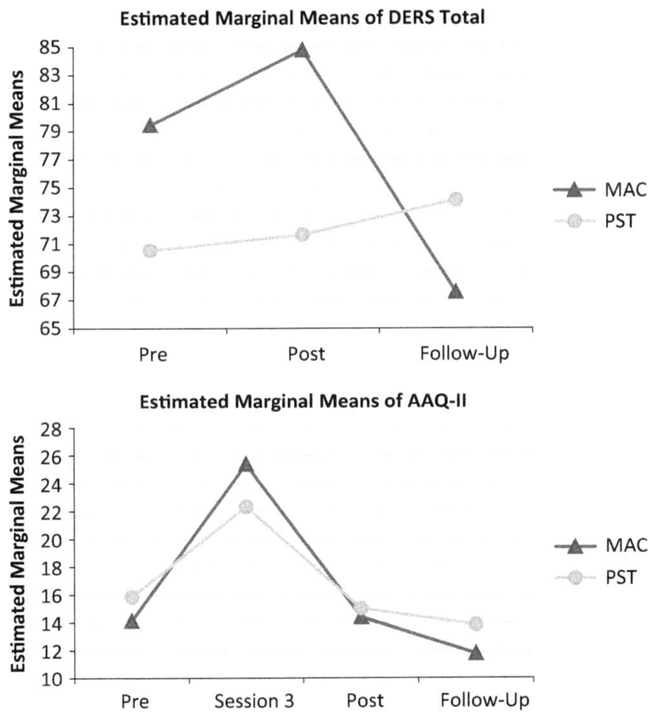

FIGURE 12.2 Estimated marginal means of DERS and AAQ-II scores by group across time.

Results also revealed within-group differences on the AAQ-II ($F (3, 36) = 6.31$, $p = .02$, $h^2p = .35$) when examining scores at four time points (pre-intervention, session three, post-intervention, and one-month follow-up). Upon examination of the pairwise comparisons, it was determined that there were statistically significant differences in AAQ-II scores for MAC participants from pre-intervention to session three ($p = .01$), and from post-intervention to one- month follow-up ($p=.04$). Additionally, statistically significant between-group differences were found on MAAS scores ($F (1, 16) = 4.69$, $p = .05$, $h^2p = .23$), with significantly higher scores in the PST group at pre-intervention ($p = .02$) and post-intervention ($p = .03$). Within-group differences were not found for DERS ($F (2, 32) = 2.21$, $p = .13$, $h^2p = .12$) or MAAS ($F (2, 32) = 0.55$, $p = .58$, $h^2p = .03$) scores (see Figure 12.2).

Sport Performance Measure

A mixed-model ANOVA was also examined for a measure of sport performance, the Overall Performance subscale of the SPQ. A statistically significant within-group main effect was identified for scores on this subscale ($F (2, 32) = 5.77$, $p = .03$, $h^2p = .23$). Consistent with our hypotheses, MAC participants experienced significant increases in sport performance from pre-intervention to post-intervention ($p = .04$).

Marlowe–Crowne Social Desirability Scale Analyses

The Marlowe–Crowne Social Desirability Scale assessed for the presence of impression management by participants. As noted, three participants were removed from the analysis based on a cutoff score of 10 or above. Out of the three participants who were eliminated from the analyses, two were from the PST group and one was from the MAC group.

Outcome Measures

A mixed-model ANOVA was conducted for each of the CCAPS-62 subscales, with the subsample of 15 participants. Statistically significant within-group differences were still found over time in the MAC group on the Distress Index ($F (2, 26) = 3.57$, $p = .04$, $h^2p = .22$), Eating Concerns ($F (2, 26) = 3.78$, $p = .04$, $h^2p = .23$), Generalised Anxiety ($F (2, 26) = 5.50$, $p = .01$, $h^2p = .30$), Hostility ($F (2, 26)=3.17$, $p=.04$, $h^2p =.20$), and Substance Use ($F (2, 26) = 4.39$, $p =.02$, $h^2p = .25$) sub-scales. Upon examination of post hoc pairwise comparisons, the MAC group had statistically significant decreases from pre-intervention to one-month follow-up on the Distress Index ($p = .05$) and Substance Use ($p = .02$) subscales. The MAC group also had significant decreases from post-intervention to one-month follow-up on the Distress

Index ($p = .01$), Generalised Anxiety ($p = .00$), Hostility ($p = .04$), and Substance Use ($p = .01$) subscales. As for interaction effects, a significant interaction of group and time was still found for the Substance Use ($F\ (2, 26) = 3.52$, $p = .05$, $h^2p = .21$) and Hostility ($F\ (2, 26) = 6.01$, $p = .01$, $h^2p = .32$) subscales.

Process and Sport-Specific Measures

Each of the process measures was also re-examined with the subsample of 15 participants, eliminating those who were likely using impression management. Mixed-model ANOVA tests revealed one significant change in the results. Differences between the MAC and PST groups were no longer found on levels of mindfulness, as measured by the MAAS ($F\ (1, 13) = 1.94$, $p = .19$, $h^2p = .13$). Several of the previous findings were still present in the subsample. First, a statistically significant interaction of group and time on the DERS was still present with the sub-sample ($F\ (2, 26) = 4.84$, $p = .02$, $h^2p = .27$). Additionally, statistically significant differences were still present in the MAC group on the AAQ-II over time ($F\ (3, 27) = 3.69$, $p = .03$, $h^2p = .23$). Lastly, statistically significant increases were still found in the MAC group from pre-intervention to post-intervention on ratings of overall performance using the SPQ ($F\ (2, 26) = 5.47$, $p = .03$, $h^2p = .25$).

Discussion

This RCT examined the effectiveness of the MAC programme for behavioural difficulties, emotional distress, psychological symptoms, and athletic performance when compared to an active treatment (traditional PST) among a sample of female collegiate athletes. This investigation was a unique contribution to the empirical literature in two ways. First, this was the first published RCT examining MAC's effectiveness when compared to an active treatment. Since the initial publication of this study, a large number of studies have provided empirical support for MAC as an evidence-based intervention for optimising performance and personal well-being (Ajilchi et al., 2022; Andersson & Nilsson, 2019; Josefsson et al., 2019; MacDougall et al., 2019; Mohebi et al., 2021; Ning et al., 2022; Robinson and Cedenblad, 2020). Given the number of RCTs resulting in positive outcomes, along with the fact that these studies have been generated through research groups unaffiliated with the developers of MAC, the intervention now fully meets criteria as an empirically supported intervention (Chambless et al., 1998; Chambless & Ollendick, 2001; Moore & Gardner, 2023). Second, when this study was first published, this was the first RCT to explore the effectiveness of a mindfulness- and acceptance-based approach with student-athletes for both sport performance and mental health concerns.

Findings from this study suggested (and have since been substantiated) that the MAC is effective in reducing psychological symptoms, behavioural difficulties, and emotional distress, while also improving sport performance among a sample of female collegiate student-athletes. As measured by the CCAPS-62, the MAC group had a statistically significant effect upon Substance Use and Hostility when compared to the PST group. The decrease in substance use among MAC participants should be particularly considered within the context of evidence suggesting that student-athletes consume more alcohol and engage in more frequent heavy episodic binge drinking than non-athletes (e.g., Knettel, Cherenack, & Bianchi-Rossi, 2021). Although studies have found slightly greater use among male student-athletes, substance use among female student-athletes is highly prevalent. According to a 2012 NCAA survey, alcohol use among female athletes increased across sports (except for women's lacrosse) from 2005 to 2009. The survey also found that in 2009, across all NCAA female sports, 20.3% of the student-athletes reported using marijuana within the past 12 months.

This study also evidenced a statistically significant decrease on the Generalised Anxiety and Eating Concerns subscales of the CCAPS-62 from post-intervention to one-month follow-up. The reduction in problems related to eating among MAC participants is a noteworthy finding, considering the high rate of eating issues among female student-athletes, and the related psychological and physical difficulties associated with this issue. It is also a notable result because student-athletes face a number of risk factors associated with disordered eating, may be less likely than non-athletes to seek treatment, and may not receive empirically supported clinical treatments when they do attend treatment (Moore et al., 2007).

In the MAC group, there was a statistically significant decrease on the CCAPS-62 Distress Index, which is a measure of overall psychological distress, from post-intervention to one-month follow-up. Importantly, when the one MAC participant who engaged in impression management was eliminated at each time point, this result became significant from pre-intervention to the one-month follow-up. While the goal of mindfulness- and acceptance-based interventions is the enhancement of personal functioning, whether experiencing or not experiencing affective states, it is noteworthy that MAC participants experienced a reduction in overall psychological distress over time, even though such reduction was not the primary goal of the intervention.

The present study also examined the process variables of emotion regulation, psychological flexibility, and dispositional mindfulness at pre-intervention, post-intervention, and one-month follow-up. Specifically, findings revealed that MAC group participants became more emotionally regulated across time when compared to the PST group. This finding is consistent with the foundational MAC theory suggesting that improved emotion regulation is a mechanism through which the MAC achieves its results (Gardner & Moore, 2007), and is particularly important because research in the clinical psychology literature has consistently demonstrated that numerous forms of psychopathology are associated with difficulties in emotion regulation. According to Werner and Gross (2010), difficulties in emotion regulation are characteristic of over 75% of the disorders listed in the (then current) DSM-IV-TR. In addition, models of eating disorders (Prefit, Candea, & Szentagotai-Tatar, 2019) and alcohol abuse (Weiss et al., 2022) consider deficits in emotion regulation to be an important process through which individuals may become susceptible to pursue food or alcohol to reduce, eliminate, or otherwise control unwanted internal states.

Results also indicate that from post-intervention to one-month follow-up, participants in the MAC group reported statistically significant increases in psychological flexibility as measured by the AAQ-II. These increases in psychological flexibility coincided with decreases in psychological distress at one-month follow-up. This is consistent with empirical evidence demonstrating that there is a negative association between psychological distress and psychological flexibility (Masuda & Tully, 2012). The findings herein are consistent with previous MAC studies, which have found similar results with respect to psychological flexibility. Specifically, Schwanhausser's (2009) case study investigating MAC's effectiveness with an adolescent springboard diver resulted in increases in psychological flexibility, as measured by the AAQ-II, as did two previous case studies in which the MAC intervention resulted in greater psychological flexibility (Gardner & Moore, 2007). Psychological flexibility is an important aspect of social and psychological well-being and overall health, and it is also associated with lower risk of psychopathology (see Kashdan & Rottenberg, 2010). As the findings of the present study noted increased levels of psychological flexibility and reduced difficulties with emotion regulation among participants in the MAC group, it appears that the MAC programme is effective in targeting core mechanisms of psychological distress and dysfunction.

In this study, it was also hypothesised that MAC group participants would achieve greater dispositional mindfulness over time when compared to PST participants. Yet, the data did not support this hypothesis. In contrast to the present study's findings, other mindfulness- and acceptance-based interventions used for performance enhancement, including MAC, have demonstrated increases in attention, awareness, and the related construct of flow as a result of these interventions (Aherne et al., 2011; Schwanhausser, 2009; Thompson et al., 2011). While prior to the intervention there were between-group differences in dispositional mindfulness as measured by the MAAS, these differences were no longer found when controlling for impression management. The lack of increase in dispositional mindfulness noted in this study may be explained in two ways. First, it may be that the dose of mindfulness included in this study was not sufficient. In fact, a study by Goodman et al. (2014) found similar positive results along with increases in dispositional mindfulness by using MAC plus a 60-minute per week yoga intervention with student-athletes. Research has yet to clearly elucidate the most effective "dose" of mindfulness practice to achieve optimal results. It will thus be interesting to replicate these findings to determine whether the MAC programme could benefit from a more intensive focus on the development of mindfulness skills. A more likely possibility is that adequate focus was not given to the mindfulness training component of MAC. In fact, between-session mindfulness monitoring forms recommended by Gardner and Moore (2007) were not utilised in the study.

In the PST group, no statistically significant changes emerged over the course of the intervention on either process or outcome measures. It is not surprising that the PST procedures did not result in mental health benefits, as they were not developed for this purpose. However, a few studies have suggested that athletes can transfer the skills they have learned in PST training into their everyday lives (Gilbert et al., 2008; Horn et al., 2011; Sheard & Golby, 2006). One potential reason why PST did not evidence similar outcomes to MAC may be because it was not specifically designed to target core mechanisms (i.e., experiential avoidance, emotion regulation) thought to underlie several of the clinical concerns measured in this study. As such, caution is warranted when interpreting the clinically oriented results, particularly because the clinical process measures that were selected were possibly more sensitive to the MAC intervention. Interpretation of the results should be considered within the context of the measures selected and may not necessarily be an indication that one intervention is superior to the other. Further, some of the concepts (i.e., using cognitive defusion rather than cognitive restructuring) may at first seem unconventional to athletes, and they may therefore initially prefer PST interventions. The acceptability of these interventions among athletes may be a worthwhile area for future research. In fact, a recent study by Josefsson and colleagues has suggested ways to make MAC concepts more easily understandable and accessible to athletes (Joseffson et al., 2020).

It was also hypothesised that participants in the MAC group would demonstrate greater increases in sport performance over time, as rated by their coach, when compared to the PST group. While this hypothesis was not directly supported, as no between-group differences emerged based upon coach ratings of athletic performance, only participants in the MAC group demonstrated statistically significant increases in overall sport performance from pre-intervention to post-intervention. This finding adds to a growing body of literature suggesting that mindfulness- and acceptance-based interventions can be effective in improving sport performance (Gardner & Moore, 2004; Goodman et al., 2014; Schwanhausser, 2009; Thompson et al., 2011;

Wolanin, 2005; Andersson & Nilsson, 2019; Josefsson et al., 2019; MacDougall et al., 2019). However, this result should be interpreted with caution, given that the pre-score of the MAC group was lower than the PST group. Additionally, the standard deviation of the MAC group was higher than that of the PST group, indicating that there was more variability in scores in the MAC group.

Combined with the mental health-related findings previously noted, the statistically significant improvement in sport performance in the MAC group suggested at the time that this intervention may be effective in simultaneously enhancing athletic performance while also reducing psychological, emotional, and behavioural concerns facing the student-athlete (a finding that has since been strongly supported, as reported earlier). This was a timely finding considering that the NCAA was at the time placing a greater emphasis on mental health awareness among student-athletes (Zillmer & Gigli, 2007) and has gradually increased it's commitment to athlete mental health since that time (NCAA, 2023a). Additionally, athletic departments continued to search for ways to obtain and maintain performance success (Wrisberg et al., 2012).

Limitations

The findings from the original study should continue to be considered within the context of several limitations. First, the study was limited by a small sample size, which increases the chances of Type II error. So, greater results could possibly have been detected with a larger sample size, particularly as this pertains to the lack of between-group differences in the present study. Second, due to the small sample size and low diversity among the sample, the results should be carefully generalised to other populations. The sample was all female, primarily African American, and from the same sport. Third, one of the groups (MAC group) was led by the original first author of the study (Dr. Mike Gross). While there is a possibility that allegiance effects influenced the results, the WAI was administered during the third session to assess whether factors attributed to the clinicians may have influenced the outcome, and no differences between groups were found on this measure. Fourth, the study did not employ random selection, although it did involve random assignment to the treatment conditions. An attempt was made to use random selection, but scheduling issues and time constraints resulted in the decision to use just one team in the present study. Fifth, there may have been pre-intervention differences, particularly those related to sport (i.e., injury) that were not measured prior to the start of the study. However, some sport-related variables (i.e., playing time, starter vs. non-starter) could not be assessed due to preseason status. Sixth, as previously described, the study did not include a no-treatment control group, which may have limited the ability to evaluate if outcomes were due to treatment effects or passage of time. Seventh, the study relied on self-report measures, and although this is common practice in empirical research, it may have limited the validity of the findings. It is possible that the power of the findings could have been increased by including other indices of change for emotional, behavioural, and sport performance outcomes. Eighth, the results of this study may have differed depending upon therapist experience and characteristics. As such, caution is advised when considering these results within the greater context of clinical practice. Future studies comparing sport psychology interventions may benefit from assessing therapist competence. For example, in a RCT comparing acceptance-based behaviour therapy to applied relaxation for generalised anxiety disorder (Hayes-Skelton et al., 2013), an expert rater viewed treatment sessions and used a 4-point Likert scale to assess therapist competence in delivering skills utilised in a particular session. Finally, when delivering PST, it is considered best practice to assess individual needs and demands prior to implementation (Weinberg & Gould, 2015). Future research seeking to build upon the present study should consider using qualitative and quantitative assessments to evaluate pre-intervention needs and demands.

Future Directions

To date, there still exists a limited research base that has systematically examined and compared the effectiveness of different intervention models in sport psychology. Further, most studies have not measured the effects of a sport psychology intervention upon both sport performance and mental health outcomes (Moore, 2007). The research provided an initial framework for conducting this form of investigation. Future research in this area is therefore likely to benefit from conducting similar studies using larger and more diverse samples. Gardner (2009) contended that while conducting RCTs with athletes can be challenging, this potentially can be accomplished via multisite investigations and multiple research teams.

The present study lends support to MAC's impact as an intervention on core mechanisms associated with a wide range of psychopathology. Future research may also benefit from examining MAC's effectiveness as a primary prevention programme for collegiate athletes. There is already some preliminary evidence that MAC is effective as a prevention tool for high school students and high school athletes (Gross et al., 2012), and thus, it would be beneficial to explore MAC's usefulness as a prevention tool among collegiate athletes, as well. Indeed, transdiagnostic prevention programmes that target shared risk factors for mental health problems via a single intervention may be particularly appealing and cost-effective at the college level (Levin et al., 2014).

Future studies should also continue to assess mechanisms of change, which have traditionally been overlooked in sport psychology research

(Moore, 2009). As the field evolves, it is increasingly necessary for sport psychologists to understand what underlying mechanisms account for intervention outcomes (Gardner, 2009).

Conclusion

Collegiate student-athletes represent an at-risk population for mental health concerns, and as such, sport psychologists have a unique opportunity to help these athletes improve both athletic performance and overall psychosocial well-being. According to Gardner (2007):

> … although performance enhancement work is a significant part of most sport psychologists' work, many NCAA institutions are seeking licensed clinical sport psychologists who can not only teach mental strategies for performance enhancement, but also address a wide range of clinical issues such as anxiety disorders, mood disorders, eating disorders, and substance abuse. (p. 207)

The original study served as an empirical investigation of the MAC approach, which was developed specifically to target the core processes that underlie mental health and performance issues. This RCT found that the MAC was effective in reducing psychological, emotional, and behavioural concerns among student-athletes, while also improving sport performance. The findings herein further show that the MAC programme can simultaneously meet the mental health and performance needs of collegiate student-athletes.

References

Aherne, C., Moran, A. P., & Lonsdale, C. (2011). The effects of mindfulness training on athletes' flow: An initial investigation. *The Sport Psychologist*, *25*, 177–189.

Ajilchi, B., Mohebi, M., Zarei, S., & Kisely, S. (2022). Effect of a mindfulness programme training on mental toughness and psychological well-being of female athletes. *Australasian Psychiatry*, *30*(3), 352–356.

American College Health Association (ACHA). (2015).*American college health association-National college health assessment: Reference group data report, Spring.* Baltimore, MD: Author.

Andersson, H., & Nilsson, M. (2019). Internet based Mindfulness-Acceptance-Commitment in sports: A randomized controlled trial. *Master's Thesis, 300 ECTS.* Umea University.

Andrews, P., & Meyer, R. G. (2003). Marlowe–Crowne social desirability scale and short form C: Forensic norms. *Journal of Clinical Psychology*, *59*, 483–492.

Barnhofer, T., Crane, C., Hargus, E., Amarasinghe, M., Winder, R., & Williams, J. M. G. (2009). Mindfulness-based cognitive therapy as a treatment for chronic depression: A preliminary study. *Behaviour Research and Therapy*, *47*, 366–373.

Bautista, T., James, D., & Amaro, H. (2019). Acceptability of mindfulness-based interventions for substance use disorder: A systematic review. *Complementary Therapies in Clinical Practice*, *35*, 201–207.
Bennett, G. (2007). The role of a clinical psychologist in a division I athletics program. *Journal of Clinical Sport Psychology*, *1*, 261–269.
Birrer, D., & Morgan, G. (2010). Psychological skills training as a way to enhance an athlete's performance in high-intensity sports. *Scandinavian Journal of Medicine & Science in Sports, 20*, 78–87.
Bond, F. W., Hayes, S. C., Baer, R. A., Carpenter, K. M., Guenole, N., Orcutt, H. K., … Zettle, R. D. (2011). Preliminary psychometric properties of the acceptance and action questionnaire-II: A revised measure of psychological flexibility and experiential avoidance. *Behavior Therapy, 42*, 676–688.
Brown, K. W., & Ryan, R. M. (2003). The benefits of being present: Mindfulness and its role in psychological well-being. *Journal of Personality and Social Psychology, 84*, 822–848.
Chambless, D. L., Baker, M. J., Baucom, D. H., Beutler, L. E., Calhoun, K. S., Crits-Christoph, P., Daiuto, A., DeRubeis, R., et al. (1998). Update on empirically validated therapies, II. *The Clinical Psychologist, 51*(1), 3–16.
Chambless, D. L., & Ollendick, T. H. (2001). Empirically supported psychological interventions: Controversies and evidence. *Annual Review of Psychology*, *52*, 685–716.
Claspell, E. (2010). Cognitive-behavioral therapies. In M. B. Andersen & S. J. Hanrahan (Eds.), *Routledge handbook of applied sport psychology* (pp. 131–140). New York, NY: Taylor and Francis.
Cohen, J. (1992). A power primer. *Psychological Bulletin*, *112*, 155–159.
Crowne, D. P., & Marlowe, D. (1960). A new scale of social desirability independent of psychopathology. *Journal of Consulting Psychology*, *24*, 349–354.
Drew, B., & Matthews, J. (2019). The prevalence of depressive and anxiety symptoms in student-athletes and the relationship with resilience and help-seeking behavior. *Journal of Clinical Sport Psychology, 13*(3), 421–439.
Eifert, G. H., & Forsyth, J. P. (2005).*Acceptance and commitment therapy for anxiety disorders.* Oakland, CA: New Harbinger.
Etzel, E. F., Ferrante, A. P., & Pinkney, J. W. (2002).*Counseling college student athletes: Issues and interventions* (2nd ed.). Morgantown, WV: Fitness Information Technology.
Gardner, F. L. (2007). Introduction to the special issue: Clinical sport psychology in American intercollegiate athletics. *Journal of Clinical Sport Psychology, 1*, 207–209.
Gardner, F. L. (2009). Efficacy, mechanisms of change, and the scientific development of sport psychology. *Journal of Clinical Sport Psychology*, *3*, 139–155.
Gardner, F. L., & Moore, Z. E. (2004). A mindfulness-acceptance-commitment-based approach to athletic performance enhancement: Theoretical considerations. *Behavior Therapy*, *35*, 707–723.
Gardner, F. L., & Moore, Z. E. (2007).*The psychology of human performance: The mindfulness-acceptance-commitment approach.* New York, NY: Springer.
Gardner, F., & Moore, Z. (2006). *Clinical sport psychology*. Champagne, IL: Human Kinetics.
Gilbert, J. N., Gilbert, W. D., Lewis, D. K., Loney, B. S., Horn, C. M., & Glynn, B. A. (2008, September). *UNIFORM: A mental skills training curriculum for high school and beyond.* Paper presented at the Association for Applied Sport Psychology, St. Louis, MO.

Goodman, F. R., Kashdan, T. B., Mallard, T. T., & Schumann, M. (2014). A brief mindfulness and yoga intervention with an entire NCAA division I athletic team: An initial investigation. *Psychology of Consciousness: Theory, Research, and Practice, 1*, 339–356.

Gratz, K. L., & Roemer, L. (2004). Multidimensional assessment of emotion regulation and dysregulation: Development, factor structure, and initial validation of the difficulties in emotion regulation scale. *Journal of Psychopathology and Behavioral Assessment, 26*, 41–54.

Gross, M., Gardner, F. L., Autera, J., & Moore, Z. E. (2012, November). *Using the mindfulness-acceptance-commitment (MAC) approach with high school student-athletes: An investigation of its effectiveness as a prevention program.* Paper presented at the Association for Applied Sport Psychology, National Harbor, MD.

Gross, M., Moore, Z. E., Gardner, F. L., Wolanin, A. T., Pess, R., & Marks, D. R. (2016). An empirical examination comparing the mindfulness-acceptance-commitment approach and psychological skills training for the mental health and sport performance of female student athletes. *International Journal of Sport and Exercise Psychology, 16*(4), 431–451. 10.1080/1612197x.2016.1250802.

Hamaideh, S. H. (2011). Stressors and reactions to stressors among university students. *International Journal of Social Psychiatry, 57*, 69–80.

Hardy, L., Jones, G., & Gould, D. (1996). *Understanding psychological preparation for sport: Theory and practice of elite performers.* New York, NY: Wiley.

Hayes, S. C., Strosahl, K. D., & Wilson, K. G. (1999). *Acceptance and commitment therapy: An experiential approach to behavior change.* New York, NY: Guilford.

Hayes-Skelton, S. A., Roemer, L., & Orsillo, S. M. (2013). A randomized clinical trial comparing an acceptance-based behavior therapy to applied relaxation for generalized anxiety disorder. *Journal of Consulting and Clinical Psychology, 81*, 761–773.

Hoge, E. A., Bui, E., Marques, L., Metcalf, C., Morris, L., Robinaugh, D., … Simon, N. (2013). Randomized controlled trial of mindfulness meditation for generalized anxiety disorder: Effects on anxiety and stress reactivity. *Journal of Clinical Psychiatry, 74*, 786–792.

Horn, C. M., Gilbert, J. N., Gilbert, W., & Lewis, D. K. (2011). Psychological skills training with community college athletes: The UNIFORM approach. *The Sport Psychologist, 25*, 321–340.

Humphrey, J. H., Yow, D. A., & Bowden, W. W. (2000).*Stress in college athletics: Causes, consequences, coping*. Binghamton, NY: Haworth Half-Court Press.

Hunt, J., & Eisneberg, D. (2010). Mental health problems and help-seeking behavior among college students. *Journal of Adolescent Health, 46*, 3–10.

Josefsson, T., Ivarsson, A., Gustafsson, H., Stenling, A., Lindwall, M., Tornberg, R., & Böröy, J. (2019). Effects of mindfulness-acceptance-commitment (MAC) on sport-specific dispositional mindfulness, emotion regulation, and self-rated athletic performance in a multiple-sport population: an RCT study. *Mindfulness, 10*, 1518–1529.

Josefsson, T., Tornberg, R., Gustafsson, H., & Ivarsson, A. (2020). Practitioners' reflections of working with the mindfulness-acceptance-commitment (MAC) approach in team sport settings. *Journal of Sport Psychology in Action, 11*(2), 92–102. 10.1080/21520704.2018.1549641.

Kashdan, T. B., & Rottenberg, J. (2010). Psychological flexibility as a fundamental aspect of health. *Clinical Psychology Review*, *30*, 865–878.

Kazdin, A. E. (2002). *Research design in clinical psychology* (4th ed.). Needham Heights, MA: Allyn & Bacon.

Knettel, B. A., Cherenack, E. M., & Bianchi-Rossi, C. (2021). Stress, anxiety, binge drinking, and substance use among college student-athletes: A cross-sectional analysis. *Journal of Intercollegiate Sport*, *14*(2), 116–135.

Kristeller, J., Wolever, R. Q., & Sheets, V. (2013). Mindfulness-based eating awareness training (MB-EAT) for binge eating: A randomized clinical trial. *Mindfulness*, *3*, 282–297.

Levin, M. E., Pistorello, J., Seeley, J. R., & Hayes, S. C. (2014). Feasibility of a prototype web-based acceptance and commitment therapy prevention program for college students. *Journal of American College Health*, *62*, 20–30.

Locke, B. D., Buzolitz, J. S., Lei, P. W., Boswell, J. F., McAleavey, A. A., Sevig, T. D., …Hayes, J. A. (2011). Development of the counseling center assessment of psychological symptoms-62 (CCAPS- 62). *Journal of Counseling Psychology, 58*, 97–109.

Loo, R., & Thorpe, K. (2000). Confirmatory factor analyses of the full and short versions of the Marlowe- Crowne social desirability scale. *Journal of Social Psychology*, *140*, 628–635.

Lopes Dos Santos, M., Uftring, M., Stahl, C. A., Lockie, R. G., Alvar, B., Mann, J. B., & Dawes, J. J. (2020). Stress in academic and athletic performance in collegiate athletes: A narrative review of sources and monitoring strategies. *Frontiers in Sports and Active Living*, *2*, 42.

Macdougall, H., O'Halloran, P., Sherry, E., & Shields, N. (2019). A pilot randomised controlled trial to enhance well-being and performance of athletes in para sports. *European Journal of Adapted Physical Activity*, *12*(2).

Masuda, A., & Tully, E. C. (2012). The role of mindfulness and psychological flexibility in somatization, depression, anxiety, and general psychological distress in a non-clinical college sample. *Journal of Evidence-Based Contemporary & Alternative Medicine*, *17*, 66–71.

Meichenbaum, D. (1977).*Cognitive behaviour modification: An integrative approach.* New York: Plenum.

Mohebi, M., Sadeghi-Bahmani, D., Zarei, S., Gharayagh Zandi, H., & Brand, S. (2021). Examining the effects of mindfulness–acceptance–commitment training on self-compassion and grit among elite female athletes. *International Journal of Environmental Research and Public Health*, *19*(1), 134–140.

Moore, Z. E. (2003). Toward the development of an evidence-based practice of sport psychology: A structured qualitative study of performance enhancement interventions. *Dissertation Abstracts International-B, 64*, 5227–5291.

Moore, Z. E. (2007). Critical thinking and the evidence-based practice of sport psychology. *Journal of Clinical Sport Psychology*, *1*, 9–22.

Moore, Z. E. (2009). Theoretical and empirical developments of the mindfulness-acceptance-commitment (MAC) approach to performance enhancement. *Journal of Clinical Sport Psychology, 3*(4), 291–302.

Moore, Z. E., Ciampa, R., Wilsnack, J., & Wright, E. (2007). Evidence-based interventions for the treatment of eating disorders. *Journal of Clinical Sport Psychology*, *1*, 371–378.

Moore, Z. E., & Gardner, F. L. (2023). Mindfulness interventions in sport. In D. Tod, K. Hodge, & V. Krane (Eds.), *Routledge handbook of applied sport psychology: A comprehensive guide for students and practitioners* (2nd ed., pp. 221–230). Routledge.

National Collegiate Athletic Association (NCAA). (2023a). *NCAA coaches report increased focus on mental health, detail personal challenges.* Retrieved from https://www.ncaa.org/news/2023/1/26/media-center-ncaa-coaches-report-increased-focus-on-mental-health-detail-personal-challenges.aspx

National Collegiate Athletic Association (NCAA). (2023b). *Overview.* Retrieved from https://www.ncaa.org/sports/2021/2/16/overview.aspx

Nelson, T. F., & Wechsler, H. (2001). Alcohol and college athletes. *Medicine and Science in Sports and Exercise, 33*, 43–47.

Ning, J. H., Hao, Q. W., & Huang, D. C. (2022). Effects of "mindfulness acceptance insight commitment" training on flow state and mental health of college swimmers: A randomized controlled experimental study. *Frontiers in Psychology, 13*, 799103. 10.3389/fpsyg.2022.799103.

Norton, P. J., Little, T. E., & Wetterneck, C. T. (2014). Does experience matter? Trainee experience and outcomes during transdiagnostic cognitive-behavioral group therapy for anxiety. *Cognitive Behaviour Therapy, 43*(3), 230–238.

Prefit, A. B., Candea, D. M., & Szentagotai-Tătar, A. (2019). Emotion regulation across eating pathology: A meta-analysis. *Appetite, 143*, 104438.

Proctor, S., & Boan-Lenzo, C. (2010). Prevalence of depressive symptoms in male intercollegiate student athletes and nonathletes. *Journal of Clinical Sport Psychology, 4*, 204–220.

Reynolds, W. M. (1982). Development of reliable and valid short forms of the Marlowe-Crowne social desirability scale. *Journal of Clinical Psychology, 38*, 119–125.

Robinson, P., & Cedenblad, M. (2020). Effects of Mindfulness-Acceptance-Commitment (MAC) intervention on self-rated levels of performance and well-being in martial arts competitors. *Bachelor Thesis in Sport and Exercise Psychology, 61-90 ECTS.* School of Health and Welfare: Halmstad University.

Schuling, R., Huijbers, M. J., van Ravesteijn, H., Donders, R., Cillessen, L., Kuyken, W., & Speckens, A. E. (2020). Recovery from recurrent depression: Randomized controlled trial of the efficacy of mindfulness-based compassionate living compared with treatment-as-usual on depressive symptoms and its consolidation at longer term follow-up. *Journal of Affective Disorders, 273*, 265–273.

Schwanhausser, L. (2009). Application of the mindfulness-acceptance-commitment (MAC) protocol with an adolescent springboard diver: The case of Steve. *Journal of Clinical Sport Psychology, 3*, 377–395.

Segal, Z. V., Williams, M. G., & Teasdale, J. D. (2002). *Mindfulness-based cognitive therapy for depression.* New York, NY: Guilford Press.

Sheard, M., & Golby, J. (2006). Effect of a psychological skills training program on swimming performance and positive psychological development. *International Journal of Sport and Exercise Psychology, 4*, 149–169.

Su, N., Si, G., & Zhang, C. Q. (2019). Mindfulness and acceptance-based training for Chinese athletes: The mindfulness-acceptance-insight-commitment (MAIC) program. *Journal of Sport Psychology in Action, 10*(4), 255–263. 10.1080/21520704.2018.1557772.

Suinn, R. M. (1986).*Seven steps to peak performance: The mental training manual for athletes.* Lewistown, NY: Hans Huber.

Sullivan, P., Blacker, M., Murphy, J., & Cairney, J. (2019). Levels of psychological distress of Canadian university student-athletes. *Canadian Journal of Higher Education, 49*(1), 47–59.

Thompson, R. W., Kaufman, K. A., De Petrillo, L. A., Glass, C. R., & Arnkoff, D. B. (2011). One-year follow-up of mindful sport performance enhancement (MSPE) with archers, golfers, and runners. *Journal of Clinical Sport Psychology, 5*, 99–116.

Tracey, T. J., & Kokotovic, A. M. (1989). Factor structure of the working alliance inventory. *Psychological Assessment: A Journal of Consulting and Clinical Psychology, 1*, 207–210.

Trindade, I. A., Guiomar, R., Carvalho, S. A., Duarte, J., Lapa, T., Menezes, P., … & Castilho, P. (2021). Efficacy of online-based acceptance and commitment therapy for chronic pain: A systematic review and meta-analysis. *The Journal of Pain, 22*(11), 1328–1342.

Weinberg, R. S., & Gould, D. (2015). *Foundations of sport & exercise psychology* (6th ed.). Champaign, IL: Human Kinetics.

Weinberg, R. S., & Williams, J. M. (2001). Integrating and implementing a psychological skills training program. In J. M. Williams (Ed.), *Applied sport psychology* (pp. 347–377). Mountain View, CA: Mayfield.

Weiss, N. H., Kiefer, R., Goncharenko, S., Raudales, A. M., Forkus, S. R., Schick, M. R., & Contractor, A. A. (2022). Emotion regulation and substance use: A meta-analysis. *Drug and Alcohol Dependence, 230*, 109–131.

Wieland, A., Chow, G. M., & Bird, M. D. (2018). Clinical issues in sport; exercise and performance: A whole-person approach to helping athletes and individuals succeed in sport and life. In A. Mugford, & J. Gualberto Cremades (Eds.), *Sport, exercise, and performance psychology* (pp. 153–174). Routledge.

Werner, K., & Gross, J. J. (2010). Emotion regulation and psychopathology: A conceptual framework. In A. M. Kring & D. M. Sloan (Eds.), *Emotion regulation and psychopathology* (pp. 13–37). New York, NY: Guilford Press.

Wolanin, A. T. (2005). Mindfulness-acceptance-commitment (MAC) based performance enhancement for division I collegiate athletes: A preliminary investigation. *Dissertation Abstracts International-B, 65*, 3735–3794.

Wolanin, A. T., Hong, E., Marks, D. R., Panchoo, K., & Gross, M. (2016). Prevalence of clinically elevated depressive symptoms in college athletes and differences by gender and sport. *British Journal of Sports Medicine, 50*, 167–171.

Wrisberg, C. A., Withycombe, J., Simpson, D., Loberg, L. A., & Reed, A. (2012). NCAA division I administrators perceptions of the benefits of sport psychology services and possible roles for a consultant. *The Sport Psychologist, 26*, 16–28.

Yau, E. K. B., Ping, N. P. T., & Kuan, G. (2021). The use of Mindfulness Acceptance Commitment (MAC) approach for Malaysian elite triathletes. *Journal of Sport Psychology in Action, 12*(4), 271–279. 10.1080/21520704.2021.1920522.

Zillmer, E. A., & Gigli, R. W. (2007). Clinical sport psychology in intercollegiate athletics. *Journal of Clinical Sport Psychology, 1*, 210–222.

Zook, A., & Sipps, G. J. (1985). Cross-validation of a short form of the Marlowe-Crowne social desirability scale. *Journal of Clinical Psychology, 41*, 236–238.

13

PASSION AND EXERCISE ADDICTION

Healthier Profiles in Team than in Individual Sports: An Update

Attila Szabo, István Soós, Ricardo de la Vega, Roberto Ruíz-Barquín, and Rita Kovacsik

A physically active lifestyle yields numerous health benefits (Anderson & Durstine, 2019; Jakicic et al., 2019). Above and beyond physical benefits, regular physical activity is associated with better mental health (Marconcin et al., 2022). Based on this widespread information, many individuals engage in physical activities to cope with the hassles and challenges of daily life (Berczik et al., 2012; Elliott et al., 2021). Ironically, physical activity, including sports and exercise, may also become a source of stress (Dinardi et al., 2021). In scholastic literature, the repeated urge to train/exercise in increasingly higher volumes, with simultaneous loss of control over it, is known as "exercise addiction" (Szabo, 2010; Szabo & Demetrovics, 2022; Szabo et al., 2015). Other analogous terms are also used in the literature. Examples are "exercise dependence" (Marques et al., 2019), "compulsive exercise" (Schlegl et al., 2022), "obligatory exercise" (Wu et al., 2023), and/or "exercise abuse" (Calogero & Pedrotty, 2004). However, Szabo and Demetrovics (2022 [Figure 9.2, p. 115]) argue that the correct terminology is "addiction" because it incorporates dependence and compulsion.

Exercise addiction often appears to be confused with *commitment* to exercise (Szabo, 2010), which involves passion for and dedication to an activity. MacLaren and Best (2007) warn that although exercise addiction is related to the volume of exercise, the latter is not an index of addiction. Indeed, a more recent investigation (Szabo & Kovacsik, 2019) revealed that exercise addiction is unrelated to exercise volume. Passion toward an activity is a notion that refers to engaging in a beloved activity that one finds essential to the self and invests time and energy into because of an emotional component attached to the activity (Mageau et al., 2009). Vallerand et al. (2003) conceptualized passion as an intense affinity toward an activity people

DOI: 10.4324/9781003459750-13

love, value, and invest effort and time in. Love and value separate this activity from others, toward which the person may show interest or even intrinsic motivation, but are less significant (Mageau et al., 2009).

Individuals demonstrate an affinity for their beloved activity in both autonomous and controlled ways, which determine the form of their passion through behavioral regulation. In the context of the latter, people could love and value their activity (i.e., sport) for autonomous reasons motivated by the inherent satisfaction generated by the activity itself or for controlled reasons serving the compensatory function of the activity (Mageau et al., 2009; Vallerand et al., 2003). Although total segregation of these two reasons may be impractical, an activity performed for autonomous reasons is characterized more by harmonious passion, while an activity undertaken for rigidly controlled reasons is characterized more by obsessive passion (Mageau et al., 2009).

Harmonious passion is, therefore, a result of autonomous internalization that generates an intense but controlled drive to be part of the activity that is freely accepted by the person, and it is in congruence with aspects of the self in which it becomes integrated (Mageau et al., 2009). Harmonious passion becomes evident when one flexibly engages in the autonomously internalized activity, which then is strongly and directly related to positive affect while being inversely associated with negative affect (Stenseng et al., 2011; Vallerand et al., 2003; Vallerand et al., 2006; Vallerand & Miquelon, 2007).

In contrast, obsessive passion surfaces in the absence of fulfillment of one's intrinsic needs that may result in the internalization of intra- or interpersonal pressures or both; it may emerge when one internalizes the activity in a rigid/controlled way when the participation is obligatory, which is strongly related to negative affect (Lalande et al., 2015). An obsessively passionate person attaches importance to activity contingencies such as self-esteem and the escape from problems (i.e., stress), which makes it difficult to stop a passionate activity (Vallerand, 2010). Thus, self-pressures may arise from contingencies attached to the activity and loss of control over the activity and/or social pressure (Mageau, 2009). Vallerand et al. (2003) propose that engaging in an activity with obsessive passion may be a substitute for self-worth that motivates the indulgence in the activity for ego-nourishment. Obsessively passionate individuals feel compelled to pursue their activity. Therefore, although the person likes or loves the activity (Vallerand, 2015), she/he feels an urge to engage in it because of one or more internal contingencies.

Consequently, extrapolating from Kenrick's and Cialdini's (1977) thoughts on romantic passion, obsessive passion, despite the intrinsic motivational aspects and love for the activity like those seen in harmonious passion, may be perceived as being primarily regulated by negative reinforcement that characterizes the compelled nature to the chosen activity, in contrast to harmonious passion that is regulated via positive reinforcement as mirrored by the freely chosen characteristic of the behavior. New research (Smith, 2023), however, criticizes the Passion Scale (Marsh et al., 2013), the tool used for measuring obsessive and harmonious passion, and there is argument and evidence for the two-dimensionality of passion leading to one passion, characterized by suffering and pleasure or "pain and gain" as reflected by high harmonious passion surfacing along high obsessive passion (Szabo et al., 2022).

Currently, there is limited empirical work connecting exercise addiction and passion. Obsessive passion was positively associated with exercise addiction in endurance sports and other leisure physical activities (Schipfer & Stoll, 2015; Stenseng et al., 2011). It was shown that obsessive passion is linked to all the dimensions of exercise addiction (time, reduction in other activities, tolerance, withdrawal, continuance, intention effects, and lack of control), which was not the case for the harmonious passion that was only related to time and tolerance (Paradis et al., 2013). Further, it was revealed that harmoniously passionate exercisers could increase the time spent on exercise without decreasing the time invested in other essential life activities, which is not the case for obsessively passionate exercisers, who spend exaggerated time on exercise while taking time away from other important life activities (Paradis et al., 2013). The gist of these findings was strengthened by a Greek study demonstrating that obsessive passion bears a stronger relationship to exercise addiction than harmonious passion (Parastatidou et al., 2014). This finding was supported later by Kovacsik et al. (2018), who reported that obsessive passion was the strongest (32%) predictor of exercise addiction. In contrast, Sicilia et al. (2017) reported that both harmonious and obsessive passion were significant mediators between goal content and exercise addiction.

The link between exercise addiction and passion, as a function of the athletic level of competition, was examined in a large sample of low- and high-level competitive athletes and non-competitive leisure exercisers (De La Vega et al., 2016). The findings suggested that obsessive passion strongly predicted exercise addiction, accounting for 37% of its variance. In contrast, harmonious passion was not a significant component of the model. While athletes in formal competitive sports scored higher than leisure exercisers on all measures, no differences were disclosed in exercise addiction and passion between athletes competing at low and high levels. Finally, De La Vega et al. (2016) found that athletes in team sports may report greater harmonious and obsessive passion than those participating in individual sports.

The objectives of the current work were to directly investigate the connection between exercise addiction and passion in team and individual sports, and because exercise volume may be related to exercise addiction (İrem & Bavli, 2016; MacLaren & Best, 2007), we also assessed the triangular link between reported weekly hours of exercise, passion, and exercise addiction. The importance of examining this link lies in the proposal of De La Vega et al. (2016) who suggested that "*The concept of exercise addiction is not a plain and independent construct and may not reflect a psychological dysfunction in the athletic population*" (p. 325), which could explain the consistently higher exercise addiction scores noted in athletes – regardless of the form of participation (i.e., individual or team) – than leisure or recreational exercisers (Szabo et al., 2015). The high exercise addiction scores in athletes could reflect a passion for sport rather than a behavioral addiction.

We hypothesized that obsessive passion and weekly hours of exercise, but not harmonious passion, will predict exercise addiction. To directly test De La Vega et al.'s (2016) findings, we hypothesized that team-sport athletes will exhibit more obsessive- and harmonious passion than athletes in individual sports. Further, given that athletes, in general (whether they are involved in team or individual sports), report higher exercise addiction than recreational exercisers (Szabo et al., 2015), and since all participants in the current study were athletes, we postulated that team and individual athletes will not differ in their risk for exercise addiction scores.

Methods

Sample Size Calculation

The required sample size (n) for regression was calculated using the G*Power (v. 3) software (Faul et al., 2007). The *a priori* test (power (1 − β = .95, medium effects size (f^2) = .15, α = .05, with three predictors (obsessive passion, harmonious passion, and weekly hours of exercise) revealed that the required sample size was 119. The minimum sample size for the group comparisons or between groups analyses (power 1 − β = .95, medium effects size (f^2) = .15, and α = .05, with three dependent measures (obsessive passion, harmonious passion, and exercise addiction) and two covariates (age and weekly hours of exercise) was 73.

Participants

The study was conducted at the Budapest University Athletics Club (BEAC), incorporating over 10 organized sports. Using a "one in three" systematic randomization method, members of three team sports (defined as individuals interacting and depending on each other while working for a shared goal) and three individual sports clubs who trained with an equal frequency (three times per week), were solicited to take part in the study. The sports were cheerleading,[1] football, and basketball, representing team sports (n = 92), and gymnastics, running, and kettlebell forming the individual sports (n = 98). We examined 190 volunteers (78 men and 112 women; mean age = 22.94,

SD = 4.64 years). They trained an average of 6.20 (*SD* = 3.30) hours per week for 6.08 (SD = 5.48) years for a minimum of one year. All participants were Hungarians. Ethical clearance for the study was granted by the Research Ethics Committee at the Faculty of Education and Psychology at Eötvös Loránd University in Budapest, which ensured that the work conformed to the ethical principles for research with human participants of the Helsinki Declaration (World Medical Association, 2008).

Materials

A demographic questionnaire was used to determine the participants' gender, age, weekly hours of exercise, and history of exercise. The Hungarian (Mónok et al., 2012) validated version of the Exercise Addiction Inventory (Terry et al., 2004) was used to assess the risk for exercise addiction. This is a six-item scale based on the components model of addictions (Griffiths, 2005). Sample items include "*Exercise is the most important thing in my life*" or "*If I have to miss an exercise session, I feel moody and irritable.*" The exercise addiction inventory is rated on a 5-point Likert scale and ranges from *"strongly disagree"* to *"strongly agree"*; the scale comes with good psychometric properties (Griffiths et al., 2015; Mónok et al., 2012; Terry et al., 2004). Its internal reliability (Cronbach alpha [α]) ranges between .68 and .80 across several international studies (Griffiths et al., 2015). The Hungarian version's internal reliability is .72 (Mónok et al., 2012).

Another paper and pencil tool used was the psychometrically revalidated Passion Scale (Marsh et al., 2013). We used its Hungarian version (Tóth-Király et al., 2017). Sample items include "*This activity is in harmony with the other activities in my life*" or "*If I could, I would only do my activity.*" The word "activity," in this case, refers to the practiced sport. The scale gauges harmonious passion on a 6-item subscale and obsessive passion on another 6-item subscale. Both subscales are rated on a 7-point Likert scale, ranging from *"not agree at all"* to *"very strongly agree."* The internal reliability of both subscales is good; Cronbach α of the obsessive passion scale is .86, and that of the harmonious subscale is .83. The respective values for the Hungarian version are .88 and .80 (Tóth-Király et al., 2017).

Procedure

After reading and signing a written informed consent form, the participants completed the two questionnaires in their usual training environments before their scheduled training. Data were entered in an SPSS (Statistical Package for Social Sciences) file (Version 22.0), verified by two experimenters and analyzed with the same software.

Statistical Analyses

Initial correlations were followed by hierarchical multiple regression analysis to test the predicting power of obsessive passion, harmonious passion, and weekly hours of training on exercise addiction scores. A multivariate analysis of covariance (MANCOVA) was used to test the null hypothesis that athletes in team and individual sports do not differ from each other in obsessive passion, harmonious passion, and exercise addiction.

Results

As expected, initial correlations yielded statistically significant relationships among all measures (Table 13.1). Fisher's r-to-z transformation determining statistical significance between two correlation coefficients showed that the strength of the relationship between the weekly hours of exercise and the two forms of passion, as well as the risk of exercise addiction, was statistically not significant. However, there was a trend in obsessive ($z = -1.56$, $p = 0.059$) and harmonious passion ($z = -1.30$, $p = 0.097$), being more closely related to exercise volume than the risk of exercise addiction.

The relationships between the dependent measures warranted the inclusion of the weekly hours of exercise and obsessive passion and harmonious passion in the hierarchical multiple regression to test the predicting power of these variables on exercise addiction. First, the standard residuals (St. Resid.) were analyzed to identify any outliers in the data. This test indicated that Participant No. 114 needed to be removed. After removing this outlier, the sample size decreased from 190 to 189. The re-test of the standardized residuals indicated that the new data did not contain any further outliers (St. Resid. Min. = −2.665, St. Resid. Max. = 2.359). Subsequently, the test of the assumption of collinearity indicated that multicollinearity was not a concern in the data (harmonious passion, tolerance = .608, *variance inflation factor* [*VIF*] = 1.644; obsessive passion, tolerance = .592, *VIF* = 1.689; weekly hours of exercise, tolerance = .672, *VIF* = 1.488). The data also met the

TABLE 13.1 Statistically significant correlations between the exercise addiction, obsessive passion, harmonious passion, and reported weekly hours of exercise (Pearson r; p < .001 in all instances)

	Obsessive Passion	*Harmonious Passion*	*Weekly Hours of Exercise*
Exercise addiction	0.599	0.493	0.391
Obsessive passion		0.582	0.519
Harmonious passion			0.499

assumption of independent errors (Durbin-Watson value = 1.946). Finally, the data met the assumption of non-zero variances (harmonious passion, variance (s^2) = 26.686; obsessive passion, s^2 = 36.393; weekly hours of exercise, s^2 = 10.896). The order of entering the independent variables in the hierarchical regression was (1) obsessive passion, (2) harmonious passion, and (3) weekly hours of exercise. The results of the regression analysis provided partial confirmation of our research hypothesis. Beta (β) coefficients for the three predictors were: obsessive passion, $\beta = .253$, $t = 6.073$, $p < .001$; harmonious passion, $\beta = .132$, $t = 2.747$, $p = .007$; and weekly hours of exercise, $\beta = .056$, $t = .789$, $p > .05$. The best fitting model for predicting exercise addiction is a linear combination of obsessive passion and harmonious passion ($R = .624$, $R^2 = .390$, F (1,186) = 9.621, $p = .002$). However, despite statistical significance, harmonious passion had a small contribution to the model (R^2 change = .032).

The 2 (type of sport: individual-, team-sport) by 2 (gender: men, women) (the dependent measures: obsessive passion, harmonious passion, exercise addiction) MANCOVA using age and the weekly hours of exercise as the covariate, yielded a statistically significant multivariate main effect for the type of sport (Pillai's Trace = .097, $F(3, 181) = 6.50$, $p < .001$, partial ETA squared (η_p^2) = .097, power ($1 - \beta = .969$). While age was not significant, the other covariate, weekly hours of exercise, was also statistically significant (Pillai's Trace = .287, $F(3, 181) = 24.34$, $p < .001$, $\eta_p^2 = .287$, $1 - \beta = 1.0$). No gender main effect, or gender by type of sport, interaction has emerged from this analysis ($p >.05$). The follow-up univariate tests revealed that athletes in team sports scored statistically significantly higher on harmonious passion than those in individual sports ($F(1, 183) = 17.29$, $p < .001$, $\eta_p^2 = .086$, $1 - \beta = .985$; Table 13.2). This finding was further examined with a Bootstrap ANOVA to determine robustness and bias (Table 13.3).

Given the group differences found in harmonious passion, we were interested in re-examining the relationship between passion and exercise addiction, now separately for the two groups, by repeating the hierarchical multiple regression analysis initially performed for the whole sample.[2] Given that weekly hours of exercise was not a significant predictor in the regression

TABLE 13.2 Means and standard deviations in brackets, F and p values (in brackets) and effects sizes (partial ETA squared (η_p^2) for three dependent measures

	Team Sport	*Individual Sport*	F, p	η_p^2
Exercise addiction	20.80 (3.21)	19.99 (3.47)	0.054 (.817, NS*)	.000
Obsessive passion	25.42 (5.01)	22.74 (6.62)	2.31 (=.130, NS*)	.012
Harmonious passion	36.35 (2.96)	32.21 (5.94)	17.29 (< .001)	.086

**Note:* NS = Not Significant.

TABLE 13.3 Result of the Bootstrap (1000 bootstrap samples) ANOVA for harmonious passion comparing team and individual sports

	Statistic	*Bias*	*Standard Error*	*Bootstrap Confidence Intervals (95%)*	
				Lower	*Upper*
Team Sport	Mean	.0049	.2947	35.771	36.968
	SD	−.0270	.2564	2.490	3.3841
Individual Sport	Mean	.0113	.6054	30.982	33.488
	SD	−.0439	.4866	5.039	6.724

analysis of the full sample, only obsessive passion was entered first, followed by harmonious passion in these hierarchical multiple regressions. After ascertaining that assumptions were met, as done for the full-sample regression described above, we found two models that were statistically significant (Table 13.4). Given the fact that harmonious passion only added 4% and 3%, respectively, to the second model in both cases, only the first model, containing obsessive passion as the predictor of exercise addiction (boxed in Table 13.4), was further tested with an analysis of covariance (ANCOVA) to verify the interaction between obsessive passion (used as a covariate) and team and individual sports groups' exercise addiction as the dependent measure. The interaction was statistically not significant, indicating that the slopes of the regression line of the covariate did not differ, merely the predictor's (obsessive passion) range was statistically significantly different in the two groups ($F(1, 185) = 84.79$, $p < .001$, $\eta_p^2 = .314$). Therefore, the relationship between obsessive passion and exercise addiction was stronger in the individual than in team sports.

Finally, we calculated the prevalence of the risk for exercise addiction (indicated by a score of 24 or more on exercise addiction [Terry et al., 2004]) in the studied samples. The overall rate of risk for exercise addiction was 15.3%. When examining the prevalence in team and individual groups, Chi-Square indicated that the groups did not differ and had an approximately equal rate of risk for exercise addiction: 15.4% in team sports and 15.3% in individual sports.

Discussion

The key findings emerging from the current investigation are that obsessive passion is a significant component of exercise addiction, especially in individual sports, and that athletes in organized team sports report greater harmonious passion than athletes in individual sports. In contrast to our hypothesis, the weekly exercise volume was not a predictor of exercise addiction, but harmonious passion was, even though it contributed only

TABLE 13.4 Summary of the hierarchical multiple regression analyses performed separately for team sports (n = 91) and individual sports (n = 98). The R^2 is highlighted in both cases to stress the difference in the predictive power of obsessive passion on (obsessive passion) the dependent variable, exercise addiction (exercise addiction), in the two forms of organized sports

		Predictor	*R*	*R²*	*F*	*p*	*B**	*SE***	*t*	*p*
Team Sports	Model 1	Obsessive Passion	.45	**.21**	22.92	<.001	.29	.06	4.79	<.001
	Model 2	Obsessive Passion	.50	**.25**	14.40	<.001	.23	.07	3.49	=.001
		Harmonious Passion					.25	.11	2.21	=.03
Individual Sports	Model 1	Obsessive Passion	.69	**.47**	84.99	<.001	.36	.04	9.22	<.001
	Model 2	Obsessive Passion	.71	**.50**	48.27	<.001	.29	.05	5.96	<.001
		Harmonious Passion					.14	.05	2.57	=.012

Note: B* = Unstandardized coefficients; SE** = Standard Error.

3–4% to the variance in exercise addiction. Exercise volume is, in general, relatively high in athletes and does not reflect exercise addiction (Szabo et al., 2015). Thus, unlike recreational exercisers (Szabo, 2010), the relationship between exercise volume and exercise addiction seems to be absent in athletes, whether they are involved in individual or team sports. However, such a relationship may be absent in general, not only in athletes.

This conjecture is supported by a study using the data from the current and another study (Kovacsik et al., 2018) combined and showing that high- and low-exercise volume groups differed in exercise addiction even after controlling for age and sex ($p < .001$), but after adding obsessive and harmonious passion as continuous predictor variables, the statistical significance disappeared, whereas the predictors were statistically significant. Moreover, when controlled for the effect of passion, the correlation between exercise addiction and weekly exercise volume was weak and negative. Thus, in contrast to exercise addiction, passion appears to be more closely related to exercise volume. In the current study, providing 38.2% of the data for another paper (Szabo & Kovacsik, 2019), a trend emerged hinting at a stronger relationship between exercise volume and passion than between the risk of exercise addiction and exercise volume. Therefore, it is understandable why Szabo and Kovacsik warned that a conceptual confound between *a presumed risk of exercise addiction* and passion could jeopardize the results of hundreds of published works in the area.

Finally, the results reveal that the rate of the risk for exercise addiction in team sports is relatively high (15%). This figure was not different from that obtained in individual sports. These findings are consistent with previous reports from studies on exercise addiction among elite athletes (Szabo et al., 2015; Juwono et al., 2022). However, as discussed in two recent papers (Griffiths et al., 2023; Juwono et al., 2022), it seems illogical to investigate addiction in *scheduled* sports settings because an addiction (driven by cravings and urges) cannot be scheduled. Athletic training and team sports are scheduled. Thus, one addicted in this sports environment should do “extra” training above and beyond the scheduled team training to fuel exercise addiction, potentially harming the athletic career (Griffiths et al., 2023).

Our findings replicate the results of De La Vega et al. (2016) in that the current results show that obsessive passion predicts exercise addiction. Indeed, obsessive passion determines more than one-third of the variance (37% in de La Vega et al. and 36% in the current work) in exercise addiction. These results corroborate past reports linking obsessive passion to exercise addiction (Paradis et al., 2013; Schipfer & Stoll, 2015; Stenseng et al., 2011). They also match the results of Parastatidou et al. (2014) and Kovacsik et al. (2018), showing that obsessive passion manifests a stronger relationship to exercise addiction than harmonious passion.

Indeed, in De La Vega et al.'s study, harmonious passion was not a significant predictor of exercise addiction, while in Kovacsik et al., similarly to the present inquiry, despite the statistical significance, it only accounted for 3% of the variance in exercise addiction. Similarly, in a recent study (Alcaraz-Ibáñez & Paterna, 2023), harmonious passion explained a significant proportion of variance in fewer exercise addiction measures than obsessive passion. Therefore, obsessive passion and exercise addiction seem to have many commonalities, while the latter bears a weaker connection to harmonious passion. However, based on recent arguments of the two-dimensionality of passion, the obsessive passion scores on the Passion Scale may simply reflect an *obsession* with the sport (Szabo et al., 2022).

The current findings expand those of De La Vega et al. (2016), who reported that the commonality between exercise addiction and obsessive passion is stronger in individual than in team sports. Indeed, in the former, obsessive passion accounted for nearly half (47%) of the total variance in exercise addiction, while in the latter, for less than half (21%) of that seen in individual sports. While these are novel findings concerning the differences between team and individual sports, it should be mentioned that the relationship between obsessive passion and exercise addiction appears to be mediated via introjected regulation (Parastatidou et al., 2014) that is a component of external motivation (Pelletier et al., 1995). Since Parastatidou et al. (2014) studied fitness participants in leisure centers, the next step is to study the moderating role of motivational factors in the relationship between passion and exercise addiction in organized sports, with an expanded focus on the differences between team and individual athletes.

Since the publication of this research, a longitudinal study (Kovacsik et al., 2021) has examined the suggested relationship in 149 novice exercisers who trained once a week for 90 min. The results suggested that the risk of exercise addiction and passion were already high at baseline and slightly increased over the 12-week study period. Several motivational factors predicted passion, while the risk of exercise addiction was predicted by female gender, team sport participation, higher exercise intensity, and identified motivation. Such findings suggest that passion and exercise addiction may show relatively independent developmental patterns associated with different motivational features. Therefore, passion and exercise addiction may exhibit a relationship, but they still could be independent constructs concerning the associated motivational determinants. Future studies should look at motivational constructs and their role in long-term habitual exercisers training with greater exercise volume than in the research by Kovacsik et al. (2021). They also should consider the two-dimensional view of passion.

The current findings reveal that harmonious passion is higher in athletes participating in team sports than in individual sports. This finding replicates the results of De La Vega et al. (2016) and agrees with the results reported by

Vallerand et al. (2003). An explanation for this finding is that in addition to the physical and mental aspects of the athletic activity found in individual sports, team sports have a social context that could affect harmonious passion. Indeed, collective motivation, shared success, and cooperation may be associated with greater harmonious passion in team versus individual sports. Further, the level of socialization, which is higher in a team- than in individual sports (Devecioglu et al., 2012), may also contribute to the greater harmonious passion in the former group. Combined with a weaker link between obsessive passion and exercise addiction, athletes in team sports demonstrate a healthier profile in these variables than in individual sports. Indeed, individual athletes are likely to exert greater internal pressure and control on their training, which may be linked to higher obsessive passion (obsession?), and do not profit from some of the social aspects of athletic training, which could mirror a lower harmonious passion in contrast to team players.

The risk for exercise addiction rate was relatively high in the present study in both team and individual sports. However, the obtained figure (15%) is lower than in some studies (Blaydon & Lindner, 2002; Costa et al., 2015; McNamara & McCabe, 2012; Szabo et al., 2013), that ranged from 17.0% to 41.4%. Still, it is higher than the prevalence reported for various sports in a review paper (Di Lodovico et al., 2019). It was argued that in team sports, the differences may be due to the different interpretations of the items measuring exercise addiction between athletes and leisure exercisers (Szabo et al., 2015; Szabo & Demetrovics, 2022). This contention remains to be tested in future research.

Limitations

The current study has limitations; using more than one exercise addiction assessment tool is warranted. While the work successfully replicates past results, how representative the selected team and individual sports athletes are of the athletic population, in general, is uncertain. Further, although the required sample size was calculated *a priori*, to generate a robust conclusion interpretable at the population level, results obtained from a larger sample would be more reliable. Finally, cultural differences in passion, especially obsessive passion, may exist (Szabo et al., 2018, 2022), which could also affect the generalizability of the current findings. Finally, future research with a greater representation of team and individual sports is necessary. The results obtained here may only be tentative but should motivate further work.

Conclusions

The study replicates limited findings in the field, revealing that obsessive passion strongly predicts exercise addiction, while harmonious passion has a limited predictive power in the latter. The present work expands past reports by showing that the connection between obsessive passion and exercise addiction is more than twice as high in individual sports than in team sports. Still, motivational factors could mediate the passion-addiction relationship, subject to future research. This work also provides evidence for higher harmonious passion in team sports than in individual sports; these findings project a healthier profile in passion and obsessive passion-exercise addiction relationship in team than in individual sports.

Financial Support

No financial support was received for this study.

Ethical Clearance

Ethical permission for the study was obtained from the Faculty of Education and Psychology Research Ethics Committee at Eötvös Loránd University.

Author Contribution

AS wrote the current update, helped in the original research design, and wrote the Methods, Discussion, and Conclusion sections of the original report. IS did the literature search, wrote part of the Introduction, and performed part of the statistical analyses; RV had primary theoretical input on passion and the data interpretation; RR took part in data analysis and reviewed the coherency of the chapter as well as he cross-checked the references; RK conceived the design, coordinated the research, and collected the data.

Conflict of Interest

The authors have no conflict of interest to declare.

Acknowledgments

The authors thank the Budapest University Athletics Club (BEAC) managers for helping with the subject requirement among its athletes.

Notes

1 *Unlike soccer and basketball that are open-skill team sports, cheerleading is an interactive closed-skill team sport in which 15 to 25 individuals work together and depend on each other.*

2 *Given that group-sample size was lower than the whole sample size, the power (1 - β error probability) decreased from 0.95 to 0.91 in the team sports group (n = 91) and to 0.93 in the individual sports group (n = 98).*

References

Alcaraz-Ibáñez, M., & Paterna, A. (2023). An exploratory examination of the relationship between harmonious and obsessive passion and specific symptoms of exercise dependence. *International Journal of Sport and Exercise Psychology*, Online first. 10.1080/1612197x.2023.2180071

Anderson, E., & Durstine, J. L. (2019). Physical activity, exercise, and chronic diseases: A brief review. *Sports Medicine and Health Science*, *1*(1), 3–10. 10.1016/j.smhs.2019.08.006

Berczik, K., Szabo, A., Griffiths, M. D., Kurimay, T., Kun, B., Urbán, R., & Demetrovics, Z. (2012). Exercise addiction: Symptoms, diagnosis, epidemiology, and etiology. *Substance Use & Misuse*, *47*(4), 403–417. 10.3109/10826084.2011.639120

Blaydon, M. J., & Lindner, K. J. (2002). Eating disorders and exercise dependence in triathletes. *Eating Disorders, 10*(1), 49–60. 10.1080/106402602753573559

Calogero, R. M., & Pedrotty, K. N. (2004). The practice and process of healthy exercise: An investigation of the treatment of exercise abuse in women with eating disorders. *Eating Disorders, 12*(4), 273–291. 10.1080/10640260490521352

Costa, S., Hausenblas, H. A., Oliva, P., Cuzzocrea, F., & Larcan, R. (2015). Perceived parental psychological control and exercise dependence symptoms in competitive athletes. *International Journal of Mental Health and Addiction, 13*(1), 59–72. 10.1007/s11469-014-9512-3

De La Vega, R., Parastatidou, I. S., Ruiz-Barquin, R., & Szabo, A. (2016). Exercise addiction in athletes and leisure exercisers: The moderating role of passion. *Journal of Behavioral Addictions, 5*(2), 325–331. 10.1556/2006.5.2016.043

Devecioglu, S., Sahan, H., Yildiz, M., Tekin, M., & Sim, H. (2012). Examination of socialization levels of university students engaging in individual and team sports. *Procedia-Social and Behavioral Sciences*, *46*, 326–330. 10.1016/j.sbspro.2012.05.115

Di Lodovico, L., Poulnais, S., & Gorwood, P. (2019). Which sports are more at risk of physical exercise addiction: A systematic review. *Addictive Behaviors*, *93*, 257–262. 10.1016/j.addbeh.2018.12.030

Dinardi, J. S., Egorov, A. Y., & Szabo, A. (2021). The expanded interactional model of exercise addiction.*Journal of Behavioral Addictions*, *10*(3), 626–631. 10.1556/2006.2021.00061

Elliott, L. D., Wilson, O. W., Holland, K. E., & Bopp, M. (2021). Using exercise as a stress management technique during the COVID-19 pandemic: The differences between men and women in college.*International Journal of Exercise Science, 14*(5), 1234–1246. PMID: 35096245

Faul, F., Erdfelder, E., Lang, A. G., & Buchner, A. (2007). G*Power 3: A flexible statistical power analysis program for the social, behavioral, and biomedical sciences. *Behavior Research Methods*, *39*(2), 175–191. 10.3758/bf03193146.

Griffiths, M. (2005). A 'components' model of addiction within a biopsychosocial framework.*Journal of Substance Use, 10*(4), 191–197. 10.1080/14659890500114359

Griffiths, M. D., Landolfi, E., & Szabo, A. (2023). Does exercise addiction exist among individuals engaged in team-based exercise? A position paper.*International Journal of Mental Health and Addiction.* Online first. 10.1007/s11469-023-01039-5

Griffiths, M. D., Urbán, R., Demetrovics, Z., Lichtenstein, M. B., de la Vega, R., Kun, B., … & Szabo, A. (2015). A cross-cultural re-evaluation of the Exercise Addiction Inventory in five countries. *Sports Medicine-Open, 1*(1), 1–7. 10.1186/s40798-014-0005-5

İrem, U. Z., & Bavli, Ö. (2016). Do regular exercises cause exercise dependence symptom on sedentaries?. *International Journal of Science Culture and Sport (IntJSCS), 4*(1), 68–75. 10.14486/intjscs487

Jakicic, J. M., Kraus, W. E., Powell, K. E., Campbell, W. W., Janz, K. F., Troiano, R. P., … & Piercy, K. L. (2019). Association between bout duration of physical activity and health: Systematic review. *Medicine & Science in Sports & Exercise, 51*(6), 1213–1219. 10.1249/mss.0000000000001933

Juwono, I. D., Tolnai, N., & Szabo, A. (2022). Exercise addiction in athletes: A systematic review of the literature. *International Journal of Mental Health and Addiction, 20*(5), 3113–3127. 10.1007/s11469-021-00568-1

Kenrick, D. T., & Cialdini, R. B. (1977). Romantic attraction: Misattribution versus reinforcement explanations.*Journal of Personality and Social Psychology, 35*(6), 381–391. 10.1037/0022-3514.35.6.381

Kovacsik, R., Griffiths, M. D., Pontes, H. M., Soós, I., de la Vega, R., Ruíz-Barquín, R., Demetrovics, Z., & Szabo, A. (2018). The role of passion in exercise addiction, exercise volume, and exercise intensity in long-term exercisers.*International Journal of Mental Health and Addiction, 17*(6), 1389–1400. 10.1007/s11469-018-9880-1

Kovacsik, R., Tóth-Király, I., Egorov, A., & Szabo, A. (2021). A longitudinal study of exercise addiction and passion in new sport activities: The impact of motivational factors. *International Journal of Mental Health and Addiction, 19*(5), 1511–1526. 10.1007/s11469-020-00241-z

Lalande, D., Vallerand, R. J., Lafrenière, M.-A. K., Verner-Filion, J., Laurent, F.-A., Forest, J., & Paquet, Y. (2015). Obsessive passion: A compensatory response to unsatisfied needs.*Journal of Personality, 85*(2), 163–178. 10.1111/jopy.12229

MacLaren, V. V., & Best, L. A. (2007). Symptoms of exercise dependence and physical activity in students. *Perceptual and Motor Skills, 105*(3 suppl), 1257–1264. 10.2466/pms.105.4.1257-1264

Mageau, G. A., Vallerand, R. J., Charest, J., Salvy, S.-J., Lacaille, N., Bouffard, T., & Koestner, R. (2009). On the development of harmonious and obsessive passion: The role of autonomy support, activity specialization, and identification with the activity. *Journal of Personality, 77*(3), 601–646. 10.1111/j.1467-6494.2009.00559.x

Marconcin, P., Werneck, A. O., Peralta, M., Ihle, A., Gouveia, É. R., Ferrari, G., Sarmento, H., & Marques, A. (2022). The association between physical activity and mental health during the first year of the COVID-19 pandemic: A systematic review. *BMC Public Health, 22*(1). 10.1186/s12889-022-12590-6

Marques, A., Peralta, M., Sarmento, H., Loureiro, V., Gouveia, É. R., & Gaspar de Matos, M. (2019). Prevalence of risk for exercise dependence: A systematic review. *Sports Medicine, 49*, 319–330. 10.1007/s40279-018-1011-4

Marsh, H. W., Vallerand, R. J., Lafrenière, M.-A. K., Parker, P., Morin, A. J. S., Carbonneau, N., & Paquet, Y. (2013). Passion: Does one scale fit all? Construct validity of two-factor Passion Scale and psychometric invariance over different activities and languages. *Psychological Assessment, 25*(3), 796–809. 10.1037/a0032573

McNamara, J., & McCabe, M. P. (2012). Striving for success or addiction? Exercise dependence among elite Australian athletes.*Journal of Sports Sciences, 30*(8), 755–766. 10.1080/02640414.2012.667879

Mónok, K., Berczik, K., Urbán, R., Szabo, A., Griffiths, M. D., Farkas, J., ... & Kun, B. (2012). Psychometric properties and concurrent validity of two exercise addiction measures: A population wide study. *Psychology of Sport and Exercise, 13*(6), 739–746. 10.1016/j.psychsport.2012.06.003

Paradis, K. F., Cooke, L. M., Martin, L. J., & Hall, C. R. (2013). Too much of a good thing? Examining the relationship between passion for exercise and exercise dependence. *Psychology of Sport and Exercise, 14*(4), 493–500. 10.1016/j.psychsport.2013.02.003

Parastatidou, I., Doganis, G., Theodorakis, Y., & Vlachopoulos, S. (2014). The mediating role of passion in the relationship of exercise motivational regulations with exercise dependence symptoms. *International Journal of Mental Health and Addiction, 12*(4), 406–419. 10.1007/s11469-013-9466-x

Pelletier, L. G., Fortier, M. S., Vallerand, R. J., Tuson, K. M., Briere, N. M., & Blais, M. R. (1995). Toward a new measure of intrinsic motivation, extrinsic motivation, and amotivation in sports: The Sport Motivation Scale (SMS). *Journal of Sport & Exercise Psychology, 17*, 35. 10.1123/jsep.17.1.35

Schipfer, M. & Stoll, O. (2015, July). *Exercise-addiction/exercise commitment- model (exercise addictionCOM)*. Paper presented at the 14th European Congress of Sport Psychology, Bern, Switzerland.

Schlegl, S., Vierl, L., Kolar, D. R., Dittmer, N., & Voderholzer, U. (2022). Psychometric properties of the Compulsive Exercise Test in a large sample of female adolescent and adult inpatients with anorexia nervosa and bulimia nervosa. *International Journal of Eating Disorders, 55*(4), 494–504. 10.1002/eat.23694

Sicilia, Á., Alcaraz-Ibáñez, M., Lirola, M.-J., & Burgueño, R. (2017). Influence of goal contents on exercise addiction: Analysing the mediating effect of passion for eExercise. *Journal of Human Kinetics, 59*(1), 143–153. 10.1515/hukin-2017-0154

Smith, R. W., Min, H., Ng, M. A., Haynes, N. J., & Clark, M. A. (2023). A content validation of work passion: Was the passion ever there? *Journal of Business and Psychology, 38*(1), 191–213. 10.1007/s10869-022-09807-1

Stenseng, F., Rise, J., & Kraft, P. (2011). The dark side of leisure: Obsessive passion and its covariates and outcomes. *Leisure Studies, 30*(1), 49–62. 10.1080/02614361003716982

Szabo, A. (2010). *Addiction to exercise: A symptom or a disorder?* New York: Nova Science.

Szabo, A., & Demetrovics, Z. (2022). *Passion and addiction in sports and exercise.* New York, NY: Routledge. 10.4324/9781003173595

Szabo, A., de la Vega, R., Kovacsik, R., Jiménez Almendros, L., Ruíz-Barquín, R., Demetrovics, Z., Boros, S., & Köteles, F. (2022). Dimensions of passion and their relationship to the risk of exercise addiction: Cultural and gender differences. *Addictive Behaviors Reports, 16*, 100451. 10.1016/j.abrep.2022.100451

Szabo, A., de la Vega, R., Ruiz-Barquín, R., & Rivera, O. (2013). Exercise addiction in Spanish athletes: Investigation of the roles of gender, social context and level of involvement. *Journal of Behavioral Addictions, 2*(4), 249–252. 10.1556/JBA.2.2013.4.9

Szabo, A., Griffiths, M. D., de la Vega, R., Mervó, B., & Demetrovics, Z. (2015). Methodological and conceptual limitations in exercise addiction research. *Yale Journal of Biology and Medicine, 88*, 303–308. PMCID: PMC4553651

Szabo, A., Griffiths, M. D., Demetrovics, Z., Vega, R., Ruíz-Barquín, R., Soós, I., & Kovacsik, R. (2018). Obsessive and harmonious passion in physically active Spanish and Hungarian men and women: A brief report on cultural and gender differences. *International Journal of Psychology*, 54(5), 598–603. 10.1002/ijop.12517

Szabo, A., & Kovacsik, R. (2019). When passion appears, exercise addiction disappears. *Swiss Journal of Psychology, 78*(3–4), 137–142. 10.1024/1421-0185/a000228

Terry, A., Szabo, A., & Griffiths, M. (2004). The exercise addiction inventory: A new brief screening tool. *Addiction Research and Theory, 12*, 489–499. 10.1080/16066350310001637363

Tóth-Király, I., Bõthe, B., Rigó, A., & Orosz, G. (2017). An illustration of the exploratory structural equation modeling (ESEM) framework on the passion scale. *Frontiers in Psychology, 8*. 10.3389/fpsyg.2017.01968

Vallerand, R. J. (2010). On passion for life activities: The dualistic model of passion. In M. P. Zanna, & J. M. Olson (Eds.), *Advances in experimental social psychology* (pp. 97–133). San Diego, CA: Academic Press.

Vallerand, R. J. (2015). *The psychology of passion: A dualistic model.* Series in Positive Psychology. New York, NY: Oxford University Press.

Vallerand, R. J., Blanchard, C., Mageau, G. A., Koestner, R., Ratelle, C., Leonard, M., Gagne, M., & Marsolais, J. (2003). Les passions de l'ame: On obsessive and harmonious passion. *Journal of Personality and Social Psychology, 85*(4), 756–767. 10.1037/0022-3514.85.4.756

Vallerand, R. J., & Miquelon, P. (2007). Passion for sport in athletes. In D. Lavallee, & S. Jowett (Eds.), *Social psychology in sport* (pp. 249–262). Champaign, IL: Human Kinetics.

Vallerand, R. J., Rousseau, F. L., Grouzet, F. M. E., Dumais, A., Grenier, S., & Blanchard, C. M. (2006). Passion in sport: A look at determinants and affective experiences. *Journal of Sport & Exercise Psychology, 28*(4), 454–478.

World Medical Association (2008). *World Medical Association Declaration of Helsinki: Ethical Principles for Medical Research Involving Human Subjects.* Retrieved from: http://www.wma.net/en/30publications/10policies/b3/17c.pdf

Wu, R., Jing, L., Liu, Y., Wang, H., Xie, L., & Deng, W. (2023). Effects of mindfulness on obligatory exercise during the return of injured athletes to sports: The mediating roles of self-criticism and competitive state anxiety. *Psychology Research and Behavior Management, 16*, 2157–2171. 10.2147/prbm.s414709

14

LONG-TERM QIGONG PRACTICE IS ASSOCIATED WITH IMPROVED SELF-PERCEIVED HEALTH AND QUALITY OF LIFE

Takashi Shimazaki, Tibor Hortobágyi, Azusa Uematsu, Hirofumi Kobayashi, Madoka Nakamura, Masataka Kiryu, and Shuji Suzuki

Historical Origin and Characteristics of QiGong

QiGong is a traditional Chinese exercise system that integrates diverse body postures, breathing control, focused intention, deep relaxation, visualization, and self-applied massage (Garber et al., 2011; Sancier & Hu, 1991). QiGong has a long history. Movements similar to those used in today's QiGong practice appear on painted artifacts made in 206 BC–220 AD during the imperial reign of the Han Dynasty (The Chinese Health QiGong Association, 2012). To date, an estimated 70 million people practice QiGong in China and many more around the world (Chen, 2000).

Feng et al. (2020) classified QiGong into two types based on its execution. Dynamic or active Qigong emphasizes body movements. Passive or meditative Qigong does not involve specific body movements. It instead involves holding certain postures, breathing, and mental focus. The combination of the motor and meditative elements favorably affects cardiorespiratory function, mobility, and mood (Garber et al., 2011; Larkey et al., 2009) and responses to QiGong correspond to those observed during self-paced walking (Larkey et al., 2009) in healthy old adults (Ng & Tsang, 2009). A recent study reported that mind-body interventions using mediative movements including QiGong can also increase healthy old adults' sleep quality, depressive symptoms, and quality of life (QoL) (Weber et al., 2020).

Health Benefits of QiGong

Compared with its ancient roots, research history of QiGong spans a much shorter period. A meta-analysis summarizing 30 years of QiGong research demonstrated its favorable effects on medical outcomes including sleep

DOI: 10.4324/9781003459750-14

quality (Cheung et al., 2021), fatigue (Yin et al., 2020), emotional disturbances (Meng et al., 2021), and QoL and well-being (Ye et al., 2022) in cancer patients. Meta-analyses focusing on other severe illnesses reported positive effects on lung function, exercise capacity, and QoL in patients with chronic obstructive pulmonary disease (COPD) (Xu et al., 2022), clinical motor symptoms, and physical function of Parkinson's disease (Chen et al., 2020), QoL of the knee osteoarthritis patients (Zeng et al., 2020), exercise capacity and QoL in patients with heart failure (Yang et al., 2023), executive function in patients with mild cognitive impairment (MCI) (Lin et al., 2022), mental health, sleep quality, and QoL in drug addiction (Cui et al., 2022). Additional meta-analyses reported positive effects on risk factors and symptoms of lifestyle-related non-communicable diseases which include reductions in systolic and diastolic blood pressure in patients with hypertension (Ching et al., 2021), HbA1c and mental health in type 2 diabetes (Luo et al., 2023), waist circumference, blood pressure, and triglyceride level of metabolic syndrome patients (Tao et al., 2023).

Systematic reviews without meta-analyses suggested that QiGong could have favorable effects on mobility disability (Jahnke et al., 2010), immune function (Wang et al., 2012), fibromyalgia (Chan et al., 2012c), neck pain (Girard & Girard, 2019), pain management in older adults (Tang et al., 2019), and on physical and psychological symptoms associated with COVID-19 (Badakhsh et al., 2021). Application of QiGong has thus been prevalent in disease prevention and health promotion, early intervention for diagnostic population, rehabilitation, and palliative care (Chan et al., 2012a, 2012b; Garber et al., 2011; Sancier & Hu, 1991).

Research Question in the Present Study

The majority of previous studies documented the acute effects of QiGong on physical and psychological outcomes. A randomized clinical trial comprising 30–60 min sessions for eight weeks to 12 months also demonstrated favorable effects on physical and psychological outcomes (Wang et al., 2014; Zou et al., 2017). However, the effects of long-term QiGong practice on physical and mental health, health promotion, QoL, and self-perceived health are unknown (Zeng et al., 2019; Cheung et al., 2021). Because QiGong practice has favorable immediate and short-term effects on a variety of outcomes, we hypothesized that long-term QiGong practice improves self-perceived health, an outcome strongly associated with mobility and survival (Burstrom & Fredlund, 2001; Idler & Benyamini, 1997). Considering modest rates of adherence to conventional exercise programs at any age (Sperandei et al., 2016), it is important to offer exercise practitioners physical activity choices that produce positive self-awareness and self-perceived health.

We conducted two studies to examine the effects of the long-term Qigong practice on QoL. Study 1 identified the self-perceived benefits of QiGong exercise and determined the relationship between long-term QiGong and QoL. Study 2 determined the relationship between QiGong practice for over 13 years and the prevalence of physical and psychological dysfunction in Japanese QiGong practitioners over the age of 50 years. Such findings would provide evidence that QiGong's practice could improve self-perceived health, including QoL.

Study 1

Purpose

Study 1 determined participants' perceptions toward QiGong exercise and examined the relationship between QiGong and QoL.

Methods

In Study 1, we collected data by administering two questionnaires. We asked 350 individuals attending QiGong classes in Saitama prefecture in North West metropolitan Tokyo, Japan, to fill in a questionnaire. Of the 350 individuals attending QiGong classes, 346 (98.9%) received the questionnaire. In Study 1, as we did not impute demographic information, we excluded 26 of 346 (7.5%) participants. Three hundred twenty participants (91.4%) completed and returned the questionnaire.

The questionnaire had one open question concerning the perceived benefits of QiGong practice, "What benefits did you expect when you started practicing QiGong?" We also measured QoL by the valid and reliable Japanese version of the WHOQOL-26, published originally by the World Health Organization (WHO) (Skevington et al., 2004; WHO, 2016). We used three domains: general, physical, and psychological QoL. In the present study samples, the Cronbach's alpha coefficients for these three domains were 0.77, 0.73, and 0.81, respectively.

The 1.0% missing WHOQOL-26 data was replaced by the grand mean value. Sample characteristics were characterized by a Chi-square test. Cohen's w was calculated to estimate size of bias and classified as 0.10 = small, 0.30 = medium, and 0.50 = large (Cohen, 1992). We applied a thematic analysis to the qualitative data, including the steps of (a) data screening; (b) data coding of information based on content by two independent researchers; (c) theme classification; (d) reviewing and modifying the classified themes; and (e) defining themes (Braun & Clarke, 2006). Two trained researchers (authors: TS, MK) conducted the thematic analyses and three researchers (authors: TS, MK, SS) resolved inconsistencies.

Part 2 of analysis for Study 1 comprised the computation of partial correlation coefficients and an analysis of covariance (ANCOVA). Partial correlation coefficients were calculated to identify the relationship between QiGong duration and QoL moderated by age, gender, and profession. We also considered whether or not the relationship between QiGong practice and QoL was linear. ANCOVA was conducted to identify differences in QoL across four levels of QiGong experience. QiGong experience was defined in quartiles of 0–3, 4–7, 8–12, and over 13 years based on data in Study 2. The model was adjusted for age, gender, profession, and QiGong duration. Cohen's *f* was calculated to quantify the influence of demographics. Cohen's *f* was categorized as 0.10 = small, 0.25 = medium, and 0.40 = large (Cohen, 1992). Sub-effect analyses were performed by Bonferroni's method. All analyses were done in IBM SPSS Statistics 24 and R version 3.3.1.

Results

In Study 1, most participants at the QiGong event were 69–75 years old (73.8%, $\chi^2 = 84.1$, $p < 0.01$, $w = 0.51$), female (85.6%, $\chi^2 = 162.5$, $p < 0.01$, $w = 0.71$), and unemployed (86.6%, $\chi^2 = 13.7$, $p < 0.01$, $w = 0.21$) (Table 14.1).

Table 14.2 shows that QiGong affords perceived physical, psychological, and social benefits. Concordance between two reviewers relative to physical, psychological, and social benefits was 86.7%, 73.2%, and 100%, respectively. Physical benefits appeared as improved physical and vital organ function,

TABLE 14.1 Participants characteristics in Study 1 ($n = 320$)

Variables	n	%
Age, years		
≤60	16	5.0
69–65	70	21.9
66–70	86	26.9
71–75	80	25.0
76–80	46	14.4
≥80	22	6.9
Gender		
Female	274	85.6
Male	46	14.4
Employment		
Employed	43	13.4
Unemployed	277	86.6
Qigong experience, years		
0–3	98	30.6
4–7	95	29.7
8–12	64	20.0
≥13	63	19.7

TABLE 14.2 Participants reporting perceived improvements in physical and mental health as a result of QiGong practice based on theme analysis (n = 320)

Identified Theme	*Theme Elements*	*Report Perceived Improvement, Number*	*Total Response*
Physical			
Motor function	Quality of life	18	73
	Move easily	17	
	Flexibility	16	
	Posture	13	
	Falls	3	
	Balance	3	
	Body mass	2	
	Effects of age lessened	1	
Fitness	Less often ill	24	41
	General strength	9	
	Leg and back strength	7	
	Recover faster from fatigue	1	
Pain	Back	11	29
	Knee	7	
	Stiff neck	6	
	Ankle	4	
	Neck	1	
Bodily function	Breathing	11	22
	Sensitivity to cold	3	
	Constipation	3	
	Blood pressure	3	
	Stomach ache	1	
	Blood profile	1	
Illness	Insomnia	6	17
	Headache	5	
	Lungs	2	
	Allergy	2	
	Autonomic imbalance	1	
	Diabetes	1	
Psychological			
Vigour, energy	Mentally satisfied	17	36
	Life is fun	16	
	Purpose to life	2	
	Desire to live	1	
Emotions	Being positive	14	29
	Mood	11	
	Fulfillment from co-engager	2	
	Vigour	2	

(*Continued*)

TABLE 14.2 (Continued)

Identified Theme	*Theme Elements*	*Report Perceived Improvement, Number*	*Total Response*
Concentration	Attention	3	5
	Fresh mind	2	
Cognition	Thinking clearly	3	3
Relaxation	Becoming mindful	1	1
Social			
Extroversion	Enjoy talking with friends	17	19
	Talking with new friends	2	

higher fitness, less joint pain, and fewer diseases. Psychological benefits were increased vigor, positive emotional arousal, better concentration, increased cognitive function, and an ability to relax. A few participants reported becoming more extrovert as a social benefit.

Partial correlation coefficients adjusted for age, gender, and employment were small to medium between QiGong duration (years) and general (r = 0.25, $p < 0.01$), physical ($r = 0.17$, $p < 0.01$), and psychological ($r = 0.18$, $p <$ .01) QoL, respectively. ANCOVA revealed a strong relation of QiGong practice duration (years) and QoL (general: $F = 6.94$, $p < .01$, $f = .26$; physical: $F = 3.29$, $p < .05$, $f = .18$; psychological: $F = 3.36$, $p < .05$, $f = .18$, Table 14.3). Participants with an exposure to QiGong over eight years had higher general QoL than the group pursuing QiGong for 0–3 years ($p < .05$ for 8–13 years and $p < .01$ for >13 years). Physical and psychological QoL was higher in the 13+ years QiGong compared with the 0–3 years QiGong group (both $p < .05$).

Discussion

The thematic analysis revealed that many practitioners perceived QiGong to exert favorable effects on motor function. In particular, 73 of 320 (22.8%) practitioners perceived the benefits of QiGong practice as improved movement-related QoL, less difficulty with movement, and greater flexibility. While QiGong, similar to Tai Chi (Tsang & Hui-Chan, 2004), involves weight shifts (Rogers et al., 2009), only 3 of 73 (4.1%) respondents in the motor category perceived that QiGong helped reduce falls. This low rate of perception may be related to our participants' relatively high health status and low fall rate at the time of starting to practice QiGong. Many QiGong practitioners reported the perception of being ill less often due to improved fitness. The composite nature of QiGong is likely to cause practitioners to perceive less pain, better bodily functions, and having fewer medical conditions. The second largest category of perceived benefits was in the domain of psychology followed by the social domain. Over 20% of the

TABLE 14.3 Difference of QOL among experience of QiGong exercise

	0–3 Years		*4–7 Years*		*8–12 Years*		*13 Years+*			
	M	SD	M	SD	M	SD	M	SD	F *value*	*Cohen's* f
General	3.09	0.68	3.33	0.58	3.48	0.54	3.61	0.72	6.94**	0.26
Physical	3.37	0.54	3.44	0.48	3.47	0.38	3.61	0.51	3.29*	0.18
Psychological	3.35	0.46	3.44	0.49	3.52	0.50	3.65	0.51	3.36*	0.18

Note: $^{**}p < .01$, $^{*}p < .05$

320 respondents named vigor, energy positivity, and good mood as psychological and emotional benefits, complementing some but not all vigor-related data. Finally, a small number of old adults reported that they perceived themselves becoming more extrovert and friend-seeking, resonating with WHO's inclusion of social factors in the definition of health and with the role peers play in adherence to exercise (WHO, 2017).

In addition, partial correlation coefficients and ANCOVA revealed a relationship between long-term QiGong practice and QoL. A previous small sample cross-sectional study observed no relationship between the number of years of QiGong practice and QoL (Ho et al., 2011). However, our data suggest that years of QiGong improve physical and psychological QoL, an observation that is in line with the conclusions of a systematic review of how physical activity affects health-related QoL in the general population (Bize et al., 2007).

Study 2

Purpose

In Study 2 we examined the prevalence and improvements of health problems as a result of QiGong practice.

Methods

Participants attended the 15th annual conference of Daoyin Yangsheng Gong (DYSG) in Yokohama, Japan in October 2014, representing the main school of QiGong exercise. Of the 1,200 conference attendees, all of whom were QiGong practitioners, 74.0% or 888 returned the survey at the end of the conference. Only surveys with complete answers were included in the analyses (n = 799, 66.7%).

We asked participants to report their age, gender, the number of years they have been practicing QiGong and the perceived presence of five physical and five psychological problems. We hypothesized that regular long-term QiGong would minimize these problems based on findings in Study 1. Physical factors were the perceived presence of (1) Physical fatigue; (2) Poor physical health; (3) Joint pain; (4) Heartbeat irregularity, and (5) Poor sleep. Psychological factors were the perceived presence of (1) Low energy; (2) Depression; (3) Poor concentration; (4) Forgetfulness, and (5) Anger. A "Yes" answer denoted the presence of a condition. In addition to documenting the presence of a condition, we also asked participants whether the condition improved after engaging in QiGong: "If you had this health problem when you started practicing QiGong, did this problem improve after engaging in QiGong". The answer choices were: "Did not improve", "Somewhat improved", and "Improved significantly".

In Study 2, we categorized responses for each of the five physical and psychological variables as "Did not improve" and "Improved" by combining "Somewhat improved" and "Significantly improved" into one category. We performed logistic regression analyses adjusted for age and gender to determine the effects of QiGong duration on prevalence and improvement of self-perceived health and psychological problems. We computed crude and adjusted odds ratios (OR) and 95% confidence intervals (CI) to determine the risk of perceived physical and psychological problems relative to 13 years of QiGong practice ("prevention effect analysis"). We referenced QiGong's health-improving effects to the 0–3 years of QiGong experience category ("health promotion analysis") including only participants who reported health problems.

Results

In Study 2, most participants at the QiGong conference were 69–75 years old (70.6%. $\chi^2 = 176.0$, $p < .01$, $w = .47$) and females (88.6%, $\chi^2 = 476.5$, $p < .01$, $w = .77$). The number of participants reporting physical fatigue (66.7%, $\chi^2 = 74.6$, $p < .01$, $w = .33$), joint pain (50.4%, $\chi^2 = 47.9$, $p < .01$, $w = .28$), problems with attention (49.1%, $\chi^2 = 13.4$, $p < .01$, $w = .14$), and forgetfulness (60.7%, $\chi^2 = 119.6$, $p < .01$, $w = .42$) was higher than those not reporting such health problems (Table 14.4).

TABLE 14.4 Participants characteristics in Study 2 (n = 799)

	n	%
Age, years		
≤60	111	13.9
69–65	156	19.5
66–70	221	27.7
71–75	187	23.4
76–80	91	11.4
≥80	33	4.1
Gender		
Female	708	88.6
Male	91	11.4
Qigong experience, years		
0–3	217	27.2
4–7	207	25.9
8–12	194	24.3
≥13	181	22.7
Health problems		
Physical fatigue		
Yes	445	66.7
No	222	33.3

(Continued)

TABLE 14.4 (Continued)

	n	%
Poor physical health		
Yes	340	52.1
No	313	47.9
Joint pain		
Yes	403	63.8
No	229	36.2
Palpitation		
Yes	187	28.5
No	468	71.5
Insomnia		
Yes	315	47.6
No	347	52.4
Low energy		
Yes	313	47.6
No	380	52.4
Depression		
Yes	225	32.1
No	476	67.9
Poor attention		
Yes	392	57.0
No	296	43.0
Forgetfulness		
Yes	485	70.9
No	199	29.1
Anger		
Yes	326	49.5
No	332	50.5

Note: Percentage of the health problems were calculated excluded missing data.

Table 14.5 shows that participants with 0–3 versus 13+ years of QiGong practice perceived to have palpitation (adjusted OR: 2.69, $p < .01$), insomnia (1.67, $p < .01$), a lack of vigor (2.08, $p < .01$), and attention deficit (1.56, $p < .01$). There was a similar trend for the same comparison for joint pain, depression, and forgetfulness. Logistic regression analyses showed that long-term QiGong practice seemed to reduce the perception of health problems.

Table 14.6 shows that long-term QiGong experience of 13+ versus 0–3 years reduced perception of physical fatigue (adjusted OR = 1.80, $p < .05$), poor physical health (1.99, $p < .05$), joint pain (1.90, $p < .05$), insomnia (2.32, $p < .05$), problems with attention (1.95, $p < .05$), forgetfulness

TABLE 14.5 Effects of QiGong experience on prevalence of health problems ($n = 799$)

	QiGong Experience, Years						
	0–3		*4–7*		*8–12*		*≥13*
	Crude OR (95%CI)	*Adjusted OR (95%CI)*	*Crude OR (95%CI)*	*Adjusted OR (95%CI)*	*Crude OR (95%CI)*	*Adjusted OR (95%CI)*	
Physical							
Fatigue	1.36 (0.85, 2.19)	1.31 (0.81, 2.11)	1.09 (0.69, 1.72)	1.06 (0.67, 1.67)	1.05 (0.66, 1.68)	1.03 (0.65, 1.65)	1
Health	1.22 (0.78, 1.91)	1.17 (0.75, 1.83)	1.38 (0.89, 2.14)	1.34 (0.87, 2.09)	1.39 (0.88, 2.19)	1.37 (0.87, 2.16)	1
Joint pain	1.51 (0.94, 2.43)	1.62† (1.00, 2.61)	1.18 (0.75, 1.86)	1.23 (0.78, 1.94)	1.10 (0.69, 1.76)	1.12 (0.70, 1.80)	1
Palpitation	2.74** (1.61, 4.67)	2.69** (1.57, 4.61)	2.07** (1.21, 3.52)	2.03** (1.19, 3.47)	1.95* (1.12, 3.38)	1.94* (1.11, 3.38)	1
Insomnia	1.64* (1.04, 2.58)	1.67* (1.06, 2.64)	1.20 (0.77, 1.87)	1.22 (0.78, 1.90)	1.57† (0.99, 2.47)	1.57† (1.00, 2.48)	1
Psychological health							
Low energy	2.10** (1.35, 3.27)	2.08** (1.33, 3.25)	1.44 (0.93, 2.24)	1.43 (0.92, 2.22)	2.01** (1.28, 3.16)	2.01** (1.28, 3.16)	1
Depression	1.58 (1.00, 2.49)	1.57† (0.99, 2.48)	0.94 (0.59, 1.51)	0.94 (0.59, 1.51)	1.10 (0.68, 1.76)	1.10 (0.68, 1.76)	1
Attention	1.51† (0.98, 2.33)	1.56* (1.01, 2.42)	1.24 (0.81, 1.91)	1.27 (0.83, 1.95)	2.14** (2.36, 3.36)	2.16** (1.37, 3.39)	1
Forgetfulness	1.47 (0.91, 2.36)	1.53† (0.95, 2.48)	1.36 (0.85, 2.17)	1.39 (0.87, 2.22)	1.26 (0.78, 2.03)	1.26 (0.78, 2.05)	1
Anger	1.00 (0.64, 1.55)	0.85 (0.54, 1.35)	0.87 (0.56, 1.35)	0.77 (0.49, 1.21)	0.97 (0.62, 1.52)	0.92 (0.58, 1.45)	1

Note: $^{**}p < .01$, $^{*}p < .05$, $^{\dagger}p < .10$; OR, odds ratio.

TABLE 14.6 Participants reporting improvements in health based on QiGong experience

	QiGong Experience, Years						
	0–3	*4–7*		*8–12*		*≥13*	
		Crude OR (95%CI)	*Adjusted OR (95%CI)*	*Crude OR (95%CI)*	*Adjusted OR (95%CI)*	*Crude OR (95%CI)*	*Adjusted OR (95%CI)*
Physical							
Fatigue	1	1.20 (0.72, 2.00)	1.19 (0.71, 1.99)	1.02 (0.61, 1.73)	1.06 (0.62, 1.80)	1.64 (0.93, 2.89)	1.80* (1.01, 3.22)
Health	1	0.98 (0.55, 1.74)	0.99 (0.55, 1.78)	1.15 (0.63, 2.09)	1.30 (0.70, 2.40)	1.68 (0.88, 3.22)	1.99* (1.02, 3.89)
Joint pain	1	1.37 (0.81, 2.33)	1.35 (0.80, 2.30)	1.17 (0.67, 2.04)	1.13 (0.65, 1.98)	2.00* (1.11, 3.59)	1.90* (1.05, 3.45)
Palpitation	1	0.83 (0.38–1.81)	0.82 (0.37, 1.80)	1.05 (0.47, 2.36)	1.11 (0.49, 2.52)	2.06 (0.80, 5.31)	2.32† (0.88, 6.11)
Insomnia	1	0.86 (0.46, 1.59)	0.86 (0.46, 1.59)	1.19 (0.65, 2.18)	1.26 (0.68, 2.32)	2.12* (1.08, 4.17)	2.32* (1.17, 4.62)
Psychological health							
Low energy	1	0.86 (0.46, 1.59)	0.97 (0.53, 1.77)	1.19 (0.65, 2.18)	0.83 (0.46, 1.50)	2.12* (1.08, 4.17)	1.28 (0.65, 2.55)
Depression	1	1.14 (0.55, 2.35)	1.10 (0.53, 2.31)	0.87 (0.42, 1.81)	0.97 (0.46, 2.04)	1.68 (0.79, 3.56)	1.78 (0.82, 3.84)
Attention	1	1.29 (0.71, 2.34)	1.26 (0.69, 2.31)	0.84 (0.46, 1.55)	0.85 (0.46, 1.58)	1.96* (1.04, 3.68)	1.95* (1.02, 3.71)
Forgetfulness	1	1.35 (0.71, 2.59)	1.29 (0.67, 2.49)	1.03 (0.51, 2.08)	0.97 (0.48, 1.99)	2.21* (1.14, 4.31)	2.08* (1.06, 4.08)
Anger	1	1.35 (0.70, 2.59)	1.53 (0.83, 2.84)	1.03 (0.51, 2.08)	1.12 (0.59, 2.12)	2.21* (1.14, 4.31)	2.85** (1.46, 5.54)

Note: $^{**}p < .01$, $^{*}p < .05$, $^{\dagger}p < .10$; OR, odds ratio.

(2.08, $p < .05$), and anger (2.85, $p < .01$). For a similar comparison, there was a trend for palpitation.

Discussion

Using 13+ years of QiGong practice as a reference, practitioners reported a reduced perception of the presence of ailments. Those who practiced QiGong for 0–3 versus 8–12 years reported the perception of 50% higher odds of having joint pain, 60% greater odds of having palpitation, 40% greater odds of having depression, and 30% higher odds of being more forgetful. The ineffectiveness of short-term QiGong practice on joint pain is similar to data reported in a review (Geneen et al., 2017). While there was a positive effect of QiGong on perceived palpitation, there was still a perception of having nearly two-fold greater odds of palpitation in the 8–12 years group, a finding reported previously (Jones, 2006). There was a lack of effect of QiGong on insomnia, energy, and attention because the odds of perceiving these problems were similar after 0–3 or after 8–12 years of QiGong practice. This lack of effect could be indicative of the presence of depression (Kvam et al., 2016). We speculate that individuals with low levels of depression started to practice QiGong, creating a potential selection bias.

Summary and Concluding Discussion

Health Benefits due to Long-Term Practice

We determined the self-perceived health benefits of QiGong exercise and its relationship with QoL (Study 1) and examined the relationship between QiGong practice and prevalence of physical and psychological dysfunction in Japanese QiGong practitioners (Study 2).

Study 1 showed only 23% of participants perceived health benefits from QiGong. In addition, the duration of QiGong practice correlated with QoL. Participants who practiced QiGong for 13+ years reported to have higher QoL than those who practiced for 0–3 or 8–12 years. Results from Study 2 confirm the findings of Study 1: participants pursuing QiGong for 13+ years consistently reported that they perceived improvements over the practice period in fatigue, health, joint pain, palpitation, insomnia, energy, attention, and forgetfulness. While numerous studies have examined the effects of QiGong on QoL or its elements in cancer (Larkey et al., 2016; Tao et al., 2016), psychosocial well-being in older adults (Chan et al., 2017), sleep (Ko et al., 2022), COPD (Xu et al., 2022), low back pain (Teut et al., 2016), and fatigue-related conditions (Li et al., 2015; Yin et al., 2020), many of these studies reported small or mixed effects possibly due to the limited duration of the intervention. Our data suggest the presence of a duration effect on health outcomes when practice duration is extended to years instead of weeks or months (Tables 14.2, 14.5, and 14.6). Even those old adults who reported to have practiced QiGong for up to 12 years, the self-perceived health benefits were statistically lower than the benefits reported by those who practiced QiGong for 13+ years, an observation also reported in relation to the effects of physical activity on healthy old adults' motor and cognitive function (Litscher et al., 2001). All in all, our data agree with the prevailing ACSM physical activity guidelines for seniors, recommending daily physical activity of at least 30 min for as many years as possible (Nelson et al., 2007).

Several participants reported that the social health benefits of Qigong practice manifested through the opportunity to socialize with friends. Previous systematic reviews reported that maintaining social relationships and social support from peers is strongly associated with mortality risk (Holt-Lunstad et al., 2010; Wang et al., 2023). Further, participation in exercise and community classes contributes to the reduction in the risk of developing functional disabilities (Kanamori et al., 2014). Taken together, although a practitioner can perform QiGong exercise alone, attending QiGong classes can enhance social participation and diminish the risks of developing functional disability. Such effects could extend health span.

Limitations and Implications for Practice

First, the cross-sectional design, i.e., post-only assessment of QiGong practice could not fully explain a causal relationship between practice duration and perceived health benefits, clinical outcomes, and QoL. In addition, the effects of QiGong practice were evaluated retrospectively. Therefore, there could be a bias in recall. Longitudinal studies are needed to demonstrate the benefits of long-term Qigong practice. Second, it was not possible to determine the frequency of QiGong practice, an important factor that can affect perceived health benefits. Third, socio-economic status (SES, income, employment) is strongly related to health condition and health behavior (Kivimäki et al., 2020; Kraft & Kraft, 2021). We did not discuss the effects of SES on health outcomes because most participants were over age 65 years and retired. Finally, our subjects were Japanese DYSG QiGong practitioners and cross-cultural differences and the style of QiGong can affect perceived health benefits.

QiGong practice affords perceived physical, psychological, and social health benefits and conversely healthy Japanese old adults also perceived that they had fewer physical and psychological dysfunctions and higher QoL. The greatest perceived benefits occurred after 13+ years of QiGong practice with some benefits also present at a dose level of eight years. QiGong is a multi-component form of physical activity, which – if practiced for prolonged periods – affords motor, cognitive, and social benefits. Forming an exercise habit may be a key factor to derive health benefits from QiGong practice. Exercise habits may be constructed according to specific action planning (Wee & Dillon, 2022), making an if-then plan which combines a set of contextual cues (i.e., timing, place) and action plan (Bieleke et al., 2021), and coping planning which is a plan of how individuals cope and overcome potential barriers to engage in exercise (Carraro & Gaudreau, 2013). Thus, QiGong practitioners and trainers should be knowledgeable about such behavioral change theories and techniques to facilitate the formation of exercise habits of QiGong practice.

Ethical Standards

Both Study 1 and Study 2 survey was conducted according to the World Medical Association Declaration of Helsinki: Ethical Principles for Medical Research Involving Human Subjects. The present study used an anonymous, blind survey. An experienced research staff constructed the questionnaire using simple-worded and mindful questions that were free of unpleasant or potentially abusive language. Participants did not write their names on the questionnaire or provide any other information that could have identified them. Participants were assured that all of the information obtained in the survey would be used for research purposes only and that the data and responses would be kept confidential. Thus, participants' confidentiality and privacy were maintained. Participants understood that filling in the survey was the act of consent.

Author Note

The authors want to acknowledge President Zhang Yu Song, Japanese Daoyin Yangsheng Gong Association, who cooperated with for participants recruitment.

References

Badakhsh, M., Dastras, M., Sarchahi, Z., Doostkami, M., Mir, A., & Bouya, S. (2021). Complementary and alternative medicine therapies and COVID-19: A systematic review. *Reviews on Environmental Health*, *36*(3), 443–450. 10.1515/reveh-2021-0012

Bieleke, M., Keller, L., & Gollwitzer, P. M. (2021). If-then planning.*European Review of Social Psychology*, *32*(1), 88–122. 10.1080/10463283.2020.1808936

Bize, R., Johnson, J. A., & Plotnikoff, R. C. (2007). Physical activity level and health-related quality of life in the general adult population: A systematic review. *Preventive Medicine*, *45*(6), 401–415. 10.1016/j. ypmed.2007.07.017

Braun, V., & Clarke, V. (2006). Using thematic analysis in psychology. *Qualitative Research in Psychology, 3*(2), 77–101. 10.1191/1478088706qp063oa

Burstrom, B., & Fredlund, P. (2001). Self rated health: Is it as good a predictor of subsequent mortality among adults in lower as well as in higher social classes? *Journal of Epidemiology & Community Health, 55*(11), 836–840. 10.1136/jech.55.11.836

Carraro, N., & Gaudreau, P. (2013). Spontaneous and experimentally induced action planning and coping planning for physical activity: A meta-analysis. *Psychology of Sport and Exercise, 14*(2), 228–248. 10.1016/j.psychsport.2012.10.004

Chan, A. W., Yu, D. S., & Choi, K. C. (2017). Effects of tai chi qigong on psychosocial well-being among hidden elderly, using elderly neighborhood volunteer approach: A pilot randomized controlled trial. *Clinical Interventions in Aging, 12*, 85–96. 10.2147/CIA.S124604

Chan, C. L., Wang, C. W., Ho, R. T., Ho, A. H., Ziea, E. T., Taam Wong, V. C., & Ng, S. M. (2012a). A systematic review of the effectiveness of qigong exercise in cardiac rehabilitation. *The American Journal of Chinese Medicine, 40*(2), 255–267. 10.1142/S0192415X12500206

Chan, C. L., Wang, C. W., Ho, R. T., Ng, S. M., Chan, J. S., Ziea, E. T., & Wong, V. C. (2012b). A systematic review of the effectiveness of qigong exercise in supportive cancer care. *Supportive Care in Cancer, 20* (6), 1121–1133. 10.1007/s00520-011-1378-3

Chan, C. L., Wang, C. W., Ho, R. T., Ng, S. M., Ziea, E. T., & Wong, V. T. (2012c). Qigong exercise for the treatment of fibromyalgia: A systematic review of randomized controlled trials. *The Journal of Alternative and Complementary Medicine, 18*(7), 641–646.

Chen, K. (2000). Chinese qigong and the qigong-induced mental disorders [response to letter]. Retrieved from http://www.bmj.com/rapid-response/2011/10/28/chinese-qigong-and-qigong-induced-mental-disorders

Chen, S., Zhang, Y., Wang, Y. T., Liu, X., Song, W., & Du, X. (2020). The effect of qigong-based therapy on patients with Parkinson's disease: A systematic review and meta-analysis. *Clinical Rehabilitation, 34*(12), 1436–1448. 10.1177/0269215520946695

Cheung, D. S. T., Takemura, N., Smith, R., Yeung, W. F., Xu, X., Ng, A. Y. M., Lee, S. F., & Lin, C. C. (2021). Effect of qigong for sleep disturbance-related symptom clusters in cancer: A systematic review and meta-analysis. *Sleep Medicine, 85*, 108–122. 10.1016/j.sleep.2021.06.036

The Chinese Health Qigong Association. (2012). *Health qigong: 12-step Daoyin health preservation exercise Doa Yin Yang Sheng Cong Shi Er Fa.* Beijing: Foreign Languages Press.

Ching, S. M., Mokshashri, N. R., Kannan, M. M., Lee, K. W., Sallahuddin, N. A., Ng, J. X., Wong, J. L., Devaraj, N. K., Hoo, F. K., Loo, Y. S., & Veettil, S. K. (2021). Effects of qigong on systolic and diastolic blood pressure lowering: A systematic review with meta-analysis and trial sequential analysis. *BMC Complementary Medicine and Therapies, 21*(1), 8. 10.1186/s12906-020-03172-3

Cohen, J. (1992). A power primer. *Psychological Bulletin, 112*(1), 155–159. 10.1037/0033-2909.112.1.155

Cui, J., Liu, F., Liu, X., Li, R., Chen, X., & Zeng, H. (2022). The impact of qigong and tai chi exercise on drug addiction: A systematic review and meta-analysis. *Frontiers in Psychiatry, 13*, 826187. 10.3389/fpsyt.2022.826187

Feng, F., Tuchman, S., Denninger, J. W., Fricchione, G. L., & Yeung, A. (2020). Qigong for the prevention, treatment, and rehabilitation of COVID-19 infection in older adults. *The American Journal of Geriatric Psychiatry*, *28*(8), 812–819. 10.1016/j.jagp.2020.05.012

Garber, C. E., Blissmer, B., Deschenes, M. R., Franklin, B. A., Lamonte, M. J., Lee, I. M., ... Swain, D. P. (2011). American College of Sports Medicine position stand. Quantity and quality of exercise for developing and maintaining cardiorespiratory, musculoskeletal, and neuromotor fitness in apparently healthy adults: Guidance for prescribing exercise. *Medicine & Science in Sports & Exercise, 43*(7), 1334–1359. 10.1249/MSS.0b013e318213fefb

Geneen, L. J., Moore, R. A., Clarke, C., Martin, D., Colvin, L. A., & Smith, B. H. (2017). Physical activity and exercise for chronic pain in adults: An overview of Cochrane Reviews.*The Cochrane Database of Systematic Reviews, 1*, CD011279.

Girard, J., & Girard, A. (2019). The effects of qigong on neck pain: A systematic review. *Complementary Therapies in Clinical Practice, 34*, 23–29. 10.1016/j.ctcp.2018.10.013

Ho, T. J., Christiani, D. C., Ma, T. C., Jang, T. R., Lieng, C. H., Yeh, Y. C., ... Lan, T. Y. (2011). Effect of qigong on quality of life: A cross-sectional population-based comparison study in Taiwan. *BMC Public Health*, *11*, 801. 10.1186/1471-2458-11-546

Holt-Lunstad, J., Smith, T. B., & Layton, J. B. (2010). Social relationships and mortality risk: A meta-analytic review. *PLoS Medicine*, *7*(7), e1000316. 10.1371/journal.pmed.1000316

Idler, E. L., & Benyamini, Y. (1997). Self-rated health and mortality: A review of twenty-seven community studies. *Journal of Health and Social Behavior*, *38*(1), 21–37. Retrieved from http://www.jstor.org/ stable/2955359

Jahnke, R., Larkey, L., Rogers, C., Etnier, J., & Lin, F. (2010). A comprehensive review of health benefits of qigong and tai chi.*American Journal of Health Promotion*, *24*(6), e1–e25. 10.4278/ajhp.081013-LIT-248

Jones, S. A. (2006). Ageing to arrhythmias: Conundrums of connections in the ageing heart. *Journal of Pharmacy and Pharmacology*, *58*(12), 1571–1576. 10.1211/jpp.58.12.0002

Kanamori, S., Kai, Y., Aida, J., Kondo, K., Kawachi, I., Hirai, H., Shirai, K., Ishikawa, Y., Suzuki, K., & JAGES Group (2014). Social participation and the prevention of functional disability in older Japanese: The JAGES cohort study. *PloS One, 9*(6), e99638. 10.1371/journal.pone.0099638

Kivimäki, M., Batty, G. D., Pentti, J., Shipley, M. J., Sipilä, P. N., Nyberg, S. T., Suominen, S. B., Oksanen, T., Stenholm, S., Virtanen, M., Marmot, M. G., Singh-Manoux, A., Brunner, E. J., Lindbohm, J. V., Ferrie, J. E., & Vahtera, J. (2020). Association between socioeconomic status and the development of mental and physical health conditions in adulthood: A multi-cohort study. *The Lancet. Public Health, 5*(3), e140–e149. 10.1016/S2468-2667(19)30248-8

Ko, L. H., Hsieh, Y. J., Wang, M. Y., Hou, W. H., & Tsai, P. S. (2022). Effects of health qigong on sleep quality: A systematic review and meta-analysis of randomized controlled trials. *Complementary Therapies in Medicine*, *71*, 102876. 10.1016/j.ctim.2022.102876

Kraft, P., & Kraft, B. (2021). Explaining socioeconomic disparities in health behaviours: A review of biopsychological pathways involving stress and inflammation. *Neuroscience and Biobehavioral Reviews, 127*, 689–708. 10.1016/j.neubiorev.2021.05.019

Kvam, S., Kleppe, C. L., Nordhus, I. H., & Hovland, A. (2016). Exercise as a treatment for depression: A meta-analysis. *Journal of Affective Disorders, 202*, 67–86. 10.1016/j.jad.2016.03.063

Larkey, L., Jahnke, R., Etnier, J., & Gonzalez, J. (2009). Meditative movement as a category of exercise: Implications for research. *Journal of Physical Activity & Health, 6*(2), 230–238. 10.1123/jpah.6.2.230

Larkey, L. K., Roe, D. J., Smith, L., & Millstine, D. (2016). Exploratory outcome assessment of qigong/tai chi easy on breast cancer survivors.*Complementary Therapies in Medicine, 29*, 196–203. 10.1016/j.ctim.2016.10.006

Li, J., Chan, J. S., Chow, A. Y., Yuen, L. P., & Chan, C. L. (2015). From body to mind and spirit: Qigong exercise for bereaved persons with chronic fatigue syndrome-like illness. *Evidence-Based Complementary and Alternative Medicine, 2015*, 1–7.

Lin, S., Guo, J., Nie, P., Chen, X., Guo, J., Lin, N., & Liu, F. (2022). Baduanjin for executive function in patients with mild cognitive impairment: A systematic review and meta-analysis. *Complementary Therapies in Clinical Practice, 49*, 101626. 10.1016/j.ctcp.2022.101626

Litscher, G., Wenzel, G., Niederwieser, G., & Schwarz, G. (2001). Effects of QiGong on brain function. *Neurological Research, 23*(5), 501–505. 10.1179/016164101101198749

Luo, X., Zhao, M., Zhang, Y., & Zhang, Y. (2023). Effects of baduanjin exercise on blood glucose, depression and anxiety among patients with type II diabetes and emotional disorders: A meta-analysis. *Complementary Therapies in Clinical Practice, 50*, 101702. 10.1016/j.ctcp.2022.101702

Meng, T., Hu, S. F., Cheng, Y. Q., Ye, M. N., Wang, B., Wu, J. J., & Chen, H. F. (2021). Qigong for women with breast cancer: An updated systematic review and meta-analysis. *Complementary Therapies in Medicine, 60*, 102743. 10.1016/j.ctim.2021.102743

Nelson, M. E., Rejeski, W. J., Blair, S. N., Duncan, P. W., Judge, J. O., King, A. C., … Castaneda-Sceppa, C. (2007). Physical activity and public health in older adults: Recommendation from the American College of Sports Medicine and the American Heart Association. *Circulation, 116*(9), 1094–1105. 10.1161/CIRCULATIONAHA.107.185650

Ng, B. H., & Tsang, H. W. (2009). Psychophysiological outcomes of health qigong for chronic conditions: A systematic review. *Psychophysiology, 46*(2), 257–269. 10.1111/j.1469-8986.2008.00763.x

Rogers, C. E., Larkey, L. K., & Keller, C. (2009). A review of clinical trials of tai chi and qigong in older adults. *Western Journal of Nursing Research, 31*(2), 245–279. 10.1177/0193945908327529

Sancier, K. M., & Hu, B. (1991). Medical applications of qigong and emitted qi on humans, animals, cell cultures, and plants: Review of selected scientific research. *American Journal of Acupuncture, 19*(4), 367–377. Retrieved from https://www.researchgate.net/publication/285693644_Medical_applications_of_Qigong_and_emit

Skevington, S. M., Lotfy, M., & O'Connell, K. A. (2004). The World Health Organization's WHOQOL- BREF quality of life assessment: Psychometric properties and results of the international field trial: A report from the WHOQOL group. *Quality of Life Research, 13*(2), 299–310. 10.1023/B:QURE.0000018486.91360.00

Sperandei, S., Vieira, M. C., & Reis, A. C. (2016). Adherence to physical activity in an unsupervised setting: Explanatory variables for high attrition rates among fitness center members. *Journal of Science and Medicine in Sport, 19*(11), 916–920. 10.1016/j.jsams.2015.12.522

Tang, S. K., Tse, M. M. Y., Leung, S. F., & Fotis, T. (2019). The effectiveness, suitability, and sustainability of non-pharmacological methods of managing pain in community-dwelling older adults: A systematic review. *BMC Public Health, 19*(1), 1488. 10.1186/s12889-019-7831-9

Tao, S., & Li, Z. (2023). Effects of qigong exercise on cardiovascular risk factors in patients with metabolic syndrome: A systematic review and meta-analysis. *Frontiers in Physiology, 14*, 1092480. 10.3389/fphys.2023.1092480

Tao, W. W., Jiang, H., Tao, X. M., Jiang, P., Sha, L. Y., & Sun, X. C. (2016). Effects of acupuncture, tuina, tai chi, qigong, and traditional Chinese medicine five-element music therapy on symptom management and quality of life for cancer patients: A meta-analysis. *Journal of Pain and Symptom Management, 51*(4), 728–747. 10.1016/j.jpainsymman.2015.11.027

Teut, M., Knilli, J., Daus, D., Roll, S., & Witt, C. M. (2016). Qigong or yoga versus no intervention in older adults with chronic low back pain: A randomized controlled trial. *The Journal of Pain, 17*(7), 796–805. 10.1016/j.jpain.2016.03.003

Tsang, W. W., & Hui-Chan, C. W. (2004). Effect of 4- and 8-wk intensive Tai Chi training on balance control in the elderly. *Medicine & Science in Sports & Exercise*, 36(4), 648–657. 10.1249/01.MSS.0000121941.57669.BF

Wang, C. W., Chan, C. H., Ho, R. T., Chan, J. S., Ng, S. M., & Chan, C. L. (2014). Managing stress and anxiety through qigong exercise in healthy adults: A systematic review and meta-analysis of ran- domized controlled trials. *BMC Complementary and Alternative Medicine, 14*, 1146. 10.1186/ 1472-6882-14-8

Wang, C. W., Ng, S. M., Ho, R. T., Ziea, E. T., Wong, V. C., & Chan, C. L. (2012). The effect of qigong exercise on immunity and infections: A systematic review of controlled trials. *The American Journal of Chinese Medicine, 40*(6), 1143–1156. 10.1142/S0192415X1250084X

Wang, F., Gao, Y., Han, Z., Yu, Y., Long, Z., Jiang, X., Wu, Y., Pei, B., Cao, Y., Ye, J., Wang, M., & Zhao, Y. (2023). A systematic review and meta-analysis of 90 cohort studies of social isolation, loneliness and mortality. *Nature Human Behaviour*, 10.1038/s41562-023-01617-6. Advance online publication. 10.1038/s41562-023-01617-6

Weber, M., Schnorr, T., Morat, M., Morat, T., & Donath, L. (2020). Effects of mind-body interventions involving meditative movements on quality of Life, depressive symptoms, fear of falling and sleep quality in older adults: A systematic review with meta-analysis.*International Journal of Environmental Research and Public Health, 17*(18), 6556. 10.3390/ijerph17186556

Wee, Z. Q. C., & Dillon, D. (2022). Increasing physical exercise through action and coping planning. *International Journal of Environmental Research and Public Health, 19*(7), 3883. 10.3390/ijerph19073883

World Health Organization. (2016, September 13). WHO Quality of Life-BREF (WHOQOL-BREF) [Website]. Retrieved from http://www.who.int/substance_abuse/research_tools/whoqolbref/en/

World Health Organization (2017). Official records of the World Health Organization no.2: Summary report on proceedings minutes and final act of the international health conference. Retrieved from http://apps.who.int/iris/bitstream/10665/85573/1/Official_record2_eng.pdf Accessed 20 January 2017

Xu, S., Zhang, D., He, Q., Ma, C., Ye, S., Ge, L., Zhang, L., Liu, W., Chen, Z., & Zhou, L. (2022). Efficacy of liuzijue qigong in patients with chronic obstructive pulmonary disease: A systematic review and meta-analysis.*Complementary Therapies in Medicine*, *65*, 102809. 10.1016/j.ctim.2022.102809

Yang, W. Y., Xu, Y., Ye, L., Rong, L. J., Feng, J., Huang, B. L., Chien, C. W., & Tung, T. H. (2023). Effects of baduanjin exercise on quality-of-life and exercise capacity in patients with heart failure: A systematic review and meta-analysis. *Complementary Therapies in Clinical Practice*, *50*, 101675. 10.1016/j.ctcp.2022.101675

Ye, X. X., Ren, Z. Y., Vafaei, S., Zhang, J. M., Song, Y., Wang, Y. X., & Song, P. G. (2022). Effectiveness of Baduanjin exercise on quality of life and psychological health in postoperative patients with breast cancer: A systematic review and meta-analysis.*Integrative Cancer Therapies*, *21*, 15347354221104092. 10.1177/15347354221104092

Yin J., Tang L., & Dishman R.K. (2020). The efficacy of qigong practice for cancer-related fatigue: A systematic review and meta-analysis of randomized controlled trials. *Mental Health and Physical Activity*, *19*, 100347. 10.1016/j.mhpa.2020.100347

Zeng, Z. P., Liu, Y. B., Fang, J., Liu, Y., Luo, J., & Yang, M. (2020). Effects of baduanjin exercise for knee osteoarthritis: A systematic review and meta-analysis. *Complementary Therapies in Medicine*, *48*, 102279. 10.1016/j.ctim.2019.102279

Zeng, Y., Xie, X., & Cheng, A. S. K. (2019). Qigong or tai chi in cancer care: An updated systematic review and meta-analysis. *Current Oncology Reports*, *21*(6), 48. 10.1007/s11912-019-0786-2

Zou, L., Sasaki, J. E., Wang, H., Xiao, Z., Fang, Q., & Zhang, M. (2017). A systematic review and meta-analysis Baduanjin qigong for health benefits: Randomized controlled trials. *Evidence-Based Complementary and Alternative Medicine*, *2017*, 1–17.

15

EXERCISE MAY BENEFIT PATIENTS WITH SCHIZOPHRENIA

Chen Chang, Chiung-Ling Chu, and Tsung-Min Hung

According to the *Diagnostic and Statistical Manual of Mental Disorders, 5th Edition* (DSM-V) (American Psychiatric Association, 2013), schizophrenia is a severe mental disorder that profoundly impacts an individual's thoughts, emotions, behaviors, and perceptions. It is characterized by positive symptoms, including delusions, hallucinations, disorganized thinking, and abnormal motor behavior. Negative symptoms such as reduced emotional expression, avolition, alogia, anhedonia, and asociality are commonly observed. To meet the diagnostic criteria, two or more of these symptoms must be present for a significant portion of one month, accompanied by signs of impaired occupational and social functioning.

The worldwide prevalence of schizophrenia is estimated to be 0.3–0.7%. This disorder not only carries a mortality rate twice that of the general population but also significantly impairs individuals' cognitive functions and emotional recognition abilities (Davidson et al., 2004). Moreover, schizophrenia typically emerges during the crucial educational and occupational years, severely disrupting learning and impacting families' livelihoods (Torrey, 2001). The associated social costs, including the burden on healthcare systems and lost productivity, are estimated to be as high as 75 billion annually (Sadock & Sadock, 2004). Consequently, schizophrenia has wide-ranging implications for society, families, and individuals.

Traditional treatments for schizophrenia primarily involve antipsychotic medications, psychosocial counseling, and coordinated specialty care. While antipsychotic medications can effectively alleviate positive symptoms, their impact on negative symptoms is limited (Faulkner, 2005). Moreover, many patients with schizophrenia often experience comorbid conditions such as anxiety and depression, with a substantial portion (13–39%) grappling with

DOI: 10.4324/9781003459750-15

social anxiety (Bermanzohn et al., 2000). Despite advancements in pharmacology, typical and atypical antipsychotics offer limited efficacy in addressing the cognitive deficits commonly observed in patients (Insel, 2010). It's worth noting that the use of antipsychotic medication may contribute to progressive brain volume reduction (Veijola et al., 2014). While valuable, psychotherapy and other interventions also have drawbacks (Faulkner & Biddle, 1999). Psychotherapy can be time-consuming and costly, necessitating the development of approaches with minimal side effects that can be applied independently or as adjuncts to traditional therapy (Martinsen, 1990).

The Neurophysiology of Schizophrenia

The etiology of schizophrenia remains elusive, but it manifests with both structural and functional brain alterations.

Structurally, individuals with schizophrenia are characterized by neural difficulties, brain atrophy, and hippocampal shrinkage (Antonova et al., 2004; Sawada et al., 2005; Steen et al., 2006). Notably, patients displayed a reduction in the number of neurons, neural subtypes, and presynaptic proteins at the projection ends of the entorhinal cortex (Harrison, 2004; Sawada et al., 2005). The hippocampal volume reduction correlates with neural shrinkage and the disruption of the neural fiber network (Harrison, 2004; Steen et al., 2006), which is directly related to memory impairment. Besides structural changes, similar impairments extend to neurogenesis, contributing to impaired connectivity between the cortex and hippocampal, consequently affecting new memory formation (Reif et al., 2006).

Evidence from neuroimaging highlights abnormalities in emotion, attention, and olfactory processing, implicating dysfunction in key regions like the prefrontal cortex (PFC), anterior cingulate gyrus (ACG), amygdala (AMG), and hippocampus. Concerning emotion, general impairment is associated with the limbic system (Gur et al., 2002), while deficits in face perception are linked to amygdala, fusiform gyrus, ventral temporal, basal ganglia, and prefrontal cortex (Williams et al., 2007). This results in the inability of patients to recognize human emotional expressions. In terms of attention, Dichter et al. (2010) discovered that patients exhibited aberrant reciprocal inhibitions compared to healthy individuals, coupled with reduced activation in the dorsal prefrontal cortex (DPFC) and ventral prefrontal cortex (VPFC) and increased dorsal activation in the anterior cingulate. Subsequent research indicated a negative association between negative symptoms and decreased anterior cingulate activation in patients with schizophrenia, suggesting a form of brain dysfunction.

Moreover, studies using event-related potentials also revealed olfactory, emotional, reading, and attention dysfunction. They are characterized by smaller amplitudes and abnormal latencies compared to healthy individuals. For instance, deactivation in PFC was observed through smaller amplitude in late ERP components (N1 & P2) in odor identification and threshold sensitivity detection. Additionally, the delayed latency of late positivity (LP) waves suggests abnormalities in their odor recognition function (Turetsky et al., 2003), and the difficulties in odor identification are associated with negative symptoms (Geddes et al., 1991).

In response to facial emotional stimuli, patients exhibited decreased LP amplitude in intense facial expressions, while no differences were observed in neutral stimuli, possibly reflecting the dysfunction of emotional recognition by reduced processing of negative stimuli or increased processing of neutral stimuli in patients (Turetsky et al., 2007). Patients also displayed reduced LP amplitudes in the emotional perception of written sentences (Kuperberg et al., 2011). Late positivity represents the intrinsic emotional salience and arousing quality of a given stimulus, it is discovered to be associated with negative symptoms (Turetsky et al., 2007). And the results indicated patients reduced immediate neural responses to critical emotional words. Concerning attention, patients typically showed a decreased amplitude and prolonged latency in P300 (Jeon & Polich, 2003; Ford et al., 1999). P300 is related to enduring negative symptoms, ebbing of attention, gray matter volume deficits (Ford et al., 1999), and recall performance (Karis et al., 1984; Polich, 2007). The abnormality in P300 suggests the dysfunction in memory and attention in patients with schizophrenia.

Benefits of Exercise to Brain Function

Exercise involves structured, planned, and repetitive bodily movements and is undertaken by an individual for the sake of improving or maintaining health (Caspersen et al., 1985). Compared to traditional psychiatric therapy, exercise is a relatively cost-effective and self-directed approach (Martinsen, 1990). For patients, exercise can serve as a complementary treatment to improve both structural and functional aspects of the brain, thereby ameliorating their overall physical and mental well-being. The following sections will provide further explanations of exercise's impact on brain structure, cerebral blood flow, and cognitive function.

Exercise has been shown to modulate cerebral blood flow and brain structure. Numerous studies have demonstrated that exercise can enhance structural volume and integrity in multiple brain regions, enhancing both efficiency and effectiveness (Erickson et al., 2015; Hillman et al., 2008). Even in older adults, a high-risk group for brain degeneration, exercise interventions yielded positive results regarding brain structure and function

(Chen et al., 2020; Matura et al., 2017). Specifically, research suggested a significant increase in the volume of PFC, temporal lobe, and anterior white matter after exercise intervention (Colcombe et al., 2006). Pereira et al. (2007) also observed a notable increase in cerebral blood volume (CBV) in the dentate gyrus, a hippocampal subregion important for neurogenesis. Moreover, exercise induces angiogenesis in the cortex and cerebellum (Black et al., 1990; Ding et al., 2006). Consequently, it can be inferred that exercise can ameliorate the issue of reduced brain volume in patients.

More neuroscience research supports the positive effect of exercise on improving cognitive and emotional function. Hillman et al. (2008) found that individuals with high physical fitness exhibited larger P300 amplitude and shortened latencies compared with those with low physical fitness. Additionally, older adults with high physical activity displayed smaller error-related negativity (ERN), suggesting a better process of action monitoring (Themenson et al., 2006). Thus, it is expected that exercise can normalize the abnormalities in P300. In terms of emotion, Colcombe et al. (2006) discovered that aerobic exercise training reduced activity in ACC and increased activation in the frontal and parietal lobes. These brain regions are closely related to attention and emotional processing. Consequently, exercise is expected to ameliorate dysfunction in the frontal and ACC regions, thereby addressing corresponding attention and emotion-related issues.

As mentioned above, exercise has the potential to modulate the brain structure and enhance cognitive function (executive function), by potentially correcting the abnormalities in P300. Thus, it can be expected that exercise plays an important role in improving overall brain function in patients with schizophrenia. The positive effect of exercise on patients' symptoms was established in the previous review (Falkai et al., 2017; Firth et al., 2017; Gorczynski et al., 2010; Wei et al., 2020). The present study will primarily focus on the benefit of cognition after exercise intervention in patients with schizophrenia.

Data Collection

The present study employed a systematic search to identify relevant articles from major electronic databases, including PubMed and Scopus. The search was conducted using a set of predefined keywords and inclusion criteria. The keywords used in the search strategy were "physical activity," "physical fitness," "exercise," "sport*," or "aerobic*," in combination with "schizophrenia" or "psychosis." The search was restricted to articles published between 2013 and 2023, and the keywords were required to appear in the title, abstract, or keywords of the articles. The inclusion criteria of the studies in this review were as follows. (1) The study must involve an exercise intervention. (2) The study must include both an experimental group and a control group. (3) The independent variables must involve cognitive function (Table 15.1).

TABLE 15.1 Systematic search to identify relevant articles from major electronic databases

Authors	*Intervention*	*Cognitive Variables*	*Results*
Malchow et al., 2015	Endurance Training (bicycle) 2 × 30 min for 6 weeks Table soccer	Verbal Learning Memory Test (VLMT) Wisconsin Card Sorting Test (WCST) TMT-A & B	Within Memory: STM: both significant increase LTM: ET but not TS Processing speed: TMT-A & B: both no significant change WCST: ET but not TS
Kimhy et al., 2015	Aerobic Exercise (AE): 3 × 1 hour/week for 12 weeks 60% HR max(week1) 65%(week2) 70%(week3) 75%(week4–12) Treatment as Usual (TAU)	MATRICS Consensus Cognitive Battery	Between AE > TAU
Bhatia et al., 2017	Treatment as Usual (TAU) (n = 92) Yoga (YT) (n = 104): 1 hour for 21 days Physical Exercise (PE) (n = 90): brisk walk, jogging, aerobic	Pennsylvania Computerized Neurocognitive Battery (Penn CNB)	Between Speed Index spatial memory, face memory, emotion: YT > TAU face memory, working memory, emotion: PE > TAU Accuracy Index face memory, working memory, attention: PE > TAU face memory, working memory: PE > YT abstraction and mental flexibility: YT > TAU

Firth et al., 2018	Exercise Group (EG) (n = 25): 2 × 45–60 min MV aerobic & resitance exercise Control Group (CG) (n = 7):	Cambridge Neuropsychological Test Automated Battery	Within EG significant changes in Verbal STM, social cognition, executive function, inhibitory control No significant change in processing speed, motor function
Choi et al., 2020	Physical Exercise (PE) (n = 29): 3 × 30 min / week Cognitive Training (CT) (n = 27) PE+CT (n = 29): PE 2 × 30 min/week, CT 1 × 30 min/week	Wechsler Adult Intelligence Scale–Fourth Edition Processing Speed Index (PSI)	Between WMI: PE, PE+CT > CT PSI: PE > PE+CT = CT
Li et al., 2020	Baduanjin Group (EG): 5 × 40 min/week for 24 weeks brisk walk Group (CG): 5 × 40 min/week for 24 weeks	Wechsler Memory Scale TMT-A Digit Symbol Substitutuin Test (DSST)	Between LM: EG > CG TMT-A: EG = CG DSST: no diff
Kuo et al., 2021	BSET (n = 14): 30 min/ 40–60% HRR CTRL (n = 14)	Symbol Digit Modalities Test	No diff. between BSET & CTRL
Gao et al., 2021	Yijinjing Group (EG) (n = 20): 2 × 40 min/week for 12 weeks Control Group (CG) (n = 20)	Mini Mental State Examination	Between MMSE: EG > CG
Dai et al., 2022	CAE (n = 26): 2 × 30 min/week for 8 weeks Aerobic Exercise (AE) (n = 25): 45 min 50–70% Max HR Control Group (CG) (n = 31)	TMT-A Symbol Coding Test (SCT) Stroop Colour-Word Test (SCWT)	Between TMT-A: CAE > AE = CG SCT: CAE > AE = CG SCWT: CAE > AE = CG

(Continued)

TABLE 15.1 (Continued)

Authors	*Intervention*	*Cognitive Variables*	*Results*
Kurebayashi et al., 2022	Exercise Group (EG) (n = 4): 2 × 60 min/week for 8 weeks 60% Max HR Control Group (CG) (n = 14)	Cognitrax Basic Version	Between EG > CG
Chen et al., 2022	Baduanjin Group (BG) (n = 24): 2 × 60 min/week for 12 weeks Brisk Walk (BW) (n = 24): 2 × 60 min/week for 12 weeks	Montreal Cognitive Assessment TMT-A,B Wechsler Memory Scale Logical Memory TUG-DTc	Within BG: WMSLM sinificant increase BW: WMSLM: sinificant increase Between TUG-DT: BG > BW
Mandini et al., 2022	Guided Walking (GW)(n = 20): 2 × 45–60 min/week for 12 months Cognitive Rehabilitation (CG) (n = 12): 50 sessions in 12months,	Screen for Cognitive Impairment in Psychiatry (SCIP) Frontal Assessment Battery (FAB)	Within GW: significant increase in SCIP & FAB CR: no improvement in both
Nuechterlein et al., 2023	Cognitive Training & Exercise (CT & E) (n = 24): 150 min/week Cognitive Training (CT) (n = 23): 2 days/week for 24 weeks	MATRICS Consensus Cognitive Battery (MCCB)	Between MCCB: CT&E > CT

Research Evidence on Exercise as a Treatment for Schizophrenia

An increasing body of research has explored exercise as an adjunctive treatment for individuals with schizophrenia. These investigations have comprehensively assessed various cognitive domains to investigate the impact of exercise interventions on cognitive function in this population. These domains include processing abilities (such as spatial processing and processing speed), attention (including simple and complex attention), memory (encompassing short-term memory, long-term memory, verbal memory, visual memory, and logical memory), and executive functions (involving inhibitory control, working memory, and cognitive flexibility).

Specifically addressing processing speed, numerous studies have employed assessments like TMT-A, TMT-B, DSST, and the Symbol Digit Modalities Test (SDMT) to gauge cognitive performance in this realm. The outcomes of exercise interventions on processing speed have yielded inconsistent results. While some studies have reported no significant impact on processing speed in patients (Malchow et al., 2015; Firth et al., 2018; Kuo et al., 2021; Li et al., 2020), recent investigations have demonstrated positive influences of exercise interventions (Choi et al., 2020; Dai et al., 2022; Kurebayashi et al., 2022). It is worth noting that the choice of cognitive tasks might contribute to the variability in exercise effects on processing speed. For example, Dai et al. (2022) observed a significant improvement in processing speed following exercise intervention but did not find similar improvements when using the TMT-A. Additionally, research has emphasized that processing speed assessments are sensitive to participant engagement levels and the nature of the tasks themselves (Firth et al., 2018). Choi et al. (2020) noted that a six-week exercise intervention led to significant enhancements in processing speed, surpassing a combined exercise and cognitive training group (three weeks of each). However, no significant differences in processing speed improvements were observed between the exercise and cognitive training group (six weeks) and the cognitive training-only group (six weeks). In conclusion, the impact of exercise on processing speed in individuals with schizophrenia appears to be influenced by factors such as the specific cognitive tasks employed and the duration and nature of the exercise interventions.

Regarding memory functions, exercise consistently demonstrates positive effects in individuals with schizophrenia. Most studies indicate that exercise interventions yield favorable outcomes across various memory domains, including short-term memory, long-term memory, spatial memory, face memory, verbal memory, and logical memory (Chen et al., 2022; Bhatia et al., 2017; Firth et al., 2018; Li et al., 2020; Malchow et al., 2015). Previous research on brain structure has revealed significant impacts of exercise on hippocampal plasticity. For example, a three-month cycling intervention resulted in a 12% increase in hippocampal volume among individuals with schizophrenia, indicating potential improvements in cognitive functioning (Pajonk et al., 2010). Furthermore, a randomized controlled trial conducted by Scheewe et al. (2013) associated improvements in aerobic fitness with increased brain white matter volume, reduced third ventricle size, and alterations in cortical thickness. These findings suggest that exercise-induced enhancements in aerobic capacity can lead to structural changes in the hippocampus, white matter, and cortical regions of the brain, ultimately enhancing memory function in individuals with schizophrenia.

Additionally, Li et al. (2020) found a significant increase in logical memory in the Baduanjin group compared to the brisk walk group after 24 weeks of intervention (five times a week for 40 minutes each). This difference may be attributed to the inclusion of mindfulness training in Baduanjin and yoga, with meditation being proven to improve memory performance in adults (Farhang et al., 2019). In the realm of executive functioning and global cognition, previous studies have also reported promising results. Several studies indicated significant improvements in cognitive flexibility (Bhatia et al., 2017; Kurebayashi et al., 2022; Malchow et al., 2015), working memory (Choi et al., 2020), inhibitory control (Dai et al., 2022), and overall executive functioning (Firth et al., 2018; Kurebayashi et al., 2022). Similar positive results were discovered regarding the effect of exercise intervention on global cognition (Gao et al., 2021; Chen et al., 2022; Mandini et al., 2022; Nuechterlein et al., 2023).

Conclusion

The present review mainly focused on elucidating the beneficial effect of exercise intervention on cognitive improvement in schizophrenia patients. As the results suggested, exercise is a promising adjunctive therapy in psychiatric treatment in practical clinical application. Through exercise intervention, it is possible to effectively enhance patients' attention, processing speed, memory-related function, executive function, and global cognition.

The articles included in this study encompass a wide range of exercise types for interventions, including aerobic exercises (such as walking, jogging, and cycling), resistance training, Baduanjin, yoga, and more. Despite the diversity in exercise modalities, there is a consistent effect observed in the research results regarding the promotion of cognitive function. Furthermore, the studies exhibited significant variability in exercise interventions, spanning from gentle exercises emphasizing body awareness and postures to moderate to vigorous intensity exercises like aerobic and endurance training. Notably, despite these differences in intervention approaches, they consistently yielded improvements in cognitive functioning. It is important to note that, several studies have provided a diverse range of exercise options during the intervention to increase patients' engagement levels throughout the intervention process and maximize the enhancement of cognitive functions. (Bhatia et al., 2017; Choi et al., 2020; Firth et al., 2018; Kurebayashi et al., 2022). Therefore, as long as exercise intervention can be implemented as an adjunctive therapy for schizophrenia treatment and enhance patients' adherence throughout the intervention process, it can have a positive impact on patients' cognitive functioning.

In the realm of exercise psychology, there has been a growing interest in "qualitative" research designs aimed at enhancing executive function within the field of physical activity studies. These research methodologies place a greater emphasis on factors like "task complexity" and "mental engagement" during interventions, as opposed to the traditional "quantitative" approach, which primarily focuses on identifying the dose-response relationships of variables such as "exercise intensity," "exercise frequency," "exercise type," and "exercise duration" concerning executive function (Mavilidi et al., 2018; Pesce et al., 2009; Tomporowski et al., 2015). The degree of mental engagement during the exercise process is a critical factor in determining its positive impact on cognition (Best, 2010). Exercises involving higher cognitive engagement tend to yield more robust cognitive outcomes compared to those with minimal cognitive engagement (Best, 2010; Fissler et al., 2013; Levin et al., 2017).

To exemplify this concept, one of the studies included in the present review incorporated the notion of cognitive engagement during exercise. In the study by Dai et al. (2022), the Cognitive Engagement Exercise (CAE) group participated in a Cognitive Control and Response Training (CCRT) program. This system comprised 30 exercise sequences dynamically adjusted in difficulty based on the patients' accuracy, targeting an 80% success rate. In contrast, the Aerobic Exercise (AE) group engaged in 45 minutes of jogging at an intensity ranging from 50% to 70% of their maximum heart rate. Lastly, the control group continued with their usual treatment regimen. Notably, after eight weeks of intervention, the CAE group demonstrated the most significant improvements in processing speed and inhibitory control. This shift toward qualitative research designs emphasizing cognitive engagement during exercise interventions signifies a promising avenue for enhancing cognitive function through exercise intervention.

However, it is essential to acknowledge the high heterogeneity in symptom severity among individuals with schizophrenia. Further research is required to determine the dose-response relationship of exercise interventions, including factors such as frequency, intensity, duration, and type, in maximizing cognitive function improvement in patients.

In conclusion, exercise interventions offer a promising avenue for improving cognitive function in individuals with schizophrenia. These interventions hold significant potential to enhance the overall well-being and cognitive abilities of patients, which could ultimately contribute to better outcomes and improved quality of life for those living with this challenging mental disorder.

References

American Psychiatric Association. (2013). *Diagnostic and statistical manual of mental disorders* (5th ed.). 10.1176/appi.books.9780890425596

Antonova, E., Sharma, T., Morris, R., & Kumari, V. (2004). The relationship between brain structure and neurocognition in schizophrenia: A selective review. *Schizophrenia Research, 70*, 117–145. 10.1016/j.schres.2003.12.002

Bermanzohn, P. C., Porto, L., Arlow, P. B., Pollack, S., Stronger, R., & Siris, S. G. (2000). At issue: hierarchical diagnosis in chronic schizophrenia: A clinical study of co-occurring syndromes. *Schizophrenia Bulletin, 26*(3), 517–525. 10.1093/oxfordjournals.schbul.a033472

Best, J. R. (2010). Effects of physical activity on children's executive function: Contributions of experimental research on aerobic exercise. *Developmental Review, 30*(4), 331–351. 10.1016/j.dr.2010.08.001

Bhatia, T., Mazumdar, S., Wood, J., He, F., Gur, R. E., Gur, R. C., … & Deshpande, S. N. (2017). A randomised controlled trial of adjunctive yoga and adjunctive physical exercise training for cognitive dysfunction in schizophrenia. *Acta Neuropsychiatrica, 29*(2), 102–114. 10.1017/neu.2016.42

Black, J. E., Isaacs, K. R., Anderson, B. J., Alcantara, A. A., & Greenough, W. T. (1990). Learning causes synaptogenesis, whereas motor activity causes angiogenesis, in cerebellar cortex of adult rats. *Proceedings of the National Academy of Sciences, 87*, 5568–5572. 10.1073/pnas.87.14.5568

Caspersen, C. J., Powell, K. E., & Christenson, G. M. (1985). Physical activity, exercise, and physical fitness: Definitions and distinctions for health-related research. *Public Health Reports, 100*, 126–131.

Chen, F. T., Hopman, R. J., Huang, C. J., Chu, C. H., Hillman, C. H., Hung, T. M., & Chang, Y. K. (2020). The effect of exercise training on brain structure and function in older adults: A systematic review based on evidence from randomized control trials. *Journal of Clinical Medicine, 9*(4), 914. 10.3390/jcm9040914

Chen, C. R., Huang, Y. C., Lee, Y. W., Hsieh, H. H., Lee, Y. C., & Lin, K. C. (2022). The effects of Baduanjin exercise vs. brisk walking on physical fitness and cognition in middle-aged patients with schizophrenia: A randomized controlled trial. *Frontiers in Psychiatry, 13*, 983994. 10.3389/fpsyt.2022.983994

Choi, J., Taylor, B., Fiszdon, J. M., Kurtz, M. M., Tek, C., Dewberry, M. J., … & Pearlson, G. D. (2020). The synergistic benefits of physical and cognitive exercise in schizophrenia: Promoting motivation to enhance community effectiveness. *Schizophrenia Research: Cognition, 19*, 100147. 10.1016/j.scog.2019.100147

Colcombe, S. J., Erickson, K. I., Scalf, P. E., Kim, J. S., Prakash, R., McAuley, E., … & Kramer, A. F. (2006). Aerobic exercise training increases brain volume in aging humans. *The Journals of Gerontology Series A: Biological Sciences and Medical Sciences, 61*(11), 1166–1170. 10.1093/gerona/61.11.1166

Dai, Y., Ding, H., Lu, X., Wu, X., Xu, C., Jiang, T., … & Huang, S. (2022). CCRT and aerobic exercise: a randomized controlled study of processing speed, cognitive flexibility, and serum BDNF expression in schizophrenia. *Schizophrenia*, *8*(1), 84. 10.1038/s41537-022-00297-x

Davidson, G. C., Neale, J. M., & Kring, A. M. (2004). *Abnormal psychology* (9th ed.). Danvers, MA: John Wiley & Sons.

Dichter, G. S., Bellion, C., Casp, M., & Belger, A. (2010). Impaired modulation of attention and emotion in schizophrenia. *Schizophrenia Bulletin, 36*(3), 595–606. 10.1093/schbul/sbn118

Ding, Q., Vaynman, S., Akhavan, M., Ying, Z., & Gomez-Pinilla, F. (2006). Insulin-like growth factor I interfaces with brain derived neurotrophic factor-mediated synaptic plasticity to modulate aspects of exercise-induced cognitive function. *Neuroscience*, *140*, 823–833. 10.1016/j.neuroscience.2006.02.084

Erickson, K. I., Hillman, C. H., & Kramer, A. F. (2015). Physical activity, brain, and cognition. *Current Opinion in Behavioral Sciences*, *4*, 27–32. 10.1016/j.cobeha.2015.01.005

Falkai, P., Malchow, B., & Schmitt, A. (2017). Aerobic exercise and its effects on cognition in schizophrenia. *Current Opinion in Psychiatry*, *30*(3), 171–175. 10.1097/YCO.0000000000000326

Faulkner, G. (2005). Exercise as an adjunct treatment for schizophrenia. In G. E. J. Faulkner, & A. H. Taylor (Eds.), *Exercise, health and mental health: Emerging relationship* (pp. 27–47). London: Routledge.

Faulkner, G., & Biddle, S. (1999). Exercise as an adjunct treatment for schizophrenia: A review of the literature. *Journal of Mental Health*, *8*(5), 441–457. 10.1080/09638239917157

Farhang, M., Miranda-Castillo, C., Rubio, M., & Furtado, G. (2019). Impact of mind-body interventions in older adults with mild cognitive impairment: A systematic review. *International Psychogeriatrics, 31*(5), 643–666. 10.1017/S1041610218002302

Firth, J., Stubbs, B., Rosenbaum, S., Vancampfort, D., Malchow, B., Schuch, F., … & Yung, A. R. (2017). Aerobic exercise improves cognitive functioning in people with schizophrenia: A systematic review and meta-analysis. *Schizophrenia Bulletin*, *43*(3), 546–556. 10.1093/schbul/sbw115

Firth, J., Carney, R., Elliott, R., French, P., Parker, S., McIntyre, R., … & Yung, A. R. (2018). Exercise as an intervention for first-episode psychosis: A feasibility study. *Early Intervention in Psychiatry, 12*(3), 307–315. 10.1111/eip.12329

Fissler, P., Küster, O., Schlee, W., & Kolassa, I. T. (2013). Novelty interventions to enhance broad cognitive abilities and prevent dementia: Synergistic approaches for the facilitation of positive plastic change. *Progress in Brain Research, 207*, 403–434. 10.1016/B978-0-444-63327-9.00017-5

Ford, J. M., Mathalon, D. H., Marsh, L., Faustman, W. O., Harris, D., Hoff, A. L., … & Pfefferbaum, A. (1999). P300 amplitude is related to clinical state in severely and moderately ill patients with schizophrenia. *Biological Psychiatry*, *46*(1), 94–101. 10.1016/S0006-3223(98)00290-X

Gao, H., Luo, C., Tu, S. J., Lu, R. P., Jiang, L. N., Qiao, H. J., … & Chen, J. H. (2021). The effect of Yijinjing on the cognitive function of patients with chronic schizophrenia. *Frontiers in Psychiatry, 12*, 739364. 10.3389/fpsyt.2021.739364

Geddes, J., Huws, R., & Pratt, P. (1991). Olfactory acuity in the positive and negative syndromes of schizophrenia. *Biological Psychiatry, 29*(8), 774–778. 10.1016/0006-3223(91)90196-S

Gorczynski, P., & Faulkner, G. (2010). Exercise therapy for schizophrenia. *Cochrane Database of Systematic Reviews*, (5). 10.1002/14651858.CD004412.pub2

Gur, R. E., McGrath, C., Chan, R. M., Schroeder, L., Turner, T., Turetsky, B. I., … Gur, R. C. (2002). An fMRI study of facial emotion processing in patients with schizophrenia. *American Journal of Psychiatry, 159*, 1992–1999. 10.1176/appi.ajp.159.12.1992

Harrison, P. J. (2004). The hippocampus in schizophrenia: A review of the neuropathological evidence and its pathophysiological implications. *Psychopharmacology (Berl), 174*(1), 151–162. 10.1007/s00213-003-1761-y

Hillman, C. H., Erickson, K. I., & Kramer, A. F. (2008). Be smart, exercise your heart: Exercise effects on brain and cognition. *Nature Reviews Neuroscience, 9*(1), 58–65. 10.1038/nrn2298

Insel, T. R. (2010). Rethinking schizophrenia. *Nature*, *468*, 187–193. 10.1016/S0925-4927(02)00126-9 10.1016/S0925-4927(02)00126-9

Jeon, Y. W., & Polich, J. (2003). Meta-analysis of P300 and schizophrenia: Patients, paradigms, and practical implications. *Psychophysiology*, *40*(5), 684–701. 10.1111/1469-8986.00070

Kimhy, D., Vakhrusheva, J., Bartels, M. N., Armstrong, H. F., Ballon, J. S., Khan, S., … & Sloan, R. P. (2015). The impact of aerobic exercise on brain-derived neurotrophic factor and neurocognition in individuals with schizophrenia: A single-blind, randomized clinical trial. *Schizophrenia Bulletin, 41*(4), 859–868. 10.1093/schbul/sbv022

Karis, D., Fabiani, M., & Donchin, E. (1984). "P300" and memory: Individual differences in the von Restorff effect. *Cognitive Psychology*, *16*(2), 177–216. 10.1016/0010-0285(84)90007-0

Kuo, Y. C., Chang, D. Y., & Liao, Y. H. (2021). Twelve-weeks of bench-step exercise training ameliorates cardiopulmonary fitness and mood state in patients with schizophrenia: A pilot study. *Medicina*, *57*(2), 149. 10.3390/medicina57020149

Kuperberg, G. R., Kreher, D. A., Swain, A., Goff, D. C., & Holt, D. J. (2011). Selective emotional processing deficits to social vignettes in schizophrenia: An ERP study. *Schizophrenia Bulletin, 37*(1), 148–163. 10.1093/schbul/sbp018

Kurebayashi, Y., Mori, K., & Otaki, J. (2022). Effects of mild-intensity physical exercise on neurocognition in inpatients with schizophrenia: A pilot randomized controlled trial. *Perspectives in Psychiatric Care*, *58*(3), 1037–1047. 10.1111/ppc.12896

Levin, O., Netz, Y., & Ziv, G. (2017). The beneficial effects of different types of exercise interventions on motor and cognitive functions in older age: A systematic review. *European Review of Aging and Physical Activity*, *14*(1), 1–23. 10.1186/s11556-017-0189-z

Li, M., Fang, J., Gao, Y., Wu, Y., Shen, L., Yusubujiang, Y., & Luo, J. (2020). Baduanjin mind-body exercise improves logical memory in long-term hospitalized patients with schizophrenia: A randomized controlled trial. *Asian Journal of Psychiatry*, *51*, 102046. 10.1016/j.ajp.2020.102046

Mandini, S., Morelli, M., Belvederi Murri, M., Grassi, L., Masotti, S., Simani, L., … & Mazzoni, G. (2022). Adherence to a guided walking program with amelioration of cognitive functions in subjects with schizophrenia even during COVID-19 pandemic. *BMC Sports Science, Medicine and Rehabilitation*, *14*(1), 48. 10.1186/s13102-022-00440-2

Martinsen, E. W. (1990). Benefit of exercise for the treatment of depression. *Sports Medicine, 9*, 380–389. 10.2165/00007256-199009060-00006

Malchow, B., Keller, K., Hasan, A., Dörfler, S., Schneider-Axmann, T., Hillmer-Vogel, U., ... & Falkai, P. (2015). Effects of endurance training combined with cognitive remediation on everyday functioning, symptoms, and cognition in multiepisode schizophrenia patients. *Schizophrenia Bulletin, 41*(4), 847–858. 10.1093/schbul/sbv020

Matura, S., Fleckenstein, J., Deichmann, R., Engeroff, T., Füzéki, E., Hattingen, E., ... & Pantel, J. (2017). Effects of aerobic exercise on brain metabolism and grey matter volume in older adults: Results of the randomised controlled SMART trial. *Translational Psychiatry, 7*(7), e1172–e1172. 10.1038/tp.2017.135

Mavilidi, M. F., Okely, A., Chandler, P., Domazet, S. L., & Paas, F. (2018). Immediate and delayed effects of integrating physical activity into preschool children's learning of numeracy skills. *Journal of Experimental Child Psychology, 166*, 502–519. 10.1016/j.jecp.2017.09.009

Nuechterlein, K. H., McEwen, S. C., Ventura, J., Subotnik, K. L., Turner, L. R., Boucher, M., ... & Hayata, J. N. (2023). Aerobic exercise enhances cognitive training effects in first-episode schizophrenia: Randomized clinical trial demonstrates cognitive and functional gains. *Psychological Medicine, 53*(10), 4751–4761. 10.1017/S0033291722001696

Pajonk, F. G., Wobrock, T., Gruber, O., Scherk, H., Berner, D., Kaizl, I., ... & Falkai, P. (2010). Hippocampal plasticity in response to exercise in schizophrenia. *Archives of General Psychiatry, 67*, 133. 10.1001/archgenpsychiatry.2009.193.

Pereira, A. C., Huddleston, D. E., Brickman, A. M., Sosunov, A. A., Hen, R., McKhann, G. M., ...Small, S. A. (2007). An in vivo correlate of exercise-induced neurogenesis in the adult dentate gyrus. *Proceedings of the National Academy of Sciences, 104*, 5638–5643. 10.1002/hipo.20157

Pesce, C., Crova, C., Cereatti, L., Casella, R., & Bellucci, M. (2009). Physical activity and mental performance in preadolescents: Effects of acute exercise on free-recall memory. *Mental Health and Physical Activity, 2*(1), 16–22. 10.1016/j.mhpa.2009.02.001

Polich, J. (2007). Updating P300: An integrative theory of P3a and P3b. *Clinical Neurophysiology, 118*(10), 2128–2148. 10.1016/j.clinph.2007.04.019

Reif, A., Fritzen, S., Finger, M., Strobel, A., Lauer, M., Schmitt, A., ...Lesch, K. P. (2006). Neural stem cell proliferation is decreased in schizophrenia, but not in depression. *Molecular Psychiatry, 11*(5), 514–522. 10.1038/sj.mp.4001791

Sadock, B. J., & Sadock, V. A. (2004). *Kaplan and Sadock's concise textbook of clinical psychiatry* (2nd ed.). Philadelphia, PA: Lippincott Williams & Wilkins.

Sawada, K., Barr, A. M., Nakamura, M., Arima, K., Young, C. E., Dwork, A. J., ... Honer, W. G. (2005). Hippocampal complex in proteins and cognitive dysfunction in schizophrenia. *Archive of General Psychiatry,* 62(3), 263–272. 10.1001/archpsyc.62.3.263

Scheewe, T. W., Backx, F. J. G., Takken, T., Jörg, F., Van Strater, A. C. P., Kroes, A. 1., ... & Cahn, W. (2013). Exercise therapy improves mental and physical health in schizophrenia: A randomised controlled trial. *Acta Psychiatrica Scandinavica, 127*(6), 464–473. 10.1111/acps.12029

Steen, R. G., Mull, C., McClure, R., Hamer, R. M., & Lieberman, J. A. (2006). Brain volume in first episode schizophrenia: Systematic review and meta-analysis of magnetic resonance imaging studies. *British Journal of Psychiatry, 188*, 510–518. 10.1192/bjp.188.6.510

Themanson, J. R., & Hillman, C. H. (2006). Cardiorespiratory fitness and acute aerobic exercise effects on neuroelectric and behavioral measures of action monitoring. *Neuroscience, 141*(2), 757–767. 10.1016/j.neuroscience.2006.04.004

Torrey, E. F. (2001). *Surviving schizophrenia: A manual for family, parents, and providers* (4th ed.). New York, NY: HarperCollins.

Tomporowski, P. D., McCullick, B., Pendleton, D. M., & Pesce, C. (2015). Exercise and children's cognition: The role of exercise characteristics and a place for metacognition. *Journal of Sport and Health Science, 4*(1), 47–55. 10.1016/j.jshs.2014.09.003.

Turetsky, B. I., Kohler, C. G., Indersmitten, T., Bhati, M. T., Charbonnier, D., & Gur, R. C. (2007). Facial emotion recognition in schizophrenia: When and why does it go awry? *Schizophrenia Research, 94*, 253–263. 10.1016/j.schres.2007.05.001

Turetsky, B. I., Moberg, P. J., Arnold, S. E., Doty, R. L., & Gur, R. E. (2003). Low olfactory bulb volume in first-degree relatives of patients with schizophrenia. *American Journal of Psychiatry, 160*, 703–708. 10.1176/appi.ajp.160.4.703

Veijola, J., Guo, J. Y., Moilanen, J. S., Jääskeläinen, E., Miettunen, J., Kyllönen, M., ... & Murray, G. K. (2014). Longitudinal changes in total brain volume in schizophrenia: Relation to symptom severity, cognition and antipsychotic medication. *PLoS One, 9*(7), e101689. 10.1371/journal.pone.0101689

Williams, L. M., Das, P., Liddell, B. J., Olivieri, G., Peduto, A. S., David, A. S., ... Harris, A. W. (2007). Fronto-limbic and autonomic disjunctions to negative emotion distinguish schizophrenia subtypes. *Psychiatry Research: Neuroimaging, 155*, 29–44. 10.1016/j.pscychresns.2006.12.018

Wei, G. X., Yang, L., Imm, K., Loprinzi, P. D., Smith, L., Zhang, X., & Yu, Q. (2020). Effects of mind–body exercises on schizophrenia: A systematic review with meta-analysis. *Frontiers in Psychiatry, 11*, 819. 10.3389/fpsyt.2020.00819

16

CONCLUDING REFLECTIONS AND FUTURE PATHWAYS

Robert J. Schinke and Alessandro Quartiroli

Fourteen accepted manuscripts were determined to belong within this special feature from the International Society of Sport Psychology's Academy of Science. The vastness of mental health writings in relation to sport and physical activity spans conceptual discussions, psychometric tools, and examinations of health status in relation to professional, elite amateur sport, developmental sport, and physical activity. There is an emerging consensus from the international community dialoging with the ISSP that there are pathways to human thriving. To present, there are rapidly growing threads of discussion that pertain to mental health, which in turn could contribute to the improved support of people seeking to excel in their daily lives. The proposed pathways to deepening our understanding and improved services must expand to include people in situ. Contextual factors such as work and recreation organizations, embedded within their subcultural and cultural contexts will provide better, informed solutions to recurring motivational challenges. Below, we offer six key, broad-based takeaways derived from the international contributors.

Postulate One: Engaging with Mental Health Must Be Proactive and Retroactive

Sport scientists, practitioners, and organizations must engage in proactive and retroactive efforts to consider the mental health of athletes, coaches, and support staff. The proactive elements should be focused on what might constitute thriving within sport and physical activity, as part of a broader human condition. Reactively, interventions should be centered on formalized mental health literacy and advocacy, coordinated with a clearly understood

DOI: 10.4324/9781003459750-16

and streamlined referral and treatment provision processes. These coordinated efforts are essential in fostering athletes' mental health at the individual and organizational levels.

Postulate Two: A Performer's Mental Health Is a Shared Responsibility Necessitating a Coordinated Effort

A performer's mental health is everyone's responsibility, from the athletes or sport participants to their affiliated coaching and support staff, and the associated clubs and sporting organizations, embedded within their national contexts. In short, the responsibility for mental health necessitates micro- and macro-level engagement. Everyone in the organization can (and should) contribute to the early detection, identification, and referral of aspects and experiences related to compromised mental health. A coordinated effort focused on triaging the management of referrals to the best versed and qualified support resource is a practical and viable approach to mental health improvements.

Postulate Three: Organizational Culture Is Crucial to Athletes' Safety and Mental Health

Organizations must develop and implement a culture uniquely theirs, that normalizes human thriving whereby mental health becomes a high priority within a culture of excellence. Therefore, organizations must dedicate the appropriate resources (e.g., human, time, and financial) to develop, implement, and monitor this culture, whilst normalizing discussions that encourage growth, introspection, support, and collaboration in relation to human conditions that will include times of optimal functioning and strain.

Postulate Four: Mental Health Is Presented, Negotiated, and Fostered Idiosyncratically

Cultural, social, political, organizational, and legislative contexts in which sport participants, coaches, and staff members operate must be considered when conceptualizing, developing, implementing, and assessing mental health interventions. Though considerable scholarship accounts for mental health of the person, the human condition ties closely with each person's social context when pursuing sport and exercise. Mental health research and models of practice should be developed and centered around organizationally and culturally sensitive and culturally grounded strategies that augment nurturing sport and physical activity environments. These environments might look and function differently in one country as compared with another. However, a shared objective of fostering human thriving using idiosyncratic strategies must be pursued. These idiosyncratic strategies might then be shared and considered by sport psychology practitioners and sport organizations across regions to expand understandings across peoples.

Postulate Five: Mental Health Research in Sport and Physical Activity Should Consider Innovative, Inclusive Methodologies to Answer Recurring Questions

Researchers must consider developing and employing innovative, ecologically friendly, and inclusive methodologies aimed at exploring, understanding, and intervening on individual and organizational risk and protective factors. Moreover, researchers must design and encourage safe spaces where individual and shared narratives, stories, and experiences can contribute to the conceptualization, detection, assessment, and treatment of performer mental health. There must be an openness to vast methodological strategies that span our professional community, with these approaches triangulating data sources and expertise to derive holistic and comprehensive solutions to prevailing questions, such as how to respond to significant life transitions, pressing psychological hardships that contribute to instability or/and resilience, and how to integrate important stakeholders in the generation of healthy performance environments as part of daily life.

Postulate Six: Athletes' Mental Health Must Be Integrated into Sport Psychology Training

There is a need for educational and training pathways to develop holistic sport psychology training encompassing knowledge, ability, and skills to support athletes' and organizational wellbeing, development, performance, and mental health. Concurrently, professional organizations must invest in continued professional development programs using an international inclusive lens, aimed to support scientist-practitioners in developing their understanding and competence related to athletes' mental health in relation to a diverse client base.

The Academy's Path Forward

This edited compilation of featured manuscripts above was narrowed to a single subject based on healthy negotiations of two partners, the International Society of Sport Psychology and Routledge Publishers. Our discussion led to a focus onto mental health in sport and physical activity. As this project culminates, the editor, ISSP Publication Committee, and the adjudicators are left to ponder about pathways forward for this burgeoning ISSP initiative. A simple and low hanging reflection is that the emergence of trending topics within sport and exercise psychology is fluid and subject to change. Change is a matter of zeitgeist. The current book reflects one among several trending topics evident within the broader domain of sport and exercise psychology. There are already discussions underway relating to two equally highly visible and frequently submitted subject areas. Though we dare not disclose our next thematic venture, these ideas are germinating among the project's stakeholders. A second reflection pertains to what the next compilation might look like in terms of the nature of the contributions. We ponder whether the invited manuscripts will be updated versions of existing accepted manuscripts with high scoring, such as we just provided, or whether new, emerging contributions will be invited from highly trending authors, derived from their submissions to the International Journal of Sport and Exercise Psychology (IJSEP). Once more, uncertainty arises as we seek to advance the ISSP Academy from its inaugural launch toward what it might yet become for the field at large. A third and final reflection pertains to the ideas expressed within this edited book. The readership might agree, partially agree, or entirely disagree with any featured manuscript, or with the concluding postulates offered above. The academy more broadly, meaning the readership and contributors to the IJSEP, will inevitably see what is offered from an equally idiosyncratic lens to the ones shared by the authors. The need for academic connoisseurship is a necessary condition within a thriving sport and exercise psychology. Discussions, agreements, and disagreements are a necessary part of a growing, legitimate profession. How we dialog, considering and welcoming disparate views from within and across regions, cultures, and social positions, is a necessary part of what we must strive for. These discussions can be in the form of societal meetings and through written manuscripts. Both avenues, reflectively undertaken, will lead to thriving within and across the International Society of Sport Psychology's membership and beyond.

INDEX

Note: *Italicized* and **bold** page numbers refer to figures and tables.

For Product Safety Concerns and Information please contact our EU
representative GPSR@taylorandfrancis.com
Taylor & Francis Verlag GmbH, Kaufingerstraße 24, 80331 München, Germany

www.ingramcontent.com/pod-product-compliance
Ingram Content Group UK Ltd.
Pitfield, Milton Keynes, MK11 3LW, UK
UKHW020153200926
475702UK00016B/2693

9781032603964